S...ity ...Na...

in the Indian Ocean

About the Book and Author

The five island societies of the Western Indian Ocean—Madagascar, Mauritius, the Seychelles, the Comoros, and the French Overseas Department of Réunion—have retained distinctive national characters while cultivating regional cohesion and the establishment of a Zone of Peace. In this study, Dr. Allen places the nations of the maritime Latin Quarter in several contexts: He discusses the historical legacies of British power and French cultural tradition, the influence of twentieth-century nationalism in Asia and Africa, the islands' vulnerability to the vicissitudes of international markets, and the competition in the region between major security systems. After sketching a millennium of Indian Ocean history, the author profiles each island, emphasizing its unique responses to the pressures of underdevelopment, dependence, and national self-determination. Arguing that the conflicting dynamics between nationalism and international dependence represent a startling irony, Dr. Allen shows that external intervention is welcomed for the sake of security but that the outside powers' pursuit of their own economic and strategic interests constrains national aspirations of the island countries and frustrates the emergence of national autonomy and regional cooperation.

Philip M. Allen was a Foreign Service officer from 1956 to 1966 and has lived and worked in the Indian Ocean area periodically since 1962. He is professor and chairman of humanities at Johnson State College and the author of *Madagascar* (Westview, forthcoming).

Security and Nationalism in the Indian Ocean

Lessons from the Latin Quarter Islands

Philip M. Allen

Westview Press / Boulder and London

Westview Special Studies in International Relations

Copyright © 1987 by Westview Press, Inc.

Published in 1987 in the United States of America by Westview Press, Inc.; Frederick A. Praeger, Publisher; 5500 Central Avenue, Boulder, Colorado 80301

Library of Congress Cataloging-in-Publication Data
Allen, Philip M.
   Security and nationalism in the Indian Ocean.
   (Westview special studies in international relations)
   Bibliography: p.
   Includes index.
   1. Indian Ocean Region—Strategic aspects. I. Title.
II. Series.
UA830.A45   1987   355'.0330182'4   86-9217
ISBN 0-8133-7171-6

Composition for this book was created by conversion of the author's word-processor disks.
This book was produced without formal editing by the publisher.

Printed and bound in the United States of America

⊗   The paper used in this publication meets the requirements of the American National Standard
    for Permanence of Paper for Printed Library Materials Z39.48-1984.

6   5   4   3   2   1

To Mother and Dave

Contents

Acknowledgments

I thank Peter Duignan for suggesting that the book be done and The Hoover Institution on War, Peace, and Revolution for a grant that facilitated the early stages of research. Other grant funds were generously provided by the National Endowment for the Humanities and by Johnson State College, which also allowed me to run off with the stipend on academic leave. I obtained invaluable advice and access to special resources at the Centre d'Etudes et de Recherches des Pays de l'Océan Indien (CERSOI) at the Université d'Aix-Marseille in Aix-en-Provence and at the Centre de Documentation et de Recherches sur l'Asie du Sud-Est et le Monde Insulindien (CeDRASEMI) in Sophia Antipolis, Valbonne, France; particular thanks go to President Louis Favoreu, Professor Jean Benoist, Marc Besson and Mme. Besson at Aix. Similar courtesies were extended by Mme. Lauret at the Centre de Documentation de l'Océan Indien at St. Denis in La Réunion and by archivists and librarians in all of the islands, France, the United States, and Montreal. Thanks go to Paul Gallagher and to Linda Kramer of the Johnson State College Library for finding and smoothing paths.

I'm especially appreciative of comments and encouragement from Sohrab Kheradi, secretary of the UN's ad hoc committee; Robert LeBlond, lately of Canada's International Development Research Centre; Ram Mannick of the University of London; Colin Legum, editor of *Africa Contemporary Record*; Guy Lionnet, of the Seychelles Ministry of Education; and my veteran collaborators, Aaron Segal and John M. Ostheimer. Larry W. Bowman opened the door for me to Westview Press, where Barbara Ellington and Bruce Kellison urged the project onward with both passion and patience. Jenney Campbell and Audrey Miller deciphered my scribbles to produce publishable scripts. Sally Searles and Roberta Heath valiantly helped unscramble the processing of words. I am thankful for the inquiring minds of students on three continents, never intimidated by claims of expertise or readily satisfied by its answers, and to Susan, who understands both the ideas and the person who strove to express them.

Philip M. Allen
Johnson, Vermont, and
Constantine, Algeria

PART ONE

Introduction

1

Security and Authority in the Indian Ocean

. . . As when to them who sail
Beyond the Cape of Hope, and now are past
Mozambic, off at sea north-east winds blow
Sabean odors from the spicy shore
Of Araby the Blest, with such delay
Well pleased they slack their course, and many a league
Cheered with the grateful smell old ocean smiles . . .

Paradise Lost, IV

To understand oceans, most of us have to turn continents inside out. The wastes of water tend to reflect cities and landscapes, people and politics, the typical imagery of their nearer shores. Sea bottoms mirror anthropomorphic mysteries, fish collect in "schools" and "banks," Atlantis becomes a Shangri-La or Paris of the deep. These great basins filled with the source and the silence of life are nothing to us if not foyers of terrestrial sociability.

Dimly perceived in our cultural imagination, the Pacific, Atlantic, and Mediterranean have distinct reputations to protect. Recall the two-dimensional characters given them by classroom maps: the Atlantic a doglegged chasm where the Americas and Africa used to fit; we see it bridged by stripes of maritime activity, the connective tissue of a coherent universe, our West. Two distinct Pacifics spill off those maps—the eastern and western margins of the world—peopled, if at all, by exotics until the water reaches California or Japan, and society begins again. The Mediterranean is an island surrounded by land, impaled on the glorious foot that had been Rome. Our archetypal memory fills all the inner seas, especially the Mediterranean, with floods of cultural force, the myths of who we are, the original structures of civilization germinating in the realm of the sun. At the antipodes of our map lie, for good measure, two hidden oceans of ice—barren, excluded from human history—at the top and bottom of life.

But consult your schoolday imagery for the Indian Ocean and you see everything jumbled together, or nothing at all. Perhaps only a mirror for the ill-conceived "third world," reflecting the smiles and grimaces of three continents disciplined by a fourth—Europe. More accurately, a great public yard at the rear of high mansions called Asia, Africa, Australia, Arabia, a place where the Orient meets for business, and Europe visits to stay.

The character of this ocean depends preeminently on our inner map, our point of view. For the sons of empires past, the sea issues an invitation into the slow, lucrative currents of the sailing trade. Indomitable—even when vanquished—Arabs, Indians, Swahili Africans, Malays, at times Chinese float on the dependable monsoons. Portuguese filibuster along the coasts to capture and lose the Indies. England puts her rowdy rivals one by one to rest and stabilizes sterling, together with an entire hemisphere, from the vantage-place of India. This courtyard behind the continents has been constantly crossed by the busiest traffics of trade and truculence the world has ever known. It still is, and the imperial invitation remains engraved on certain inner maps.

But, if we peer more closely, the Western imagination falters before the complex odors and obscure truths playing upon these waters. Everything is half-familiar to us, and half-forbidden. To readers of today's instant history-by-headline, the Indian Ocean opens at the Persian Gulf (it used to be Suez) where armies and terrorists strike in the dark. It balloons hugely out from there to the south and east, as the world economy blows life-giving petroleum into it. The courtyard rings with great ideals—of true community, of self-fulfillment in the sacrifice of self, the unity of God, and the thrilling multiplicity of nature. Yet famine stalks here, and life is wasted by obscure fanaticisms. Despotic governors torture innocents to ensure the longevity of their privileges, and faceless armies squabble over glaciers and deserts.

We aren't alone in our discomfort. Never completely at home here, even China and Japan tread discreetly into the region from their Pacific points of departure. Lofty monarchies in Iran and Afghanistan perch precariously on high balconies, isolated from their neighbors, including one another; today, rid of those monarchs, societies quiver in the agitated air of revolution south of Siberia. From Moscow, a live enemy of that Islamic revolution, the ocean is a backstage crossover between European and Siberian extremities, studded with political affairs en route.

We all seek to control the unknown, and in our encounters with it, we insist more than ever on remaining ourselves. Various masters have swaggered into this place from century to century, for commerce or possession, shifting left and right to spot trouble, leaving when trouble became too wearisome, carrying little understanding home with them.[1] Few English or royal Frenchmen, Venetian Polos, or cross-bearing Portuguese consented to change their spots on the dramatic journey to and from the Orient. Europe acquired territory, commodities, self-imposed responsibilities, aesthetic bric-a-brac. Arabs brought souls and spices home to Islam, as Japanese bring oil to power plants. Surmounted and subdued, the colossal continents south and east of Suez remained ineluctably remote from Europe. Westerners found "home" only in selected spots where they accumulated permanently in sufficient numbers to determine an entire culture, not merely to transform politics. Such places are of great interest, but they are few: South Africa's white enclaves, the Kenya and Rhodesia (Zimbabwe) highlands, Australia, the Mascarene and Seychelles archipelagoes, perhaps Israel and, tentatively, urban Mozambique. These are the classic colonies, and their privilege caused the surrounding societies to suffer in imperial neglect. In such places, reversion to rule by non-Europeans has proved particularly difficult, at times impossible. But they don't add up to a Westernized, or "global" region.

For their part, Asian and African notables sent their fortunate children to Europe's schools, procuring for them the facility of cultural miscegenation, the role of mediators, and ultimately, the privileges of local authority. This book seeks the point of view of those elites, to depict the Indian Ocean according to their culturally hybrid inner map. For the courtyard now abounds with their "nation" states, all produced in the name of popular self-determination, all pledging fidelity to greater combinations of societies, all by and large seeking security for particular regimes identified somehow with the nation. The irreducible nationalism that got them to this point has had to compromise itself in the process. Popular self-determination has been baffled by the imperatives of state security; the independence which it claimed as a birthright is deferred in exchange for the protection of external powers; the prosperity that is part of that claim requires further sacrifices of autonomy. Finally, the solidarity that all pledge as a principle of third world destiny is nullified by the exigencies of discreet states, competitive among themselves, insecure within their own societies, tributary to overseas patrons of economic, political, military, and/or ideological stability. These are among the ironies of nationalism and security treated in the ensuing chapters—using the islands of the Southwest as a relatively clear laboratory, for they alone stand untrammeled by continental theatrics; Madagascar, Mauritius, Comoros, Seychelles, and Réunion alone belong to the ocean; it is their continent, turned inside out.

With difficulty, the shapers of contemporary policy have tended increasingly to treat the entire basin as a unit. Since the independence of India and Pakistan in 1947 (itself an example of fragmentation), statesmen, scholars, and rhetoricians have envisaged the ocean as an organic zone, with a heartland of littoral peoples (usually grouped around India) and a reciprocating hinterland. The United Nations has pronounced the region in perpetuity to be a zone of peace, and its delegations have sought for over a decade to shape a diplomatic reality fit for that declaration. Sea-minded patriots in Washington urge the consecration of a "fifth" Navy to warrant the permanence of American force throughout an "arc of instability" passing through the Arab-Persian Gulf. The Soviet Union needs an entire ocean as a traversable counterpart of its hard land-mass between Black Sea and Kamchatka. More recently, certain Western commentators have discovered the "heart of the world" transplanted to the Indian Ocean, from wherever it may have once been.[2]

In truth, the Indian Ocean scarcely qualifies as the world's own heart. The oceanic "center" remains an open realm of passage, a medium for commercial and other energies among the various circumferential theatres—the Gulf and Arabian Peninsula, the Horn and coastlands of Africa, the volatile lands above the Cape of Good Hope, the seaboards of South and Southeast Asia. This "periphery" often runs deeply inland, forming sub-regional arenas for rivalry. Two generations of triumphant nationalism have precluded coalescence of these theatres into the larger unity of their aspirations. Nationalism, redefined for the security of governing elites, has even invited the powers of the high seas to participate in the affairs of the littoral states, rendering this exclusively third world zone into the most international area of them all.

Of course the Indian Ocean cannot claim regional homogeneity in the literal sense. It is a huge, diverse parabola of peoples, from Cape Town through the long East African coast and Arabian Peninsula to South and Southeast Asia, crossing to Australia and the Pacific. This is not a continuous area of gradually transmitted values or universally shared institutions. It is nevertheless more than a mere geographic expression or a sentimental construct of historical linkages. Regional solidarity and collaboration are matters now for states, not for migrating people, or markets, or ideas. And regional cohesion represents a kind of motivating myth, a genuine political cause for the leading classes of Indian Ocean states. They keep touch with each other across the sea (or, more concretely, across the tribunes and benches of UN conferences), even when the dynamic of national interest diverts their main attentions to troublesome continental neighbors or formidable overseas partners. At the otherwise impotent assizes of the zone of peace, and elsewhere, they have managed to strike concerted approaches to common problems of conflict and development. In chapter eight, we note some of the vicissitudes of this rather recent development, justifying acknowledgement of an incipient region, on the diplomatic level at least.[3]

As an international construct, the ocean encompasses a congeries of natural and political interests which have combined and split over the ages. For more than a millennium these societies have failed to produce their own unifying power. For a half-millennium, they have been vulnerable to intrusion, trailing in the wakes of European history. An ancient story is being repeated, as each new intruder contributes to a climate of insecurity which can be alleviated only by the "protection" of other outsiders. In the seventeenth and eighteenth centuries, great foreign trading companies offered sanctuary from local enemies, and from the other great trading companies—all in order to export for company profit to Europe. Later, European governments arrived to protect the companies. Today, great global powers still offer protection and participation in the larger, expanding systems of Western trade and finance, or of socialist institutional organization, or even both. As the fortunes of external patrons changed during the past two decades, the ocean's economic and strategic assets began to rise in value. Local circumstances came into the light and heat of international concern. Internecine conflicts erupted and had to be extinguished, like brushfires close to the settlements. Major power protects those settlements, even if they are not called colonies any longer.

If the exertions of external power raise local anxieties, they do so in the very name of stability.[4] This perception allows the enlistment of indigenous nations for their own good into masterful systems serving non-indigenous ends. Understandably, perceiving their own purposes (including zonal solidarity) as essential and perceiving global designs as incidental if not pernicious, resident regimes fall back on the rhetoric of nationalism—or their equally futile opponents do so. They insist on the rights of "the South" to bargain collectively on principles, but to contract separately on practicalities. They urge joint eviction of the intruders, but without sacrificing their individual prerogatives of external protection. Nor have they as yet renounced the privilege of national enmity which gives foreign powers a pretext for protective intervention. This is a capital irony of the zone of peace, and surely the saddest of all.

Under such circumstances, no eviction of intruders is even conceivable. And in fact, no feat of this kind has ever succeeded. All foreign masters have either been expelled by new arrivals, or they have abandoned claims to domination in the ocean on their own account.

The Shape and Story of an Ocean

External powers are once again redefining the region's importance and vulnerability for its one and one-half billion people. This population inhabits thirty-six littoral and insular states and several dependent island territories. Their societies abut 20,000 kilometers of coast on three sides of a maritime triangle encompassing seventy-five million square kilometers. Twenty-five of those thirty-six countries obtained independence since World War Two, seventeen of them since 1960. With a population rising at well over two percent a year, the region includes many of the world's poorest nations. Although seventeen resident countries, eight of them in the Persian Gulf area, register per capita annual incomes of over $1,000, only four—Australia, South Africa, Singapore, and Israel—obtain major portions of that revenue through industry. The remaining thirty-two, and all twelve land-locked nations in the immediate Asian and African hinterland, rely principally upon overseas sources of manufactured goods, services, and markets for relatively undifferentiated primary products. Dependent and vulnerable, Indian Ocean societies share an unwelcome identity as competing components of a region in need not of autonomy but of patronage.

Like the Mediterranean, the Indian Ocean and its littoral are contained within strong natural boundaries. It is marked off, if not exactly sealed, by the closed Antarctic to the south, the Rift Valley running inside Africa's coast from the Red Sea to the Zambezi, the Arabian desert and the Himalayan barriers to the north, and the contrapuntal sequence of Malaysian and Indonesian territory leaping down to Australia in the east. Two great bays project northward out of the ocean on either side of India's 4,000 kilometers of coastline into the great Asian monolith. The Red Sea and Persian Gulf act as vast rivers connecting the ocean with Europe and Western Asia along the flanks of Arabia. Otherwise, the basin's topographical and climatic barriers virtually forbid extensive inland penetration. Successful invasions from interior to coasts have been rare and diservedly celebrated. Cyrus brought Persian armies to the Indus River and Alexander reached the Oxus by what is now Pakistan. Islam was carried into the Subcontinent and the Malay orient by land as well as by sea. Bantu migrations populated the East African coasts over a milennium after the time of Christ. Subsequently, predominant seapower allowed a succession of modern European hegemonies: Portugal in the sixteenth century was challenged by Holland, France, and Muscat Oman, then replaced by Great Britain at the turn of the seventeenth. Japanese armies failed to reach the Indian center from Burma in 1942 and the projects for overland conquest by Napoleon's France, Czarist Russia, and Hitler's Germany did not materialize.

The region's coastlines are sliced seawards by a multiplicity of state borders, emphasizing the importance of the ocean as an essential medium for mobility and, some day perhaps, for unity. While politically and geographically partitioned, the ocean has sustained a dynamic intercourse of civilized behavior for almost as long a period as the Mediterranean, far longer than the Atlantic or Pacific. Twenty centuries of commercial contact and multitudinous migrations have woven the East African coast and neighboring islands into relations with India, Indonesia, the Arabian Peninsula, China, and the peoples beyond the Red Sea. Entrenched populations from Malaysia, India, Pakistan, China, and Arabia are found in broadly dispersed diasporas from one corner of the sea to the other.

The romance of seafaring on the monsoons from northeast to southwest and back has yielded to more prosaic pilgrimages of oil tankers, trawlers, deep-sea drilling rigs, merchantmen of grain, and military gray. Still, the loose-knit fabric remains, the lines connect across the sea without uniting, the roads cross that only lead away. Despite chauvinisms to the contrary, there are no solid precedents for Indian Ocean unity. Elaborate networks of commercial and cultural interchangehave left fundamental loyalties fragmented along personal, ethnic, class and caste—occasionally national—demarkations, without establishing the political nucleus for an Indian Ocean civilization. If the outside world has rediscovered this ocean as a shambles to be kept under control, the invitation and the response are nothing new. For the last five-hundred years, the ocean's inhabitants have answered new interventions by disdaining to unite.

Great as they often were, none of the indigenous powers ever seems to have entertained serious thalassocratic ambitions of the kind pursued by China, Portugal, France, Britain, and Japan. They usually kept naval strength within the scope of domestic purposes, at best manifesting limited defensive notions about the greater oceanic arena. They protected their own coastlines, fishing grounds and avenues of commerce, sailed to the aid of friendly neighbors, and pirated to a fare-thee-well. But they left the vast Indian Ocean trade structure as a parallelogram of interlocking systems, never undertaking to reorganize the terms under which they and their neighbors produced, traded, and defended their own peace. That organization was left to Europe, once Europeans were sufficiently strong to rule what had already been divided for them. The result has been almost five centuries of continuous clientage for the Indian Ocean societies. The modern vocation of this densely populated, technologically underprivileged region has been the provision of raw materials, labor, and cheap manufactures to markets dominated by external powers. The region today remains tributary in both international security and world economics.

For centuries before the arrival of aggressive European technology and mercantile ambitions, traffic beat two principal itineraries on the ocean surface: a coastal trade route from China across the northern tier and southwestward on the appropriate monsoon as far as southern Tanganyika using highly advanced maritime technology; and a still mysterious pathway of Indonesian canoes intrepidly propelled for purposes of settlement as far as Madagascar at least.

On the first of these trajectories, monsoon-borne traffic linked the coasts of Asia and Africa with a flow of trade goods south- and westward from November to April and back in the summer semester. Starting or pivoting at Aden (or less often, Djibouti, Berbera, or Mukalla), Arab dhows and baggalas linked Bombay, Basra in the Persian Gulf, and Zanzibar. They exchanged honey, furs, ivory, precious stones, dates, grain, sugar, and goats, and slaves. With these commodities came arts and techniques, ideas of godhead, mutually intelligible ways of thinking and acting, language, and some cultural homogeneity. Yemeni and Omani Arab influences became vivid in Zanzibar and Pemba; they later reached the Comoros and Madagascar. Mediterraneans participated in this trade at several maritime concessions on the shores of northeast Africa and the Arabian peninsula. Enough documentation and materials of exchange have reached us to permit reliable scholarly accounts and stirring romances on the subject.[5]

The precise routes, timing, motives, and outcome of the Indonesian migrations remain largely unrecorded and subject to vigorous controversy. Current speculation persuades us that the first Javanese, probably intermixed with Bantu or other Africans, arrived in uninhabited Madagascar from East Africa and/or the Comoro Islands between the third and eighth centuries A.D. A second wave of Indonesians seems to have arrived on the Malagasy east coast from India by the twelfth or thirteenth century, after Arab domination had been established over the eastern monsoon itineraries. Malayo-Polynesian language and culture, strongly mixed with Bantu in the west, represents the foundation of Malagasy society, but scholars disagree over the hypothesis that Indonesians also took up residence in East Africa. The traces of their presence there could have originated in Madagascar, perhaps via the Comoros, after permanent settlement of the island.[6]

A third major force spread over the region on the southward tides of Islam from the late seventeenth century, particularly from the tenth. Part of that movement, the ancient Arab import trade of African slaves for military, domestic, and industrial services, continued into the late nineteenth century. But the Arab impact on India, Malaysia, and the Indonesian archipelago was more constructive, political, and evangelical, than it proved to be in East Africa. Integrating smoothly into the oceanic commercial system, the new religion came as a spiritual and political commodity over the tradewinds and land routes of Persia, Afghanistan, and India. Seventh and eighth century Arab conquests in the Mediterranean had separated Christian Europe from western Indian Ocean shores where Europeans had once traded freely. Europe's acquisition of luxury goods, the circulation of gold from Sofala and the eastern Sudan, the silver of southeast Asia and the spices of the Orient all depended on the consent of Arabs, interrupting the normal commerce between continents. Islam was able to colonize to the south as well as the north and west from southern Arabia. They even came to settle. Dissident Arabs from Hadhramaut and Persians from Shiraz conquered and resided along the familiar East African coast and the Comoro islands from the end of the seventh century. Their African descendants ruled a loose maritime league of autonomous Swahili cities between Mogadishu and Kilwa until after 1498, when the plundering Portuguese destroyed for a time the so-called empire of Zenj.[7]

Arab blockage of Red Sea and Persian Gulf transhipment led to circumvention, counter-attack, and ultimate domination by Atlantic Europeans eager to assure supplies to their markets at the source. The great commercial land routes across Asia stayed firmly in Muslim (Ottoman) hands. But, strong only in its home waters, the colossal land power of the Turks sputtered before the southern seas and could not defend Islam against an Atlantic European naval resurgence from the south. The Ottomans ventured only into the extreme northwestern extensions of the ocean, and did not establish themselves even there for very long. Smaller invading and marauding forces from various points of the ocean attacked all the grand targets of southern Asia and East Africa over centuries, softening them for Europe. Persia, Mogul India, and the empires of Indonesia, Malaya, and Burma restored their traditional economic and military authority over parcels of South Asia until the late seventeenth and early eighteenth centuries, but they eventually disintegrated under European pressure from the sea.

The African interior powers, Buganda, Monomotapa, and eventually Zanzibar, sustained autonomy well into the nineteenth century. This coastal trade policy nevertheless had to comply with Portuguese or British ways of merchandising and mobilizing. Beginning in the late eighteenth century, the triumphing Europeans even resumed the mass migrations of labor that had sent waves out of teeming Java and arid Arabia into the western ocean. Under their new industrial aegis came Muslims and Hindus from the overpopulated Subcontinent into Africa and the southwestern islands on coolie labor contracts with repatriation clauses as easily honored in the breach as the observance. Together, these movements have left large Asian and Arab minorities in East Africa, Asian majorities in Madagascar and Mauritius, and Asian minorities in South Africa, as well as strong African influence in the Subcontinent, the Maldives, Madagascar, and the Creole Mascarenes and Seychelles.

Once Portuguese caravels began probing eastward from the Cape of Good Hope in 1498, a long season of insecurity blew across the ocean. For the first time in history, sea power became sufficient to permit imperial ambitions over the whole expanse of seaboard and vital waterways. Up to that moment, slightly less than five centuries ago, Arab and Indian navies were used exclusively for mercantile and coastal defenses. A Chinese armada, constructed in the grand imperial spirit of the Middle Kingdom, never applied itself to the task. Invasion by Mongols brought that force home in 1433. By 1507, when Albuquerque's Portuguese fleet had invested the entire Orient with the powder and smoke of militant Christianity, the Indian Ocean entered its long tributary course to the European mainstream. While identities have shifted significantly, that subordination prevails under the polarizations of the late twentieth century.

Passing under the great bulk of the Muslim Middle East and stopping short of Chinese Asia, the Portuguese power supplanted Arab and other local suzerainties. At its zenith, it operated across the seas from the shores of Mozambique to Bab-el-Mandeb and Hormuz to India and Indonesia. The search for spices and precious metals once identified simply with "Araby," the ardor of a resurgent royal Catholicism in a vain search for Christian allies, and the exaltation of nascent transport and military technology sustained a monopoly over the seas and a genial if brutal management from Albuquerque's headquarters at Goa. Portuguese control fell far short of universal efficacy, however. Arab and Malay warlords and Indian potentates gnawed at the empire intermittently, but it was rival European power and later Muscat Arabs who ultimately bludgeoned overseas Portugal to dimensions commensurate with its slender Iberian motherland.

Portugal had considered her mission inspired by divinity. Pope Alexander VI had decreed her right to the spiritual and temporal wealth of the East in 1494 and, a year later, Spain recognized Lisbon's title in the Treaty of Tordesillas. Her opponents arrived after a century with less exalted purposes but with similar results. The Protestant Dutch flung their new sea energies against the entire Portuguese edifice from 1595 in the august name of commerce. The British and French were to follow in 1600 and 1664, respectively. For all contestants, the state depended both materially and mythically upon the wealth amassed by force. Preoccupied by competition in the European and American theatres, the new powers entrusted Indian Ocean security to special mercantile companies. The profit drive emerged from the mind of seventeenth century mercantile imperialism with a militant global verve comparable to its "multinational" dynamic of today.

The eighteenth century came upon an uneasily partitioned ocean buffeted by sea skirmishes and pillaged by Arab, European, and even American pirates.

Europeans did not subdue a major Indian Ocean land power until Britain completed her conquest of India during a period of extreme decadence in the late nineteenth century. Like the Arabs before and after her hegemony, Portugal was weakened by land wars at home. She had been unable to develop a strong base from which to repel intruders. Mogul India, which possessed that asset, renounced the concomitant of a sea force. Britain proved that both were necessary to longterm domination of the ocean. Access to her vital Malabar possessions virtually monopolized Portuguese attention after the loss of Arabian and East African territories as far south as Mozambique to the Sultan of Muscat between 1698 and 1715. Although capable of reconquest, the Portuguese navy could not expect to maintain control over so vast an empire without land forces. These proved unavailable for what were, after all, secondary colonies.

Following defeats in the naval wars of the seventeenth century and beleaguered by the financial drains of an unproductive empire, the Dutch consolidated their holdings on the Malay (Indonesian) archipelago. Founded in 1621, their single great base at Batavia was served from 1652 by a refreshment station on the Cape of Good Hope. Mauritius was left to the French, East Africa to the Portuguese, Arabs, and, ultimately the English. The Omani Sultanate shifted its location to Zanzibar in 1837 and, to save its livelihood through piracy and slave trading, played alternatingly subservient and insubordinate roles to reticent England along the western shores of the monsoons.

Successive European wars between Britain and France, beginning with Louis XIV's confrontation with the League of Augsburg in 1688 and the dispute over the Spanish throne in 1702, involved not only the rest of Europe but the overseas dominions of the participants as well. So it was that the British navy, originally an Atlantic machine, became committed to the eradication of Indian Ocean privateering, as it was later to devote itself to suppression of the slave trade. England ran inevitably against the ambitions of the French, based on the Ile de France (Mauritius). Compagnie des Indes Governor Mahé de Labourdonnais (1735-1746), was a master of peaceful as much as the naval arts, and Admiral Pierre André Suffren defeated the British in several important battles from 1778-1782. Yet, France could not sustain the necessary weight of conquest while also battling a fluctuation of enemies in Europe and the New World. Company and Crown fleets were reinforced and eventually replaced by royally commissioned corsairs among whose best clients and suppliers were tradesmen of the new American merchant marine. But without concerted naval force, France could not hold her subcontinental territories. Suffren's triumphs were offset by more telling losses in the Atlantic. Britain gradually neutralized the assets of France's Dutch and Iberian allies, and by the time of the French Revolution, she was virtually unchallenged on the Asain mainland.

The Napoleonic period began with a vague threat of French resurgence in the area but again the absence of a fleet nullified the Corsican's oriental ambitions after the capture of Egypt in 1798. Failure to commit state power against England reduced the Indian Ocean to a minor theatre of activity during the mighty wars that ensued. Nevertheless, French privateer attacks on British shipping to and from India obliged England to evict the Dutch from their Cape of Good Hope station in 1806. She also neutralized Batavia in 1811 after seizing the Ile de France (Mauritius) in an invasion of the enemy's Mascarene and Seychelles colonies. Having neutralized these perches along the sealines between the Cape and the South Asian coasts, England had little to fear from Gallic buccaneers in the oriental seas.

In the general post-Napoleonic settlement, England restored to France, Spain, and the Netherlands all but the most strategically critical conquests of the previous decade. She was able to supervise the ocean with relative serenity from points in Australia, the Malay peninsula, India, Mauritius, the Cape, Aden, and subsequently, Kenya and Zanzibar. The appearance of an expansive Germany in the 1880s stirred the celebrated "scramble" for continental territory in the ancient but amorphous bailiwick of the Sultans of Zanzibar. Although eventually closed out of the continent, France regained some prestige by acquisition of the strategic port of Djibouti in 1888 and the invasion of Madagascar in 1895, ten years after imposing a spurious protectorate over the Merina-ruled Great Island. Retention of base rights on the Somali coast gives France a vantage point over the "super powers" today in the Arabian Sea and neighboring areas, but neither Djibouti nor Madagascar or the Comoros could replace Mauritius as a springboard against British supremacy west of Indo China. No power was able to mount such a challenge until World War Two, although Britain was continually obliged to counter the untoward growth of Russian, Italian, German, and Japanese ambitions.[8]

The glamor of foam-borne battalions, pirate republics and endemically restive indigenous societies, gave way in 1814 to a calmer century in which commerce dutifully tracked its flag. The continental powers settled willy-nilly for a subordinate role to Britain's thalassocracy in the enjoyment of free trade and oriental favors. Control of the Suez Canal, even while shared with France, gave Britain mastery over the fifth gateway to the ocean, after the Cape of Good Hope, the Persian Gulf, the Malaccan straits and the passages around Australia. Britain thus decided the nature and price of Indian Ocean accessibility, security, and economic exploitation. But it was from India, and mainly for India, that England protected her interests in Persia, Nepal, Tibet, and Afghanistan, in East Africa, the Burmese and Singapore territories, the Malay protectorates, and neutralized Siam (Thailand).

Equilibrium under England enabled a full imperial process to transpire in the Western ocean. Australia, South Africa, Rhodesia, Kenya, the French Mascarenes, and Seychelles all had transcendant settler concentrations. Portuguese Mozambique, the Dutch East Indies, French Madagascar, and German Tanganyika obtained substantial dispersions of rural colonists and headquarters officialdom. Mid-nineteenth century trade and missionary activity required new accretions of functionaries in India, Zanzibar, Italian Somalia, and the southern Arabian coast. East Africa continued to export gold, ivory, and even slaves (despite British surveillance of the abominable traffic) to Arabia and South Asia. But the opening of the Suez Canal in 1869, and the subsequent establishment of new, highly capitalized charter companies to exploit mineral and agricultural concessions, began a reorientation of Western Indian Ocean trade northward via the Red Sea. Intra-European competition became intense once again toward the end of the nineteenth century. Footholds were "negotiated" in new territories, favoring complaisant local groups against opponents less accommodating to the Europeans. Ports were opened, railways built, forts and factories established, armies and administrators dispatched to keep the holdings secure. Subsidiary imperial systems of France, Germany and Italy were perfected from 1895 into the years before World War One. Labor shortages induced programs of forced work and the importation of "coolies" from India.

Imperial stability was sharply but temporarily disrupted in the two World Wars. During the first, Britain successfully opposed Ottoman attempts to dominate Middle Eastern oil supplies. German warships operated from Tanganyikan bases against West European shipping until the major raiders were finally eliminated by the Royal Navy. The Allies thereupon used India as a base for the conquest of German East Africa.

Japan's sudden massive surge in Southeast Asia and Indonesia seemed during the early phases of the second World War to augur an assault upon India and the domination of the entire ocean by an entirely new Asian power. The imperial forces advanced as far as the Andaman and Nicobar islands in the Bay of Bengal. They secured the eastern part of Burma, but proved incapable of gathering for the decisive effort after the spring of 1942. This "Malay barrier" could hardly satisfy Japan, for the Allies' vital lines ran as always, westward from India. And the west was relatively stable: Italy had been driven out of Somalia in 1940-1941; Suez was protected against Rommel's eastward drive; Mombasa became a major port and supply station; Aden was a useful base; Iraq held firm and Iran was neutralized by British and Russian forces in 1943; by then, Djibouti and Madagascar had been rendered harmless. Axis submarine raids, while prejudicial, failed of themselves to sever the lines of supply.

Hence, like China five hundred years earlier, Japan decided in midcourse that it could not guarantee its most crucial assets in and near the homeland while completing conquest of a less vital Afro-Asiatic hemisphere. Britain and its allies profited from this renunciation. They used Madagascar and the Comoros for anti-submarine activity against German depredations. Reconstituting a fleet in India, the West prepared for a projected invasion of Japan. Today, Japan has effected its Indian Ocean presence ironically, as a vested, not a revolutionary power, relying on the latest versions of Western strength to safeguard Japanese interests.

Britain continued to preside over Indian Ocean destinies through the transitions of decolonization from the close of World War Two until the mid-1960s. Her subsequent retirement coincided with Soviet and American conversion into Indian Ocean powers.

At the same time, the ocean remains inveterately, monumentally, a succession of third world theatres. It was in regional foyers like Bandung, Colombo, New Delhi, Cairo, Addis Ababa, and Dar es Salaam that the self-awareness of nations variously identified as "nonaligned," the "seventy-seven," or "the South" became inspired and expressed. No world power enjoys immediate geographical access to the area—although the island territories excluded from decolonization by Britain and France give them claim to status as riparian proprietors. Its straits and capes are therefore points of demarkation between the ocean and the major interests which use it. Geographical alienation has ultimately undone all external hegemonies, and the ocean has sooner or later restored itself, as the alien conquerors wearied of managing its immensities. From the still enigmatic repatriation of the Chinese armada in 1433 to Britain's declaration of retrenchment east of Suez in 1968, each has eventually chosen to protect more vital interests closer to home. China, Portugal, Holland, Turkey, France, Japan, England all had successively to leave the ocean to its devices—whether competing local interests or the dicates of new external suzerains.

A Region's Assets and Liabilities

Today, a marvelous diversity of Indian Ocean people subsists in great stretches of poverty, patched in places by fragments of wealth. They have by and large little use for their own resources, few skills, and scant mobilizable capital. Nevertheless, the notable distinctions of any part are taken by the world as an index for the whole. For one thing, just getting there and getting back entails long passages through zones of untamed water, desert and mountain waste, and intractable societies. To obtain spices from Malay Indonesia or gold from Monomotapa, the Portuguese, Arabs, and Dutch had to dispute one-another across the entire expanse of ocean. India's size, wealth, and political incoherence gave Britain and France cause for competition far to the west and south of the Subcontinent. Today, access to petroleum in the northwest corner of the sea dictates enormous military and diplomatic investment across its entirety.

For this ocean is indeed a reverberation of its parts, a region in metaphor if not in institutions or internally shared values. There are metals, woods, condiments and fish, people for agriculture, labor for industry, an abundance of grand cultures, a technological legacy of seafaring and cultivation. These endowments are distributed with ruthless unevenness across the gigantic crescent of littoral and its contiguous hinterland and hinterseas. The ocean is richer at its four corners—in South Africa, the Persian Gulf, Singapore, and Australia—than anywhere in its interior or along the connecting perimeter. Only the partly European enclaves of Australia, South Africa, and Israel—all in temperate zone extremities of the region—are adequately diverse, well-endowed, industrial, and efficient to manage their own affairs in relative independence from external coercion and with capacity for regional economic influence. India is approaching that status; Singapore lacks the specific gravity for it; Iran, Egypt, and Iraq are falling away from it. Everywhere else lies a tropical, usually undercapitalized, underdeveloped third world. Its attractions periodically catch and lose the attention of major investors, purveyors of technology, and guarantors of commercial stability, as marketable assets come into and out of international favor. For the moment, of course, the universal eye is on petroleum—and an industrial shopping list of metals.

More than half of the known world petroleum reserves lie beneath the sands and waters of the Persian Gulf. The endowment is distributed among eight countries which together account for nearly forty percent of world annual production.[9] Market glut, price stagnation, and tribulations in the Organization of Petroleum Exporting Countries (OPEC) notwithstanding, world energy needs for the next several decades will remain keyed to the availability of oil. Most of these states also account for major quantities of natural gas. Under peaceful circumstances, a tanker passes every half hour through the Strait of Hormuz connecting the ocean with the Gulf via the Gulf of Oman. Forty ships navigate the Mozambique Channel each day, 25,000 turning the Cape of Good Hope in a year, bound to or from Europe and the Western hemisphere. Combined with Indonesia's production of seventy million tons, these sources supply four-fifths of Japan's petroleum needs. They can pump at present rates for another century, far beyond the estimated capacity of Eastern European, North Sea, or Western Hemisphere sources. The long-term security of these supplies has conditioned most of the West's strategic policy in the Indian Ocean region as a whole.

In addition to energy, the region provides quantities of metals, valuable agricultural products, and marine resources, including deep-sea reserves of fish. South Africa and Australia are among the world's great resources of industrial, strategic, and precious metals. The ruling European minority of South Africa determines the disposition of most of the world's gold, much of its platinum, manganese, uranium, chromium, asbestos, industrial diamonds, nickel, and soft coal, as well as many specialized metals. Australia is the world's largest producer of bauxite, with important shares of its iron, lead, zinc, coal, nickel, and manganese. India is sixth among producers of iron ore, manganese, and titanium. Malaysia is first in tin, while Indonesia ranks fourth and Thailand fifth. Indonesia is eighth in nickel, Malaysia fourth in cobalt. South Africa, Australia, India, and the tin-producing nations have developed the industrial capacity to transform their mineral ores, although India's steel production is limited by scarcity of coal and energy.

Agriculture has flourished in the highly capitalized temperate environments of Australia, South Africa, and Israel. Australia is first in wool, third in meat, and ninth in sugar, while South Africa and Israel have high exportable productions of citrus fruits and other foodstuffs, including processed foods. In the third world's most vital foodstuff, rice, China's production leadership is closely followed by India, Indonesia, Thailand, Bangla Desh, and Burma. However archaic in some places, plantation technology in Malaysia, Indonesia, Mauritius, and Réunion, and efficient export farming in India, Sri Lanka, Kenya, and Sudan, give the region a roster of leading trade products which contrasts glaringly with its overall misery, stagnation, and turbulence. Without having overcome these afflictions, India stands first in production of tea, jute, groundnuts, millet, cattle, and cane sugar, second in rice, bananas, and sorghum, fourth in cotton, wheat, and copra, sixth in manganese, iron, coal, titanium, and fish. While per capita industrial output remains low, India has been industrializing rapidly through effective adaptations of technology and exploitation of its enormous labor supply, advanced educational output, and extensive domestic market. It has already begun impressive programs of technical and capital exchange with less developed and overly specialized neighbors throughout the region.

The uneven distribution of this endowment suggests that, under different political realities, the Indian Ocean economies could benefit from intraregional development strategies stressing specialization, liberal trade on the basis of comparative advantage, and monetary compatibility. Recalling centuries of integrated commerce in a simpler, yet still decentralized Indian Ocean, regional patriots rage over the ocean's tributary economic plight today. Most of its resources have been exploited in modern times thanks to industrialized Western and East Asian interest in them. The operation of that interest continues, even after the collapse of empires, to ensure the selective viability of economies, externally determined terms of trade, and political fragmentation.

Engaged one by one with stronger overseas partners, the separate riparian societies have few resources to use for regional or sub-regional economic combinations. They can exert little leverage against the options of overseas sources of capital, technology, industrial goods, and markets—even when their own privileged groups are willing to relinquish the benefits of prevailing patterns of investment, foreign trade, technology transfer, development subcontracting, and cultural distinction. They do rhetorical homage to the cause of regional coherence and neighborhood collaboration without affording the sacrifice of access to the overseas sources and markets—most of them within the Organization for Economic Cooperation and Development (OECD). Whatever her ambitions, India is scarcely equipped at present to replace those major partners at a level significant for the process of regional integration. Even the ocean's conspicuous geopolitical asset as a zone of transit for vital commodities is hardly exploitable so long as local states maintain crucial rivalries of their own—thus needing external sources of security more than the external strategies need them. Their tendency to blame external powers for their failure to overcome longstanding, often aggressive heterogeneity, discussed in our concluding chapter, only dramatizes their fundamental dependence on those powers.

The ocean basin remains relatively unpolluted, thanks to the low industrial levels of its littoral. Metallic nodules are found in great density on the ocean floor, although their mineral composition is regarded as less rich than comparable deposits in the Pacific. Abundant fish resources are exploited today chiefly by Soviet, Scandinavian, Japanese, and other East Asian fleets, while the resident populations (including even India's) are restricted to poorer opportunities in coastal waters. Virtually all littoral states have had recourse to the two-hundred mile economic zone, but without tangible benefit until their harvesting, processing, and law-enforcement capacities improve.

Despite the existence of modest maritime fleets, particularly under the flags of the major oil producers, intrazonal cooperation has barely begun in merchandise trade and transportation. India's facilities occasionally serve neighborly needs in technology and banking services; Arab oil funds reach into some important (but Western-controlled) development projects; Tanzania has supplied internal security assistance and rural development inspiration to several neighbors; Australia has expanded economic partnerships in the ASEAN complex. But in the crucial markets for vital goods and services, even well-endowed residents remain subservient to wider international market forces. Two-thirds of India's economic exchanges are transacted with the industrialized West. Despite their evident assets, Israel and South Africa remain excluded for political reasons from ideal conceptions of an integrated Indian Ocean economy.

Transactions in world markets consist increasingly of weapons transfers by one side or other, in exchange for raw materials, privileged investment, and other dispositions by the host state. The arrangements also call for guarantees of protection to the weaker partner through military investment, training, and overt defense ties.[10] Less privileged clients reciprocate by extending military stationing and leave privileges, port and airfield facilities, and other concessions, as in the case of Egypt, Somalia, Kenya, and Oman in the American interest sphere, South Yemen (PDRY), Ethiopia, and Mozambique for the USSR.[11] Many other resident states have less elaborate understandings with one or both major powers. France maintains its independent "third alternative" with bases in Djibouti, its Overseas Department of Réunion, and Mayotte territory withheld from Comorean independence since 1975.

Thus, parallel North-South systems of bilateral arrangements tie the policies of weaker states to external powers, dividing them rigorously from one another, and influencing the evolution of their institutions—including, as Shepherd stresses, the status of prevailing third world elites. The actions of secondary external powers, including the old imperial states as well as new participants (Cuba, North Korea, China, the Scandinavian and Arab states) tend to reinforce the bipolarization of these arrangements. As constituents of major systems, they too obtain access to energy and other raw materials, markets for exports, and local influence through arms and technology transfers, loans, and credits which consolidate institutional alignments.

The emergent system sustains Indian Ocean security—containing local conflicts and protecting national regimes at the price of autonomy and regional cohesion. That security then depends largely on the way in which the major powers envisage their own relations and the extent to which they can control destabilizing behavior on the part of their respective clients. Enjoying positions of exceptional independence, Israel, South Africa, and Iraq have proved less tractable in this respect than most clients, and Iran has escaped from the tributary role almost entirely since 1979. Few Indian Ocean neighbors are able, or inclined, to follow those examples, however.

Most of those states have accepted dependence as part of the price paid for security, economic and military. They have declined to jeopardize that security by over-audaciously exploiting the rivalry between the two "blocs." Thus, the Soviet claim of identity of interest with the third world is welcomed for the political support it entails without being accepted as a depiction of reality. While both global powers have a stake in maintaining the bimodal tributary system, keeping the South as a whole from challenging overall Northern prerogatives, they compete for primacy within that dual system. The great powers may eventually dispute the direction of strategic trade as Eastern Europe comes to seek new Third World markets and sources of supply and as their constant argument rages over which elites are entitled to administer which third world societies.

Exceptions to this discipline have been dramatic, but not of notable success. Ethiopia's revolutionary regime and its rival, Somalia, as well as Pakistan, Mozambique, Mauritius, and others have been obliged to choose sides, whatever their preferences. Others like Tanzania, Seychelles, Madagascar, Maldives, and Burma have defended the virtues of categorical nonalignment. India probably belongs in a class by herself, bulk and position enabling New Delhi to play virtually any side against its rival. What India and her potential collaborators have not as yet achieved, however, is a regional counterforce to the over-weening tribute system itself. Observing that "the littoral nations do have a considerable power of restraint upon global power policy, especially when they act together ...," Shepherd concedes that collective self-reliance nonetheless requires an arduous "step-by-step process . . . through nonalignment and through building alternative sources of arms and goods."[12] Those alternatives may be available to help some Indian Ocean states shore up national autonomy from outside the global system—as, for instance, in Tanzania's acceptance of Scandinavian and Chinese aid. It is not clear, however, that such recourse contributes to collective solidarity. So long as congenital rivalries separate the region's residents, without effective security strategies from inside, they seem destined to be ruled from abroad.

Notes

1. See Auguste Toussaint, *History of the Indian Ocean*, trans. June Guicharnaud (London: Routledge and Kegan Paul, 1966); Alan Villiers, *Monsoon Seas: The Story of the Indian Ocean* (Boston: Houghton Mifflin, 1928).

2. Philippe Leymarie, *Océan Indien: le nouveau coeur du monde* (Paris: Karthala, 1981); Amiral Henri Labrousse, "Océan Indien 'nouveau coeur du monde,'" *Monde en Développement* 21 (1978): 131–148; J.P. Langellier, *Le Monde du Dimanche*, 15 February 1981, p. xix; Philip M. Allen, "The Indian Ocean: A new Area of Conflict or a Zone of Peace?" in Colin Legum, ed., *Africa Contemporary Record (ACR) 1980–81* (New York and London: Holmes & Meier, Africana Publishing, 1981), pp. A 72–79.

3. For the "region" issue, see Ashok Kapur, *The Indian Ocean: Regional and International Power Politics* (New York: Praeger Special Studies, 1982), pp. xvi and passim; Dieter Braun, *The Indian Ocean: Region of Conflict or Peace Zone?* trans. Carol Geldart and Kathleen Llanwarne (New York: St. Martin's Press, 1983), Parts I and IV; Ferenc A. Váli, *Politics of the Indian Ocean Region: The Balances of Power* (New York: The Free Press, 1976), esp. Ch. 2; G.S. Bhargava, *South Asian Security After Afghanistan* (Lexington, Mass.: D.C. Heath, 1983), Ch. 11; William L. Dowdy and Russell B. Trood, "The Indian Ocean: An Emerging Geostrategic Region," in *International Journal* (Toronto), 38:3, Summer 1983, pp. 432–458.

4. See Braun, *The Indian Ocean*, Ch. 3; Kapur, *Regional and International Power Politics*, Introduction and Ch. 1; and the author's essays on the Indian Ocean: "New Area of Conflict?" "Very Much at Sea," "Rocks Between the Hard Places," "All Quiet in the Zone of Peace," and "A Year of Disasters" in *ACR 1980–81, 1981–82, 1982–83, 1983–84* and *1984–85*, respectively.

5. For historical accounts of this long, great season of mercantile exploration, see, in addition to the "Thousand and One Nights," *Periplus maris Erythraei: The Periplus of the Erythrean Sea: Travel and Trade in the Indian Ocean by a Merchant of the First Century*, trans. and annotated by Wilfred H. Schoff (London: Longmans, Green, 1912); Toussaint, *History*, Chs. 1–6; Alan Villiers, *Sons of Sinbad* (New York: Charles Scribner's Sons, 1969); E. B. and C. P. Martin, *Cargoes of the East* (London: Elm Tree Books, 1978); H. Neville Chittick and Robert I. Rotberg, eds., *East Africa and the Orient: Cultural Syntheses in Pre-Colonial Times* (New York and London: Africana Publishing, 1975).

6. For controversial assessments of data, see P. Vérin, "Madagascar," in G. Mokhtar ed., *UNESCO General History of Africa*, Vol. 2, *Ancient Civilizations of Africa* (Berkeley: University of California Press, 1981), Ch. 28, pp. 693–717; Vérin, "Austronesian Contributions to the Culture of Madagascar: Some Archaeological Problems," in Chittick and Rotberg, *East Africa and the Orient*; Aidan Southall, "The Problem of Malagasy Origins," in ibid. (see also Introduction to that volume); Michel Mollat du Jourdin, "Les contacts historiques de l'Afrique et de Madagascar avec l'Asie du Sud et du Sud-Est: le rôle de l'Océan Indien," paper presented at UNESCO conference, Port Louis, Mauritius, 1974, reprinted in *Archipel, Etudes Interdisciplinaires sur le monde Insulindien*, No. 21, Paris: CNRS-SECMI, 1981, pp. 35–53; Jean Poirier, "Problèmes de la mise en place des couches ethniques et des couches culturelles à Madagascar," in *Mouvements des populations dans l'océan Indien* (Paris: Honoré Champion, 1979); Raymond K. Kent, *Early Kingdoms in Madagascar, 1500–1700* (New York: Holt, Rinehart and Winston, 1970), pp. 2–4.

7. S. Labib, "Islamic Expansion and Slave Trade in Medieval Africa," in *Mouvements des populations*.

8. Ballard, *Rulers*, Ch. 14; Toussaint, *History of the Indian Ocean: A Study of Maritime Enterprise, 1810–1850* (Oxford: Clarendon Press, 1967); C.S. Venkatachar, *Sea Power in the Indian Ocean*, Eastern Economic Pamphlets, no. 22 (New Delhi: Eastern Economic, 1953).

9. Saudi Arabia, Kuwait, Iraq, Iran, The United Arab Emirates, Qatar, Bahrein, Oman; see James H. Noyes, *The Clouded Lens: Persian Gulf Security and U.S. Policy* (Stanford: Hoover Institution Press, 2nd ed., 1982), Ch. 6; "Oil and the Gulf: a Survey," supplement to *The Economist* (London), July 28, 1984.

10. George W. Shepherd, Jr., "Demilitarization Proposals for the Indian Ocean," in Larry W. Bowman and Ian Clark, eds., *The Indian Ocean in Global Politics* (Boulder, Colorado: Westview Press; Nedlands, W.A.: University of Western Australia, 1981), pp. 223–247.

11. Ibid. See also Allen, "The Indian Ocean: Very Much at Sea."

12. Shepherd, "Demilitarization Proposals," p. 241.

PART TWO

The Southwestern Islands: Latin Quarter of the Indian Ocean

The western ocean bears scatterings of coral, volcanic rock, and granite organized into five notable entities and a spray of what the French call "imperial confetti." The south-western archipelagoes—Comoros, Mascarenes, and Seychelles—punctuate their ocean around and away from big Madagascar. Yet they stand in no shadow, belonging historically and culturally neither to the Great Island nor to the neighboring continent. If anything, they reflect in different ways the power and overseas personality of imperial Europe with an intensity unusual even for this long subordinate oceanic region. The central section of our study follows those three archipelagoes and Madagascar, from the westernmost Comoros standing at arm's length from southern Tanzania, to Mascarene Réunion, Mauritius, and Rodriguez on the farther side of the Great Island, northward to the broadly cast Seychelles, all deeply marked by France. These twelve million islanders issue from a variegated broil of African, Asian, and European influences stabilized, established, and still frequented by the cosmopolitan spirit of the Franks.

Other islands in the western ocean lie outside the "Latin" imprint of our central subject. East from the northern Seychelles, the tiny Chagos atolls are inhabited today only by rotating Anglo-American military and construction crews on Diego Garcia atoll. Since 1965, the archipelago has belonged to the British Indian Ocean Territory (BIOT), established for strategic purposes by amputation from the then colonial administrations of Mauritius and Seychelles. The western part was returned to the Seychelles at independence in 1976, leaving the Chagos as sole constituent of the BIOT. Shortly after the 1965 transfer, the atolls were emptied of their population, consisting of about 1,200 Creole fishing folk and coconut plantation workers employed by Mauritius-based concessionary proprietors. Britain dumped them peremptorily in Mauritius without any effort at consultation. Both the companies and the evicted families have received indemnities from the Crown. However, the quantity and circumstances of compensation for the resettled Creoles engendered more than a decade of recrimination against both heartless England and laggard Mauritius. In 1982, a second subsidy on more generous terms ended public controversy for the forlorn Chagos "ilois."

Before obtaining notoriety for this questionable case of depopulation and as a site of the West's main oceanic naval and air base, the Chagos had entertained sugar cane plantations, guano mining, steamship coaling operations and the derring-do of pirates. Today, a British naval administrator exercises civil jurisdiction on Diego Garcia, acting as landlord for the U.S.-built harbor, port, airfield, and barracks installations and as host to some 2,000 service and civilian construction personnel. In addition to the facilitation of routine crossings of carrier fleets, reconnaissance aircraft, and submarines, the Diego Garcia base serves as supply warehouse and offloading station for the evolving American Rapid Deployment Force. Seventeen cargo ships, including eight newly converted "roll-on-roll-off" container vessels, are stationed at the island with "pre-positioned" supplies for whatever emergency the RDF is commanded to tend.

A thousand kilometers north of the Chagos, the chain of Maldive Islands dangles off the Malabar coast of the Indian peninsula. Until recently, a medieval sultanate at Male in the north ruled these two hundred islands strung over eight hundred kilometers. Islamic since the twelfth century, the Maldives fell under the benign "protection" of Britain in 1870. Retaining control primarily to keep other powers away from India, London was content to allow the Government of Ceylon (Sri Lanka) to administer the Crown's prerogatives over Maldivian external relations, and to permit communal tradition to determine local politics and economic distribution on the archipelago. During the second World War, the British built a port and airbase on Gan island in Addu atoll, creating a southern nucleus for employment and modern communications. In 1956, the southern islands rebelled against the Sultanate, objecting to the diversion of substantial royalties from Britain away from the immediate area of Gan. Their secession as the Suvadivan Republic was suppressed by 1959, however, and Male retained its centralized authority and metropolitan privileges.

The Maldives became independent in 1965 during England's general abdication east of Suez. By 1968, republican sentiment abolished the Sultanate by referendum but without fundamentally disturbing patriarchal relationships among the republic's 160,000 inhabitants. Traditional (Shari'ah) law, communal precedent, caste determination of occupations, clan loyalties, and face-to-face politics prevail despite growing state power in the economy. Insisting on neutrality and exercising a considerable pragmatism in external affairs, Maldives has refrained from organizing a military institution. It has kept scrupulously away from the various bouts of animosity among its larger neighbors—despite religious affinities with Pakistan and Bangla Desh, linguistic and historic affiliation to Sri Lanka and a new, broad-gauged financial and technological relationship with India. At independence, the Sultanate declined to join the Commonwealth, although it does belong to the United Nations, the Colombo Plan and several utilitarian international agencies. As Diego Garcia developed, the Gan base became gradually inoperative. It was formally retroceded by Britain in 1976. A Soviet offer to lease the facilities for trawler fleet support was politely declined, and the erstwhile port of war has become an obscure but thriving accommodation for northern Europeans wintering in its steamy, pacific climate.

Changing Sri Lanka's position as metropole for a richer, more promising attachment to India, Maldives seeks to modernize its principal fishing industry, to establish efficient communications among the constituent islands, to improve occupational skills and to enlarge and occupy its short-range merchant marine—mostly through banking, technical, and other services from India. The islands still export dried fish to Sri Lanka, usually in exchange for rice, and their Islamic identity provides access to Pakistan and the wealthy states to the northwest. Thus, for all its insular originality, Maldives stands economically and culturally in close proximity to the Asian continent. This affinity distinguishes the republic from the Euro-Afro-Asian islands to the southwest, from the Chagos through Madagascar.

The western sea also contains its share of offshore islands whose destinies are even more closely tributary to the continents they face. This satellite relationship generally holds true for the Laccadives off India's west coast, the strategically conspicuous Persian Gulf and Omani islets, Socotra in the Gulf of Aden, and the Swahili speaking settlements on the fringes of East Africa. Even Zanzibar, once suzerain of a continental patrimony, has succumbed more or less to offshore subordination as Tanzania's truculent junior partner. Such continental identity simply does not apply in any significant measure to the truly oceanic, cosmopolitan societies of the "Frankish Quarter" studied in our ensuing chapters.

For Madagascar, Comoros, Réunion, Mauritius, and Seychelles, the Indian Ocean is not merely a medium of transmission between theatres of concentration: it is their theatre, their real region, their reality. So oceanic are they that the smaller spots were scarcely noticed in the early records of commerce and conflict in their sector. Even Madagascar, fourth largest island on the globe, is only vaguely acknowledged in the ancient Periplus writings and the mapmaking of medieval geographers. The Arabs tossed various names at these places, some of them finding their mark, until the new European victors pushed their own nomenclature into the area as spoils of competitive technology. Thus the names for Madagascar, Mascarenes, Chagos, and the more powdery points were Latinized by Portugal, while Mauritius became Dutch; Réunion, Seychelles and eighteenth century Mauritius (as Ile de France) held fast in French, whereas Comoros like Zanzibar has stayed Arabic.

Despite their slenderness and political fragility, these islands have assumed considerable responsibility for attracting attention to the ocean as an ensemble. Their spokesmen proclaim the region's special character and its will to integrate. Through bilateral and multinational diplomacy, they have done their best to forge their own affiliations of zonal security and solidarity. The achievements and frustrations of the campaign for an Indian Ocean regional identity represent a continuing preoccupation of this study. Our more immediate purpose in the six ensuing chapters is to characterize the evolving national identity of each southwestern island entity against a background of post-colonial dependence and the distractions of insecurity.

2

Comoros:
The Contumely of Patriarchies

Four volcanically raised chunks of ocean bed, Grand Comoro, Moheli, Anjouan, and Mayotte lie like giant stepping stones across the northern opening of the channel between northernmost Mozambique and the top of Madagascar. Varying in topography, soils, and population density, the Comoros have nonetheless shared more than a century of common obscurity. In the latter 1970s, colonial neglect gave way to impecunious under-development. At the southern end of Islam's reach, these four societies have developed along classbound lines sanctified in all sectors of life by powerful, insular versions of Muslim ritual.

For all its proximity to the shores of East Africa and its predominantly Swahili-speaking population, the pre-colonial archipelago dwelt in benign detachment just outside the principal business of monsoon shipping. The islands are as susceptible to summer cyclones and nasty seas as to benevolent trade winds, and they seem to forbid maritime access as much as they entice the lover of seascape. Only southernmost Mayotte, called Mahore (or Maore) in old accounts of the affairs of the Zenj, offers fair shelter for shipping in its punctured circumference of reef. Political spill from Arab-Swahili Zanzibar was responsible for the ruling oligarchies and their religious legitimacy on each island. During the nineteenth century the strongest emirate in touch with French, British, or Zanzibari patrons imposed suzerainty on older chiefdoms in each island, all in intense rivalry with one another. Freebooting, imported firearms, and slave trading supported the presumptuous insular sultanates in these backwaters of empire.[1]

This combination of legitimate and illicit contact with Indian Ocean traffic has worked its will through the Comorean bloodstream for a millennium. The predominantly Bantu Antalaote majority on all four islands bears strong admixtures of Omani, Shirazi, and other Arab sources, with Polynesian influences arriving both from the Sakalava west coast of Madagascar and (probably) from Africa and the eastern ocean as well. The archipelago offers virtually all its 450,000 souls to Sunni Muslim orthodoxy, albeit with distinctive variations in custom and liturgy. Arabic is still used in the ubiquitous mosques and Koranic schools, but Comorean Swahili (spoken in slightly differing dialects from island to island) is both the official and popular language. Business gets done in French, and Malagasy circulates freely.

A hereditary aristocracy, related to the former Muscati sovereigns of Zanzibar and calling itself Sharifean (in the lineage of the Prophet), enjoys lofty proprietary and ceremonial privileges above the Antalaote population. A few civil servants, artisans, school teachers, and others outside the aristocracy compose an incipient middle class. Mayotte's distinction, flagrantly exaggerated in French debates over Mahorais self-determination, consists in a higher proportion of Malagasy ethnic and cultural influence, and a tiny but economically and politically powerful "Creole" community of Roman Catholics. The little island's creole presence owes its existence to relatively early French interest in Mayotte's strategic advantages. In 1841, that southern island became an acquisition of the Monarchy of July. These few European settlers and their mulatto descendants have long enjoyed commercial and social privileges on Mayotte, often in communication with French holdings in northern Madagascar and Réunion. In the early 1970s, the prospect of impending Comorean independence stimulated Mayotte's Creoles to campaign for French sympathy on behalf of Mahorais separatism.

Fully ninety percent of the Comorean population depends on a fragile agricultural economy for its livelihood, and on international donations for survival. Where rainfall is dependable, adequate, and retainable, both subsistence and export crops prosper. The old forests of Grand Comoro and Anjouan, respectively the largest and most densely inhabited of the four, have been devastated, however, partly in the quest for fuel, partly in the march of population up the volcanic slopes toward open land. That population grows at three percent each year even now, and the best land remains out of bounds for subsistence farmers. Potentially fertile but porous lava soils permit few streams or springs except on geologically older Mayotte. Water-retention technology is rarely available. Grand Comoro has a lofty rain forest on the slopes of the Karthala (2,400 meters) but no permanent streams. Erosion and dessication have given it the appearance and organic aptitude of a vast, undulating cinder block. The most fertile soils are devoted everywhere to plantations of cloves, vanilla, coconuts, and ylang-ylang, all grown for export production by French companies on concessionary lands of the aristocracy. Paradoxically, these tree crops crowd the readier coasts, so that food must be grown on the less ingratiating, eroded upper terrain where trees would have prospered.

Livestock and fisheries production remains rudimentary in Comoros and even the plantation crops are inefficiently cultivated, subject to climatic vagaries and price pressures from abroad. Colonial French subsidies for ylang perfume essence, vanilla extract, and clove oil have been replaced primarily by the price stabilization mechanism (STABEX) of the EEC's Lomé convention with African, Caribbean, and Pacific partners. The mountainous islands have yielded no exploitable minerals, and a modern educational structure has only begun to replace (or supplement) the anachronistic

Koranic schools. Trade unions are virtually nonexistent, and political parties reflect prevailing class relationships.

The priorities of export agriculture, subject to whims of overseas markets and declining terms of trade, have thrown the Comorean economy into a chaotic cycle of insufficiency and serfdom. The islands have suffered increasing balance of trade deficits and food shortages over the past two decades. Their best manpower seeks employment abroad, generating remittances to help stabilize the domestic economy. The diaspora also furnishes recruits for the ranks of a political opposition in exile. Habitual indifference by the distant metropole began in the late 1960s to strike numbers of Comoreans as a cause of, not a remedy for, their chronic poverty. Independence came to represent a real solution for metropolitan default. The dramatic revolution in 1972 on nearby Madagascar, homeland of 50,000 Comoreans, helped arouse local nationalism. Comoros crossed the 1960 sill to statehood some fifteen years late, erupting forthwith into revolutionary socialism.

A stirring history of insular emirs besieging and under siege came to a close with the acquisition of Mayotte by France in 1841 and the subsequent assertion of French "protection" over Anjouan, Moheli, and Grand Comoro. France had lost Mauritius and Seychelles in 1810 and was to renounce her continental East African ambitions in favor of Britain and Germany. She understandably cultivated compensatory interest in Madagascar, and by implication in the Comoros as a way of keeping others away from the Great Island. The archipelago had also served since the French Revolution as a quarantine site for exiled Europeans. Its several sultans provided exploitable terrain for opportunistic planters and export-minded concessionaires.

After purchasing Mayotte, the French found pretexts for intervening in the other three islands, until, tiring of the game, they declared protectorates over them in 1886, one year after making a similar claim in Madagascar. Direct control increased until it was ratified by formal annexation of the archipelago in 1904. Absorbed initially into the administration of Réunion, then into greater Madagascar, the islands became an Overseas Territory of their own in 1946. Fifteen unremarkable years later, the territory obtained some rights of domestic self-government, sufficient to its leaders at the time, while most other places in Africa were reaching independence. The new status conveyed intimations of improved treatment for island economics and society, but so little did the archipelago contribute to French interests in the early Fifth Republic that General DeGaulle could warn Comoreans during his 1958 overseas tour that a choice of independence would result in cancellation of all metropolitan support. However modest this French buttress, the island electorate understood the implications of imperial abandonment: they voted overwhelmingly to stay in DeGaulle's republic at the October 1958 referendum.

During France's century of responsibility, the islands wallowed in neglect. With half the total population of the Overseas Territories, they obtained less than a fifth of the public investment in those dependencies during the

1950s and 1960s. The former self-sufficiency of the battling emirates had given way to the conventional colonial "dual economy." Comoreans exported sons and daughters as well as perfume oils and other tropical commodities to the metropole. Accessibility of the French passport benefitted them primarily by allowing the brightest and most vigorous to emigrate, under French Government protection.

Original colony though it be, little Mayotte fared only slightly better than the rest of the archipelago. Dzaoudzi rock, a minuscule, waterless satellite of Mayotte, offers a sheltered harbor which helped recommend the island as naval and administrative headquarters from 1843. But Dzaoudzi never had a real chance of becoming France's austral answer to Gilbraltar.[2] While the little rock was territorial capital, however, Mayotte alone of the Comoros voted in favor of independence from France in DeGaulle's 1958 referendum—a shocking phenomenon considering the piety of Mahorais francophilia today.

In the constitutional shift of 1961, colonial administration and communications were transferred from Dzaoudzi to Moroni on more populous Grand Comoro in the extreme northwest. Losing capital status aggravated overall Mahorais alienation, not so much from the offending French administration as from their grasping Comorean neighbors. Mahorais particularism reappeared in the early 1970s in an adroit campaign to exploit metropolitan French affinities for overseas wards who professed loyalty while the other islands were seeking to leave the bosom of France. Expressed through the island's leading political party, the Mahorais Movement (MM, later retitled Mahorais People's Movement, MPM), these professions of tory faith proved most effective after 1973, when most of Western Europe's oil became theoretically vulnerable to attack as it passed through the archipelago on its way around the Cape of Good Hope. Suez remained closed until 1975, and a revolution in Madagascar and the imminent independence of Djibouti began to shake France's position at its traditional Indian Ocean bases. The strategic seas shuddered once more as Mozambique surged out of Portuguese control into nonalignment during 1974–1975. "Mayotte Française" appealed strongly to conservative French popular sympathies, pleased with the illusion that the distant little island was peopled mainly by close relatives.

Dominant political force in the archipelago of the 1960s, the "Green" party, later established as the Democratic Union of the Comoros (UDC), represented the great families in the traditional and colonial status quo. The UDC's leader, Prince Said Mohamed Cheik, was a master of domestic political dynamics, based largely on family loyalties and rivalries.[3] This approach to politics as an arena for stabilizing elite relationships inspired not only the usual rival aristocratic parties—the mildly liberal Democratic Assembly of the Comorean People (RDPC) and, after Cheik's death in 1970, the loose, opportunistic People's Party, or Umma, of Prince Said Ibrahim. It also stimulated a more popular modernist movement taking shape amid the protest politics of the Comorean diaspora.

Nationalist activity was dominated during the 1960s by the National Liberation Movement of the Comoros (MOLINACO), an expatriate party of young Comoreans based in Dar es Salaam. There, MOLINACO had access to decolonizing patronage away from French police control, while yet keeping in contact with developments on the stagnating islands. A first effort to establish MOLINACO in archipelago politics during the early 1970s failed when its local offspring, the Party for Comorean Evolution (PEC) was devoured by the UDC. Cheik's party was then dominated by Ahmed Abdallah, an agile plutocrat from Anjouan with a reputation for deviousness. Beginning in 1972, in half-hearted alliance with the RDPC, Abdallah eventually preempted the radical MOLINACO's national program and brought the islands to self-government, albeit more abruptly and painfully than he had anticipated.

Self-Determination, With or Without Mayotte

Watching anxiously during the late 1960s as enterprising immigrants arrived in Mayotte from relatively unproductive, over-populated Anjouan and Grand Comoro, the MPM became spokesman for its island's particular interests, distinct from those of the archipelago. Party leaders, many of them women, are drawn from the tiny Mahorais middle class. Creoles of mixed European, Malagasy, and Arab origins effectively control the political options of the 50,000 Antalaotes on the Island. They seek primarily to secure exploitation of Mayotte's agricultural and fisheries resources, to profit from French military and development contracts, and to avoid ethnic and class upheaval.

Working skillfully in Parliament and the press, MPM spokesmen managed to appeal to French patriotism against the decolonization that was approaching in the early 1970s. Their Gaullist sympathizers, holding parliamentary power in Paris until 1981, were allowed to portray the island's loyalty as a mass resistance of supposedly Christian Creoles against senseless incorporation into a black Islamic Comorean majority.[4] This distortion of reality survived long enough to divert the French Government away from its initial pledge to follow the plebiscitary will of the overall territorial majority in determining its future. Although the Pompidou Government had considered "island by island consulations" in 1972, President Giscard himself assured the continued unity of the archipelago on October 24, 1974. The reversal of Giscard's commitment began immediately in the Gaullist-dominated French Senate and, as tory sentiment rose on Mayotte, the Government declined to contest the issue against its parliamentary majority.[5]

On November 6, 1974, to placate Mahorais particularism and its sympathizers, the French administration conceded a change in referendary language. It authorized a plebiscite on December 22 to determine the will of "the populations" with respect to independence. Pluralism was thus suddenly recognized in Comorean self-determination, and the avenue was juridically opened to detach Mayotte. As expressed through the customary oversimplification of the referendary process, two separate "wills" did indeed emerge: overwhelmingly in favor of independence (eighty five percent) when taken as a single "population," the Comorean nation split between a quasi-totality for independence on Anjouan, Moheli, and Grand Comoro, against a sixty-four percent majority on Mayotte in favor of "staying free with France," as the MPM liked to characterize the option.

Trying to determine the next step, Comorean leadership in Moroni was paralyzed by the dispute between partisans of conciliation for the Mahorais and advocates of categoric, unqualified independence. The French Government temporized but the Gaullists continued to insist on deference to the MPM's loyalism. The MPM itself was working to erase Mayotte's 36 percent minority vote in favor of independence. It engineered the deportation of over 2,000 Anjouanais and Grand Comoreans (and some Mahorais political opponents) from Mayotte. Its propaganda mobilized Mahorais fears of further inundation by settlers from the other islands after independence. Hence, by February 1976, fourteen months after the first referendum, the party was able to contrive a 99.4 percent majority for remaining with France. By that time, the Comoros had seized independence and France had belatedly recognized it—for three, not four, of the islands.

This MPM flair for the main chance recurred in June 1981. The grateful party had showered a ninety percent majority upon Giscard in the presidential elections of May 11, but it knew how to catch the spirit of François Mitterand's victory over the incumbent. Within less than a month, the MPM had replaced its Gaullist parliamentary deputy with the more leftward-leaning J.P. Hory, who easily won the seat in the June legislative elections. Hory thereupon claimed affiliation not with the MPM's Gaullist soul-mates, but with the Mitterand Socialist majority in the National Assembly. After some understandable hesitation, the majority caucus accepted Hory, who has played an important role in legislation affecting Overseas France.

Astonished by French willingness to change the rules of the 1974 referendum to accommodate Mayotte, the Comorean leaders in Moroni and Paris were unable to concert on any initiative whatever for half a year. The expatriate nationalist MOLINACO had warned the U.N.'s Decolonization Committee of the impending perfidy well before the 1974 referendum, but responsible leaders in Moroni, enjoined by their Assembly to seek independence in amity with France, considered themselves betrayed. The radical opposition, still largely in exile, proved more resolute. Sensitive for the past two decades to the sounds of change outside the impassive isles, expatriate groups sought international attention for what they apprehended as an impending injustice to their nation. France was about to sunder a dependent territory's integrity in violation of its right to self-determination. Paris was going to reserve the choicest Comorean morsel for itself in perpetuity before offering the remainder of the plate to its rightful consumers.

But the French were themselves unable to resolve the stalemate. On July 3, 1975, the parliament voted to postpone independence out of respect for the five percent minority which had voted against it: that minority happened to be concentrated on one island, where it represented a nearly two-thirds majority.[6] Continuing to run well ahead of Giscard's executive policy, the legislators circled back to the approach espoused by Pierre Messmer, Pompidou's Gaullist Prime Minister (and, previously, Overseas Minister) authorizing the presentation of an independence constitution to the Comorean electorate in still another referendum, the results to be tabulated on an "island by island" basis. This was self-evident encouragement to Mahorais secession. It provoked the Comorean Chamber of Deputies to force its own executive to an inhabitually peremptory response. On July 6, three days after the French parliamentary resolution, the Government Council, headed by France's self-styled "best friend," Ahmed Abdallah, proclaimed the archipelago independent, and intact.

The prevailing politics of prudence, which since World War II had always yielded to the interests of a gracious and unperturbed metropole, was suddenly transformed into a nationalist movement. Urbane, amiable, adept with proverbial lore, merchant prince of Anjouan, former Senator of France, Ahmed Abdallah had been chosen for the premiership in 1973 because of his facility about Paris. Now, incapable of conciliating the French-loving Mahorais, he ironically became President of a rebellion. Abdallah's Gaullist friends were astounded, while his socialist denigrators cheered—for a few days.

Mayotte, understandably, would not budge, for France was still there, and while avoiding confrontation with the renegade Comoreans, the French would continue to treat Mahorais separatism as an accomplishment. Truncation of a territory prior to final decolonization has a full, if not always honorable, past. What empires have joined, their liquidators can sunder. Great Britain had partitioned India, Palestine, and Malaysia, as well as Mauritius, prior to yielding authority. France had separated certain islets from Madagascar before granting a transfer of sovereignty to the Malagasy Republic in 1960. Such amputation has been contested elsewhere, if seldom in the courts. While French power dominates the field, Comoros' grievance has the moral advantage of world opinion and apparent justice. Reserving to itself the right to partition a territory before independence brings France into conflict with item six of U.N. General Assembly resolution 1514 (XV) of 14 December 1960, which condemns such acts as violations of the integrity of a decolonized territory.

But the several stakes in the Mayotte case should be scrupulously disentangled, for both sides have defensible claims. And it is precisely the imperative of decolonization that is being challenged here. In Mayotte, as in many dependent territories, a privileged minority of the population vigorously opposed the transfer of sovereign powers to a disadvantaged majority. The socio-economic distinctions also happen to follow ethnic and cultural lines of demarcation and, as in notorious instances like Southern Rhodesia (Zimbabwe), Algeria, and, indeed Ulster from the 1920s, the minority succeeded in enlisting political sympathies among a closely related metropolitan population, usually including business and military interests.

In Mayotte's case, the minority was able to identify its position with a geographically separable unit. Opinion in that unit could thus cause fragmentation of an ensemble that had been administered as an entity for seventy years. Even discounting the inveterate flimsiness of the plebiscitary process among a largely illiterate population, Mayotte's toryism bears reasonably close resemblance to the spirit of self-determination. After all, Mayotte had been French for four decades in the mid-nineteenth century before the other Comoreans entered the empire.

Nevertheless, the case for partition depends on sympathy with a minority which wishes to maintain its socio-economic advantage over the majority—comparable, then, to the unsuccessful secessionary movements in Katanga (Shaba) and Southeastern Nigeria (Biafra) after independence, and even to the ideologically rationalized apartheid program of Bantustan creation in South Africa. Few archipelago states could survive if relatively favored units were juridically entitled to separate from the disadvantaged mass. Britain had no real hope of holding a half-hearted Caribbean Federation intact through independence in the 1960s. On criteria of ethnicity and culture, however, the Katangan, Biafran, Basque, and Singapore secessions have greater merit than that of the Mahorais. The difference being not that Mayotte's separation took place before independence: technically, it didn't, for French occupation of the island in July 1975 merely blocked enforcement of the unilateral declaration which was eventually recognized even by France. The distinction consists in the de facto efficacy of that occupation in frustrating the Comorean declaration, a fact of superior force, not of juridical right.

Apart from the truculence in Mayotte, France reacted with restraint to the Comorean rebellion. Another impoverished dependency had graciously taken itself off the French taxpayer's books. Mayotte was strategically important and Mayotte could be comfortably held so long as the military garrison was considered to be acting on the manifest will of the Mahorais. Independence for the "three Comorean islands" was recognizable by the French parliament, notwithstanding general international endorsement of the Comorean claim to the entirety of the archipelago. After gradually removing most of its personnel, equipment, and "life-support" technology from Grand Comoro, Anjouan, and Moheli, France was prepared to negotiate cordial relations and economic assistance on the customary bilateral basis without prejudice to the destiny of Mayotte. On December 30, 1975, the French Council of State declared the amputation of Mayotte to be constitutional, on the ground that the Comorean territory had itself been assembled piecemeal over time during the nineteenth century.[7]

In February 1976, France avoided U.N. Security Council condemnation by vetoing a resolution in favor of the Comorean irredenta. Since then the French invariably cast an annual lone vote against similar (non-binding) General Assembly resolutions while their allies abstain in embarrassment. French military and police had stood by on October 24, 1975, when MPM squads forceably deported the Anjouanais and Grand Comoreans, as well

as some Mahorais partisans of archipelago unity. The 99.4 percent majority
was ready for the new plebiscite of February 8, 1976. Still another referendum
on April 11 found a majority of Mahorais impatient over the pace set for
the island's re-integration into France: while Paris was still only asking
whether they wished to retain their status of Overseas Territory, eighty
percent of the electorate followed MPM instructions to file a separately
(hence illegally) printed ballot demanding to become a Department of the
French Republic on the example of Réunion, Guadeloupe, Martinique, and
Guyana. Such status would entail a far more deeply engaged integration as
a province of France, as well as a gigantic infrastructural and social investment.
The MPM's novel second ballot could not be endorsed in French law; the
island slipped into the anomalous but flexible status of "territorial collectivity."
But Paris got the point of the petition and has been trying ever since to
persuade the world that its treatment of Mayotte has been honorably
responsive to popular sovereignty.

"The world" has had difficulty accepting the validity of such claims. Not
only is a self-respecting people expected to prefer total decolonization to
any other form of status, but the obvious advantages reaped by French
contractors and the MPM's commercial leadership suggest that Mahorais
self-determination has been remarkably convenient for metropolitan interests.
Mayotte has relatively abundant resources as well as some strategic value.
Although smaller than Grand Comoro and Anjouan, it boasts a superior
abundance of free arable land, a richer garland of fisheries, and the only
large natural harbor in the island chain. Population density is only 174 per
square kilometer, as opposed to 322 in Grand Comoro and 448 on Anjouan.
(While also capable of development, Moheli is too small to represent as
considerable a solution to Comorean demographic and production problems.)

The reality of the Mayotte case transcends simple bourgeois rapacity by
the MPM or neocolonial power-grabbing by Paris. However distorted its
ethnic and cultural distinction has been in political rhetoric, Mayotte, like
most islands, does have a particular sensibility which sets it at odds with
the other Comoros. Historically, the Mahorais have lived in greater proximity
to Madagascar. The Majunga-Sakalava dialect and other elements of Malagasy
culture permeate their island as an important secondary culture, although
Comorean Swahili and Comorean Islam dominate Mahorais life. As France's
"old colony" in the Mozambique Channel, with twice as many European-
residents as the other Comoros combined, Mayotte also enjoys an undis-
putable affinity with the metropole. Longer familiarity with Europe and
with Madagascar has caused some important deviations in Mahorais society.
Women play a more influential, even conspicuous, role in public life, for
instance, than they do in the stricter Koranic paternalism of the other
islands.

Nevertheless, Mahorais particularity remains a matter of degree, not of
"race," or *Weltanschauung*. Apart from its Europeanized elite, the mostly
rural population has never experienced the degree of Francophone facility
or identification with France displayed, for instance, by the four original

urban "communes" of Senegal (St. Louis, Rufisque, Gorée, Dakar) or by the Creoles of Mauritius or the Antilles. What has penetrated Mayotte's population through its leadership is the double message that (1) independence in the ensemble would entail a sharing of poverty with the three sister islands, even inviting avid Comorean settlers bearing no capital, technology, or respect for Mahorais idiosyncrasies to flood Mayotte's vacant, fertile landscape and ply its fragile fisheries; and (2) staying with France, whether formally integrated as a Department or otherwise, would sustain dramatic improvements in construction, public works, education, and other social services, facilities for investment and security undertaken since 1976 by the French authorities. Some Mahorais also respond to Tory arguments that third world independence jeopardizes political and human liberties, invoking the revolutionary tribulations of Zanzibar, Madagascar, and Seychelles as nearby cases in point.

France thus appears as guardian of Mahorais peace, freedom, and hopes for prosperity. That self-determination in this island does not conform perfectly to the ideology of decolonization disturbs MPM stalwarts very little. Nor does the anomaly disquiet the conservative majority now governing France with a different conscience from that of the 1981 Socialist regime. Given a clear choice between being ruled from Moroni or from Paris, the Mahorais majority (which might well prefer neither alternative) has taken the latter option. Without having been manipulated any more flagrantly than voters in most third world elections, many Mahorais know that their option permits European, Arab, and Creole elites to retain control of land-use, commerce, and administrative services, acting as Paris' surrogates on a loyal little island. Still, MPM leaders and French residents (military and civil servants) yearn for an approximation of the Overseas Department relationship which has endowed nearby Réunion with the highest standard of living of any society between South Africa and Saudi Arabia. Mayotte's advantageous position in the Mozambique Channel and its superior harbor at Dzaoudzi provide geopolitical benefits appreciated in Paris, notwithstanding French Socialist insistence from 1975 that the Comoros be reunified.[8] During its five years in power, however, the Mitterand regime treated the Mayotte question in much the same manner as its Gaullist-Giscardist predecessors. Acknowledging that Mayotte could return to the Comorean state once the Mahorais felt sufficiently secure to reverse the direction of the earlier plebiscites, the Giscard and Mitterand policies have counted on time to heal alienated sensibilities. They have encouraged Comorean constitutional and political adjustments to help bring about a more conciliatory consensus on the separate island. This eventuality remains vigorously contested by the MPM as well as by local French residents, metropolitan Gaullists, and Réunionnais conservatives.

Continuing to classify the island in limbo as a "territorial collectivity" allows Paris' prefect to adapt overseas legislation to suit the island's circumstances. France is thus not obliged to finance the considerable socio-economic infrastructure presupposed by departmental status to which the

MPM leadership aspires. It also gives France freedom to make Mayotte available to Comorean reunification if time comes for that decision, without requiring the two-thirds majority of both Mahorais and French electorates specified for the alienation of department territory.[9]

In their transitional situation, the Mahorais can participate in French elections as citizens, pay taxes to and obtain benefits from France as decided by deliberate legislative or administrative determination, and be consulted periodically on what they wish France to do with them. They remain, of course, under French security and in the Franc Zone. They have obtained considerable improvement in roads, schools, public works, technical development, and guaranteed investment, while watching small contingents of the French Navy, Foreign Legion, and Gendarmerie deploy on and around their island. Their economic links with Réunion have multiplied and the Réunionnais establishment continues to regard Mayotte with avuncular affection. Dzaoudzi has become a kind of headquarters again, although it has to share the distinction across the harbor with Mutsamudu, principal town on Mayotte island proper.

While becoming deeply implicated in the "separate development" of Mayotte, the French government awaits a change of atmosphere on the archipelago as a whole which would encourage the Mahorais back into the Comoros without prejudice. International opprobrium, while mild for the present, could encumber French policy, particularly in the third world, if Paris should appear to be clinging to Mayotte on motives of military interest or to appease the French Right.

Like other powers which retain overseas dependencies, Paris cannot concur with the U.N. majority's dictum that self-determination must inevitably result in the conventional form of independent state. In the current tortured process in New Caledonia, for instance, Mitterand himself even proposed a limited form of "independence," in association with France.[10] Nevertheless, France seeks to minimize conflict with world opinion. Mayotte appears far more dispensable than, say, Réunion or the Caribbean Departments, or even the Pacific territories of Polynesia and New Caledonia which allow France to stretch her grandeur to global lengths. Mayotte is too small and too woefully undeveloped to promise much of a return on investment. Its authentic claims to Tricolor loyalty have been blatantly manipulated by a self-serving minority. It is claimed by a friendly third world state in relatively good standing within the U.N. and OAU, and it is surrounded by other third world countries, most of them genuinely non-aligned and all of them of value in the evolution of French relations in Africa and the Indian Ocean.

The strategic assets of Mayotte exert less attraction for Paris than the MPM and its champions claim. Réunion and Djibouti offer adequate alternative base accommodations for a modest military presence and there are new hopes in Paris for a return to Madagascar's great harbor at Antseranana (Diego Suarez). Even should the strategic value of Dzaoudzi harbor rise, its use might be better secured by cordial agreement with an accommodating regime in Moroni, as in the example of Djibouti, than by defying Comorean sensibilities through flagrant deployment of military force. Frustration over the irredentist case could eventually jeopardize Comorean accommodation, turning the Abdallah regime or a more nationalist successor away from France in vengeance. This is a consequence which French diplomacy has strenuously resisted in Madagascar, which the British have sought to avoid in Mauritius and Seychelles, and which would in effect isolate Réunion within a cauldron of Afro-Asian radicalism.

Notwithstanding the overriding logic of a policy favoring Comorean reunification, France cannot at present commit the reluctant Mahorais to the appetites of a dubious Comorean state seeking outlets for excess population and a taxable bonanza. Respect for the particular character of each island in the federal state has been thetorically assured by Comorean leaders since before the first referenda. It has been embodied, at French behest, in the Federal Constitution of 1978. But Comorean federalism leaves much to be desired in practice, and the unsavory reputation of Moroni's leadership diminishes the international pressure on France to act precipitously.[11] Mayotte the collectivity probably hovers in constitutional uncertainty until the next plebiscite, already indefinitely postponed from its 22 December 1984 deadline.

Instant Revolution, Prompt Thermidor

The dubious comportment of Comorean leadership since 1975 has helped France endure her dilemma over Mayotte. After its first reaction, a state of emergency backed by a showing of the Legion at critical points on the archipelago, Paris relaxed. Regrouping its forces on Mayotte, France proceeded to make public life impossible for Moroni by withholding budgetary subsidies pending reconciliation. A long month went by without perceptible progress toward resolving the state of rebellion.

On August 3, a coalition of notables, radicals, and technocrats deposed Ahmed Abdallah in a genteel coup d'état without bloodshed. Abdallah's reputation as "reactionary, obscurantist, corrupt, nepotistic, and anti-French," above all, suddenly and surprisingly, anti-French, condemned him in the estimation of powerful conservatives like Said Ibrahim and Said Mohamed Jaffar. He thus became the crucial obstacle to reconcilation over Mayotte and the benevolent recognition of their sovereign republic. They were shortly to be undeceived on the nature of French reticence as well as on the character of their own junta. The unilateral declaration had not only given the French a pretext for forsaking an onerous colonial burden while maintaining control over its most attractive component. It had also transformed Comorean politics from an imperially protected tourney of medieval Muslim barons into a seething ideological arena. While the lords of the old jousting parties retained nominal leadership for a time, the real force of their coup d'état maneuvered behind a young, middle class agricultural engineer named Ali Soilih, who had once led the left wing of Said Ibrahim's Umma party.

On August 3, Soilih became Minister of Justice and Defense in a state without judges and without an army. His first achievement was to unify the three accessible islands under the junta. This required the application of force to dislodge the deposed, unreconciled Abdallah from his bailiwick on Anjouan island, where he had surrounded himself with a small, yet in Comorean terms, formidable Praetorian guard. On September 21, in a move that was to set an ironic precedent against him, Soilih dispatched a company of hastily trained commandos led by a half-dozen European mercenaries to Anjouan, evicting and exiling the "Father" of Comoros' infant independence.

Soilih's second accomplishment consisted in allowing the junta's Francophile aristocrats time to fail in their own supplication to France over Mayotte. That failure achieved, Soilih could replace them in the name of national efficacy. Inevitably suspected of complicity in the August 3 coup to punish the ambivalent Abdallah, France cooperated very little with his replacements. While still in negotiations with the new regime, they began evacuating civil servants and teachers from all except Mayotte.

Allowing MPM militants to expell the Anjouanais and Grand Comoreans from Mayotte, the Gendarmerie also helped defeat a Gandhi-like attempt by Soilih to assert Comorean authority on that elusive isle. Arriving on November 21, after the failure of Jaffar's negotiations in Paris, fifty unarmed men with no mercenaries in their midst this time, were summarily turned back by the Mahorais at Dzaoudzi airfield, still wearing their red and white kerchiefs of unrequited reconciliation.[12]

Nor did the prolonged negotiations in Paris succeed in normalising relations or reunifying the territory. In October, France announced its intention to satisfy the MPM with a second referendum on Mayotte. While withholding its own recognition, France noted the international endorsement, if not assistance, which the Comoreans had received for their Mayotte grievance. On July 30, the young republic was admitted by the OAU, with the U.N. following suit on November 12, against French objections to language implying the inclusion of Mayotte. On December 10, France finally recognized the *fait accompli*, extending recognition explicitly to three, not four, islands.

This gesture seemed to hurt more than it helped the government of President Jaffar. During the interim, France had been considering herself relieved of obligation for the survival of the new, virtually helpless republic. Financial subsidies were suspended in July and 2,000 French officials and family members were evacuated by early December, leaving the Comoros without an administration. As in the case of Guinea after the fateful referendum of 1958, France was fulfilling DeGaulle's prophecy that those who abandoned her would renounce the capital, technology, services, labor market, and communications hitherto assured by the French presence. Amounting to eighty percent of public expenditures, France's regular twenty million dollar subsidy had never been enough to satisfy Comorean administrative needs, but it was indispensable. On its own, the republic was able at best to amass no more than four million dollars in state revenues; and massive help was not visible on any of its horizons. Loyal Mayotte was to benefit, but the three Comoros had declared themselves sovereign without adequate preparation for the future and must henceforth take the consequences on their own.

After five months behind Jaffar, using the noble President for his symbolic value in domestic cohesion and his acceptability to France, Soilih took charge. In the National Revolutionary Council (CNR) meeting of January 2, 1976, he ousted the incumbent by sixteen votes to six (with three abstentions). France declined to react to this third instance of illegitimacy, but Paris could not have been overjoyed by the new turn to the left. Soilih's mission soon became clearer: it was an original, almost wildly accelerated program of administrative, cultural, economic, and political reconstruction, a practically suicidal act of total decolonization. Virtually all the French-trained indigenous civil service was discharged, central administration reduced to a skeleton, archives demolished to obliterate the colonial past, and a new system of decentralized authority inaugurated.

A commoner with technical training, Ali Soilih sought within a few months to reverse not merely a century of French rule but a millennium of Comorean history. He had seized control over a somnolent administration abandoned by its indispensable European operators, and he proceeded to assault both the modicum of modernity represented by France and the indigenous tradition which had supplied Comorean identity. The paternal French having abandoned their part of the structure, Soilih's principal enemy was the anachronistic oligarchy of "Sharifean" families. Cooperating with clearly defined French interests in security and in plantation export-import commerce, this landed aristocracy monopolized Comorean society from political leadership to domestic market trade. In the name of Islam, but in recondite patterns of custom not readily recognizable farther north, they sanctioned the elaborate and costly ceremonies of the Mosque without which no Comorean could be considered eligible for social distinction. They thus governed the liturgically defined channels of educational, professional, and political mobility. Young men could not progress in any respect without endorsement through the appropriate "grand marriage" ceremony under the presidency of the patriarchs.[13] These families dominated the Comorean civil service, colonially trained to think of itself as a consumer elite rather than a social utility. They nurtured economically vital alliances with European concessionaires and international trading interests who in turn controlled allocations of the islands' scanty economic and fiscal resources.

To escape the prejudice of this exotic feudal system, thousands of Comoreans had emigrated to France, Madagascar, and East Africa. Those who returned after 1975 joined Soilih and the few remaining technicians, intellectuals, and schoolboys in an alliance against family privilege and class collaboration with the foreigners. Their campaign was deliberately modeled on the Chinese Cultural Revolution of 1966, yet remained without the transcendental authority of a Mao Tsetung or the ancient disciplinary traditions of China's army and bureaucracy. To effect a genuinely secularizing revolution, Soilih knew he would have to operate not only against the prevailing structures of property and politics, but on the atavistic cultural foundations underlying the objectionable system. Naively, he thought he could uproot that system by abolishing its objective manifestations, that to prohibit the veil of modesty for women and the turban of devotion for men, for instance, would eradicate the human sources of female subordination and class privilege. The aim of the program was a rapidly ordained modern socialist community carried on the overriding spirit of a presumed popular revolution. The metamorphosis may have been calculated from the *Little Red Book*, but it lacked the depth and the patience needed to accomplish a national upheaval in a society not yet permeated by revolutionary impulses. Some conditions of revolution may have been perceptible but the self-awareness of being "damned of the earth" had not emerged.[14]

In practice, all stages of the revolution were lugubriously telescoped into matters of months, like a simulation game played on a cybernetic reproduction of social process. Phase one of the program consisted of political emancipation from "foreign and bourgeois" control of productive resources. The objective was allegedly achieved by simple seizure of power from the corrupt Abdallah and the reactionary Jaffar, facilitated by France's evacuation in alacrity. But what were the productive resources remaining to the triumphant people and how were they to make use of them?

Phase two entailed an equally expeditious victory for modernization over the oligarchist "medieval mentality" by banning the flamboyant liturgies and the symbolism of atavistic tradition. The revolution thereupon turned to implementation of a decentralized system of government by village units, called *mudirias*. Directed by what Soilih called an "administrator-educator," in a curious echo of the revolutionary pedagogy of Paolo Freire,[15] the mudiria was designed as a veritably autarchic complex, with agricultural, commercial, cultural, judicial, police, and civil jurisdiction. Land was declared national property, to be distributed to a suddenly productive peasantry; education to be liberated from the dead hand of the Mosque and from the intimidation of French culture; the national diet to be emancipated from costly dependence on imported rice through large-scale cultivation of corn. Comorean Swahili became the sole official language. The voting age was lowered to fourteen years.

Its three phases compressed into a copybook caricature of the struggle that took China twenty years and Algeria at least eight to complete, the Soilih revolution foundered on its own chimerical ambition. Land allocations encountered fierce proprietary disputes and all administrative reforms fell into procedural pitfalls. The few schools which remained open depended on French-speaking teachers, some of them Comorean, others from Belgium, Senegal, and Algeria, all of them living from hand to mouth. Agricultural production withered, particularly in the vital export sectors, from an absence of funds to hire replacements for the evacuated French. Even the construction of the mudiria buildings, an important visible sign of revolutionary progress, faltered for want of cement—which eventually had to be imported from detested South Africa. People of experience and means melted away, alienated by the regime's inability to meet its payroll or its debt, alarmed by the impetuosity of its reforms. Their defection left adolescents and ideologues in charge of the vestigial civil service, the mudirias, and the ultimately irrepressible "Commando Moissi," Soilih's version of Mao's Red Guards.

Refugees from Soilih's revolution soon reached Mayotte, Madagascar, and Reunion, recounting tales of repression and misery. The Moissi vigilantes, although more or less trained by Tanzania, were behaving like Tonton Macoutes. Four attempts were reported on Soilih's life. Epidemic hunger had become starvation. In December 1976 and the following January, 17,000 Comorean refugees were repatriated after bloody riots in Majunga where Malagasy had risen (some say with Government encouragement) in resentment against the relative affluence of the long established Comorean community. The luckless regime had thus to absorb a new, impecunious population equal to some five percent of the Comorean totality. Human rights violations abounded, although trials of political prisoners were few and executions rare. Not surprisingly, refugees and their predisposed French correspondents denounced the ubiquity of "gulags," of torture and official terrorism in a fascist state.

Although Soilih insisted that by eliminating "social charlatanism" and other abuses, he was in fact defending the purity of Islam, his regime was vilified by the devout and his application for membership in the Arab League was refused. The Giscard regime, secure in its protection for Mayotte against barbarism, felt under no obligation to rescue a tyranny approved nowhere. Some help had come from China for the organization of rural communes, from Tanzania for military and police training, from Libya for Muslim education. A few international aid programs continued operating minimally, but most of the assistance obtained at the outset from U.N., European, and Arab sources evaporated as the revolution spun out of control. External agencies could get little collaboration from Soilih's rudimentary administration. The regime lost sympathy in East Africa and among Comorean students abroad whose ideological dispositions became rapidly diverted by the failure of their scholarship remittances from penurious Moroni. Food and other necessities became dangerously scarce. In Fall 1977, Moheli was in open rebellion. The state was living at best from day to day.[16]

In October 1977, Soilih made an extraordinary public confession of his personal failure to bring the revolution to fruition after two years of struggle. The mudiria scheme lagged behind schedule; phase three was not succeeding. He did not acknowledge the imprudence of his conceptions for phases one and two. Asking the Comorean people to pardon him for his "conceptual error," he sought by referendum to renew his mandate until the mudirias could be completed, after which he would retire and allow a successor to organize the first elections in the independent state. The Comorean electorate responded to this refreshing act of self-sacrificial candor by an equally unusual manifestation of divided public opinion: Soilih received his authorization with 65,906 votes, only 55 percent of the ballots cast on October 28.

In early 1978, fifty-seven *mudirs* were appointed to operate the partially constituted local organizations, but the vestigial economy and the state's security deteriorated even further. Riots were suppressed with brutality on all three islands. Soilih became a recluse, rarely seen during the final months of his regime. He was arrested at his residence on the night of May 12-13, 1978 by a squadron of the fifty European mercenaries hired by Abdallah in France. Even the Moissi commandos had fled and the 2,000-man Army, after being neglected in favor of the "red guards," willingly laid down its arms. Abdallah was recalled from exile on May 21 to find only four million CFA francs (about $16,000) in the state treasury, against overdue liabilities of more than 600 million. On May 28, the revolution's leader was shot and killed while conveniently indulging in the classic act of "trying to escape" from detention. He was undone by some of the same hired guns whom he had himself engaged as Defense Minister in order to deliver the new state from Abdallah in September 1975.

Although resumption of Abdallah's mandate returned Comoros to its constitutional status quo ante, the restored President's mercenaries have added a new chapter to the great grotesque romance of Indian Ocean illegitimacy. Their leader, the French Gilbert Bourgeaud, alias Bob Denard, had helped Soilih evict Abdallah from Anjouan. He was thus engineering his own previous victim's revenge and his erstwhile patron's assassination. Denard could also boast of freebooting exploits in Biafra, Rhodesia, Algeria, Zaire, Cabinda, Yemen, and Gabon, and probably in Benin and Seychelles, but his only distinct success occurred in Comoros. So he and his cohorts of 1978 decided, like so many buccaneers before them, to make a home in the southwestern Indian Ocean. Denard even changed his name once more, to Colonel Said Mustapha M'Hazou, taking a Comorean wife and joining Abdallah's political-military directorate. Several dozen of his colleagues in the adventure against Soilih also blended as well as they could into Comorean society. Many of them appropriated real estate and business franchises as the state turned back to private property and other forms of normalcy. Others stayed on to train and command the army and police force.[17]

In October 1978, Abdallah who had been sharing authority with Mohamed Ahmed, another wealthy merchant exile under Soilih, stood alone for reelection. He was depending by then on France to resume benevolent responsibility for finance, social services, and the restoration of Mayotte, now that the frightful Soilih was out of the way. But he found that somebody else was still in it: Denard. He did everything he could to ingratiate his regime with the colonizer whom he had offended in the 1975 declaration. He allowed French jurists to draft a new constitution with federal guarantees to facilitate Mayotte's return with due respect for its distinction. He accepted French replacements to train the army, shifting the mercenaries to his own palace guard. The Guard thereupon became the principal security force, relegating the army once again to ceremonial status. But the influential audience in France and the third world refused to tolerate the company he kept. His delegation was rejected by the OAU meeting at Khartoum in August not because it represented a government which had overthrown Soilih, but because it had employed unsavory non-Africans of the kind who used to frequent Katanga's Moise Tshombe. Denying any responsibility for helping Abdallah come back, the Giscard government delayed recognition until July 1, and then declined to discuss such things as Mayotte until the mercenaries stopped enjoying their conspicuous favors on the islands.

Denard-M'Hazou had to leave, and he did so in a grand show of personal regret and national gratitude, on September 28. Or, at all events, he agreed to transfer his principal residence to Bordeaux and thence to Johannesburg where he operates businesses which take him frequently to the third world, including of course his beloved Comoros. At least two dozen of his less notorious comrades remained and Abdallah continued to suffer the prejudice of their association. Among their enterprises, according to authenticated press accounts, is a steady transhipment of arms, medicines, and other supplies at Moroni and Anjouan airfields for the Mozambique National Resistance (MNR or ReNaMo), even after March 1984 when South Africa formally undertook to end its own support of the guerrillas. Intimacy with Pretoria, enhanced in December 1984 by a clandestine visit to Moroni by South African Foreign Minister R.F. ("Pik") Botha, includes cooperation in airline flights, tourism, and overall investment.[18] European mercenary colonists enjoy central roles in this new network of international liaisons, largely beyond Abdallah's control.

From the beginning of his renewed tenure, Abdallah demonstrated his intention to restore the pre-revolutionary domestic situation as it had been. Private property was returned to its owners, veils and turbans to their rightful bearers, the Koran to the schools and national radio, the minimum voting age to eighteen years, and the state to what its President called "non-ideological" normalcy. The Comoros recovered gradually from their thirty-three month revolutionary stampede. Arrests, summary executions, and disappearances cleared out the remaining enthusiasts for Soilih's experiment. The new "federal" constitution, establishing Islam as state religion, was adopted by over 99 percent of the 187,000 votes cast in another referendum, on October 1, 1978. It fails to provide for a second legislative chamber or other institution to represent the interests of the several constituent islands of the federation. Administrative practice—and court decisions—have favored central authority over the governors and island councils which nominally administer economic and public affairs.[19]

In November 1978, normalization with France was consecrated by five bilateral agreements, a vehicle familiar to all who experienced the francophone decolonization process of the 1960s. The accords provide for privileged relations; economic and financial assistance through French institutions and Franc Zone facilities; assignment of French technicians and teachers; cultural and educational exchange; mutual aid against external aggression as well as military assistance and training for the reconstituted Comorean army.[20] They ignore the problem of Mayotte.

On his own islands, the President enjoys only casual esteem, and he has had a bumpy career since 1978. He is forthrightly denounced on Mayotte and is regarded by some as an impediment to the consensus change which France seeks in order to repair the secession. The only authorized news media in Comoros, the state radio and sycophantic press agency, are carefully adjusted to sustain artificial adulation and keep general information to a minimum. But the army, civil servants, teachers, and other organized groups have resisted Abdallah tenaciously. In October 1980, the Federal Assembly voted an extraordinarily weak resolution of confidence which not only shocked constitutionalists, but also revealed shakiness in the President's grip. Rather than reaching the unanimity customary in a still party-less state, Abdallah obtained only twenty-three of the thirty-eight votes; six deputies abstained and nine declined to participate in the confidence resolution vote.[21]

Several attempts to overthrow Abdallah have been discovered and thwarted by his friends. In 1983, Australia and France cooperated in aborting a third round of mercenary machinations against the young republic; this time, the plot evidently originated in a vociferous but heterogeneous opposition coalition based in Paris.[22] On March 8, 1985, the non-Anjouanais contingent of Abdallah's palace guardsmen bungled an attempt to reverse the regime during one of the President's frequent prolonged absences from home. The putsch was easily foiled by loyal yeomen and their resident mercenary officers who had evidently been forewarned. Rather than hasten back to Moroni to reinforce his authority in the aftermath of the emergency, the insouciant Abdallah thanked his rescuers by radio from Paris and proceeded to Mecca on pilgrimage, his political debt to fortune's soldiers having become ever deeper.[23]

Outside the archipelago, opposition has become more forceful, even strident, during the Abdallah mandate. Protagonists of the Soilih revolution have joined with conservative Islamic patriots in France and East Africa to prepare appropriate retribution for Abdallah's alleged tyranny. The overseas French press and authoritative spokesmen permit little expression of fondness for the Comorean President, who remains caught between his failure to recover Mayotte from France and his inability to sever ties with his mercenary benefactors.

The combination of mercenary cronyism, avowed subservience to French interests, and rededication to the discredited pre-revolutionary social system continued for some time to alienate Madagascar, Seychelles, Mauritius, and East African socialist states from Abdallah's Comoros. Diplomatic isolation in turn hampered otherwise credible international campaigns to recover Mayotte. It has ironically thrown the archipelago even more deeply into dependence on France.

On the arrival in power of the French Left in May 1981, Abdallah's own character became an increasing liability in Paris. The President has matched his distinguished career in public service with equally notable business success. He and his family became conspicuously wealthy through a virtual monopoly on external trade in certain major commodities in and out of their home island, Anjouan. They made substantial profits from subsidized Asian rice imports during the previous decade while most Comoreans were suffering privation and malnutrition and the island economy slipped farther than ever from self-sufficiency. The leader whom Moroni taxi drivers contemptuously call "President Export-Import" joined the French Left's list of rapacious third world despots, together with central Africa's egregious "Emperor" Bokassa and other unmentionables. François Mitterand and his Socialist Party had commented publicly in the past on the Comorean President's penchant for authoritarian, nepotistic, and opportunistic behavior. The platform under which they campaigned to victory in 1981 called for the return of Mayotte but denial of other French concessions to Comoros while the repugnant Abdallah governed.[24] This formula has allowed Paris to withhold both Mayotte and other factors until Abdallah changed policy or character, or both.

Professing more philosophic regret than anger, and more patience than either, the Comorean chief of state nonetheless persists in his courtship of a former metropole which refuses to understand him. He has offered Paris anything it wants on Mayotte, if only the island is returned to Comorean sovereignty. This solution is anathema to the Mahorais political leadership of Mayotte, at least while Abdallah governs the Comoros. Since the only likely alternative is a return to the chaos of Comorean radicalism, France is wedded to an uncongenial but acquiescent partner in Moroni.

Paris' reluctance to accede to Abdallah's suit has increased pressure for greater progress in internal change, the principal object of French policy in Comoros. In February 1982, Abdallah responded by recasting his governmental structures and personnel, dissolving the Federal Assembly and appointing as Prime Minister Ali Mroudjae, known for his competence and probity. Despite a legislative ban on political parties for twelve years from 1978, Abdallah founded the Union for Comorean Progress (UPC), to carry out presidential behest. Some of the new single party's charge was shifted from the bulbous federal civil service, which was reduced by one-third of its personnel on the draconian advice of French experts. In the general campaign for regime credibility, a new parastatal import company was created in 1982 to handle the rice business which had theretofore made the President rich. By 1983, cheerful complaisance wore out the resistance. France's Socialists stopped treating Abdallah an anathema; Tanzania, Seychelles, and even Madagascar began to consider him there to stay. In January 1985, no longer ostracized from the neighborhood, the Comoreans were finally inducted into the Indian Ocean Commission (IOC), joining Madagascar, Seychelles, Mauritius, and France (sitting for Réunion) in a modestly hopeful sub-regional combination in search of international aid and standing.

In addition to sustaining profitable good will from France, Abdallah has obtained substantial financial and technical assistance from Egypt and other Arab donors, the OPEC funds, the African Development Bank, the UN agencies, and the European Communities. South Africa has become a conspicuous source of investment in a country desperate for capital, expertise, and revenues to offset a woefully lopsided trade imbalance. Comoros exported the equivalent of $18.4 million in 1983 against imports of $32.5 million. In 1984, as the vanilla market collapsed, Comorean exports fell by 58 percent, while rising prices for "dollar" products like rice and petroleum drove imports up by 43 percent, raising the trade deficit to $34 million (about 35 percent of GDP for that year). External assets dwindled, and the estimated balance of payments was $7 million in arrears.

The difference between the trade and payments deficits is achieved by substantial financial aid commitments from France, other European, and Arab donors. Virtually all agricultural development is externally financed. A new surge of concessionary international loans has put the archipelago on the long list of third world debtor states. Thanks to such overseas transfers, per capita income exceeded $300 in 1983 for the first time in Comorean history. The state has also begun to build a medical service and started a gamut of new educational and training programs (removing health and education from island administration in favor of federal jurisdiction). Public works projects, agricultural cooperatives, and other new institutions have been designed to bring Comoros into the contemporary developing world.[25]

Abdallah's aim is to inspire national solidarity and developmental dynamics without sacrificing entrenched French import-export business or the traditional anachronisms which assure stability to a highly conservative society under stress. The strategy breeds its own contradictions. New food and export crops can encroach only with utmost deference on archaic landholding prerogatives, and a shockingly inadequate educational system can improve only without offending canonical patterns of traditional schooling.[26] The federal structure must seem to permit expression of Mayotte's particularity before the lost island can be lured toward reunification. Yet decentralization cannot be permitted to disturb the sedate anarchy of Comorean political relationships. The mercenary barons of 1978 (and some later arrivals and replacements) fit into these patterns neatly, if at the sacrifice of political liberties and of popular aspirations for prosperity and self-determination.

While the results of these shifts under pressure remain in doubt, France has clearly reasserted responsibility for the archipelago's security and macroeconomic fortunes. Repeating an earlier success in Djibouti, Paris organized an international consortium of major public and private investors in Comoros during 1984, internationalizing developmental burdens while maintaining the privileged rapports guaranteed in the cooperation accords. French personnel keep their eye on indigenous institutions and exile opposition machinations, protecting regime stability, containing Comorean nationalism, juggling mercenaries and patriots, and maneuvering over Mayotte for as long as necessary. With that insular bit of advantage, France retains status as a principal power in the southwestern Indian Ocean.[27]

Notes

1. The scanty Comoros bibliography includes Hervé Chagnoux and Ali Haribou, *Les Comores*, Que sais-je? no. 1829 (Paris: Presses Universitaires de France, 1980); Thierry Flobert, *Les Comores: évolution juridique et socio-politique*, Travaux et mémoires de la Faculté de Droit et de Science politique d'Aix-Marseille, no. 24 (Aix-en-Provence, France: CERSOI, 1976); Malyn Newitt, *The Comoro Islands: Struggle against Dependency in the Indian Ocean*, (Boulder, Colorado: Westview Press; London: Gower, 1984); *The Comores: Problems and Prospects of a Small Island Economy*, World Bank Country Study (Washington: The World Bank, 1979); *Etude succinte des caractéristiques économiques et sociales du milieu rural comorien* (New York: UNICEF-FAO, 1980); Colin Legum, ed., *Africa Contemporary Record* (ACR) (New York and London: Holmes & Meier, Africana Press, annually since 1968–69); *Annuaire des pays de l'Océan Indien* (APOI) (Aix-en-Provence, France: CERSOI, periodically since 1974).

2. For France's Gibraltarean ambitions re Dzaoudzi, see Flobert, *Evolution juridique*, pp. 57–69 and Newitt, *Comoro Islands*, pp. 3, 25–26.

3. For Comorean party development, see Flobert, *Evolution juridique*; Newitt, *Comoro Islands*, Ch. 3; and John M. Ostheimer, "The Politics of Comorian Independence," in John M. Ostheimer, ed., *The Politics of the Western Indian Ocean Islands* (New York: Praeger Publishers, 1975).

4. See "Comoro Islands," in ACR, *1974–75*, pp. B 154–55; *1975–76*, pp. B 178–182; *1976–77*, pp. B 171–72; Chagnoux and Haribou, *Les Comores*, pp. 53–57.

5. ACR, *1975–76*, pp. B 178–181; Thierry Michalon, "Mayotte et les Comores," in *Le Monde Diplomatique* (Paris), December 1984 and subsequent exchange of correspondence in *Ibid.*, April 1985, p. 29.

6. ACR passages cited in note no. 4.

7. *Le Monde* (Paris), August 5, 1975, November 23–24, 1975, February 8–9 and 10, 1976; *Marchés Tropicaux et Méditerranéens* (MTM) (Paris), August 8, 1975, October 24, 1975.

8. For conditions on Mayotte, see Michalon, "Mayotte et les Comores;" Ian Hamel, "Mayotte entre deux eaux," in *Jeune Afrique* (Paris), 1276, 19 June 1985, pp. 15–20; J.P. Langellier, in *Le Monde*, 25 April 1981; Sadio Lamine Sow, "En attendant Mayotte," in *Jeune Afrique*, 27 January 1982; ACR articles on Comoros, annually, 1975–76 to date.

9. The reference is to Articles Two and Fifty-three, para. 3 of the French Constitution which require consent of "the populations concerned" for any territorial addition or deletion. See Jean-Paul Négrin, Le Fédéralisme à la Comorienne," APOI, Vol. 7, 1980; Hamel, "Mayotte entre deux eaux."

10. For the so-called "Pisani Plan" for New Caledonia, see *New York Times*, 8 January and 26 April, 1985, as well as virtually daily coverage in French press from early January through the year.

11. *Ibid.*

12. *Jeune Afrique* no. 778, December 5, 1975.

13. Chagnoux and Haribou, *Les Comores*, pp. 51–52.

14. See Frantz Fanon, "On National Culture," in Fanon, *The Wretched of the Earth*, trans. Constance Farrington (New York: Grove Press, 1968), pp. 206–248.

15. See Paulo Freire, *Pedagogy of the Oppressed*, trans. Myra Bergman Ramos (New York: Seabury Press, 1970), Ch. 3.

16. For a favorable assessment of the Soilih regime, see Chagnoux and Haribou, *Les Comores*, pp. 70–81.

17. ACR, 1978–79, pp. B 186–190; Philippe Leymarie, "La nouvelle vogue des mercenaires," in Le Monde Diplomatique (Paris), January 1982; François Soudan, in Jeune Afrique, no. 1264, 27 March 1985, pp. 36–37.

18. See Economist Intelligence Unit (London), Quarterly Economic Review: Madagascar, Mauritius, Seychelles, Comoros (EIU), no 1, 1985, pp. 8–9; Africa Confidential (London), Vol. 26, no. 15, 17 July 1985, pp. 3–6; Jeune Afrique, no. 1265, 3 April 1985, p. 27; ACR, 1983–84, p. B 108. For Nkomati accords, ACR, 1983–84, pp. B 670–672; Allen Isaacman, "After The Nkomati Accord," Africa Report (New York), vol. 30, no. 1, Jan-Feb 1985, pp. 10–13.

19. Négrin, "Le Fédéralisme;" ACR, 1978–79, p. C 42.

20. Chagnoux and Haribou, Les Comores, pp. 96–100; ACR, 1980–81, p. B 150; Claude Gaspart, "The Comoro Islands since Independence: An Economic Appraisal," in Alex Kerr, ed., The Indian Ocean Region: Resources and Development (Boulder, Colorado, Westview Press, 1981), pp. 123–143.

21. See Africa Now, April 1983 and September 1983; Afrique-Asie, June 20, 1983; Drum, June 1983; Daily Times (London), October 19, 1983; Agence France Presse from Perth, December 12, 1983. For background on exile opposition, see ACR, 1981–82, pp. B 131–132. EIU, no. 1, 1985, pp. 8–9; Africa Confidential, Vol. 26, no. 15, 17 July 1985, p. 6.

22. Négrin, "Le Fédéralisme."

23. For accounts of the March 1985 attempted coup, see Agence France Presse (Moroni), 14 March and 18 April 1985; Africa Confidential, Vol 26, no. 15, 17 July 1985; Le Monde, 21 May 1985; François Soudan, in Jeune Afrique, no. 1264, 27 March 1985, pp. 36–37.

24. Parti Socialiste Français, "Manifeste de Créteil," press release, Paris, January 24, 1981; "Le parti socialiste et l'Afrique sud-saharienne," Le mois en Afrique 186–87 (June-July 1981), pp. 16–42.

25. World Bank, Problems and Prospects, pp. 86–91; Chagnoux and Haribou, Les Comores, pp. 10–123; ACR, 1981–82, pp. B 130–132, B 138–141; ACR, 1982–83, pp. B 117–121.

26. The World Bank, The Comoros: Current Economic Situation and Prospects. A World Bank Country Study (Washington: The World Bank, 1983), passim (note all data are 1980 or earlier).

27. ACR, 1983–84, pp. B 105–107; ACR, 1984–85; Africa Confidential, Vol. 26, no. 15, 17 July 1985; Hamel, "Mayotte entre deux eaux;" "S.A.," in Jeune Afrique, no. 1257, 27 March 1985; Ibid., no. 1265, 3 April 1985, p. 27.

3

Réunion:
Assimilation Vindicated

First and final society of Indian Ocean France, Réunion was created in 1665 as a supply station on the routes of empire. It had been known to Asian seafolk and sixteenth century Portuguese mariners as a beautiful uninhabited watering spot without secure harbors in an often insecure ocean. A Portuguese captain awarded his own name to the trio of "Mascarenes" strung in a line eastward from Réunion through Mauritius to distant Rodriguez. Seven hundred kilometers to the west, Madagascar casts its great shadow seaward toward this bobbing, double-peaked, volcanic island.

Serious settlement of Réunion followed a badly managed attempt to insert French East Indies Company colonists among the uncongenial populations of southeastern Madagascar. Bourbon, as the island was originally called, developed slowly into a quiet haven of family subsistence, providing food, water, and wood for passing vessels of the company and the Crown. By 1715 it was using slave labor from Madagascar and elsewhere to convert substantial virgin land to the cultivation of coffee for continental breakfasts. Mauritius (Ile de France), Rodriguez, and subsequently the Seychelles archipelago to the north followed Bourbon as foundations of France in the hitherto unpopulated waters east of Madagascar.

Crucible of Dependence

These were the settlements of Crown and company under seventeenth and eighteenth century conceptions of colonies as extrapolated repositories of metropolitan grandeur. They represented an ingenious virtue made of two prime necessities—overpopulation (or social ferment) at home and maintenence needs along the spokes of global mercantile networks. To serve both purposes, Europe created exclaves of their own folk operating distantly but in commercial and cultural touch with the original civilization. This approach corresponds to the way Greek and Phoenician home states envisioned their own western Mediterranean settlements before such colonies became sufficiently strong for autonomy or sufficiently weak for absorption into new, greater empires. Eventually, Comoros and finally Madagascar were to follow the Seychelles and Mascarenes into French domination, but these were previously populated countries and, besides, the illusions of empire had changed radically by the later nineteenth century. Territory was then taken for whatever it was worth in a panic of possessiveness called the "scramble for Africa."[1]

No object of scramble, this proud Bourbon. Western star of the three glittering Mascarenes, Réunion is now an Overseas Department, France's oldest and most constant outpost in the eastern hemisphere, her most populous patrimony outside continental Europe. With Mayotte, the controversial "collectivity" destined eventually to be returned to the independent Comoros, Réunion is also the last remaining territory of European population in the huge zone between Spanish Melilla and Hong Kong.[2] Réunion-Bourbon has remained steadily French in thick and much thin for over three centuries. Its reward for a half million citizens today is perhaps the highest general standard of living in the Indian Ocean south of the Persian Gulf.

Distinguished as its destiny is, Réunion has had no easy time in serving French purposes, hanging on to survival and ultimately attaining relative material prosperity. It has not been an easy place for France to favor. A second thought after Madagascar, Bourbon displayed no natural resources of economic importance. With only 2,500 square kilometers of area, most of it in forbidding volcanic highland, it is 230 times smaller than its western neighbor. This space barely satisfied the original 220 company settlers sent there in 1669 to flag and refresh its ships along the southern tradewinds to the Indies. An intimidating coastline without reefs or beaches, and a spectacular vertical topography to this day impede communications within the island and with the outside world. Gentler contours and two secure harbors only 200 kilometers to the east recommended Mauritius over Bourbon as administrative headquarters for mercantile and military operations. The slightly smaller Mascarene was promptly occupied and renamed Ile de France after the departure of the Dutch way-station which had occupied it from 1638 to 1715. Thenceforth, the Bourbon colony stagnated while its handsomer sister grew into a tropical metropolis, surveying the passages to and from India. It was the Ile de France which joined the futile fight against Britain for domination over Southern Asia in the latter eighteenth century.

The role assigned to rustic Bourbon, particularly after the failure of the island's coffee export vocation by midcentury, was to provide food, cotton cloth, and tobacco for the Ile de France and her cosmopolitan callers. The great Mahé de Labourdonnais, Governor of the Mascarenes and Seychelles from 1735 to 1746, fortified Saint Denis and made it the capital of the island. But Mahé seldom visited or paid any other heed to the countrified sibling of his extroverted Ile de France. Even the Revolution of 1793 changed little except her name, replacing the late royal lineage by the hopeful but vain promise of "Réunion." Revolutionary France stirred local politics vigorously, but failed even to emancipate Bourbon's slaves.

In the peace settlements that followed Napoleon's wars, only Réunion of all the previously conquered Mascarenes and Seychelles was relinquished by the victorious British. This was a gesture to the defeated empire without much geopolitical cost to England. Bourbon France took the island back in 1814–1815 without bothering to reverse the revolutionary name change. What the restored monarchy obtained was an impoverished rural society of 15,000 peasants (habitants) and 50,000 slaves producing wheat, rice, corn, cassava, beans, peas, and cotton, coffee, and cloves for their own use and for occasional sale to a hastily passing ship. Decades of neglect and of debilitating warfare, ruinous landholding policies, favoritism for the Ile de France and bad weather in cyclone season had exhausted the island's productive assets. The coffee plantations operated feebly through the latter eighteenth century and barely survived the cyclones of 1806–1807. By 1836, two-thirds of the white population was officially indigent.[3] Systematic poverty had been driving many of its Europeans, debt-ridden and landless, into military service, to other colonies and—characteristic phenomenon of the place—into the glowering hills; there they survived in miserable freedom as squatters and sharecroppers alongside former slaves and other fugitives. This rural "proletarianisation" of many European settlers has facilitated the remarkable blending of ethnic and social class lines of the Réunionnais Creole today. In good times and bad, during its entire life as a colony, the population of Réunion grew relentlessly larger.[4]

Slavery had been introduced into the original Bourbon as a reflex of the times. Despite the vicissitudes of servitude on the island, the slave population grew to three times that of the European by the mid-eighteenth century. During the course of that century, the descendants of bondsfolk from Madagascar, and subsequently from East Africa, came to outnumber the communities of formerly unfree and indentured coolies from India. Although small numbers of European women had been delivered to the island in its first century as a colony, the process of interbreeding among ethnic groups and castes began producing a predominantly Creole society of color from the outset.

In periods of famine and social misery, as during the French Revolution and subsequent British occupation (1809–1814), some slaves obtained their freedom by regular or other means. Many of them joined the poor whites in the inhospitable highlands. By 1848, when slavery was abolished throughout the French Empire, Réunion's population included some 8,000 "freed" persons whose rights had been made theoretically equal to those of whites in 1833. Interbreeding on plantations and intermarriage in the hill country transformed the denotation of "Creole" to a majority population of mixed ethnic origins with its own linguistic and social adaptations of fundamental French colonial institutions. Since France declines to partition its censuses in racial terms, the dimensions of the Creole majority remain imprecise; it is probably equivalent to eighty percent of the 510,000 Réunionnais.

Although it took time to make a difference a new productive system was eventually imposed on the island in the early nineteenth century. Loss of Mauritius and of Haiti induced the French Crown after 1815 to pay greater attention to Réunion's capacity for becoming a major supplier of sugar. For better or worse, the island turned once again into an export factory, bound to France by tight restrictions on external trade, sacrificing food production prospects for the fluctuating allure of the new export crop. To some extent, the hitherto inexorable proliferation of smallholds reversed direction. Canefields became concentrated through the subsequent century around the most efficient sugar mills and a new class of large landowners emerged from the prevailing structure of peasant microtenure.[5]

Immigration and a rising birthrate tripled the population from 36,000 in 1778 to 110,000 by 1848, but progressive manumission and the final abolition of slavery required new sources of plantation labor. Some 60,000 former slaves preferred share-cropping, fishing, and hill-farming to continuation of canefield labor. Indentured workers came from East Africa and Madagascar and, after 1859, from British India under varying contractual circumstances. Most of the Asian coolies left the island at the expiration of their contracts, unlike the majority of those imported into British Mauritius where land and cultural survival were more readily assured. The descendants of those who remained, called "Malabars," have become strongly integrated into the Creole majority. Smaller numbers of Gujerati-speaking Indian Muslims and of Cantonese Chinese arrived during the latter nineteenth century, moving rapidly into prominent positions in the island's retail trade. In contrast to the African, Malagasy, Hindu ("Malabar") and Chinese immigrants in the Réunionnais melting pot, the Muslim middle class of about 7,000 has tended to preserve its identity intact.

Through the end of World War Two, the fortunes of the cane economy oscillated between relative prosperity and ponderous misery, determined by the needs of its distant French market. Réunion may have ranked as an old settler colony but its fate was to depend, like that of any undifferentiated imperial conquest, on metropolitan demands for its cash crop. While the island's coastlands and lower slopes became monopolized by cane, ambitious government schemes for secondary crops and for food-cultivation in the hill country failed for reasons of soil deficiency, inadequacy of communications, or peasant recalcitrance. Some alternative cash crops did take hold in the highlands; the most successful is geranium, the leaves of which are distilled to make perfume essences. Vanilla was introduced along with a variety of other perfume plants (ylang-ylang, vetiver, lemon grass) to help small planters survive the vicissitudes of the sugar market cycle. Other experiments failed utterly—tea and cloves, for instance—and tobacco disappeared only to re-emerge recently as a small cash crop. Good land was consistently reserved for cane, however, which was too valuable a speculation in favorable times for it to be abandoned in poor.

For more than a century, the island sank ever deeper into dependence on its principal export to earn the imports needed to keep the population alive.[6] Completion of the canal at Suez in 1869 and the opening of Madagascar to French colonization and trade in the 1880s reduced Réunion's advantages as a stage in the European journey to the Indies and a focus for French overseas investment.

Sugar prices rose with World War One and the industry continued in relative prosperity until the next war, but Réunion's population was increasing more rapidly than its income. There were 220,000 Réunionnais in 1941 and the sugar bonanza sweetened life for only a small minority of them. Despite the process of creolization, Réunion remained a colonial "dual society," a world of little people (ti moun)—indigent, malnourished, illiterate, subsisting beneath an empyrean of well-educated, cosmopolitan grands blancs. Enough of the latter were actually black or "colored" and enough of the ti moun white, to prevent the confirmation of a system of castes that would have embarrassed assimilationist France.

Controlling most of the productive land as well as the processing of sugar and the import-export links with France, the Bourbon plutocracy and its metropolitan partners called all tunes, determined all social privileges, delivered all services required by state and society.[7] In a curious process of concentric class formation, the aristocrats became a colony within the original colony, favored against the interests of the peasant and laboring majority. It was almost as though that majority constituted some aboriginal or at least alien population subjected to imperial control, as in Algeria, Senegal, or Indo China. The larger Creole colony that had once urged the subjugation of Madagascar as its own dependency retained only the universal right to vote as token of its old status.

Réunionnais have enjoyed French citizenship and political rights since 1792 and they have been sending deputies to the parliaments of Paris since 1870. Statesmen and poets have issued in large numbers from the battered coasts and seething mountains of the remote Mascarene to enliven the atmosphere of nineteenth and twentieth century France. From 1885 to 1896, politicians from the island played a powerful if self-deluded part in urging Paris to emasculate the Merina monarchy and subsequently annex Madagascar. Metropolitan capital and settlers soon chose the Great Island next door in preference to the old, small colony which had engineered its incorporation into the empire. Réunion thus obtained an anticipated source of beef and rice, but not at the price structure or the investment terms its champions had anticipated. Attempts to settle surplus Réunionnais in the empty stretches of Madagascar were largely repudiated by Malagasy and proved more costly than durable.[8]

Still, Réunion persisted in its French institutions and its vital dependence on Paris. The island played no remarkable role in World War Two. Loyal to France even after the capitulation of June 1940, Réunionnais welcomed DeGaulle's Free French administration in November 1942, after the British and South African occupation of strategically preferable Northern Madagascar and the Comoros. To survive in the absence of their customary metropolitan market, the Réunionnais were obliged to plant food crops on valuable canefields. But self-sufficiency proved a mere last resort.

Its export-oriented economy in shambles by war's end, Réunion began a laborious political metamorphosis in 1946. The obscure island society integrated itself into the French Republic and its standard of living rose without corresponding expansion or diversification of productive capacity. During more than three post war decades of relentless "decolonization" of the world around it, the old Bourbon colony finally achieved its distinction as an inveterate outpost of Europe. At 9,000 kilometers from Paris, Réunion became the eastern headquarters for France's remaining global pretension. It remains today on the periphery of the Europe which it represents, virtually cut off from the third world neighborhood produced by decolonization.

The 1946 statute declaring the island an Overseas Department of France, together with Caribbean Guadeloupe and Martinique and the venerable South American colony of Guyana, merely formalized a relationship which had never been seriously questioned on the island. Nor is it seriously questioned today. While the United States parries outsiders' decolonization initiatives on behalf of Puerto Rico, and Great Britain goes to war to keep the Falklands out of the third world, France serenely maintains jurisdiction over the Creole populations of the Indian and Caribbean seas. Theoretically, departmental status entails indiscriminate application of all national legislation to the erstwhile colonies. As interpreted at the time by the Fourth Republic's political Left, identification with France meant veritable emancipation of the overseas society from domination by their "feudal suzerains." This was an acceptable achievement gained at the price of deeper integration of those societies into European market capitalism. The vitality of that market system, and the ability of the landed oligarchs to retain their privileges in it, may have been underestimated during the departmentalization debates of the 1930s and 1940s.[9]

In any event, the island's fourth decade as a department now testifies to the durability of Réunion's fundamental subordination to metropolitan private sector interests. The Bourbon aristocracy participates intimately with French business in deciding investment, resource and labor allocation, export and import pricing, and the direction of trade. Departmentalization enables this relationship to prevail without risking flagrant exploitation; a broad portfolio of social amelioration is administered by the state in partial compensation for the effects of market subservience. While the export plantation base of the island economy assures continuity of the essential class structure of Réunionnais society, the gap between landed commercial aristocracy and the "little people" is now mediated by a strong new middle class of civil servants and tradesmen. Many of them have been transferred from continental France to operate the major government programs and contractor branches established on the island—the core of departmentalization. These metropolitans (called Z'oreilles in the creole pejorative) stand beside the small prosperous Muslim Indian bourgeoisie (called Z'arabes). The Muslims continue to conduct the importation of textiles and oils and to dominate retail sales of those commodities as well as household goods.

Passing through the kaleidescope of French politics in the Fourth Republic, Réunion's destiny changed little. The state had little tolerance for new departures in the loyal Creole provinces while attending to crises of authority in Indo China, Algeria, and the African territories, including Madagascar. The metropolitan bureaucracy torpidly attended to the overall harmonization of legal and regulatory conditions demanded by departmental status. Still, public investment grew from year to year during the 1950s, creating roadways, expanding the artificial port at Pointe des Galets and the airport at Gillot, providing hydro-electricity, raising the miniumum wage, and beginning the rationalization of the sugar industry.

Four regimes of the Fifth Republic inaugurated by DeGaulle in 1958 have altered the island's circumstances dramatically, however. Infrastructural development leapt ahead; agricultural production and pricing became the object of elaborate overseas dialogue; social programs have redesigned the physiognomy of the island, if not its immortal soul; and the military has been installed in modern facilities at Pointe des Galets, Gillot, and Saint Denis. Sugar has remained the central fact of economic life, using 70 percent of the island's arable land. Production reached 273,000 tons in the peak year of 1978, accounting for eighty-three percent of export revenues, although only a tenth of Gross Domestic Product (the bulk of which is in services). The number of sugar mills has been reduced for the sake of efficiency from fourteen to five conglomerate-owned regional establishments, offering smaller growers little opportunity to exploit competition. The 1983 planning target of 300,000 tonnes has proved unattainable, as that year's harvest yielded only 223,700 and the subsequent year's tally managed a mere ten percent improvement. But the European Community's quota-price mechanisms reward the island's sugar planters with higher revenues than they could expect on world markets.

Organized into several strong associations which differ according to scale of operation and ideological commitment, those planters dispute their trade interests with European sugar-beet competitors, with importer-refiners in France, and with one another. Together, they have pressed successfully for financial and technical concessions underwritten by the French Government and the results have sustained sugar as the most profitable alternative for productive investment. But at 6,000 miles from "home," Réunion's economic needs cannot be fully satisfied with a highly specialized role inside a compensatory national matrix. Department or otherwise, Réunion remains outside the metropolitan economy (let alone the European) and must continue to fend for itself, unlike, say, the wine-growing or sheep-raising regions of the metropole. Cane remains king but other things must be produced in supplement or as insurance. Agricultural diversification, proverbial illusion of many developing economies, has been approached in Réunion not by invasion of land dedicated to the lucrative cane, but through efforts to bring the hitherto neglected highlands under cultivation for food crops and livestock. Despite some significant breakthroughs in small husbandry, fishing, garden vegetables and potatoes, the program has failed to overcome bureaucratic inefficiencies, imperviousness of terrain, and the reluctance of the hill population to adapt to new farming practices without guarantees of sustained income. Agriculture, apart from sugar, contributes only two percent of GNP.[10]

Grand schemes for production have been promoted and implemented largely by public grants in the absence of private risk capital. Investors are discouraged by the remoteness of the place, the high costs of transportation and (by third world criteria) of labor, the paucity of raw materials, the impossibility of achieving economies of scale, and the absence of regional Western Indian Ocean markets. Réunionnais and metropolitans have preferred to place funds in sugar, in the booming real estate markets, and subsidized new tourist and other service industries—or to stay away from Réunion entirely. They thus perpetuate the artificiality of the economy, rendering it all the more dependent on public transfers to bridge the chasm—now running at five to one—between the money value of Réunion's imports of manufactured goods and foodstuffs, and its revenues from unrefined sugar, molasses, vanilla, and perfume oils.

Those exports are themselves buffeted by climatic vagaries and overseas market dictates. These systematic disadvantages apply even to geranium of which Réunion is the world's largest producer and vanilla where it has the advantage of metropolitan stabilization devices over its competitors in Madagascar, Comoros, and Mexico. Trade in these commodities remains dominated by a small number of non-competitive entrepreneurs working in a collaborative market. On occasion, the oligopoly exerts systematic pressure against local initiatives for import substitution and export diversification.[11]

An economy founded on production for export and self-sufficiency began in the late 1960s to manifest chronic dependence on imports and the dole. Terms of trade and productivity have declined so badly that exports, which in 1954 covered 97 percent of the island's then modest import burden, now purchase only 13 percent, forcing the French taxpayer to compensate for the enormous balance through public transfers. A huge increase in purchasing power from public welfare expenditures has in itself stimulated the consumer import sector and the corresponding export industries in France. Labor has responded along parallel lines. The very mystique of departmentalization has increasingly alienated workers from rural life where economic development requires them most.

Some 68 percent of the island is occupied in service sectors (half the entire labor force on the government payroll), with industry accounting for only 16 percent, and agriculture, once the overwhelming mass employer, taking less than fifteen of every hundred Réunionnais workers. Unemployment, expected to reach 40 percent by the early 1990s, is aggravated by the mechanization of cane production on the larger plantations and the ultra-modern mills, and by the seasonal character of cane cultivation and harvesting.[12] Despite government inducements, Réunion's Creoles prefer urban employment to the traditional discomforts, isolation, and uncertainties of rural peasant subsistence. Attracted and yet demoralized by public welfare allocations, which have risen rapidly to the virtual level established for such services in metropolitan France, they appear chiefly interested in employment opportunities in government and service trades, or in France itself.

The sudden arrival of welfare economics in a still colonial peasant society has provoked mass defection to the towns with their subsidized levels of consumption. The countryside has also been depleted by publicly sponsored emigration of the more dynamic elements of the labor force to largely menial, but well-organized, job markets in France.[13] Their absence helps keep insular unemployment manageable and their remittances contribute to the payments balance. Réunion's capital, Saint Denis, has expanded to over one-fifth the total island population as families drain out of the hinterlands. Most of the immigrants occupy low-cost public apartments built along the lovely folds of hillside and the drained lowlands to the south and east of the old colonial village.

More than 60 percent of the island population receives some form of social assistance (including family allowances), costing the French treasury about $400 per Réunionnais each year. These and other metropolitan transfers have raised mean income above $4,000, a standard equalled in Africa only by Libya and Gabon. The half-million islanders enjoy a life expectancy of sixty-eight years. They are driving ten times as many automobiles as the million Mauritians nearby; expensive as it is after the long sea journey from Marseille, the family car is as important to Réunion as it ever was to the metropole. Communication networks and transportation facilities, financed largely through Defense Ministry allocations, are the envy of the Afro-Asian world—or would be if they provided contact with that world. Apart from South African businessmen and tourists and some affluent Mauritians, Réunion's eyes and ears are for the generous metropole alone.

Given its impressive endowment of schools, housing, medical services, and family subsidies, with a minimum wage pegged only 22 percent below the metropolitan French level, Réunion must reckon the blessings of departmental dependence against its less tangible costs. Employment is problematic and self-sufficiency a figment of imaginative planning. Development of the hills to popular satisfaction costs too much and so does hired labor, so that government must take all the risks. Nearly 100,000 Réunionnais have gone to work in France and probably 60 percent of the remaining labor force is un- or under-employed. Managers and entrepreneurs are imported like manufactured goods. One third of the 1500 to 2500 new jobs emerging each year are claimed by Europeans who cost more but who demonstrate the requisite skills. Construction and equipment contracts go, often by default, to metropolitan firms, so that two-thirds of the state's investment in the island returns forthwith to France.[14] But the circulation of funds, opportunities for remunerated emigration, and guaranteed wage levels represent inalienable components of a web of departmental security which virtually no Réunionnais advocates abolishing in favor of the unknowns of self-reliance. This monumental social trade-off has occupied the polemical energies of Réunion's vigorous political factions for two decades.

A Microcosm of Politics Writ Large

In organizational terms, the island's political parties reflect their metropolitan paternity, and their coalitions tend to follow European dispositions to Left and Right. An isolated polity with the population of a medium-sized city also offers special opportunities for maverick personalities and for intimacy between municipal and island-wide politics. Réunion's twenty-four towns represent power bases for virtually all important politicians, most of whom occupy mayoral as well as departmental or national legislative office. The principal exception is Michel Debré, a unique example of a metropolitan political figure grafted successfully onto the insular political structure. A year after losing his metropolitan parliamentary seat in 1962, DeGaulle's faithful wartime companion and first Prime Minister of the Fifth Republic shifted to a "safe" constituency and thus re-entered the National Assembly through a special by-election in Réunion's first district, which includes Saint Denis and the island's north.

While retaining his mayorality at Amboise on the Loire and moving in and out of ministerial positions in subsequent national administrations, Debré has debated, negotiated, and editorialized skillfully to defend the cause of uncompromised "Réunion Française" for the past quarter century. He has used his prestige in metropolitan affairs to lead a coalition of landed and business interests, joined to new urban professionals and service employees. These island conservatives share a recognized stake in the departmental import-export system and the predominance of metropolitan French culture. This political Center and Right advocates the tightest possible identification of overseas and metropolitan departments. They insist that French legislation be implemented regularly in Réunion with at most marginal adaptations to accommodate the island's remoteness and relative underdevelopment. Réunion is constitutionally and culturally French, no more distinct, they argue, than Brittany or Savoie.

Although agreeing that Réunion's distinctions fall short of separate national identity, island Communists and Socialists argue that the vulnerability of the economy, the rigidity of its class structure, and its cultural pluralism all require particular attention in French law and administration. For decades the Left advocated departmental status as a structural corrective for abject colonialism (which the conservatives were then seeming to prefer). However, the Communist Party of Réunion (PCR), enjoying the irreducible adherence of about one-fourth of the electorate, has more recently urged an evolutionary process to break the grip of metropolitan priorities on its socio-economic transactions. According to PCR analysis since 1976, popular and democratic autonomy within the French Republic would correct the subjugation of Réunionnais by a colonial-capitalist class which depends on the benefits of those external priorities.[15]

The decentralization project of the Mitterand regime, conferring executive authority on departmentally and regionally elected councils throughout France, has been regarded auspiciously by the PCR as at least a first step in the "decolonization" process. This endorsement permitted a tentative Socialist-Communist alliance to survive on the island. Nevertheless, the Socialists have persistently avoided the PCR's autonomist option, regarded as ultimately "separatist" by all but its Communist sponsors. After the departure of Communist ministers from Mitterand's cabinet in mid–1984, PCR chairman Paul Vergès seems to have lost patience with the regime's apparent failure to develop Réunion as a full, vital, yet distinct component of "progressive" France. Yet, his party has been unwilling to break neatly with Paris' moderate socialist promise to the island.

A fringe of extreme Left parties without firm footing in the electorate seeks to transcend what they regard as PCR equivocation, advocating outright independence as the only self-determined route to dissolution of the island's oppressive class structure. One of these factions, the People's Movement for the Liberation of Réunion (MPLR), was welcomed before the OAU's Liberation Committee in 1979, despite its insignificance in island politics. Another negligible splinter, the Movement for Independence (MIR), participated in the first "independentist conference" of Overseas France in Guadeloupe during early 1985, earning some reflected distinction from association with the more powerful decolonizing movements of New Caledonia, Guyana, and Guadeloupe.[16]

Despite the appeal to French loyalties by the principal "progressive" parties, the island's majority has traditionally voted in favor of shifting coalitions of conservatives. These interests agree primarily (and sometimes only) on the perils of anything like "autonomy" as a deceptive lure away from the motherland and the security she provides.

Whatever the merits of the particular candidates and issues of the moment, each election occurs in fierce heat and recrimination on this highly politicized island. Considering the general untouchability of departmental status, it is surprising to outsiders that every campaign at the polls turns into a plebiscite on the degree of "Frenchness" advocated by the contestants. The PCR must defend its "decolonization" program against the charge that seeking autonomy is inherently disloyal. It has to respond to the unenviable examples of independence used by the Right as living admonitions against the perils of any weakening of the umbilical. These failure-stories inevitably include the tribulations of nearby Madagascar, Mauritius, Seychelles, and the Caribbean neighbors of France's other Overseas Departments, all of whom must envy Réunion's political freedom and standard of living.

In its defense, the PCR concedes that independence under current international realities merely substitutes multilateral for bilateral dependence without allowing a new nation to arrive at the level of socio-economic satisfacton needed for the enjoyment of sovereignty.[17] The party's sometime Socialist ally (the PSR, less often and even less willing an ally here than in the metropole) won't entertain such ideas as autonomy for fear of the stigma of separatism. Self-determination is satisfied for the PSR through President Mitterand's republic-wide program of administrative decentralization without questioning Réunion's fundamental Frenchness. Having ridden

Mitterand's coattails out of oblivion since 1981, the PSR commands a constituency about half the size of the PCR's. It operates programmatically on a sliver of Center-Left ground remaining between the skillfully nuanced reformism of the Communists and the dogged moderation of the Center factions who usually vote with the Réunion-Française Right. Poor electoral showings by PSR candidates and a number of local scandals have narrowed that ground considerably since 1981.

François Mitterand's accession to the Presidency in May 1981 and the victory of his Socialist-Communist parliamentary alliance a month later changed the texture, if not the direction, of political debate on Réunion. Seven years earlier, the islanders had given Mitterand a slim majority over the victorious Valery Giscard d'Estaing as a protest vote, but they became predominantly Giscardist during the incumbent's "seven fat years" as provider for the island's welfare needs. The Réunionnais majority thus endorsed Giscard's re-election bid in May 1981 against Mitterand and two other challengers. Finding themselves once again on the losing side of a presidential contest, they adapted as well as they could toward the allure of the victorious. Within a month, voters in the southernmost of the island's three parliamentary districts had turned their normally conservative National Assembly seat over to Wilfrid Bertile, mayor of Saint Philippe and leader of the hitherto feeble PSR.

Bertile and the Socialists could not have won the June 1981 election alone, no matter how compelling the sudden triumph of their presidential candidate. Conforming to national party guidelines, the PCR also threw its support en bloc to Bertile in the June 21 run-off vote after its own candidate had failed to survive the first round a week earlier. Indeed, had the Socialists followed suit in the second district after their candidate was eliminated, PCR Secretary-General Paul Vergès would probably have ousted independent rightist incumbent Jean Fontaine. Such a result would have given the Left two of the three seats in the Assembly, only Debré's District One constituency remaining relatively unassailable. Despite national directives to cooperate with the Communists, however, the PSR was unwilling to endorse Vergès, champion of "autonomy." Fontaine won in the run-off by just 500 votes.[18]

In the departmental legislative elections of March 1982, which the Overseas Left had vainly hoped to postpone in favor of rapid decentralization reform, the PCR and PSR were able to combine hesitantly to reduce their opponents' majority of seats, but not to reverse the balance. With one-half the General Council places at stake, the Left obtained a net increase of four, from six to ten. The equally uneasy coalition of Debré's Rally for the Republic (RPR) with the demoralized Giscardist Union for French Democracy (UDF) and various nonpartisan conservatives now holds a twenty-six to ten majority in the Department's legislature. One year later, in the municipal elections which went so disastrously against Mitterand's forces on the continent, the Left increased its combined tally of City Council majorities from four to ten (seven PCR, three PSR), leaving the conservative opposition with fourteen municipal majorities. In a bitter, unsuccessful race to unseat UDF Mayor Jean-Paul Virapoullé (of a consecrated rival political family) at Saint-André in March 1984, Paul Vergès' son Vincent was a victim of the CPR's electoral erosion among marginally leftist groups.[19]

Obliged by the courts to add a second legislature, the Regional Council (demanded by Debré and other plaintiffs to make Réunion conform to the rest of France), the Government was gratified by confirmation of the leftward movement through a slender majority given its forces in the February 1983 balloting for that new chamber. In reapportioning jurisdiction between the Overseas General and Regional Councils, it thus naturally favored the latter (which it originally hadn't wanted to create) with substantial authority over budgets, taxes, and socio-economic programs. The decentralization process has thus become a reality for Réunion and its sister departments, and the Left has opportunity for policy making. Considering the complexity of problems and programs, however, local politicians are obliged to rely more than ever on metropolitan administrators and technicians. The decolonization of expertise remains for the future to solve.

Auspicious as the Mitterand program was, it failed to redeem the island's inchoate Socialist forces in the March 1986 elections. While the conservative alliance duplicated its metropolitan feat of absolute majority in the legislative vote, the substantial remainder went in Réunion not to Bertile and the PSR, but to Vergès and the Communists. Although the Socialists have held their seats in the Regional Council, the Réunionnais voice in Paris has once again become polarized between the Gaullist-Giscardist Right and the Communist Left. And it is indeed in Paris where that voice makes itself heard.

Important as the disputes of local fiefdoms are, the objective of the Right since 1981 has been to challenge Mitterand's program of socio-economic change as part of the national opposition, rather than as the island's vested majority. This role has been played effectively in the Paris arena. Debré, Fontaine, Senators Georges Repiquet and Louis Virapoullé have exploited the parliamentary forum, the metropolitan press, and sympathetic business channels. They enjoyed unusually free access to the Socialist President, defending the value to French interests of the island's present status. Favored since March 1986 by the advent of their own majority in parliamentary Paris, they continue to urge France to demonstrate her international standing from Réunion, one of her few remaining secure vantage points outside Europe.

Independence, instability, exotic despotisms, and human misery inevitably accompany one another throughout the third world, so the Right maintains. Réunion remains immune to that syndrome and has demonstrated its vital affinity to France in every conceivable form. Réunionnais have welcomed the naval and air contingents once based in Madagascar, and they have solicited metropolitan business investment in good conscience. Their contributions to French intellectual and political life bespeak fruitful integration over more than a century. Their living standard, envy of the neighborhood, is a source of credit to France. The island is so far from representing another "nation" that it must be treated juridically without significant discrimination under the French Constitution, allowances made solely for temporary differences of degree connected with its state of under-development. This argument carried in December 1982 before the French Constitutional Council (the supreme constitutional court) which aborted Mitterand's special plan for unicameral legislatures in the Overseas Departments.[20]

Local conditions certainly corroborate much of the argument of Réunion-Française, for the island has been transformed dramatically from colonial somnolence over twenty years of metropolitan activity. In Saint Denis, an old town with voluminous new outskirts, Europeans feel entirely at ease. Creole architecture, dress, and cooking, like exotic flora and fauna, exist as objects to be sought out, no longer as the atmosphere for life in the capital. Africa scarcely survives in the towns and Asia remains there largely by its wits. The contrast with Mauritius and its capital, Port Louis, is profound. There, England had circumscribed the particular "races" and allowed an oriental majority to determine the conditions of a nation. France took the nations in and converted them to Francophonia. Rural life may be "retrograde," but that is a corrigible state—simply being less French, rather than something else—subject to the refining fires of modernization. The vanishing countryside culture of the island is no less part of France than the undeveloped Mezzogiorno is Italian.

Réunion's incorporation into the metropole has cultural importance and more. From Saint Denis, France is able to survey the circuits of vital cargoes passing beneath the continents, and to administer a dispersion of auspiciously situated islets in the austral seas and the Mozambique Channel. The arduously constructed harbor at Pointe des Galets, a parallel port under construction at nearby Possession, and the modern airfield at Gillot represent a southern Indian Ocean strategic asset to complement the French naval and air installations in Djibouti and the small contingents at Dzaoudzi (Mayotte) on the Comorean side of Madagascar. Some 3,000 military personnel are permanently stationed on the island. France's twenty-six ship Indian Ocean navy, with 3,000 more men, sends detachments regularly into the southern waters for surveillance, training, missions of mercy, and Tricolor displays along the strategic sea lanes. The Navy is welcome in Comoros, grievances over Mayotte notwithstanding, and it made itself symbolically useful in socialist Seychelles after the aborted mercenary invasion of the islands from South Africa in November 1981. The Government Commissioner (Prefect) of Réunion is civilian administrator of Tromelin island to the north, the Glorieuses between Comoros and Madagascar, Juan de Nova, Bassas da India, and Europa islands in the Mozambique Channel, all of them claimed by independent Indian Ocean states; he also governs austral Kerguelen, Saint Paul and Amsterdam islands, and the Crozet archipelago. These dispersed outposts are manned by small Gendarmerie or military contingents. All are used for such legitimate purposes as fishing, meteorological research, and wildlife conservation, and all "report" to headquarters at Saint Denis.[21]

Socialist France did not presume to renounce this deployment of national destiny, however reminiscent it might be of outright imperialism. The Navy continues to work its southern beat from Pointe des Galets, linking with the main French Indian Ocean forces based at Djibouti and doubtless maintaining discreet contact with United States forces in the zone. With some concern on its conscience, the Mitterand regime proved willing to debate Madagascar on its various irredentist claims, Mauritius over Tromelin, and Comoros on the Glorieuses and Mayotte, referring to such discussion by the name of negotiation. Paris is also prepared to share scientific and navigational information with neighbors and with the world at large. But the Socialist Government showed no more predilection than its Gaullist and Giscardist predecessors-successors to amputating these dispersed bits of Overseas France.

At the center of this gossamer system, Réunion is a substantial prize, far more than any of the islands which it administers. It is not surprising, therefore, that the appeal of *Réunion-Française* is held in Paris to be consistent with the Left's commitment to "decolonization"—synonomous here with social and economic reform. Thus, Mitterand granted almost equal attention to the options of the island's conservatives, even while in the national opposition, as to the decolonizers of his own persuasion. All in fact agree that French global prestige is clearly linked to the status of Réunion, and the island's Creoles are generally accepted as French. Metropolitan defection would be both constitutionally complicated and politically improbable in the absence of international pressure on Paris to give the island up.

Nevertheless, whatever they declare in the heat of political battle, all of Réunion's parties function on the unquestioned premise that France is infinitely more important to Réunion than the island is to France—or at least that the unequal relationship is seen that way by most metropolitan Frenchmen. They thus draw the conclusion that any restiveness displayed by Réunionnais against the circumstances of their position in the Republic could result in peremptory abandonment by an oblivious metropole. Even the insecure Left does not presume, therefore, to strain the umbilical too far. Recent crises of nationalism in Guadeloupe and Martinique have not been reproduced in the Indian Ocean department. The conservative island establishement contends vigorously against Paris' inclination to restore Mayotte to the Comoros (see chapter two), and almost all Réunionnais watch the vicissitudes of self-determination in New Caledonia with trepidation over the formula proposed by Mitterand for "independence in association with France."

Socialists and Communists insist, however, that the overseas price for being French must no longer entail the social inequity and cultural obliteration associated with sheer colonialism. Without categorically repudiating the progress induced by metropolitan modernization programs in education, health, and housing, the island Left advocates removal of institutional barriers to opportunity for Creoles and the creation of incentives for rural productivity and prosperity. They seek re-alignment of price and interest rate structures to reward local initiative and convey capital into light industry and smallhold farming. A majority of the island has been stultified into stagnation, they contend, by the easy palliatives of consumerism without inducement toward productivity. Welfare bureaucracies and import-export traders flourish in a fetid atmosphere impoverished by the siphoning of nearly 100,000 of Réunion's most vigorous workers and family members to laboring jobs in France under the Overseas Department Bureau of Migration (BUMIDOM).

The Left deplores the monopoly of managerial and professional posts enjoyed by some 6,000 European French "expatriates" on quasi-colonial administrative assignment with augmented salaries and emoluments. Decolonization entails conversion of such job opportunities for the benefit of Réunionnais, few of whom have appropriate qualifications at present. This demand corresponds to primary nationalism as we have identified it elsewhere in the formally independent third world. Unless it is blocked by legalistic opportunism or reversed by the new majority in Paris, decentralization in the Socialist schema would allow the island to modify these circumstances through the control of budget allocations, educational-training programs, and contracting for public projects.

With Paris' support, the parties of the Left have succeeded only recently in effectively raising the political issue of language in what they regard as a rigorously stratified insular society. Réunion has been a prime experiment in rendering a Western culture available to an entire overseas population presumed, however inaccurately, to be universally French because it started that way.

Seeking the perfect replication of a classic settlers' colony, imperial France stumbled over the idiosyncrasies of exploited non-European labor. This occurred first in the typical overseas patterns of slave holding, then in the relegation of the earth-bound ti-moun of Afro-Asians, Creoles, and déclassé whites. Unlike the European exclaves of Australia, British Canada, South Africa, and the Northeastern United States, where the elimination or strict segregation of indigenous people allowed early white colonists to evolve within their own pluralities, French Réunion became, like Algeria, most of Spanish America, and even the American South—a closed class society in which Europe could see its reflection only by peering into the very top levels of the glass. Yet, French policy differed from the unabashedly racial (or "communitarian") pluralism of the British in Mauritius and Seychelles. There, non-white labor was "settled" not to become a microcosm of Europe, but strictly as a segregated convenience for the white minorities. In their remaining Mascarene, the French have behaved at the behest of the Franco-Réunionnais (or Bourbon) minority under the assimilationist illusion that the rest of the island society somehow mirrored the metropole in its essential cultural physiognomy.

The encounter of French civilization with what Dupon calls insular constraints and colonial reality has generated a dual pattern of cultural activity. The Francophone illusion fails to incorporate the Réunionnais majority. It sustains the distinctions of a usually affluent elite thoroughly at home in authentically French institutions, customs, and aesthetic forms. Equating national loyalty with Francophone identity, the overseas system has refused cultural integrity to Creole oral literature, Sega music, and the old craft traditions of the *habitants*, which have been allowed to degenerate under the withering heat of orthodox disapproval.[22] In reaction, the Creole poor and their children must strive for achievement within authentic metropolitan standards and against strong handicaps. Like colonized indigenous people elsewhere, they are urged to adapt from a patronized folk tradition into a European milieu without being given the means of doing so. The island's schools have an examination failure record two to four times the rate of comparable institutions in European France, and the adult population is still 40 percent illiterate. In settler Réunion, assimilation is supposed to be a given, when it has not yet even become an aspiration.

The pedagogical transition to metropolitan French from the langugage used universally by ninety percent of the population is not as smooth as it might appear. Recommended correctives include recourse to pre-school and adult language training in French. The political Left, however, advocates the recognition of Creole as a respectable medium of educational and occupational transaction. Partisans of unqualified *Réunion Française* necessarily denounce such concessions to Creole as both atavistic and secessionist. Creole would represent in their view an inferior vehicle for intercourse and creativity, one that emphasizes the distance, not the affinity, between the island and the motherland. Moreover, Réunion, the anti-Creolist argues, has known issues of class and of ethnic assimilation, but never a race problem. The advocates of Creole linguistic status and of autonomy based on cultural difference are therefore charged with encouraging false nationalism, inviting the kind of social conflict which French culture has always served to obviate.[23]

The defense of Creole stresses the costs in social justice given up by the poor for the benefits of social tranquillity which favor the Francophone rich. The language debate, like the issues of capital investment and job formation, manifests serious contradictory conceptions of security. The France that has guaranteed stability and a rising standard of living for the island population over twenty-five years of ferment in the third world is also the source of special privileges and distributive inequities which themselves engender such ferment.

Maintaining the "dual society" of rich and poor, correlated with Francophone and Creole, urban and rural, tory and nationalist, simply reduces Réunion to the status of any object of empire. It ineluctably raises the issues of self-determination for the majority and redefines the debate over decolonization. Policies of social transfer, urbanization, universal education, and generally rising opulence may avoid the most painful implications of these issues. But such policies engender expectations of social mobility among the Creole poor. Government policy either neutralizes protest to the extent that those expectations can be gratified (or disguised) or aggravates it to the extent that they are frustrated. Even when public policy succeeds in rewarding the blessed state of "being French," something is sacrificed. A gain in democratic participation, prosperity, and social justice may be achieved at the expense of an entire living insular culture the richness of which has always been denied before beginning to be assessed.[24]

Notes

1. For the historical process, see Robin Hallett, *Africa Since 1875* (Ann Arbor: University of Michigan Press, 1974), Ch.9; Philip M. Allen and John M. Ostheimer, "Africa and the Islands of the Western Indian Ocean," *Munger Africana Library Notes*, No. 35 (Pasadena: California Institute of Technology, 1976).

2. Allowance made for the British Indian Ocean Territory (BIOT), political identity of the Diego Garcia air-naval base in the Chagos archipelago, the permanent population of which was evacuated to Mauritius by Britain after 1965.

3. André Scherer, *La Réunion*, Que sais-je? no. 1846 (Paris: Presses Universitaires de France, 1980), p. 35.

4. *Ibid.*, pp. 32-35, 57-61; Jean-François Dupon, *Contraintes insulaires et fait colonial aux Mascareignes et aux Seychelles*, 3 vols. (Lille, France: Atelier de Reproduction des Thèses; Paris: Librairie Honoré Champion, 1977), Vol. 3, Ch. 1.

5. Scherer, *La Réunion*, pp. 55-56; Dupon, *Contraintes insulaires*, Vol. 1, Ch. 4, part 2; Jean Benoist, "Ajustements et ruptures du système de la plantation à la Martinique, à la Guadeloupe et à la Réunion," in Raj Virasahmy, ed., *Characteristics of Island Economies* (Port Louis: University of Mauritius Press, 1977), pp. 22-42.

6. Scherer, *La Réunion*, pp. 80-85.

7. *Ibid.*, pp. 95-96; J.M. Boisson, Edmond Lauret and Serge Payet, "Emergence historique et adaptation des rapports de production dans le cadre d'une économie de plantation insulaire: le cas de la Réunion," in Virasahmy, *Characteristics*, pp. 103-163; Jean Benoist, "Perspectives pour une connaissance des sociétés contemporaines des Mascareignes et des Seychelles," in *Annuaire des Pays de l'Océan Indien (APOI)* (Aix-en-Provence, France: CERSOI, 1976), 1:1974, pp. 232-233.

8. Hubert Deschamps, *Histoire de Madagascar* (Paris: Berger-Levrault, 1961), pp. 183-189, 252-53; Phares M. Mutibwa, *The Malagasy and the Europeans: Madagascar's Foreign Relations, 1861-1895* (Atlantic Highlands, N.J.: Humanities Press, 1974), pp. 59, 206-208; Nigel Heseltine, *Madagascar* (New York: Praeger Publishers, 1971), pp. 113-118; Jean-Pierre Raison, *Les Hautes Terres de Madagascar*, 2 vols. (Paris: ORSTOM-Karthala, 1984), Vol. 2, Part 3.

9. Scherer, *La Réunion*, pp. 97-99; Dupon, *Contraintes insulaires*, vol. 1, p. 866; vol. 3, p. 1209; Benoist, "Ajustements et ruptures."

10. Boisson et al., "Emergence historique;" Dupon, *Contraintes insulaires*, vol. 1, Part 2; M.L. Rieul, "Un Plan de sauvetage pour la société rurale de la Réunion: Le Plan d'Aménagement des Hauts," in *Dossier Réunion*, bulletin d'Information du CENADDOM, no. 48 (Paris: Centre National de Documentation des Départements d'Outre-Mer), pp. 10-18; Colin Legum, ed., *Africa Contemporary Record (ACR) 1981-1982* (New York and London: Holmes & Meier, Africana Press, annual), pp. B 322-334.

11. Scherer, *La Réunion*, pp. 110-111; Philippe Legros, "L'huile locale mal digérée," in "La Réunion sous le vent du changement," (Paris: *Le Monde* supplement, March 13, 1982), p. 18.

12. Schérer, *La Réunion*, pp. 112–115.

13. Dupon, *Contraintes insulaires*, Vol. 3, conclusion; *Marchés Tropicaux et Méditerranéens (MTM)* (Paris), December 21, 1979.

14. Dupon, *Contraintes insulaires*, Vol. 3, pp. 1600–1604; ACR *1981–82*, pp. B 331–336; "La Réunion, un 'modèle' menacé d'éruption," *Le Monde* special section on Réunion, September 12, 1984, pp. 9–17.

15. André Oraison, *Le Parti Communiste Réunionnais et l'Autonomie démocratique et populaire* (Saint Denis, Réunion: n.d.); Alain Rollat, "Un certain consensus face au défi du développement," in *Le Monde* supplement, March 13, 1982, pp. 11–12; Martin Espérance, "Chronique politique et constitutionnelle: Ile de la Réunion," in *APOI*, 6:1979, pp. 351–363; ACR *1981–82*, pp. B 323–327; Bertrand LeGendre, in *Le Monde*, April 9, 1985.

16. See Alain Rollat, in *Le Monde*, April 9, 1985.

17. "Interview avec Paul Vergès," in *Le Monde* supplement, March 13, 1982, p. 16.

18. ACR *1981–82*, pp. 324–327.

19. "La Réunion, un 'modèle,'" p. 10; LeGendre, *Le Monde*, April 9, 1985; *Ibid.*, May 31, 1985; ACR *1984–85* (Réunion chapter).

20. Rollat, "Un certain consensus;" "Interview avec Michel Debré," in *Le Monde* supplement, March 13, 1982, p. 13; "Interview avec Wilfrid Bertile," *Ibid.*, p. 14; ACR *1982–83*, pp. B 333–335.

21. Philippe Leymarie, *Océan Indien: le nouveau coeur du monde* (Paris: Editions Karthala, 1981), Ch. 10.

22. Jean Benoist, "Perspectives;" Robert Chaudenson, "La situation linguistique dans les archipels créolophones de l'Océan Indien," in *APOI* 1:1974, pp. 155–182; Christian Barrat, "Rites et croyances," in Michel Albany, ed., *A la découverte de la Réunion: Tout l'univers réunionnais de ses origines à nos jours*, 10 vols. (Saint Denis, Réunion: Favéry, 1980), vol. 8; Dupon, *Contraintes insulaires*, vol. 3, Ch. 2.

23. Scherer, pp. 119–120, 125; Dupon, *Contraintes insulaires*, vol. 3, Ch. 2; G. Degoix, "La Réunion: pôle de rayonnement de la culture française dans une zone d'affrontements entre les grandes puissances," in *Bulletin d'Information du CEN-ADDOM*, No. 48, 1979, pp. 27–29.

24. Chaudenson, "Situation linguistique;" Barrat, "Rites et croyances;" Dupon, *Contraintes insulaires*, Vol. 3, Ch. 2.

4

Mauritius:
Refractions of the Nations

Flung onto the high seas without conspicuous natural endowments or even an indigenous population, Mauritius has managed in two and one-half centuries to collect a million people from three continents onto its 700 square miles of plateau and plain. The bright little nation of 1968 has also begun writing its own page in the books of modern statecraft. What the Mauritians have done in history they usually did well, considering the size and remoteness of their place and its social and economic fragility. Juxtaposed in separate, ethnically defined "communities" with discrete religious, occupational, and political identities, Mauritian society grew into an odd insular microcosm of the imperial East, a transition from Europe to Asia via southern Africa and Madagascar. Those communities had to discover the prospect for a Mauritian nation after having established a state: the hard way. That it can be done at all gives Mauritius a new importance beyond the island's geopolitical dimensions.

This is the old Ile de France, Britain's mid-ocean war prize of 1810. Until then, it was a tiny rendezvous for rakish French gentility, dubious lords and ladies, and declassed desperadoes. They cavorted over the Ile's no longer savage eighteenth century landscape of plantations and towns, romantic lakes and grottos, through brisk winds of war and commerce. It was, and remains still, a place of poetry, where Bernardin de Saint Pierre set his tragic pastoral, *Paul and Virginia*, and where the bountiful National Library holds rank upon rank of imaginative Mauritian literature in French and English.[1] In 1815, only a century after the foundation *ex nihilo* of its original glittering French society, Mauritius subsided into the more sedate mundanity of British rule. The island emerged by 1968 into problematic independence, "a flotsam left behind by the wreck of the colonial world," as one of her scholars has called the twice erstwhile colony.[2] Today, Mauritius exemplifies both the tribulations of an obscure, polyglot, over-populated, acutely dependent microstate and the remarkable determination of a free people to find their own solutions.

During a critical decade before independence in 1968, Mauritius' Asian majority overcame the often violent resistance of an apprehensive, relatively

privileged minority—primarily Europeans and Creoles of mixed origins—
in order to obtain statehood from Britain. In the equally critical decade
which followed, a dialectic of class conflict and national cohesion began to
give form to this colonial congeries of mutual strangers, ruled from their
own midst. Intolerable demographic pressures were reduced; political process
replaced much of the old bear-garden bullying among hostile ethnocentric
factions; economic diversification became measurable; and the serious temptations of third world despotism were successfully resisted. The island has
definitively solved neither its sectarian nor its economic troubles. The
integration of unreconciled "communities" remains incomplete, and au-
thoritarianism may yet afflict its politics. But, considering the odds against
stabilty and civil liberty in a dense, confused society under stress, Mauritius
has managed extraordinary progress in both directions.[3]

Modern Mauritius has made this mark by itself without apt models,
grand partnerships, or even much good luck. International attention has
been benign but skeptical. The crucial climatic and market fortunes of
Mauritius' imperious sugar crop turned catastrophic after some favorable
seasons in the early years after independence. Yet, Mauritian national
prospects survive in an original, plucky, self-confident showcase of pluralism.
In mid-1982, this Asian-African-European electorate registered a wholesale
change of government freely at the polls. Then in August 1983, it changed
its mind and restored some of the ancient regime to power.[4] In both
episodes, the defeated incumbents left office without disorder. The Indian
Ocean has seen such self-discipline before—in India and Sri Lanka, for
example—but, generally, the artificial political cultures of the third world
aren't supposed to be ready for so much popular sovereignty.

From France's Isle to Its Own Right

The only independent Mascarene began its social life, like Réunion, as
a total creation of Europe. Unlike Réunion, its European founders have
now surrendered their political kingdom to the majority. That majority,
again unlike Réunion (or Seychelles, or its own dependency of Rodriguez),
has for long been Asian, not Afro-Malagasy or Creole.

While known to Arab map-makers for centuries, the island stood too
distant from the frequented Asian and African coasts to rouse colonial
instincts from north or east. It awaited Europe's entry from the southwest
to begin playing its special cameo role in history. The Ile de France took
social shape from 1721 on a lovely oval island of forest, plateaux, peaks
and craters. Portuguese had been there in 1510, but didn't stay. Dutchmen
then named the island after their Prince Mauritz of Nassau, and for several
decades served his Highness' East Indies ventures with food and ships'
provisions. They abandoned the place in 1710 (after exterminating the edible,
overly accommodating dodo bird), preferring the Cape of Good Hope as
a service point for their long-breathed merchant marine bound to and from
what is now Indonesia.

For the French, Mauritius had the advantage of a position near the Cape-to-India route. It enjoyed the blessing, denied to Réunion, of two reasonably sheltered harbors, at Grand Port (now Mahébourg) and Port Louis, facing south and north, respectively. Under the East Indies Company Governor Mahé de Labourdonnais (1735–1746), the Ile de France became a crossroads for Europe and Asia. Original French settlers, using Indian, African and Malagasy slaves, occupied a once fully forested, volcanic landscape, carving plantations for cereals, spices, sugar cane, cotton, indigo, cassava, vegetables and livestock behind the burgeoning port towns. Labourdonnais gave the island definition as a society and an overseas imperial headquarters. His administration encouraged cultural institutions, started a shipbuilding and repair industry (denuding the plateaux for further plantation expansion), extended agriculture to export crops with virtual self-sufficiency, and gave commercial life to the ports. The population tripled in his first four years to number 3,000, two-thirds of them slaves.

Labourdonnais even turned to hounding the British in and out of their India domain. He devised brilliant, if unappreciated, projects for French settlements in Madagascar, Seychelles and East Africa, and for the establishment of a fleet at France's only secure Indian Ocean base, the Ile de France. His improvised forces had indeed seized Madras from there in 1746. Had his ideas been followed, France might have challenged Britain more successfully for control of the Indian Ocean, but as Toussaint observes, "while France was chasing after a chimera in India, she was neglecting a region where, with a little perseverance, she could have created a real France in the South Seas."[5] Policy disputes with French officials in Pondicherry ended his career in unwarranted disgrace, but Labourdonnais had established the Ile de France indelibly as a thriving molecule of Europe in an exotic web of activity.

The island had 19,000 inhabitants (15,000 of them slaves) in 1767. Its incipient thalassocracy extended to Bourbon (Réunion) and Rodriguez in the Mascarenes, the ninety previously uninhabited Seychelles, the Cargados Carajos shoals, Agalega, Tromelin and the Chagos (now British Indian Ocean Territory) in the north, spots of Madagascar 800 kilometers to the west, and several dispersed islets in the surrounding seas. The long process of dismantling this "empire" has left Mauritius with Rodriguez, copra-producing Agalega, the unpopulated fishing banks of Cargados Carajos (St. Brandon), and with unsatisfied claims to French Tromelin and the British Chagos.

At its end in 1763, the Seven Year War had exhausted France in Europe, weakened her in India and ruined the East India Company. Impoverished and forlorn, the Ile de France was purchased in 1766 by the French Crown, which gave it a new vocation. The island became a turnstile for Indian Ocean commerce and fortune hunting, an emporium for venal officials, speculators, and cavalier freebooters, and a refuge for questionable expatriate gentlefolk. In 1781, French Admiral Suffren used the island as a base for renewed naval operations against the British during the wars of the American

Revolution, but he deplored the immorality of the society and declined to bring his fleet back there after his alarums and excursions were done.

The impious islanders' fortunes rose nonetheless upon the transfer of France's Indian Ocean administration to Port Louis from indefensible Pondicherry. Business and speculation flourished in spirals and the population jumped by 1794 to 59,000 (49,000 slaves). So strong was the island politically that, following a brief period of revolutionary fervor, it actually seceded from France in 1796, rather than yield its slaves under the revolution's emancipation acts.

By that time, a third generation white planter elite controlled the Ile de France Assembly and the institutions of society, opposed from time to time by urban commercial, professional and military classes. The landed aristocrats reasserted their influence in Paris once French administration had been restored at Port Louis under Napoleon in 1803. The slave labor institution on which they believed their livelihood to depend continued until 1835 and the 10,000 "freed persons" of African, Asian or mixed blood enjoyed less than full rights of citizenship. Regular exports by the close of the century included sugar, coffee and tea, as well as fruit, vegetables, and timber from the rapidly vanishing forest endowment. Port Louis had been declared "free", presuming thereby the right to trade liberally with the world, including the new United States, rather than exclusively or by tariff preference with France.

For most of the next century, through good times and bad, the open character of the port attracted a buckle and swash of South Seas sailing, encouraging the emergence of a cosmopolitan merchant class which frequently challenged the interests of the old plantocracy. As early as 1778, Bernardin de Saint Pierre could admire the island's cosmopolitanism, if not its manners:

> I know no other corner of the earth which extends its needs so widely. This colony brings its dishware from China, its linen and clothing from India, its slaves and livestock from Madagascar, part of its food from the Cape of Good Hope, its silverware from Cadiz, and its administration from France.[6]

During its brief independence, as before, the Ile de France subsisted by both regular commerce and the disposal of cargoes snatched by corsairs from the hulls of English and Dutch merchantmen.[7] But in the final decade of a near century of war with France, English might was put to the defense of shipping, eventually wiping out the licensed pirates of the Ile de France. By 1808 Britain had little to fear from freebooting. France had again been evicted from India, this time for good, and the British could turn to the capture of their enemy's well fortified island headquarters. Bourbon, Rodriguez, and Seychelles had already been taken by December 1810 when, after a failure at Mahébourg in the south, sixty ships landed an army of 10,000 Grenadiers in the north. Although the defense of Port Louis has permitted a few proud paragraphs in the annals of French imperial history, the Ile yielded to superior force and its capitulation was sealed in the 1814 Treaty of Paris.

Controlling both India and the Cape, Britain scarcely needed the island for the administrative purposes it had served under the French. Nevertheless, the place had proven its nuisance value in enemy hands, and the British had no faith in their inveterate rival's professions of pacific intentions. So England restored the island's Dutch name and decided to keep Mauritius in perpetuity, while throwing strategically useless Réunion (Bourbon) back to France.

A most chivalrous capitulation was exacted of the vanquished French. No prisoners were taken, private property was scrupulously protected, and the colonists were explicitly permitted to "preserve their religions, laws and Customs." The imperial abolition of the slave trade was theoretically extended to Mauritius but slavery itself remained among the island's preserved "customs" for more than a quarter century of British rule. Britain's first Governor, Sir Robert Farquhar, made his sovereign peace with the preeminent planter interests of the island and it was Farquhar who in 1820 threw the island's economy everlastingly into the dominion of the sugar cane.

Introduced by Labourdonnais eighty years earlier, sugar had been sharing priority with coffee, spice, and other products of a balanced colonial export economy. It emerged as a particularly important commodity for France after the loss of Haiti in 1804. Having noted technical improvements in milling sugar from raw cane and the superior resistance offered by cane plants to the cyclone of 1818, Farquhar encouraged the expansion of sugar estates. Even after his retirement, he succeeded in obtaining from Parliament three concessions which for a time favored Mauritius over its West Indian competitors in the colonial rush to sweeten England's diet. Disadvantageous tariff differentials in England were substantially reduced; prolongation of free trade privileges enabled Port Louis to continue buying, selling and shunting French, American, and Dutch cargoes along with British; slave labor continued to work the island's French-owned plantations despite Anti-Slavery Society agitation to apply the laws prevailing throughout the older empire. England was industrializing and even so versatile a mercantile entrepot as Mauritius had to begin to specialize.

These remarkable concessions represent the start of a highly ambivalent but fruitful relationship between the Franco-Mauritian planter-millers and their new Anglo-Saxon administration. It was a rapport which lost precious little love and which yet respected to perfection the accumulating privileges of the one and the imperial prerogatives of the other.

The expansion of sugar under favorable economic circumstances sustained the illegal importation of slaves, estimated at more than 20,000 between 1807 and 1835. Most of them were brought into distant Seychelles, which remained under Mauritian administration, and were transferred to the main island as "naturalized." The planters procrastinated successfully over London's abolitionist anxieties, demanding due compensation for the human "property" to be freed once the redoubtable legislation was applied in the island. They ultimately won their case: when the 66,000 slaves were declared free in 1835, the Crown paid the 7,000 owners over two million pounds (half the selling price demanded). Moreover, a four-year apprenticeship obligation kept former bondsmen on the plantations until 1839.[8] At that time, the freed people burst en masse from the abhorred canefields, taking to the towns, to fishing villages or to independent farming on marginal land. Thanks to the extension of King Cane, there were no great orchards of palm trees to go to tend, as their counterparts were doing in the Seychelles.

The descendants of the freedmen, together with an older class of often distinguished urban professionals and artisans, form the largest minority in Mauritius today, the Creole community. Their language, derived from nineteenth century French, and roughly comparable to the Réunion majority's Creole, remains the lingua franca of Mauritius today, used among Asians, Africans, and Europeans alike. Creole fisherfolk and small farmers compose virtually all of the 20,000 people on Rodriguez, Mauritius' main dependency 560 kilometers to the east where they rent 90 percent of their land from the state. That island was first colonized by emancipated Mauritian black people who took up farming there in the late eighteenth and early nineteenth centuries, to be joined later by Creoles of mixed heritage, most of whom went into fishing.

To replace the black workers in the canefields and sugar mills, the British Government undertook forthwith to transfer large numbers of coolie labor from India under strict five-year indenture contracts. Altogether 450,000 laborers were brought to Mauritius from several major points of origin on the sub-continent between 1829 and 1909; five-sixths of them were Hindu. As a labor system, the project worked well and the Franco-Mauritian plantations prospered. Dispossessed only of their preferred nationality by Britain, the French aristocrats managed to keep their cultural distance from the small British establishment and from the burgeoning new class of Asian laborers as well. Ackowledging nothing to share, not even poverty and powerlessness, Coolies and Creoles also kept apart, the one among the cane, the other in urban trades, fishing, and subsistence farming. Yet the latter's language was used by all, plantocracy and proletariat, too. A few thousand southern Chinese were also imported to Mauritius as coolie laborers. They stayed on and their 25,000 dependents now buy and sell most of the food-stuffs and household goods consumed on the island.

By mid-century, despite the misery in which they worked and suffered, most Indians were choosing to remain in Mauritius, rather than return to even greater insecurity on the Subcontinent. Their numbers multiplied from one-third of the population of 158,000 in 1846 to two-thirds of 316,000 in 1870, gradually transfiguring the old Ile de France into a reflection of the modern third world. It is this late-immigrated laboring majority which pressed over a century toward social justice and, ultimately, political dominion.[9]

Both objectives proved attainable only slowly and arduously, however. The first labor law in 1878 remedied some flagrant abuses but more extensive ameliorations came only in 1922. A measure of participatory government arrived on the island in 1885 with a narrowly restricted franchise which was to become enlarged into universality only in 1959. The first Indo-Mauritians were not elected to the Colonial Assembly until 1926, although by that time some Hindus and Muslims (the latter a predominantly middle-class commercial minority) had been meeting electoral qualifications for three decades. Communal self-help organizations emerged during the early years of the twentieth century, particularly among the Hindu rural mass. Labor organizers and overseers (called *sirdars*) obtained the status of entrepreneurs and property owners from the early periods of indenture. Frugality and assiduity produced in time a substantial propertied class among them. A professional middle class emerged and Indians have joined Europeans, Creoles, and Chinese in the civil service. Eventually, an insular variation of the continential caste system took shape from the largely low-caste original Hindu population. Indians now own nearly half the cultivated land, albeit little of the best, in plots ranging from microholds of a single acre to large plantations purchased from Franco-Mauritian families.

In 1869, the Suez Canal displaced the Indian Ocean's access and egress routes northward, isolating the entire Southwestern sea in maritime backwaters for a full century. The weight of isolation was relieved neither by the explosion of mineral-based prosperity in South Africa nor by relatively ambitious French investment in Madagascar after 1885. Mauritius turned to South Asian markets for her sugar, importing quantities of rice from India in exchange. Rice continues to be the island's food staple and a now independent rupee its domestic currency. Prosperity returned to Mauritius with World War One, thanks to rising sugar prices in England, but the island remained isolated for another half-century. Closure of the canal from 1967 to 1975 and the obligatory deployment of the largest oil tankers over the long route around South Africa restored some of its participation in east-west traffic patterns.

During the vicissitudes of global depression and World War Two, social movements acquired distinctly political form among the island's Hindu fieldworkers and mill hands. Politics had heretofore taken root only among the Franco-Mauritian elite who alone were able to induce London to rain or shine on that distant, dishevelled garden. A lineage of titled nineteenth and twentieth century colonial Governors exchanged courtesies with that most Parisian aristocracy—the next best company they could find in Mauritius to the real society of British India. Generations of educated professional Creoles climbed as high as they were allowed on Europe's cultural rigging, playing French so astutely that they persuaded themselves, if no one else, of their impeccable Western credentials. Increasingly affluent Muslim, Chinese, and Hindu families remained in partly voluntary segregation, however.

Colonial politics evolved slowly through both World Wars, becalmed by London's apathy and the class-consciousness of Franco-Mauritians and their Creole acolytes. The rare Hindu representatives appointed, and subsequently elected, to the councils of government from 1886 tended on major social issues to behave like their elite Creole counterparts and the Creoles like the European oligarchs.[10] Notwithstanding paternalistic gestures by some Governors and planters during moments of prosperity, the Mauritian majority had no politically resonant representation of any kind until the mid–1930s. Even trade unions were slow to start, obtaining recognition only just before World War Two.

For Britain, Mauritius was an easy territory to divide and rule. The interests of an impotent urban proletariat (mainly Creole) and a suppressed mass of Hindu canefield labor could be safely ignored so long as those communities overlooked the political affinities between them. Eventually, they did converge, however, in a precarious twenty-year long alliance within the Mauritius Labour Party. The MLP was founded by the Creole physician, Maurice Curé, and others in 1936 to defend the unheeded grievances of rural and urban workers against a monolithic paternalism of British raj and Franco-Mauritian gentry. Responding to a fluid yet inexorable urge, the party became the protagonist of both social and constitutional concessions, acting originally as both unrecognized trade union and unauthorized political party. It was this force which gradually achieved labor redress, electoral reform, liberalization of the franchise, progressive self-government and, ultimately, independence for a majority-ruled island.

A single political party proved unable to embrace the interests of an emerging majority through the crucial 1960s. The MLP was obliged to negotiate its independence program among a welter of communally motivated factions. During the 1970s, when the party failed to regenerate its multi-ethnic appeal, it was gradually replaced by a new force for communal convergence, the Mauritian Militant Movement (MMM). But for two generations, the MLP performed exemplary service to Mauritian nationalism. That example deserves some amplification.

Recognized as a party just before the War, Labour commanded only a fraction of the tiny qualified electorate, and its strikes were still illegal. It was persistently bullied by contemptuous island authorities, hounded by police and ignored by the courts. With negligible help from British Labour Party and trade union mentors, the MLP survived the depression and war years on the crude integrity of its "populist" mission. For a time during the war, it lost its balance between Creole and Hindu leaders, urban and rural militants, agitators and intelligentsia. Urban Creoles kept the faith behind founding intellectuals (Curé and Guy Rozemont) and labor organizers (Emmanuel Anquetil). As an alternative to Labour politics, some Hindus remained with Harryparsad Ramnarain's multi-ethnic "industrial association," but more of them tended to drift into easier ethnocentric welfare alternatives like Basdeo Bissoondoyal's Hindu Cultural Revival.

After the war, inspired by new men, including Seewoosagur Ramgoolam, the party re-emerged as protagonist of constitutional reform, the higher road to social justice. All the grievances of fieldhands, dockworkers, craftsmen, and peasant remained to be filed from a century of post-slavery exploitation. Low wages were keeping Mauritian sugar competitive in the best and worst of world markets. Middlemen, including *sirdar* labor contractors, were taking their share from beneath their station, not from their wealthy clients.[11] For over a decade, the MLP was able to combine proletarian, humanitarian, jacobin and anti-colonial subplots into a passionate melodrama of plural politics. All MLP viewpoints focussed on a monolithic adversary, the established Franco-Mauritian planter-miller aristocracy which dominated all intermediate classes including the supercilious bureaucracy of Great Britain. The Constitution of 1886 still substantially protected that structure. Fifty years later, Mauritius remained divided more flagrantly on ethnic-communal than on class lines.

Colonial Mauritius was not entirely isolated from the world. Independence for India and Pakistan in 1947 stimulated political enthusiasms among (and often between) Hindus and Muslims on the island diaspora. Mauritius' communal chauvinism thereupon acquired international poles for development. While Hindu politicians tugged at the MLP and Bissoondoyal kept his welfare movement oblivious to politics, the Muslim bourgeoisie agitated among Creoles and Europeans for administrative attention to its own interest. Giving slight way to popular pressure, the British Labour Government offered electoral reforms in 1948, abolishing economic qualifications and thereby opening the franchise to men and women on simple literacy criteria. The MLP then began remarkably successful pressure for universal education as well as further liberalization of the vote.

A surge of Hindu successes in the 1948 elections and the momentum achieved thereafter by the MLP forced the island's European and middle-class Creole minorities together with Muslims of property and Chinese tradespeople. In 1952, they formed a conservative alliance called the Ralliement Mauricien, which became the Parti Mauritien (PM) three years later. At first, the coalition sought through political campaigns and an obedient, imaginative press to identify MLP nationalism alternatively with New Delhi hegemony (via Seewoosagur Ramgoolam), Soviet imperialism (via the leftist Rozemont), the instability of Malaysia, the terror of Kenyan Mau Mau, and the anarchy of Guyana.[12] Its approach became more sophisticated, but the PM was fervently and effectively opposed to Mauritian independence until the very end.

PM was dominated for its first decade by the white planters and professsionals, vaguely linked through Roman Catholicism and francophone affinities to the party's urban Creole constituents. But it was Creoles who conveyed the PM's image, if not its spirit, to laborers, artisans, and lumpenproletariat of the towns. And those Creoles eventually dominated the party. In 1963, the name was enlarged to Mauritius Social Democratic Party (PMSD) partly to reflect this popular appeal, partly to obtain a moderately progressive international audience as a counter to British Labour support for the MLP's independence program.

Communal polarization became perfected in the early 1960s with the rise of Gaetan Duval, lawyer, protean demagogue, and vaunting "King Creole," as the PMSD's leader. Although Duval's appeal drew away most of the MLP's remaining urban workers and intellectuals, the resulting consolidation of Creoles within the PMSD helped cause a compensatory flight of Muslims into alliance with Labour through Abdool Razack Mohammed's Muslim Action Committee (MAC). From 1957, the MAC hoped to control the balance between Hindu-dominated Labour and the Franco-Creole PMSD. It sought political alliance and demanded some form of proportional representation, since its own "community" was too widely dispersed throughout the island's town-village network to swing many electoral constituencies on its own.

For the decade through independence in 1968, each notable community thus had its own party, and each articulate economic or cultural faction its own caucus within a party. Mauritian politics reflected the deployment of class and ethnic interests across a crowded, complex chessboard. Franco-Mauritians, intransigeant against both universal suffrage and independence, retired into the wings behind the PMSD's street melodramas. Muslims dickered and temporized for ethnic and cultural protection in league with the majority MLP.

The Hindu majority was itself subdividing. "Lower-caste" spokesmen successfully exploited popular distrust of the land-owners, industrialists, professionals, and other notables identified increasingly since 1948 with Labour's successes. In growing numbers from 1958 they joined the Independent Forward Block (IFB), Sookdeo Bissoondoyal's political incarnation of his brother's cultural movement. For a time (1964–1967), they participated in the All-Mauritian Hindu Congress (AMHC), a new, ephemeral expression of sectarian chauvinism. Numerous Tamil- and Telegu-speaking Hindus also formed political parties in the universal campaign for minority protection before independence. The Chinese middle class of 20,000, concentrated in Port Louis, played both sides of the major-party dialectic, gravitating largely toward their urban cohorts in the PMSD.

Political alignments fluctuated somewhat in this city-sized constituency where personalities and local issues strongly influence national options. The rural Hindu IFB even collaborated briefly with Creole elites in the PMSD to oppose their own elites in the MLP. During most of the 1960s, however, the IFB, Congress, and MAC joined Labour in an essentially Indo-Mauritian independence front, representing some 69 percent of the population. Ultimately, it was Ramgoolam's ability to maintain contact with Mohammed's Muslim Committee and the low-caste Hindu factions which ensured his majorities in the 1963 and 1967 elections, making independence inevitable.

Indo-Mauritian unity was obtained at considerable cost, however. Alienation of the Creoles, nepotism, low-political haggling over jobs, and the distribution of favors imposed a pall of prejudice and corruption over the entire political process. Minority rights degenerated into a consecrated ritual of ethnocentric spoils-sharing, demonstrating the nasty advantages of communal, rather than national, loyalty. Despite Labour's origins and Ramgoolam's devout efforts for unity, Creoles remained by and large beyond the pale, and, through the PMSD, turned implacably against full self-government under majority rule.

Constitutional negotiations, conducted in London in 1961 and 1965, readily betrayed the inconsistencies in Mauritius' popular will. Having decided on retrenchment in Asia, Britain gladly honored the victorious electoral margins recorded by Ramgoolam's forces from 1948 through 1963. The UK had long since identified the MLP as the appropriate "moderates" to receive power in an orderly transfer, without shocking the colony's essential orientation. Nevertheless, the vociferous clamor of the minorities augured trouble for any abrupt act of decolonization. Creoles and Franco-Mauritians campaigned bitterly against the grain of history for continued association with Britain, while the Asian minorities were seeking elaborate safeguards for their own electoral representation and social rights. The negotiations proved arduous, with electoral and judicial details referred to a battery of investigative commissions.

Refused recourse to an outright referendum on the issue of independence, the PMSD boycotted the concluding sessions of the 1965 conference and demonstrated in the streets of Mauritius against Whitehall's betrayal. British troops were summoned to quell riots between Duval's Creoles and Hindus, and later between Creoles and Muslims. This turbulence seemed to argue for PMSD's position against a hasty conferral of authority on the political leadership of an unprepared, inchoate society. In a characteristically audacious gamble to make the point legitimately, the swashbuckling Duval pledged to mobilize "brother Hindus" in such numbers at the next elections that even apathetic England would reverse the momentum of independence. Taking the election as an indirect plebiscite, Britain would have to renegotiate the island's status. At the least, he thought, London must be compelled to guarantee domestic tranquillity and the rights of property, to protect minorities, assure export markets for sugar, and welcome the immigration to Britain of those loyal subjects who wished to leave the festering island.

Duval and his tory confrères were doubtless underestimating the mood of withdrawal in a never enthusiastic metropole determined to reduce its global role beyond Suez. The PMSD argument contradicted Labour's contention, supported by Governor J.S. Rennie, that the island's economic and cultural dilemmas could not be resolved without the cultivation of a national self-consciousness based on the certainty of independence. Rationalising as it sounds, this position held true. In any case, Duval did not succeed in winning his "plebiscite" gamble, although he came remarkably close.

Prospects of a Duval juggernaut, together with discouraging seasons for the sugar economy, induced an anxious Ramoolam to delay the crucial elections from June 1966 until August 1967. Even then, using all the available instruments of government and aided by a complicated system of voting in three-member constituencies which forced party, rather than communal discipline, the MLP emerged with one Legislative Assembly seat more than the PMSD (24 to 23). Labour candidates suffered a shocking reduction in ballot percentages, from 42.3% in 1963 to 33.7%, compared to PMSD's rise from 18.9% to 43.1% under Duval's incandescent leadership. Duval's party carried all city and town electorates, emphasizing the serious urban-rural cleavage in Mauritius' identity. But the MLP had combined as the Independence Party with IFB and MAC, an arrangement which obtained eleven and four additional seats, respectively (with 15.1% and 6.3% of the total vote). The alliance held firm, yielding an indisputable Indo-Mauritian majority of forty-three to twenty-seven, which was readily interpreted as a popular endorsement for independence.[13] In effect, however, an internationally unprecedented 44 percent of the electorate had opted against that final stage of self-determination.

Although the communities' worst violence took place in late 1967 after the elections, the Hindus remained under self-control while urban Muslims and Creoles took their apprehensions out internecinely against one another. As Simmons summarizes,

> Fighting between the Muslims and the Creoles was bound to be limited. If, on the other hand, the Muslims and Creoles had united against the Hindus, a civil war could have resulted. In January 1968 civil war was not a danger, but Muslims and Creoles grew terrified of one another. The Muslims turned to the Hindus for support, and middle-class Creoles looked for jobs outside Mauritius.[14]

Mauritius the Independent

Independence arrived only a few weeks later, on March 12, 1968, without fanfare but in social tranquillity. The Union Jack departed, but British troops stayed on, to keep that peace. Mauritius remained within the Commonwealth, with a Muslim Mauritian Governor and Ramgoolam as the Queen's Prime Minister. Mauritius and Britain had signed a six-year Mutual Defence and Assistance Agreement to help assure continuity of institutions and the stability of the fragile order bequeathed to the new nation. With encouragement from the Gaullist regime in France and Réunion, the PMSD soon abandoned its truculence over independence. It joined a "grand coalition" with the MLP in 1969, enabling the latter to discard its embarrassingly chauvinist partner, the radical IFB, without whom it could not have beaten Duval in the elections of 1967.

For all the fears of Hindu vengeance and MLP radicalism, independence made few structural changes in Mauritian social-economy. The sugar goose continued to lay her exportable eggs.[15] The economy had grown, and living standards had risen with due regard for established practicalities. Politically crucial goals of full employment and rising wages have been approached, when possible, outside the sugar industry which has been allowed to merchanize, to rationalize its milling and transportation facilities, and to resist labor pressures, all in the interest of maximum production at highest cost-efficiency. As the pre-eminent cultural geographer of the Mascarenes and Seychelles wrote,

> The most equitable management of scarcity would have engendered fearful results, a decline in agricultural productivity which would have subjected these minuscule nations more than ever to external control.[16]

Hence, the radical program of decolonization attributed to Labour by the anxious opponents of independence was never fulfilled.

But social successes engender their own jeopardy. Postwar modernization had so improved public health that by the late 1950s Mauritius was threatened with an alarming surge in population. After the eradication of malaria in the late 1940s, the population climbed at the rate of three percent a year, increasing by 46 percent between 1944 and 1958. During more than two decades, Mauritian society was the world's Exhibit A for the perils of unchecked demographic growth. A combination of nineteenth century immigration and twentieth century hygiene appeared to be reissuing Thomas Malthus' 1798 *Essay on the Principles of Population* within the tight boundaries of a mountainous island already consecrated to expansive agriculture. Family planning at first failed to take hold among the communities, each politically suspicious of increases in its rivals' populations. Various schemes proposed by the Governors, heeding scholarly warnings of Mauritius' future, remained ineffective until the late 1960s.[17]

Today, Mauritius enjoys the extraordinary, perhaps unique distinction among agricultural countries of a population condensed at 530 to the square kilometer. But idiomatic family planning programs have been devised and, over two decades, fertility has been dramatically lowered. The island's rate of increase declined from over three percent to 1.44 percent in 1977, and has stayed near that level since then. The death rate continues to fall along with the rate of birth, however, both subject to highly effective technology aimed against the traditional proclivities of Hindu, Muslim, and Roman Catholic communities.

The political economy of over-population rings clearly and cogently in Mauritius as anywhere else. People must be fed and protected, or they must be exported to more congenial environments. Mauritius has followed the demographic textbook as faithfully as any, and with considerable success. Dependent for better or worse on maximum production of sugar to earn foreign exchange and validate capital investment, the island's economic realities preclude the removal of any prime acreage from cane cultivation. A technologically advanced, relatively productive industry is able, barring climatic disasters, to mill upwards of 700,000 tons of sugar annually, at favorable extraction rates. This level of production, sold largely at guaranteed prices under EEC and other agreements, earns the island $300 million in export revenues during good years. Price vicissitudes affect a sizeable portion of the island's export earnings nevertheless and Mauritius' production represents too small a proportion of world sugar to exert its own influence on prices. Sugar is the source of both security and insecurity for Mauritius, considering its economy's sensitivity to fluctuations of production factors, demand, world price, and freight costs. The best Mauritius' open economy can do is adjust to change, and this it has done well.

Preoccupation of 90 percent of agricultural land (and all the best land) by cane cannot be readily reversed. Sugar involves substantial investment even on good land. Fixed costs in milling and overall technological progress take large commitments of capital, which private owners have been willing to make. Cane plants produce over multi-year cycles, and a large, specialized work force depends on seasonal activity in the plantations. One-fifth of the cane is grown on 30,000 family smallholds occupying a full third of the acreage under cane. Using an entire family during harvest periods, these plots (almost all of them owned by Hindus) are even more thoroughly integrated into the metabolisms of credit and labor allocation than the large, milling plantations. Sugar production employs 30 percent of the labor force and (with molasses) accounts for 70 to 80 percent of export earnings, depending on price and climatic fortunes. Acreage could be removed from cane and regenerated over a ten-year cycle, but Mauritius has no prospect for immediately profitable yields to tide families and companies over the interim.

In the search for remedies to chronic food shortages, quite a few innovations have appeared above Mauritian ground, only to vanish against revenue competition from sugar, or from imports, or from the hostility of entrenched political and commercial protection. These failures have kept the island's dairy industry at rudimentary levels, for instance, and rendered Mauritians entirely dependent on external sources for cereal grains. Most schemes for diversifying agriculture have evolved against opposition from an imperious Chamber of Agriculture, a powerful Franco-Mauritian lobby for the primacy of sugar. Alternative agriculture must not only avoid drawing resources from the mighty monocrop. It must also be able to resist cyclones, minimize foreign exchange needs, and adapt to microhold farming. It should also tend to need labor, mainly in the (austral) summer after the harvesting, milling, and transporting of sugar have ended. Established, efficient, supported by insurance and banking enterprises, intensive research programs, public services, international market arrangements and interlocking import-export commercial structures, the sugar industry carries an entire island society on its broad, billowing back.[18]

If principles of political economic prudence declare the canefields off-limits to intervention, Mauritius has nonetheless had fruitful recourse to supplementary cultivation and more recently to urban job promotion for its growing, restive population. Divers crops are grown on marginal lands relatively unsuited to cane and in precious footage between sugar rows when cane plants lie low enough to the ground. Since 1886, tea has been successfully farmed on the hot highlands beyond the normal reach of sugar. Tea resists cyclone damage better than most alternative crops, but its Mauritian labor is costly in competition with mainland Asain economies. Current production averages 5,000 tons and is sold at negotiated prices to South Africa, compensating for less than one-fifth of the island's imports from that source.

Tobacco has been produced in small quantities for domestic purposes since colonial times. Many of Mauritius' sugar sacks are locally fabricated from native aloe (hemp) fibers, grown at relatively high cost per acre (again when compared to sugar). Mauritius has sought to develop livestock herds and is self-sufficient in poultry, but it must import virtually all its feed, as well as other animal products, from South Africa. With 2,260 square kilometers of reef-protected lagoon, the island has usually been able to satisfy its needs in fish. The industry remains pitifully under-capitalized, however, and the lagoon has become sorely over-fished by small boatmen, most of them in deep debt to local traders. Japanese, Taiwanese, Soviet, and South Korean trawlers exploit the island's best fisheries off Saint Brandon (Cargados Carajos), beyond the reach of island fleets. The Chagos grounds lie even farther away and have been closed by their British proprietors at Diego Garcia. In Rodriguez, fishing has ceased to be the prime occupation; people now raise vegetables and livestock for the main island.

In other productive sectors, Mauritius has proved more resourceful. A fortunate interaction of public and private investment has multiplied housing and recreational facilities for an increasingly urban population. In tourism as in agriculture, domestic capital from sugar profits has been mobilized productively, beyond mere speculation. Europeans, South Africans, and Réunionnais have come to the island's glowing beaches in rapidly mounting numbers, exceeding 118,000 in 1983. The growth of facilities in tourism has posed few opportunity-cost dilemmas for the island's investors, fiscal managers, or labor force. Sharing in lucrative tour routes, Air Mauritius has also been consistently profitable.

Mauritius' most ingenious investment promotion has been devoted to small, labor-intensive export industries. Beginning in 1970, the island's traditional freeport policy was revived. An Export Processing Zone (EPZ) benefits from highly advantageous conditions for importation of materials, taxation, access to credit, utility rates, repatriation of profits and, indeed, low-cost, literate, adaptable, and undemanding labor. Clothing and other textiles, cut diamonds and micro-jewels, toys, furniture, electronic appliances and components, optical instruments, and other commodities are produced at Port Louis for export primarily to the European Economic Community, where Mauritius enjoys market privileges under the African-Caribbean-Pacific (Lomé) agreement. Participation in the micro-state light manufacturing arena earns nearly $100 million for the economy, with 23,000 jobs opened in eighty-seven European, South African, and Asian firms. Surplus Franco-Mauritian and Indo-Mauritian sugar capital has been placed in joint ventures as well. In 1981, a poor year for sugar, EPZ products accounted for 25 percent of Mauritius' exports.[19]

The international recession of the early 1980s hurt the EPZ in addition to lowering demand for sugar and for tourist services. Indecent wages and working conditions have been tolerated for Mauritians (mostly women) in the export industries to sustain the island's competitive position. Political critics have also deplored the acceptance of EPZ capital from South Africa. They consider the island implicated in the endeavors of an outcast state to penetrate otherwise inhospitable European and third world markets through "made in Mauritius" labels. The argument in defense of such compromise insists on the growing labor force which the economy must somehow occupy while its land and processing facilities remain monopolized by an increasingly mechanized sugar industry.

Emigration for Mauritians has provided a sporadic and not altogether acceptable recourse for surplus population. Manifestation of modern skills, bilinguality, capital, and/or white skin renders an emigrant welcome in certain new homelands, but few Mauritians have those assets. India and Britain long ago closed doors to homeless Hindu masses from the oceanic diaspora. Muslims and Creoles are invited to several prosperous Middle Eastern and African destinations, respectively, if they are bilingual or technically qualified, or both. Many Creole women recruited as brides are among the estimated 15,000–18,000 Mauritians legally or otherwise immigrated into France since the late 1960s.[20] Some 300 carefully selected Mauritians go to permanent residence in Australia each year. Franco-Mauritians have been able to open bank accounts abroad, legally and otherwise, and can move with relative ease, but their capital, like the technology of the fortunate Creole or Muslim, is sorely needed on the island itself. Unlike Réunion, Mauritius has never had an industrial metropole willing to absorb a steady flow of immigrant labor, but it at least enjoys the mixed consolation of retaining her more dynamic youth at home.

Like most recent colonies, Mauritius struggles toward visions of economic productivity against the cultural grain. Efficiency in human resource allocation is hindered not merely by the atavism of some traditions, but also by an educational system erected to proliferate a professional and white collar elite for which employment has become scarce. Universal educational opportunity arrived in the early 1960s, arousing expectations which could be fulfilled for only a few. Mastery of European languages (English as well as French) and satisfaction of Western educational standards remain the key to upward mobility in this polyglot third-world microcosm. So strong is the dominance of European cultural norms that Mauritius' exceedingly vigorous literary production includes virtually nothing of importance in the Asian and Creole languages of the vast majority of the population.

To reduce the legitimate clamor for high-level employment, and to retain rough parity with metropolitan educational standards, state examinations have been pegged at levels beyond what an inferior-to-mediocre secondary school system can satisfy. The resulting high failure rates entail considerable economic and emotional waste. Most of the 9,000 young people entering the economy annually are thus forced to choose between laboring jobs and no jobs at all. Vocational training and pedagogical reform have had modest results. The island's higher education and advanced research institutions remain pragmatically linked to its agricultural lifelines. But most students in Mauritius do not attend these institutions. And even for those who do, opportunity remains identified with the illusion of a professional or administrative career. Once admitted to that career, prospects for advancement encounter the longevity of a still young generation of incumbents in professional and managerial positions. To the mass of unemployables, politics provides an outlet, if not a solution, for frustrations. Students have demonstrated and protested since before independence, but they soon thereafter found an effective political channel in a new party, the Mouvement Militant Mauritien (MMM).

Once the Mauritian state had become an accomplished fact, the Mauritian nation did begin to take shape. The fruition of the process was destined, however, for another generation and a different politics than the independence movement built by Ramgoolam and the MLP. Born in a year of international upheaval, 1968, independent Mauritius pulled its assets together and shook some of its liabilities off. Totally unreconciled whites and Creoles emigrated, some to Europe, others to Australia, South Africa, and beyond. A few Muslims found work in the Middle East and Africa. The bulk of the minority population had little choice but to stay, and the majority had none.

The independence constitution was designed to prevent flagrant under-representation of minorities in the unicameral Legislative Assembly. Each of the twenty constituencies elects three representatives. The Governor, with Supreme Court advice, has the discretion to appoint up to eight additional MPs who had qualified as so called "best losers" in the electoral contest. While not necessarily guaranteeing the communities a proportionate share of Assembly votes, the system worked in 1967 to allocate equity points to minorities roughly equivalent to their proportion in the population. An Ombudsman and access to Privy Council adjudication were also part of Mauritius' original constitutional assurances.

Once in power, the Indo-Mauritian majority behaved most responsibly toward the conservatives who had feared its mob radicalism. Despite the remonstrances of the MLP's Hindu socialists, Ramgoolam tread very softly in the carpeted halls of the sugar industry. Only one of the twenty-two estates was nationalized and social legislation never exceeded the carrying capacity of the industry. Projects for mechanization, horizontal concentration, and liberal financing were largely unrestrained by Government, while administrative schemes for modernization, export marketing, job creation, and even agricultural diversification encountered little effective opposition in the private sector. While sugar prices held and EPZ output grew, GNP rose through the 1970s at an annual rate of 11 percent, adjusted for inflation, far better than the average third world economy. Exports almost quadrupled in the decade after independence, earning over $500 million in 1979. Tourism brought $40 million that year and the EPZ accounted for $90 million. The Ramgoolam regime was succeeding, despite criticisms of bureaucratic incompetence and favoritism, and despite insistence from the PMSD "social democracy" on greater inducements to free market forces.

By 1970, the PMSD argument was coming from within the Government. After losing the struggle for continued political association with Britain, the Creole party joined its enemies in December 1969. They thus reproduced a shortlived "grand coalition" that had been imposed by Governor Rennie in 1964 as a fraternal front for constitutional negotiations. That coalition was to break up and reform twice again, each time sacrificing a measure of grandeur as Mauritius' electoral weight swung leftward, away from the regime's two major parties.

Duval, who had always kept his personal lines open to Ramgoolam, became Foreign Minister in 1969. Often at cross-purposes with his chief, he inaugurated a four-year cycle of casuistry and contradiction in Mauritian diplomacy. Duval openly fostered close economic relations with South Africa, for example, while the Head of Government was denouncing apartheid in UN and African forums. He co-sponsored the United States' 1970 "two Chinas" UN resolution just as the Prime Minister was recognizing Peking. The Foreign Minister oriented ideological openings in the direction of Gaullist France and the French-speaking Organization of African and Malagasy States (OCAM) while MLP leaders were espousing nonalignment and third world patriotism in South Asia and East Africa. Although exports depended strongly on British purchases, the UK's share of Mauritius' imports was allowed to decline below 20 percent, as Duval found a range of suppliers to compete with Britain.

While Duval courted these sources, as well as markets and tourists in the West, Ramgoolam toasted friendship with Soviets, Chinese, and Indians. "However self-contradictory these approaches seemed," the author commented in 1974, "Mauritius was actually composing an eclectic portfolio of foreign relations calculated to assure the new nation's security."[21]

For the island remained isolated, sociologically fragile, economically at the mercy of whirlwinds. Its Government joined every organization in sight, sought assistance from any quarter consistent with Mauritius' integrity, as Ramgoolam understood it, as a sovereign Afro-Asian state. Duval concurred, without excessive scruple on the matter of integrity, provided private property and market opportunity were respected. Mauritius remained cordial with Israel until 1976, by which time Ramgoolam as OAU chairman did what his position seemed to demand. The two leaders clashed in November 1970 over the Prime Minister's limited four-year fisheries agreement with the USSR; Duval had himself been offering the UK a "base" in Mauritius in the place of South Africa's Simonstown.

The fisheries agreement contained no privileges not already enjoyed by Soviet trawlers in the island and other locations. It nevertheless scandalized Western press and official commentators, and sent Duval into brief resignation. Years later, the Soviet invasion of Afghanistan provided Ramgoolam an opportunity to denounce the inoffensive agreement, which was dissolved in January 1980. The Prime Minister had long since repudiated Duval's naval base offer to Britain. Incidentally, London showed little interest in the idea, having put its limited strategic interests into Diego Garcia on the Chagos. England also declined to renegotiate the 1968 Defense Agreement after its expiration in 1974; the Royal Navy's telecommunications station on the island was subsequently closed. But for several months after the 1970 incident, Mauritius was kept busy denying alternating rumors of similar offers of military facilities to France (by Duval) and the USSR (by Ramgoolam).[22]

Years earlier, while still political opponents, Ramgoolam and Duval had quarrelled over the Prime Minister's complicity in the separation of the Chagos archipelago from Mauritius for military purposes. Consent to the sale of the islands for the modest price of three million pounds had been extracted from Ramgoolam at private meetings in London with British Prime Minister Harold Wilson during the constitutional negotiations of September 1965. Apparently, no minutes exist from those meetings, but once the transfer was announced on November 19, the PMSD was able to accuse Ramgoolam of trading the Chagos for British acquiescence in his independence designs, making Whitehall appear to have been a reluctant donor of self-government.[23] Britain proceeded to combine the archipelago with remote islands drawn from the Seychelles colony (subsequently given back) to form the British Indian Ocean Territory (BIOT). Under lease from the British, the United States has developed its main Indian Ocean naval-air base on Diego Garcia, a Chagos atoll, over 2,000 kilometers from Mauritius. Subsequently, as Foreign Minister, no longer complaining of perfidy in the alleged independence deal, Duval welcomed the Anglo-American base as a boon to Western influence in the central Indian Ocean. Ignoring the (now accepted) prize of self-government, he criticized only the niggardly pecuniary price which the 1965 Mauritian negotiators had exacted for so precious a morsel of patrimony. Pressed by Indian and other Zone of Peace advocates in the early and mid-1970s, Ramgoolam had claimed that he never agreed to the erection of a monumental base on Diego Garcia; a "communications facility," first stage in the atoll's strategic evolution, was as far as he expected the allied plans to go.

Ambiguity over Diego Garcia prevailed to the end of Ramgoolam's tenure in 1982. Official Mauritian jurists maintained that Britain obtained only usufructory rights to the Chagos in 1965, allowing Mauritius to extend its 200-mile economic zone rights to the distant archipelago, a contention which London categorically rejects. Although anxious to cultivate credentials in the nonaligned forum, Ramgoolam nonetheless declined to command Britain and the United States out of Diego Garcia. At one time, he even suggested that Washington could "lease" the base directly from Mauritius once Britain relinquished its claim to ownership.[24] Moreover, his Government has been seriously embarrassed by revelations that it had tolerated Britain's eviction of 1,200 Chagos islanders from the archipelago without their consent and that it failed to provide for humane resettlement of the expellees even after receiving subsidies from London for that purpose.[25]

This reign of anarchy in Mauritian foreign affairs was interrupted in December 1973 when Ramgoolam lost his proverbial patience with his Foreign Minister. Duval had made an unauthorized pledge that new excise taxes and export duties would be annulled if the EEC agreed to donate 10,000 tons of rice that year in lieu of costly imports of the staple. Wanting to have both the rice and his new revenues, the Prime Minister fired Duval, and the PMSD returned to opposition. Duval thus bequeathed Ramgoolam two permanent foreign accomplishments: lucrative arrangements with South

Africa for tea exports, tourism, imports of favorably priced food and other consumer goods, which made South Africa second to Britain as Mauritius' main supplier; and broadscale Francophone solidarity, entailing substantial French assistance in education, cultural exchange, transportation, energy and tourist facilities, and labor emigration to French shipyards. Timely French approval of the island's affiliation with the EEC opened new guaranteed outlets for sugar even before Britain's entry into the Market. Mauritius was the first Commonwealth member to join both the EEC overseas consortium and Paris' various African clubs, including the OCAM community (the "M" of the title referring to that island after the 1972 defection of Madagascar).

Ramgoolam's construction of a pragmatic governing consensus depended primarily on his capacity to make minute policy concessions to local interests. Ethnocentrism by IFB and MLP Hindus, PMSD Creoles and MAC Muslims was absorbed into a quotidien process of favors and sanctions, carrots and sticks. While the world ignored or tolerated adolescent contradictions in foreign policy by a ministate, and while the economy enjoyed reasonable per capita growth, Mauritius subsisted admirably. The limits of international indulgence were exceeded, however, when the island had to account for its confusing external commitments and to face a crisis of getting and spending. That point was reached in the aftermath of the 1973 Middle East War, the surge of OPEC petroleum prices and the subsequent international economic decline. It was then that the opportunism of Mauritius' diplomacy and the shabbiness of its improvised political and administrative apparatus became unmistakable. By meting and doling, enticing self-serving opponents across the lines, satisfying claims, however meretricious, to right and left, the manipulated system floated. But it was drifting without direction or conviction, clarity of policy, consistency of execution, or audacity in initiative.

The prosperity induced by successful sugar harvests and EEC-protected sales to Britain had encouraged the Government to anticipate full employment by 1980. Reaching this objective would entail the creation of 76,000 new jobs in agriculture, industry and tourism during the latter half of the decade. Despite publicly financed "work for all" projects, the economy simply could not accumulate the capital to finance such development once the cost of imports rose and the fortunes of sugar encountered structural vicissitudes. The balance of trade turned negative halfway through the decade, compensated less and less well by tourist expenditures and other "invisibles." Even the diminished employment projections of the 1980–1982 Plan—22,600 new jobs, half of which were to emerge in manufacturing alone—remained out of reach. Higher wages and increased Government welfare spending, food subsidies for urbanites and bonuses for organized labor had begun to affect productivity and to drain liquidity into unproductive imports bought at inflationary rates. The wily Prime Minister was able to repair his diplomatic fences with help from Duval's loyal and effective successor, the veteran Creole Labourite Harold Walter. Ramgoolam managed to keep his shambling domestic machinery operating into the early 1980s, but through his last decade in office a new majority was developing to the left of his contrived and meticulously maintained consensus.

That challenge, embodied in the Mauritian Militant Movement, was variously interpreted through the 1970s as progressive or fascist, nationalist or Soviet controlled, inevitably successful, or bound to shatter. By keeping the MMM outside his otherwise comprehensive apparatus, holding his course in expectation of the collapse or the miraculous disgrace of his adversary, Ramgoolam wore his own forces down, exposed their fatigue and impotence and in effect abandoned the Mauritian nation to their opponent.

Born like independent Mauritius itself in the global ferment of 1968, the MMM grew into a new incarnation of the original MLP. It posed the very alternative that Labour had represented during the thirty years before its climactic triumph at independence. Like the old MLP, it stood for redistributive justice in a hierarchical class structure and for a "Mauritianism" transcending sectarianism.

> It brought the sense of 'confrontation politics' and 'direct democracy' into a Mauritian political spectrum vacant on the left. And it came at a time when, thanks to Ramgoolam's handling of the independence dilemmas, Mauritius was prepared for political controversy that cut across purely ethnic-communal lines.[26]

The MMM scored its first successes among city youth cheering its rallies for educational and land reform, nationalization of sugar, and the universal use of the Creole language. The party soon formed a true power base in labor organizations of civil servants, sugar- and dockworkers, and other parts of the private sector. Its organizers were bluntly excluded from the pampered, low-wage EPZ industries.

Although starting as a radical alternative to an aged establishment in league with the accursed sugar barons, the MMM has joined the more constrained parallelogram of orthodox Mauritian politics which had already domesticated the MLP. Like Labour, the new party was a loose coalition of moderate and revolutionary factions soldered together by mutual antagonisms against vested interests ("neo-colonial" having replaced "colonial" in nomenclature alone). Like the early MLP, it was sustained by competent leadership drawn from all the communities. Its first parliamentarian, Dev Virahsawmy, and its leader from the late 1970s into 1983, Aneerood Jugnauth, are Hindus, while the founding Secretary General and chief strategist, Paul Bérenger, is Franco-Mauritian and its most effective publicist, Hervé Masson, is a Creole.

The party's original program of structural change has been persistently modulated since 1970 as its leaders sought pluralistic, participatory and cooperative solutions, rather than ideological or authoritarian formulas, for Mauritius' problems. Nevertheless, the street demonstrations and barely legal work actions of the early 1970s gave the MMM a reputation for subversion. This undeserved image lured the Ramgoolam Government into violations of the very liberties of free labor and the press that it had once gouged from its own oligarchic adversaries. Party leaders were persecuted and imprisoned, like Labour and Bissoondoyal champions of the 1940s before them. Both generations of Mauritian nationalism were turned on the same wheel of reform, constraint, and non-communalism.

In late 1971, following a particularly destructive series of strikes, police repression, allegations of industrial sabotage, and improvised charges of foreign power machinations, the MMM seemed ready for the anathema. Ramgoolam's harried administration swerved from its hard-won legitimacy and counter-attacked with ferocity. After losing to the MMM in a by-election—held, shockingly, in his own bailiwick—Ramgoolam cancelled the general elections constitutionally due by August 1972. The Government thus operated upon its old mandate dating from before independence, treating its new opponents as seditious rather than as political rivals deserving their chance at parliamentary legitimacy.

Identifying the particular interest of an insecure political establishment with the integrity of the state, Ramgoolam invoked a new Public Order Act to declare a six-month state of emergency on December 16, 1971. Regularly renewing this security order, he was able to postpone all elections indefinitely, to suspend fourteen labor unions, proscribe political assembly, enable extraordinary search and seizure, introduce press censorship under which the MMM's *Le Militant* could be banned for a year and its editor, Masson, placed under surveillance. To preclude further unwelcome surprises at the polls, Government appointees were substituted for elected officials on the expiration of each local administrative term. On March 10, 1972, some hundred Mouvement leaders, including Secretary General Bérenger, and the party's lone MP, Virahsawmy, were arrested (some for a second time) under suspicion of subversion, although no charges were filed. They were kept conveniently out of sight during Queen Elizabeth's first visit to Mauritius later that month and remained in detention, without trial, until December.[27]

Ramgoolam's security measures aroused live controversy. The PMSD and some of the business community applauded them as manifestations of protective authority, but both the Democratic Union of Mauritius (UDM), a conservative PMSD splinter opposed to the coalition with Labour, and the radical Hindu IFB voted against emergency powers as dictatorial in-struments which could cut both left and right. Virahsawmy, who vacated his parliamentary seat in August 1972 to form his own party, was not replaced, for another by-election threatened only to insert a different MMM nose under the trembling tent. This refusal of electoral tests precipitated an intragovernmental dispute with the MAC which had been chafing against its claimed under-representation in the 1967 Assembly.[28] However, in 1974, once the PMSD was again outside the Government, the IFB moved back in. This adherence began a progressive absorption of that communally-based party within the MLP, causing the defection of some of its younger adherents to the MMM. Thus Ramgoolam's older nationalist party became increasingly

Hindu while its new challenger strengthened its national representation by appealing to Hindu rural voters.

Furthermore, civil libertarian consciences in and outside the MLP revolted against the abuses of state security weapons to suppress dissent. Several ministers left the Cabinet in protest. One of them was MLP Vice President Harryparsad Ramnarain, an authentic man of the canefields, vintage labor leader and champion of the poor since the mid-1930s.[29] An earlier MLP defector, Aneerood Jugnauth, once Ramgoolam's Minister of Labor, emerged during the early years of repression as principal attorney for his new MMM colleagues. The first Ombudsman, a Swedish jurist, also resigned in January 1972, accusing the Prime Minister himself of interfering on behalf of officials accused of malfeasance. After less than four years of self-government, Mauritius appeared to be conforming to the lamentable authoritarian pattern exemplified in several other unweanable third world democracies of the 1960s.

Once the detainees were freed, however, MMM tactics changed, and legal opposition survived in Mauritius. The Mouvement depended on the trade union machinery within its General Works Federation. Moreover, it organized strong party units in the towns, preparing for eventual national elections. Ramgoolam also had a critical choice. He had benefitted three times at precise three-year intervals from the application of irregular powers— in 1965 and in 1968 to suppress internecine rioting and protect the independence cause, and in 1971 to overcome MMM dissent. He might have readily listened to the appeal of class and party loyalties, abolishing political activity entirely and prolonging the exercise of emergency powers in the name of stability. Conceivably, had Mauritius possessed a military institution, the 1971 crisis might have produced another example of the public safety dictatorships which litter the Afro-Asian landscape in the wake of nominal decolonization. The temptations of single-party rule are said to have rung in the Prime Minister's ear,[30] but he did not, finally, heed such voices, nor did he have to face a fronde of generals or lieutenants demanding protection of the sacred state.

In the early 1970s, as Mauritius entered its critical constitutional adolescence, Ramgoolam did the characteristic thing; he compromised. The state of emergency obtained its semester-long renewals through the fifth year, ending in December 1976. The MMM and its affiliated organizations chafed under surveillance. Press censorship remained in effect until May 1976 and political meetings were proscribed until November of that year. The elections were postponed, not indefinitely, but for four years. This extension of the regime's life, obtained by convenient constitutional amendment in 1971, represented perhaps a coalition concession to Duval, as Simmons suggests,[31] but the PMSD was to leave the coalition in December 1973 and still no elections were scheduled. Postponement was an artifically legal device to buy time to construct an economic buttress for the amorphous political majority forged in the late 1960s.

But economic policy was becoming more conservative and less coherent. A wage freeze aimed at enhancing capital accumulation and business confidence. The unions were kept away from the EPZ incubator and the Government denounced MMM strikes as responsible for food shortages, rising costs, and lapses in exports. Planter and business interests, always interconnected in Mauritius, became increasingly influential in the councils of government, even after the departure of the PMSD in 1973. Charges of neo-colonialism and questions like "*what* independence?" became watchwords for a rising generation of aspirants alienated from workplace, markets, and government authority.[32] In the end, Ramgoolam's economic buttress failed and his use of police tactics, petty politics, and clumsy constitutionalisms backfired. The collapse came in time for the electorate to attribute its misfortunes not to the impetuous "radicals" of the street and union hall, but to the venerable wielders of power themselves. In finally deciding to face an electoral accounting, Ramgoolam allowed Mauritian democracy to regenerate itself, but the rescue was ultimately performed for the benefit of the MMM.

That party survived its desert passage of the early 1970s much as MLP had weathered the 1940s, through fidelity to the interests of both rural and urban labor, refusal to take sides in ethnic-communal partnership and acquisition of a reasonably attentive international audience. While Ramgoolam's party had the ear of British Labour and the PMSD continued to claim a hearing among moderates and world business interests, their post-independence antagonist managed to appeal to a range of listeners from Mitterand socialists in Europe to Qaddafi rejectionists in the third world. As the Mouvement strenghtened its hold on trade union and municipal positions, its policies became more temperate while, paradoxically, its revolutionary bedfellows became more conspicuous. The older parties sought at each electoral stage to discredit the MMM by reference to actual or imagined links with Moscow, Tripoli, or any other presumed exporter of subversion. That the Mouvement could take these charges in stride testifies as much to the tactical skills of Bérenger, Jugnauth, and other leaders as to the legitimacy of its protest against the Mauritian status quo.

After the world crisis of 1973, Mauritius' hitherto fortunate independence began to suffer the fate of the resourceless third world polity dependent on limited export opportunities for its livelihood. Sugar production and prices held firm until 1975 when a malignant conspiracy of weather and recession drove both indices down at once. In 1975, with its export-processing revenues also depressed by declining world demand and competition from new Asian sources, and with imported food and fuel prices rising rapidly, Mauritius suffered its first trade deficit since independence. The Government response was to finance essential imports and social programs through international borrowing and deficit spending, eventually siphoning off the investment capital which had kept its industries competitive and its external debt negligible. Major devaluations of the rupee in 1979 and 1981 facilitated commodity exports and tourism, but at inflationary costs. Sugar makers warned that rising wages, taxes, and interest rates had carried their costs beyond the price they could obtain.

World sugar prices had indeed fallen from 630 pounds (sterling) per ton in 1974 to 119 two years later, rising only to 275 pounds in 1981. Even at the advantageous rates paid by the UK under EEC guarantees for 500,000 tons (and other favorable prices negotiated with the United States and Canada), half the 1981 earnings from sugar went to pay for food imports alone. Although wages were inclining upward, they remained inadequate to maintain the island's creditable standard of living against the rising tides of vital high-cost imports. Four cyclones attacked Mauritius during the 1979–1980 season, one of them the most devastating storm on record. Sugar production in 1980 barely met the island's EEC quota of 500,000 tons, and it rose only slightly in 1981. Stagnating production, rising energy prices, budgetary deficits and inflation, declining reserves, and mounting unemployment rendered the 1975–1980 Plan inoperable.

Nevertheless, Mauritius' complaisant foreign policies, its successful campaigns against population growth and its overall international development project record retained the favor of major aid partners. These included the World Bank and International Monetary Fund, the European Communities, Britain, India, France, Japan, and the Scandinavian countries. Rapidly becoming Mauritius' principal supplier of commodity imports, South Africa provided "soft" loans and credits for development of tea production and fisheries.

But the resourceful island was running out of workable ideas. The civil service had become over-saturated and although population growth was under control, a constant flood of unemployable labor entered the markets as the children of the fecund 1950s and 1960s matured. The goal of food self-sufficiency by 1982 vanished like a dream. Students and teachers went on strike. Despite rising wages and mounting competition from Sri Lanka, Kenya, and the ASEAN states, industry was to be the answer. The EPZ, employing 23,000 workers in eighty-seven firms and contributing only seventeen percent of GPN, would somehow have to account for most of the 150,000 new jobs required by the embattled economy in the last two decades of the century. Among the IMF's requirements for a 730 million rupee balance of payment credit in 1979 was a politically embarrassed 27 percent devaluation of the rupee, as well as the customary fiscal restraint and curbs on the money supply. Yet the payments deficit grew to 589 million rupees in 1980, even counting tourist contributions and other "invisibles." Another twenty percent devaluation was ordered in September 1981, after a Western consortium inspired by France supplied an additional 2,000 million rupees in 1980.

During this decline in the island's economic fortunes, Mauritius' politics continued to undergo transformation, disguised by the suffocation of overt political activity through the prolonged state of emergency. Although the Ramgoolam regime found its options largely obliterated by necessities—to keep the private sugar producers and export processors afloat, to make food and other essentials available at subsidized prices—it had to do so within a tightening corset of austerity. Not all of Mauritius' economic tribulations matured in time for the first political rendering of accounts in 1976. The Prime Minister decided to try his electoral luck, rather than apply further legalisms to sustain the 1967 parliament and his own dessicating coalition. General elections were scheduled for December 20, 1976, the first since before independence, and the first parliamentary contest since the disaster in Ramgoolam's home Triolet district in 1970. Ramgoolam had been host of the 1976 OAU summit, thus enjoying the prestigious organization chairmanship for the year. By that time however, he had given the MMM a magnificent present by lowering the voting age from twenty-one to eighteen years, enfranchising some 80,000 constituents, most of them for the opposition.

The 1976 campaign transpired in traditional multi-party fashion, with Ramgoolam's MLP and Mohammad's MAC occupying a shrinking center under their venerable coalition title of Independence Party. The MMM attacked from the left and was assaulted in turn as "communist." Duval's PMSD, despite its populist rhetoric, shared the Right with bitter ex-comrades in the UDM. Ideological schematizations exaggerate the extent to which Mauritian politics had changed by 1976, however, for communalism still dstermined much of the electoral alignment. Most small parties among the thirty-one in the lists remained ethnically identified and even the MLP underwent fierce upheavals in the antagonisms among Hindu castes.[33] To defeat the older parties and the numerous new seedlings in their communally defined constituencies, the MMM nominated Hindu candidates in rural districts and Muslims or Creoles in urban areas corresponding to respective ethnic composition. Thus even the party of class conflict and national consensus seemed obliged to defer to ethnocentrism.

However questionable this strategy was in ideological terms, it paid off politically. Emerging with a plurality of thirty seats (out of sixty-two) and 40.1 percent of the vote, the MMM actually helped shatter the correlation of communal constituency with party (if not as yet with candidate). Those parties which remained ethnically identified either disappeared (the Hindu IFB and Creole UDM, for instance) or lost seriously. The PMSD dropped from 43.5 percent of the vote in 1967 to 16.5 percent in 1976 and from twenty-three to seven seats. It was badly beaten by the MMM in Port Louis and other urban constituencies although it continued to control the two seats allocated to Creole Rodriguez. The MAC lost three of its five seats. The MLP wing of the Independence ticket returned twenty-three candidates, all but four of them Hindus, a net loss of eleven seats, with only 38 percent of the votes. Some of Labour's major personalities were defeated, as were Duval, Mohammed, Bissoondoyal, the most senior leaders of the PMSD, MAC, and IFB respectively. In a 90 percent turnout and with little irregularity or violence, the rejuvenated Mauritian electorate had shifted away from the accustomed pantheons of property, pragmatism, and post-colonialism. Their votes in 1976 went to new faces, new solutions to social problems, new orientations in the world at large.[34]

After allocation of the eight "best loser" seats, aiming a communal balance, however obsolete the standard, no party had a parliamentary majority. The

MMM fell short by only two seats, holding a thirty-four to twenty-eight plurality over the MLP-MAC Independence group. A decimated PMSD held the eight-vote swing. His minority position forced Ramgoolam to choose between the ideological anathema of partnership with the "Marxist radical expropriator" and another governing coalition, the third in eleven years, with the enfeebled but more congenial PMSD. The latter's support gave him a two-vote margin for governing a nation in crisis. Accepting this option demonstrated again how the MLP, once a party of labor reform, had evolved through the exercise of power into an "establishment" of managerial, professional, and property interests, losing in quantitative appeal, along with the PMSD and MAC. The MMM had profited from this evolution but was not prepared to lead, and the Governor seems to have given little thought to breaking continuity by looking leftward to Jugnauth and Bérenger for a governing formula. The second Ramgoolam mandate under self-government lasted until June 1982, very much against the preference of the MMM plurality. During those five and one-half years, policies followed courses established earlier, but the quality and credibility of government deteriorated. This was surely the period to recall some of the ingenuity and calculated inconsistency that had animated the first years of statehood—with the organization of the EPZ and the tourist industry, the achievement of birth control programs, adherence to both Commonwealth and Francophone associations, open doors to east and west, and bold projects of public works and agricultural diversification.

Ramgoolam was nearly eighty, however, and his veterans were weary. They remained wedded to each other in ossification, defying the demands of a new population as well as the standards of efficacy. Their strategies sustained the cautious, eclectic, bungling, welfare-dominated programs that had taken the island into the problematical second half of the 1970s, there to break down. Industry, tourism, and agriculture fell short of the job creation required by successive tides of school leavers. Mauritians were consuming revenues, not investing them. Inflation began to sting as fluctuating sugar prices failed, even in the best years, to keep international payments in balance. Pressure for emigration rose again, but Australia, South Africa, and the Arab states would select only fractions of the Mauritians who wished to leave—and of course these included some of the best qualified to cope with problems at home.[35]

Mauritius declined under these burdens, but did not collapse. Political life remained hectic and the preferences of the people in a close-knit plural society were written on their faces, their sleeves, the walls of their buildings. For all its hurley-burley of emergency legislation and wolf-crying politics, Mauritius had stayed an admirably open society. The abundant, highly political press resumed its customary bumptious spontaneity and labor unions remained as vigorous as anywhere else in the organized world. Even the closets of coalition politics stayed open. Several official reports alerted the entire public to the prevalence of malefactors at all levels of government.[36] After failing to effect purgative reform from within the party, a significant

Hindu fragment bolted the MLP in revulsion over the venality and exhaustion of the governing complex. Regrouping behind the "gandhian" Harish Boodhoo as the Mauritius Socialist Party (MSP), they also took exception to the regime's concessionary pro-Western attitudes and moved into par-liamentary alignment with the MMM. This conversion transferred three seats to the opposition, but Ramgoolam hung on nonetheless, for the once monolithic MMM had by then revealed its own weaknesses under the pressures of legislative responsibility. The Mouvement had lost seven MPs to Ramgoolam since its 1976 success, and the Government majority settled at thirty-seven to thirty-three.[37]

A week long general strike in 1979 demonstrated both MMM strength and its questionable strategies of disruption. The new MSP provided a congenial repository for traditional Hindu activists and moderate socialists disillusioned with both MMM and MLP. Intra-parliamentary jockeying may have reduced its vote total, but the opposition was to emerge strengthened in the electoral arena.

Ramgoolam walked skeins of tightropes between his middle class and aristocratic patrons and the working class he had always presumed to represent. Despite continual fissures within his PMSD, Duval popped in and out of Government again in 1980. He claimed that his party would at least always control Rodriguez, where the almost totally Creole electorate blamed Hindu prejudice for systematic neglect of their drought-striken, weather-beaten, impecunious island. An MMM victory in subsequent elec-tions, warned Duval, would lead to secession of the Rodriguans. Even out of office, the PMSD leader offered his advice freely through the party press and incessant rallies of his supporters. The PMSD stood ready at all times to help Ramgoolam fend off "the Communists" and assure continued friendships in the West.[38]

The Prime Minister was seeking to outflank his opposition, initiating in 1980 a more nationalistic foreign policy line than Duval could tolerate. With unanimous OAU approval, Ramgoolam demanded return of the Chagos by the British, accused of betraying Mauritius' trust by turning their BIOT into a major military base. He even lodged a claim to French-held Tromelin, 700 kilometers to the north, inducing Madagascar to give up its competing claim to the island. These campaigns took place for third world audiences without jeopardizing the English market for sugar or French cooperation in development projects, education, police training, and payments equilibrium. Vociferous advocacy for Palestinian rights during a visit to Tripoli in 1980 earned approval of Arab states which translated into capital and jobs for Mauritians. South Africa grew into a primary source of imports, tourists, and investment capital, using its discretionary ability to buy or refuse expensive Mauritian tea as a means of reacting to the island's denunciations of the apartheid system.

At home, the government was muddling through. The Prime Ministerial succession became an open tug of war between Ramgoolam's favorite, Finance Minister Veerasawmy Ringadoo, garlanded with the unenviable albatross of rising taxes, and Agriculture Minister Satcam Boolell, a Hindu communal patriot whose original IFB rural following was enlarged by new Hindu adherents from the towns. Boolell successfully blocked backroom discussions which the Ringadoo faction had begun in 1979 with the MMM, aiming at an eventual replacement of the volatile PMSD conservatives by a grander coalition of the two major parties. Hurt by the defection of Boodhoo's Hindu socialists, Boolell was assigned the reorganization of the MLP in 1981, but the system of favors and friendships had become too deeply entrenched. The Prime Minister was considering constitutional change to make himself non-executive President of a Republic, but he feared that the MLP would collapse without his direct authority.

At election time in June 1982, the Mauritian economy had once again refused to campaign for Ramgoolam. At least 20 percent of the work force was unemployed, many more of them under-employed. Inflation had reached 25 percent. The public debt had quintupled in five years to over $600 million, with a debt service ratio equal to 15 percent of export earnings. The balance of payments deficit rose by another 36 percent in 1981, despite improvements in tourism and EPZ revenues. Construction had slowed and domestic consumption was declining.

To capture Ramgoolam's vulnerable center, the MMM softened its avowedly socialist campaign. It reassured the sugar industry against expectations of grandiose expropriation, pledged to maintain the economically critical elements of the despised South African "connection," and promised purely legitimate diplomatic activity in the execution of nonaligned foreign policies, including the recuperation of Diego Garcia. Under prodding by the astute Bérenger, the radicals of 1971 had converted their program by 1980 into a pragmatic, anti-authoritarian approach to a complex, regulated, democratic-socialist system. Therefore, government charges of Soviet masterminding and Libyan financing of Muslim votes for the MMM seemed to affect the Mouvement's credibility little, if at all. Even the announcement in March of a new agreement with Great Britain committing an additional four million pounds in assistance to the unhappy Chagos expellees, failed to improve the fortunes of MLP and MAC candidates.

The election was a tidal wave. Ramgoolam himself finished fourth best in his home district of Triolet, which like all districts has only three seats to fill. With 63 percent of the vote, the MMM-PSM alliance swept all sixty seats in the twenty districts on Mauritius and even carried Rodiguez' two places through its local ally, the Organization of Rodriguan People (OPR). By pre-arrangement, the MMM took forty-two of the seats, the PSM eighteen. As party leader, Aneerood Jugnauth became Prime Minister, with Boodhoo Vice Premier. The MMM's Jean-Claude de l'Estrac took the External Affairs portfolio and Bérenger became Finance Minister.

Only four of the maximum eight "best loser" seats were allocated by the Governor in 1982, after Supreme Court determination that the country's ethnic proportions had been adequately reflected in the election. Duval reentered the Assembly through one of these appointments, thus assuring a semblance of opposition.

As though embarrassed by it, Prime Minister Jugnauth acknowledged the dangers of so massive a victory. Democratic institutions and fair play would be scupulously respected, he assured, freedom of the press held inviolate. Elections would occur regularly, at least once every five years. Under a new scheme of decentralized authority Ramgoolam's local administrative appointees would be replaced by elected officials.[39]

The coalition pursued the carefully modulated economic reform program on which it had campaigned. Two sugar estates with mills were nationalized, leaving eighteen in private hands. Eight thousand additional hectares of good land were purchased by the government for distribution among food-growing cooperatives. Under a 1982–1985 economic plan, a State Finance Corporation was established to supply liquidity loans to cooperatives and enterprises with public equity participation, among other beneficiaries. The state took a majority share in the capital city's port and in management of the major tourist establishments, as well as the hitherto privately operated bus lines and Air Mauritius. Gradual compensation of private owners would admittedly weigh heavily on the budget for a two-year period, said Jugnauth, but the economy would enjoy reasonable taxation and fiscal restraint in the expectation of an increase in private and public investment.

In external affairs, the new regime anticipated broader relations with nonaligned neighbors Madagascar and Seychelles, Tanzania, Mozambique, and Socialist France, while preserving the prevailing intimacy with India and the United Kingdom. Policy swung unambiguously toward the Polisario guerrillas in the Western Sahara and the Palestine Liberation Organization. Mauritius favored Colonel Qaddafi's efforts to assert chairmanship of the OAU. India's Prime Minister Gandhi visited the island for the third time in August 1982, re-emphasizing her country's substantial stake in Mauritius' industrial and diplomatic development. Jugnauth returned the call in February 1983, referring to uniquely privileged relations with the northern colossus and joining India in celebrating the verities of "active nonalignment." A broadened portfolio of economic cooperation with India includes a joint shipping venture, a new fully equipped hospital, and substantial credits for Indian export products some of which (fruit, for example) were to replace politically less appetizing South African commodities. India also plays an important role in Mauritian cultural life, having endowed the Mahatma Gandhi Institute, a major center for education, pedagogical research, and the arts addressed to Hinduism in a kind of counter-balance to the established French dynamic. Relations with South Africa were discreetly trimmed wherever possible without risking further unemployment through retaliation against the island's export processing industries, tourism, or tea sales.

Major international patrons also continued to supply resources to the island after the regime changed. The IMF released a 1982 thirty-three million dollars standby credit in regular *tranches* and negotiated a new balance of payments facility for 1983. The World Bank agreed to a forty million dollar structural adjustment loan. International options swung gently into neutral gear, consistent with the nationalism of the MMM regime.

The new Government declared the island's strategic assets off-limits to all external military powers, thus indiscriminately closing Ramgoolam's indiscriminately open door. Since Soviet intervention began in Afghanistan, the MMM has castigated Moscow's strategic designs with nearly as much vehemence as it denounces Washington's machinations. While preferring a republican constitution modeled somewhat on India's system, the MMM proposed to achieve this change of status through amicable negotiation with the British guardians of the Queen's sensibilities.

Restitution of the Chagos and Tromelin were also pursued fruitlessly through cordial negotiations. On July 7, 1982, the Legislative Assembly declared the Chagos a formal component of Mauritius and discussions ensued in London and Washington, albeit without consequence. Equally desultory conservations on Tromelin also began with the French. On July 17, Mauritius joined Madagascar and Seychelles in a new Indian Ocean Commission, developing out of a less formal grouping in which the MMM had previously participated as a "progressive party." Since then, the IOC has grown to include Comoros and France (for Réunion). It aims at closer intra-regional cooperation with Western assistance, subordinating earlier progressive political platforms to more critical economic purposes.

Within six months of its inauguration, the new regime suffered its first of several crises. MMM members had protested in October over Bérenger's austerity plan, which entailed lower subsidies (and thus higher consumer prices) for imported rice and flour. The Finance Minister resigned his post rather than yield, and was ritually persuaded to return to it a week later. The PSM's five ministers then left the Government on October 22, as the Bérenger-Boodhoo feud burst into the open, this time over control of the Mauritius Broadcasting Corporation (a Boodhoo portfolio) and Bérenger's insistence on increasing Creole language broadcasts. Jugnauth patched that breach, too, and led the MMM-PSM to victory in 115 of 126 municipal council seats filled by elections throughout the island in December.

By late March 1983, Bérenger had forced the Prime Minister to choose categorically, and the option went against the MMM secretary general. The Mouvement split in two. Bérenger and eleven ministers joined the detested communalist Duval in opposition. Jugnauth reorganized his government with ten loyal Mouvement people, five Boodhoo Socialists, and a Rodriguan Creole. The nearly all-Hindu cabinet represented a weakening of the non-sectarian nationalist cause which had triumphed only nine months earlier. Even in opposition, however, Bérenger retained control of the party apparatus. He engineered the expulsion of Jugnauth and cohorts from the Mouvement, forcing new elections against the Prime Minister's will. With his remaining MMM faction, Jugnauth formed the Militant Socialist Movement (MSM) which promptly merged with Boodhoo's PSM. The next step was inevitable. They opened contact with Ramgoolam's convalescent MLP in preparation for the parliamentary electoral contest of August 21, 1983.

To win those elections, Jugnauth had in effect reproduced Ramgoolam's Independence-Party Hindu coalition of the late 1960s, including in it even the old Prime Minister himself. Together, the nationalist Jugnauth, the Gandhian Socialist Boodhoo, and the veteran accommodator appealed effectively across the spectrum of Hindu opinion. They obtained a majority of thirty-seven Assembly seats against nineteen for the retrenched Militant Movement and four for Duval's vestigial PMSD. Hindu solidarity once more carried the day. Ramgoolam was appointed Governor General on January 1, 1984. If a Mauritian republic had been negotiated with England, the eighty-five year old Labourite leader stood to become its (largely ceremonial) first President—an honor which Bérenger also would have certainly offered him. But the grand old man of Labour and independence died before any such change could be contrived; in January 1986 he was replaced as Governor General by Ringadoo, his heir-apparent who was never able to succeed to the Prime Ministry.

Apparent ideological, ethnic, and class distinctions notwithstanding, Jugnauth and Duval negotiated the PMSD's post-electoral entry into the Labour-Socialist coalition. For a time, the MMM's proletarian Creoles and Muslims dwelt in solitary opposition, denouncing Jugnauth's obtensible treason to the Right—and toward Hindu chauvinism.

Downplaying ideological and communal differences, Jugnauth characterized the upheaval in his former party as a revolt against Bérenger's dictatorial style, not a rupture over substance. Indeed, Jugnauth's own 1982 reassurances had established the mode of continuity in economic policy, both domestic and external, which his revolutionary Finance Minister dutifully followed— to the astonishment of MMM ideologues. Bérenger maintained deferential relations with France, India, and the EEC, refrained from antagonizing Britain, and didn't even overturn the South Africa market. He made Mauritius more responsive than heretofore to World Bank and IMF development strategies, imposed severe austerity on Government accounts, campaigned for wage restraint and tax incentives for business, while forcing a new five percent sales tax on consumers.[40] The Mouvement militants might well ask what had become of the program of national independence and power to the people.

The answer, of course, was that Mauritius could not afford that program. This logic had also appeared inescapable to Ramgoolam, to the Réunionnais Left, and to the Malagasy and Seychellois regimes which we study next. It was a lesson which the Comorean Soilih fanatically would not learn. "Decolonization" in weak Indian Ocean countries permits a dispersion of dependence among non-competitive external patrons, a modest redistribution of jobs and privileges at government command, but not a revolution of sovereignty. Indian Ocean nationalism has been constrained to established routes of survival. The eggs of the goose may not be solid gold, but the animal has to live to lay them. Mauritius' international rhetoric changed and some of its affinities shifted, but the realities of sugar exports, corporate industrial processing, and Western (including South African) sources of goods, capital, and technology prevailed.

As Bérenger's sudden "realism" won friends among the island's elites and middle class, the MMM lost some of its radicals, most of them Hindus, to the Jugnauth-Boodhoo MSM. This proved to be no sanctuary for them, either. The defectors seem to have felt all the more uncomfortable sharing power with Labour Old Boys and the friends of Gaetan Duval, who had become Deputy Prime Minister for having delivered his four Creole deputies to the Jugnauth team. In 1984, some of them followed the old Hindu nationalist champion, Satcam Boolell, out of the coalition; others defected a year later with the ever-dissatisfied idealist Boodhoo, thus splitting the Labour-MSM bloc, and leaving the Government with a decided Center-Right tilt. This migration of the Hindu Left enriched the opposition's communal scope, linking Bérenger in ideological solidarity with the old left wing of the MLP. Now, both Government and opposition span the range of communities. Hence, within a half-year of elections conducted largely along ethnic chauvinist lines, parliamentary maneuvering reasserted the primacy of ideological and class alignment over communal sectarianism. Begging for a moment the question whether ideological and class options have much chance of real competition over policy, Mauritius has once again shown (although not at the polls) that it remains "on top of the little league of functioning African multi-party democracies."[41]

That record is as always, in jeopardy. Jugnauth's insecurity was exposed in expulsions of Libyans and public disapproval of Soviet diplomats for tampering with the 1983 elections. It became all the more conspicuous in a new legislative campaign against labor unions and the island's multifarious, ebullient press. Censorship powers were expanded in 1984 and the imposition of expensive "security bonds" threatens many papers with insolvency. Pro-government politicians have been implicated in international drug trafficking, and Catholic clergymen have traded sharp criticisms with Jugnauth's regime. The fortunes of Mauritian pragmatism were again tested by natural calamity. The year 1983 brought both the worst drought in three decades and another devastating cyclone. Most of Mauritius' sugar could still be sold at the negotiated EEC (Lomé) price, now two and one-half times higher than prevailing world prices, but little tonnage remained over for sales windfalls or prudent storage. Import needs rose to compensate for the weather's ravages in construction and general agriculture. Depletion of foreign reserves and mounting unemployment continue to cause anxiety through 1986, even as sugar production rose, and EPZ and tourist revenues helped boost the 1985 payments ledger into surplus for the first time in nine years.

Once again, India came to the aid of her insular admirer; among other things, a new joint shipping line was scheduled for operations in late 1984. Arab and South African contacts were maintained through Duval and his brother, Labor Minister Hervé. True to the pattern of cooperation set, however ironically, by Bérenger, Jugnauth's administration met IMF conditions for a fifty-three million dollar stand-by balance of payments credit: it tightened its 1984 budget and lowered politically sensitive subsidies on imported wheat, flour, and rice. In March 1985, the IMF agreed to another stand-by loan (Mauritius' fifth): forty-nine million SDR's were committed to help increase foreign exchange reserves, correct 1984–1985 payments imbalance, and adjust debt-service ratios which had reached 25 percent of GNP.

As usual in modern Mauritius, long-term solutions were sought in expanded industrialization and increased sugar production. Already a major exporter of cotton shirts and knitwear, the EPZ energetically seeks French, German, British, American, and South African capital to take advantage of its position between the continents and its access to European community markets. Tourism continues to grow satisfactorily, and the 1984 tea season saw a record of ten million kilograms exported at enviable prices. But sugar, the economy's mainstay, remains preoccupying. An independent study commission reported a 25 percent decline in real wages throughout the sugar industry over the four years through 1983. It called nonetheless for further government-aided modernization and expanded profit margins to sustain sugar's productivity and its appeal to investment. Unable to satisfy either Left or Right regarding public control over its economic mainstay, the Government compromised. In March 1985, the legislature approved gradual reconcentration of the milling apparatus into five regional companies, with increased worker and planter participation in decisions, abolition of export taxes on sugar, new by-product technology (especially as sources of energy), and greater interlinear food cultivation. The state hopes to restore the industry's 700,000 ton annual production standard by 1986–87 with enhanced productivity and profit margins, but without aggravating unemployment. To effect such reforms, Mauritius must raise an additional seventeen million dollars from external sources.[42]

The year 1982 still represents an important watershed in Mauritian political culture. The island has for better or worse joined the third world as a nation in its own right. No longer the erstwhile Ile de France, pampered and neglected in turn by a patronizing Europe, it has an Asian and an African vocation in the lonely center of the Indian Ocean. Europe's little far-off creation now epitomizes something besides the transplantability of Western civilization—namely, the ability of an ethnic patchwork to make communal coexistence a premise of life.

Mauritius is an independent, still largely agricultural society with a deep financial and institutional commitment to a mono-crop. It cannot solve its development problems as Singapore has done, by becoming an industrial city-state on the busiest of modern highways. Nor can it evade them, as in Réunion, by calling on a totally engaged metropolitan patron to reward its patriotism. What it can do is detribalize—creating a feasible nation state out of a congeries of ethnicities. And it has begun to do that. The national prism slowly reclaimed its communal fragments during an arduous decade of heated economic and political experiment before 1982. Then came a powerful democratic seachange from out of the borrowed tides of Westminister. The victors of June 1982 fell apart over the spoils, but the resignation of the vanquished is remarkable, and more noteworthy still is the recomposition of both majority and opposition across the island's communities. After a generation in power, the victims of 1982 had failed to recognize in time the quality of the new national sensibility or the thrust of class conflict. Those who had defined these peaceful revolutions thereupon lost the next round, and they, too, relinquished power. The constellations shifted again in 1984 and the priority of national, not communal, interest reasserted itself. The reconciliations of the past four years make the achievement of a Mauritian nation and the preservation of its open political economy all the more impressive.

Notes

1. See Auguste Toussaint, *Bibliography of Mauritius, 1502–1924* (Port Louis: Esclapon, 1956); Adele Smith Simmons, *Modern Mauritius: The Politics of Decolonization* (Bloomington: Indiana University Press, 1982), pp. 227–230.

2. Jean Houbert, "Mauritius: Independence and Dependence," *Journal of Modern African Studies* 19 No. 1 (1981): p. 75.

3. For background, see Philippe Lenoir, "An Extreme Example of Pluralism: Mauritius," in *Cultures* (Paris: UNESCO), 6: No. 1, 1979, pp. 63–82; A.R. Mannick, *Mauritius: The Development of a Plural Society* (Nottingham, England: Spokesman, 1979); Louis Favoreu, *L'Ile Maurice* (Paris: Berger-Levrault, 1970); Burton Benedict, *Mauritius: Problems of a Plural Society* (London: Pall Mall Press, 1965); Simmons, *Modern Mauritius*, Ch. 10; Mannick, *Mauritius*; Joyce and Jean-Pierre Durand, *L'Ile Maurice: quelle indépendance? La reproduction des rapports de production capitaliste dans une formation sociale dominée* (Paris: Editions Anthropos, 1975).

4. See Colin Legum, ed., *Africa Contemporary Record* (ACR) (London and New York: Africana Publishing, Holmes & Meier, annual), *1982–83*, pp. B 223–233; *Ibid.*, *1983–84*, pp. B 208–219.

5. Auguste Toussaint, *History of the Indian Ocean*, trans. June Guicharnaud (London: Routledge and Kegan Paul, 1966), p. 157; for Bernardin de Saint Pierre's more jaundiced opinion, see his *Voyage à l'Isle de France, à l'Isle de Bourbon, au Cap de Bonne Espérance, etc.*, par un Officier du Roy (Neuchâtel, France: Imprimerie de la Société Typographique, 1778), pp. 221–223.

6. Bernardin de Saint Pierre, *Voyage à l'Isle de France*, p. 220; see also Auguste Toussaint, *La Route des îles: Contribution à l'histoire maritime des Mascareignes* (Paris: Ecole pratique des hautes études S.E.V.P.E.N., 1967).

7. Toussaint, *History*, pp. 160–163; Hubert Deschamps, *Les Pirates à Madagascar* (Paris: Berger-Levrault, 1949), Chs. 11 and 12.

8. Simmons, *Modern Mauritius*, pp. 24–25; Mannick, pp. 41–44; Patrick Beaton, *Creoles and Coolies: or Five Years in Mauritius*, 2nd ed., 1859 (Port Washington, N.Y.: Kennikat Press, 1971); William Law Mathieson, *British Slave Emancipation, 1838–1849* (London and New York: Longmans, Green, 1932).

9. Burton Benedict, *Indians in a Plural Society: A Report on Mauritius* (London: H.M. Stationer's Office, 1961); K. Hazareesingh, *Histoire des Indiens à l'Ile Maurice* (Paris: Librairie d'Amérique et d'Orient Adrien Maisonneuve, 1973).

10. Simmons, *Modern Mauritius*, pp. 46–51; Mannick, *Mauritius*, pp. 50–54.

11. Simmons, *Modern Mauritius*, pp. 55–56; T. Balogh and C.J.M. Bennett, *Commission of Inquiry (Sugar Industry 1962)*, Sessional Paper No. 4, 1963 (Port Louis, 1963).

12. Simmons, pp. 117–118; Philip M. Allen, "Mauritius on the Eve," *Africa Report*, May 1966, pp. 16–24.

13. After the distribution of eight communally allocated "best loser" seats by the Governor four of them going to PM, two to MLP, and one to each of the

other Independence coalition partners; thus the final tally gave the PMSD 27 M.P.s; the MLP 26 with 17 seats contributed by IFB (12) and MAC (5).

14. Simmons, *Modern Mauritius*, p. 188.

15. Houbert, "Mauritius: Independence and Dependence;" Joyce and Jean-Pierre Durand, *L'île Maurice: Quelle Indépendance?*

16. Jean-François Dupon, *Contraintes insulaires et fait colonial aux Mascareignes et aux Seychelles*, 3 vols. (Lille, France: Atelier de Reproduction des Thèses, and Paris: Librairie Honoré Champion, 1977), vol. 3, p. 997.

17. *The Luce Report: A time for Decision*. Sessional Paper No. 8, 1958 (Port Louis, 1958); J.E. Meade and others, *The Economic and Social Structure of Mauritius: A Report to the Government of Mauritius* (London: Methuen & Co., 1961); Richard M. Titmuss and Brian Abel-Smith, assisted by T. Lynes, *Social Policies and Population Growth in Mauritius*, Sessional Paper No. 6 of 1960 (London: H.M. Stationery Office, 1961).

18. For studies of the Mauritius sugar industry, see Balogh and Bennett, *Commission of Inquiry*; Vidu Nababsing and Raj Virahsawmy, "The Characteristics of the Small Planter Class in a Small Plantation Economy: The Case of Mauritius," in Raj Virasahmy [sic], ed., *Characteristics of Island Economies* (Port Louis: University of Mauritius, 1977), pp. 43–74; A. Hakim Hossenmamode, "Formulating an Industrial Strategy for Small Island Plantation Economies," in Ibid., pp. 93–103; J.M. Paturau, *The Sugar Industry of Mauritius* (Port Louis, 1962; Jean Benoist et al, *Regards sur le monde rural mauricien* (Port Louis: Université de Maurice, Doc. No. 15, February 1981).

19. For EPZ, see Mannick, *Mauritius*, Ch. 3; *ACR 1973–74*, pp. B 231–232; Ibid. *1979–1980*, pp. B 275–276; Catherine Hein, "Jobs for the Girls: Export Manufacturing in Mauritius," *International Labour Review*, Vol. 123, No. 2 March-April 1984, pp. 251–265.

20. Martine Perrot, "L'émigration des femmes mauriciennes en milieu rural français: stratégie migratoire contre stratégie matrimoniale," *Annuaire des pays de l'Océan Indien (APOI)*, (Aix-en-Provence, France, CERSOI, 1983), Vol. 8, 1981.

21. Philip M. Allen, "Mauritius: The Ile de France Returns," in John M. Ostheimer, ed., *The Politics of the Western Indian Ocean Islands* (New York: Praeger Publishers, 1975), p. 209.

22. Ibid., pp. 208–211; Mannick, *Mauritius*, pp. 160–161; *ACR 1973–1974*, p. B 229.

23. Houbert, "Mauritius: Independence and Dependence;" *Financial Times*, November 11, 1965.

24. Christian Louit, "Chronique politique et constitutionnelle: Ile Maurice," in *APOI*, Vol. 7, 1980, pp. 394–399; André Oraison, "Les avatars du B.I.O.T.: le processus de l'implantation militaire américaine à Diégo Garcia," in *APOI*, Vol. 6, 1979, pp. 177–209; Houbert, "Mauritius: Independence and Dependence," pp. 83–86.

25. Louit, "Chronique politique et constitutionnelle," p. 399.

26. Allen, "Mauritius: The Ile de France Returns," p. 207.

27. *ACR 1972–1973*, pp. B 210–213; Mannick, *Mauritius*, pp. 140–141.

28. Mannick, *Mauritius*, p. 141; Raymond Delval, "La communauté musulmane de l'île Maurice," in *APOI* Vol. 6, 1979, p. 73.

29. Simmons, *Modern Mauritius*, pp. 77–82.

30. Allen, "Mauritius: The Ile de France Returns," p. 212; *Marchés Tropicaux et Méditerranéens (MTM)*, October 13, 1974.

31. Simmons, *Modern Mauritius*, p. 191.

32. Joyce and Jean-Pierre Durand, *L'île Maurice: Quelle Indépendance?*, Ch. 4: Yin Shing Yuen (Tian Shung), *Pour une intégration régionale entre l'Ile Maurice et d'autres îles du Sud-Quest de l'Océan Indien (Les Comores, Madagascar, La Réunion, les Seychelles)*, (These de Doctorat 3ème cycle, Université de Lyon II, 1980), Part I.

33. Mannick, *Mauritius*, pp. 147–148.

34. *Ibid.*, pp. 148–149; ACR, *1976–1977*, pp. B 277–281.

35. Simmons, *Modern Mauritius*, pp. 197–198.

36. ACR *1980–1981*, pp. B 261–264.

37. Godfrey Morrison, "Balancing Act in Mauritius," *Africa Report* Vol. 24, No. 6 (November-December 1979), pp. 48–51.

38. For instance, *Le Rassemblement*, July 22, 1981.

39. Jean-Pierre Langellier, series in *Le Monde*, June 15 and 17, July 2, 1982; see also Note No. 4.

40. *The Economist* (London), April 2, 1983; *Africa Confidential*, March 30, 1983; *Africa News*, March 30, 1983.

41. *The Economist*, August 27, 1983, p. 24.

42. ACR *1984–1985* (chapter on Mauritius); *Johannesburg Star*, February 11, 1985; Agence France Presse, Port Louis, March 17 and 18, 1985.

5

Seychelles:
A Place in the Sea

Sprinkled over the western ocean a thousand miles from everywhere else, these younger cousins of Mauritius were once a relaxed, lotus-eating Eden of decaying cocount plantations and gentle fisherfolk. Nature provided all and human needs complied with her modest bounty. Now in that idyllic sanctuary, a republic stands, armed and bristling, in a strange climate of insecurity. Seychelles has become organized and drilled—sanctioned, if not entirely governed, by ideology. The gentle little cousins have grown up tough.

These ninety-two islands add up to only 440 kilometers of land arranged in a narrow arabesque curving from northeast to southwest. The several archipelagoes of the chain command a million square kilometers of oceanic economic zone. In the north, the Seychelles proper, a close-knit group of forty unique pre-Cambrian granite islands, start the arabesque from just below the Equator. They include Mahé, the largest fleck of land, its 150 mountainous square kilometers containing almost 90 percent of the republic's 66,000 people. The remaining 7,000 inhabit Praslin, La Digue, and a few other members of the granite archipelago north of Mahé.

A few hundred contract workers and their families are scattered over the southerly coral atolls where coconut palms, fisheries, turtle beds, and vanishing guano patches support a sweet austerity of oblivious, still "colonial" actuality. Dozens of solitary coral places and sand cays were attached for purely administrative convenience to the granitic archipelago, but they endow the little republic with an extent of Indian Ocean territorial waters second only to India's among the indigenous states. The southern bits include low-lying arid atolls in the Amirantes group; at the southwest extremity just north of Madagascar and the Comoros lies the international nature sanctuary of Aldabra, the world's largest atoll holding some of Seychelles' inimitable flora and fauna of air, land, and sea.

This idiomatic blend of nature and society languished through two centuries of half-hearted colonialism, first under France, then Great Britain. An original mid-eighteenth century settlement of Frenchmen and slaves soon became a neglected ward of England while remaining in Mauritius' administrative shadow. Nudged to independence by Britain in 1976 against the preference of its major political party, the islands have quickly become a centralized, presidential microstate. The islanders conduct their politics within webs of intimacy comparable to those of a rural town surrounded by colossal wastes of space. While subject more to the logic of circumstance than of choice, they have nonetheless forged institutions to work their largely service-oriented economy, to regulate powerful foreign fleets in their vicinity, and to keep an army busy in conflict against both mutineers and mercenaries. They beckon European and South African tourists toward a sandy, palm-fringed Sybaris periodically beleaguered by enemies, both real and imagined. Taking even whispered instabilities for real, the tourists sometimes decide not to come, and Seychelles encounters economic crisis.

Behind its smiling facade, the Republic is managed in delicate circum- spection by a solemn, austere socialist authority. Originating in Seychelles' nationalist movement, the regime issued from an extended contest for power in 1977, one year after independence. It has had to contend with the unruly sequels ever since. Its President, France Albert René, has promoted popular mobilization for development, psychological conversion of youth from de- pendence to initiative, and an outspoken neutralist foreign policy. Nationalist energies are leavened by due regard for the profitable prerogatives of private property, speculative investment, predominantly Western sources of capital, and heliotropic vacationers. This combination of national assertiveness and acquiescence has made Seychelles a fascinating laboratory of political culture. A fragile colonial microcosm has been precipitated into the street life of the contemporary third world. Minuscule and vulnerable, Seychelles must play the international repertoire of needs and options, grievances and priorities, nonpartisan high politics and obligatory economics.[1]

The Place and Its People

Early mariners and cartographers recognized most of the islands sprinkled over wide portions of relatively uninteresting sea. Although frequented by maritime wayfarers, they remained empty of permanent human population until decades after the more southerly Mascarenes received their first inhabitants. Before entering international concourse, they might have been perfect images of the archetypal desert isle. Portuguese had landed on them in the early sixteenth century, and the Dutch seem to have tried occupying some of the smaller sites in the seventeenth. Madagascar's pirates used them for refuge and refreshment until the latter half of the next century when power polarized between the British and French crowns, and privateering was subsumed in a decidedly official cast. Then, even the most obscure islands of the age were destined to be controlled by one or another power, either for its own mercantile glory or for the pleasure of frustrating the pretensions of a covetous rival.

France began charting and combing the seascape in the 1740s, finally claiming the several island groups in 1756, and naming them all after the most enlightened of the French East India Company's governors, Bertrand François Mahé de Labourdonnais (1735-1746). It was Labourdonnais who had foreseen prospects of a grand French empire in the southwestern sea and thus begun the charting and claiming process.[2] Even after his undeserved disgrace in 1747, his first surname "Mahé" continued to designate the principal island. The ensemble of archipelagoes was nevertheless prayerfully renamed for Louis XVI's Controller of Finances shortly after the first permanent settlement in 1771.

Thus, Seychelles was born as an outpost of vague imperial visions, christened into the royal bureaucracy, and raised in the slow eddies of imperial neglect for the next 200 years. Ile de France (Mauritius) authorities occasionally paid enough attention to deliver seed spices and livestock, trying to think of something useful for the colonists to do. But the population neither grew rapidly nor prospered intrepidly in the soft tropical air of the sub-colony. They scarcely looked after their spice groves and food gardens, preferring to apply labor to the collection of timber and land tortoises for infrequent callers from the Ile de France. Eventually, a rough system of land tenure began the orderly development of plantations for food crops and for coconut and spice exports. Shipbuilding and repair claimed most of Mahé's precious timber and the islanders harvested an abundance of fish and turtles from the accessible waters. Slave labor from East Africa and Madagascar performed the work, even after the formal abolition of slavery by the French Revolution in 1794. Typically, the colonists ignored the decree and were in turn ignored by revolutionary Paris.[3]

After two decades spent just above survival, the islands became caught in the more perilous tangle of Franco-British strategic rivalry. Undefended and innocuous, they were in fact "captured" seven times by British naval squadrons between 1794 and 1810. Unlike the proud Ile de France, which insisted on its right to blockades, bloody battles, and permanent military occupation, Seychelles were merely visited by coercive naval patrols in search of water during these wars, every British arrival enjoying an appropriate surrender, an appropriate welcome, and the appropriate flag, each departure serving as occasion for a return to the colors of France. Between their seven visits to the protean port, England honored the capitulations contrived by the wily Governor Jean-Baptiste Quéau de Quinssy, and allowed the Seychelles to conduct business as though they were under lasting British rule. This fiction enabled the islanders to penetrate Britain's blockade of the Ile de France, to give shelter to fugitive French corsairs, and to trade with both sides, as well as with Americans, Dutch, Portuguese, and anybody else who happened along those sea-lanes. Thus was maritime nonalignment ingeniously practiced within the purview of Ruling Britannia. Preserving Seychellois freedom of initiative by alternating capitulations and apostasies, de Quinssy gave Seychelles more commercial company than they have enjoyed before or since.

By 1810, however, the Ile de France and Réunion (Bourbon) were both out of combat, and Seychelles' seventh capitulation became final. Suspected of fickle-hearted inclinations, especially toward resumptions of French privateering along the Cape routes to India, Seychelles were retained by Britain along with Mauritius in the 1814 Treaty of Paris. They experienced neither a change of name nor of governor, however, so insignificant did they appear in the ranks of empire. De Quinssy remained in office under the trusty old Union Jack he'd been intermittently flying for twenty years, and the archipelago continued to honor in name the obscure French royal functionary who had helped fund the original settlement. French language and other institutions governed society and the English adaptations of French indifference remained the cardinal principle of colonial policy in Seychelles for the next century and a half. Mahé's only town, the friendly seaport of all the fleets, had no distinct identity until 1841. Then, young Queen Victoria generated enough popular enthusiasm there to break Francophone precedent and lend her name to the capital.

Some other realities did change, however. African and Creole slaves were emancipated in the 1830 British decree aimed at Mauritius' larger peculiar institution. When the act took effect five years later, 5,000 freed people left the Seychelles' modest sugar, coffee, spice, corn, rice, and cotton plantations. Some definitively turned to fishing and artisanal trades, smallhold farming, and town jobs, like their Mauritian counterparts. Most subsisted on upland garden plots and the abundant coconut palm. As in Mauritius, the slave defection caused serious declines in agricultural production, both for local consumption and export. The need to import food and other essentials into both the Mascarenes and Seychelles has become perpetual, allowing South Africa a powerful if politically embarrassing role in the islands today. But unlike Mauritius and Réunion, Seychelles never received the economic impetus requiring introduction into the senior colonies of a new laboring mass from Asia.

While Mauritius and Réunion were being converted by different metropoles into substantial producers of labor-intensive sugar cane, the Seychelles farms adapted to the less lucrative but less demanding palm. Coconut oil and subsequently, by 1850, dried cononut "meat" (copra) became the principal export. Coconut meat, milk, fibers, and trunks dominated the diet, labor, and housing of the rural people. Whereas Mauritius retained its landhold pattern based on large family estates (and Réunion reconsolidated plantations after a period of fragmentation), multigeniture carved Mahé and Praslin into still smaller farms, only a few of them substantial enough to produce surpluses for export.

Some orchards of cloves and cinnamon remained intact—France having introduced them in her eighteenth century intrusion on Holland's East India spice trade. The islanders added vanilla, patchouli for perfumes and soap, tea in the Mahé highlands and desultory cultivation of vegetables and livestock to cover subsistence needs. Reforestation has rejuvenated much of Mahé's steep slopes after the main island's great virginal tree cover disappeared in an extraordinarily brief period of ship-building and housing construction. What remains of the archipelago's unique biological endowment requires strenuous protective efforts to satisfy scientific inquiry, attract tourist admiration and justify speculation about the location here of the Biblical Eden.[4]

Britain's operation of a "limited liability" empire kept the islands in obscurity, oblivious to both the joys and sorrows wrought by colonial investment elsewhere on the globe. Education was entirely managed by the Catholic Church until 1944 when the first public schools opened, instituting a sudden wartime transfer from French to English as compulsory language.[5]

While Mauritius' demography was being reshaped by the installation of indentured Hindu canefield workers, and Réunion was undergoing a slighter process of pluralization, Seychelles retained the formula which had originally created the Creole or "colored" populations of all three places. Its Creoles represent a majority between the white planter and professional aristocracy and a small residual African minority. Tiny merchant classes of Indian Muslims and Chinese have settled here as in Mauritius, Réunion, and Madagascar, and there are a few "poor whites" among the Creole mix, but the bulk of the Seychelles is the result of a relatively uninhibited and perhaps unprecedented blending of all ethnic sources. The "high" culture of European France remained far more restricted in its appeal to Seychelles than in Mauritius or Réunion.

Unlike pluralistic Mauritius and ambivalent Réunion, Seychellois miscegenation has produced a coherent nation, diminutive but self-aware.[6] As in the older Mascarene colonies, "creolization" of the Seychelles has produced its special cultural hybrids, including a flexible language which evolved from pidgin French into a congeries of Europe, Asia, and Africa. Roman Catholicism, left unshaken after tepid nineteenth century missionizing from the Church of England, has been practised by virtually all Seychellois, often without benefit of clergy. Left to itself for so long, Seychellois Christianity assumed a decidedly syncretistic form. Passionately faithful to Catholicism as a "way," the Seychellois also tended like many other crossed cultures to respond to the spiritual signals of their natural and ancestral environment. Despite canonical disapproval, religious practice has absorbed powerful intrusions of earth and spirit rituals from the popular religions of Asia, Madagascar, Bantu Africa, and eighteenth century Europe.[7]

Family life also has a refreshing, often deplored, originality throughout these islands. A wide diversity of extra-marital, yet viable and ethically regulated unions is responsible for the majority of households and childbirths in Seychelles to this day.[8] Food, music, language, and medicine (physical, psychological, and sociological) all reflect the refusal of a free hybrid population to restrict its cultural resources.

The black and colored population of Seychelles has been stigmatized for generations by unflattering portraits of indolence, superstition, and promiscuity. Yet in the 1970s that population responded with marked energy and acumen to sudden opportunities of wage employment, urbanization and self-government. The stereotype of the smiling, supine Seychellois never did justice to this congenitally impoverished insular blend of Europe and

Africa. Whether the current socialist image of the communally responsible worker will be more accurate remains to be seen.

Economic and cultural decolonization in Seychelles is identified with class conflict by the post-1977 nationalist regime. In public policy, however, this "radical" vision has been translated into the gentler terms of social democracy. Progressive taxation seeks footings of equality among the classes emergent from Britain's colonial matrix. Kreol (Creole) has been designated sole national language, replacing an uneasy tandem of English and French. The spread of public education over the past three decades has created an almost universally literate population in the age groups below fifty years. Mahé's elite secondary school has given way to a cluster of technical institutions idealistically designed to expand vocational aptitudes and encourage only utilitarian academic pursuits. The cooperative movement is now important, labor's compensation is protected, "capitalists" are tolerated but in disapproval. While still eating their socio-economic cake, Seychellois expect to keep it in the socialist long-run too.

A thoroughly mixed economy, with attendant confusions in political culture, appears an inevitable stage in Seychelles' hastily expedited national evolution. The islands have had precious little preparation for the process. Political development only trickled through Britain's century and a half of passive rule, teaspooned out in moments of necessity. In 1889 Seychellois nominees began serving on newly instituted government councils. By 1903, the islands' personality was sufficiently pronounced to permit separation from Mauritius as a Crown Colony of its own. Nevertheless, the first elections occurred only in 1948 among a constituency of 2,000 propertied and literate subjects. Political parties appeared fifteen years later, and the franchise was not extended to all adults until 1967. The Legislative Council had by then been enlarged from four to eight seats.

The old Seychelles Taxpayers' and Producers' Association, which had furnished all the parliamentarians until the mid-1960s, dissolved into an aristocratic caucus within the new Seychelles Democratic Party (SDP). Led by Attorney James Mancham, the SDP carried the 1967 elections with four seats against three for its more nationalist opponent, the Seychelles People's United Party (SPUP) of France Albert René. The eighth seat went to an independent supported by SDP. The Council grew to fifteen seats and obtained modest executive authority under a new constitution in 1970.

Originally formed as a loose welter of politically ambitious men seeking to outpace local rivals, each party eventually staked out ideological grounds, and altered them almost as quickly. Representing landed and commercial interest, and standing for continued rule by Britain, Mancham retained his majority in 1970, with ten seats to five, although SPUP's popular vote represented 44 percent of the electorate. Mancham thereupon became Chief Minister in a limited Home Rule system which his party had been cultivating without for a moment entertaining the prospect of another step toward independence. SPUP on the other hand insisted on the logical conclusion of the constitutional process, at first through somewhat ambiguous calls for domestic autonomy. By 1968–70, the SDP was reluctantly abandoning its preference for full integration with England, on the examples of Réunion with France or Hawaii with the United States. London's distaste for such arrangements obliged Mancham to endorse self-government, thereby preempting SPUP's domestic autonomy platform. Casuistry thus displaced SPUP toward advocacy of outright independence.[9] In May 1973, René's party thereby earned designation as a "liberation movement" in the decolonizing assizes of the Organization of African Unity and the United Nations.[10]

The SDP-SPUP quarrel over self-determination may have been taking place in a vacuum, for Britain was bound to treat the colony as she always had, negligently. Eventually, the cat put on its own bell, without asking the opinion of the mice. Seychelles obtained independence in 1976 as a gesture to inevitability, not to political consensus.

But that quarrel between the parties reflected a primordial dispute among old and new elites for the levers of state security. Representing newly enfranchised peasants, fishermen and a tiny but important alliance of urban labor and young professionals, SPUP nurtured little sentimentality for England's casual patronage. It identified its SDP rivals with a colonial class structure and with the economic and social privileges which the English colonial authorities had left intact among the French planter oligarchy. The nationalist obligation was to denounce economic stagnation and stultification of opportunity. These consequences of colonialism caused social and moral alienation, accounting for large scale emigration of Seychellois labor. René insisted that the 1970 elections were not to be seen as a plebiscite against independence and that Britain should draw no conclusions on self-determination from the relative strength of the parties. SPUP kept in close touch through Seychellois expatriates with the East African nations acceding to statehood at about the time politics was being born in the islands. Its declarations underscored the Africaneity of the islands' majority, their hopelessness as a vestige of dying empire, and their putative prospects as an agricultural and commercial participant in the developing world.

Once the islands' first airport was opened in 1971, the external world actually began arriving on the hitherto oblivious archipelago. The concomitant boom in construction, public works, and tourism transmitted sudden shocks to a no longer inert society. Labor troubles and even bomb threats startled Victoria town in 1972. Blaming SPUP for instigating disorder, Mancham began pressing Whitehall for expanded security power aimed at official repression of his opponents. Politics hardened in the once sea-locked enclave and the two parties began to use radically different frames of reference.[11]

Contending that Seychellois stability and economic equilibrium depended on continued deference to British authority, the SDP followed the loyalist precedent designed, albeit without success, by Gaetan Duval's Social Democratic Party (PMSD) in the mid–1960s in Mauritius. Britain had admittedly done little for the Seychelles since 1810, but its nonchalant paternalism had at least prevented mass starvation and civil strife. Failing metropolitan incorporation on the Réunion or Hawaii model, Mancham saw the colonial subordination of Gibraltar, Bermuda, or Puerto Rico as worthy of emulation. With the intrusion of other major powers into the ocean, Mancham reasoned, British strategic interests would at least appreciate having their own quiescent, inexpensive outpost along the routes of trade. Seychelles' importance to Western interests had been demonstrated since 1963, with the relocation of the United States satellite tracking station from turbulent Zanzibar to Mahé. Even the neutralist SPUP has tolerated the station as a major employer and a harmless witness of nonalignment.

Mancham was nevertheless exaggerating Seychelles' strategic advantages. Britain could scarcely be expected to extend the umbilical so far into the Creole Indian Ocean as the SDP was urging. Seychellois were simply not a colony in the same sense as the English enclaves in the South Atlantic Falklands or the North Atlantic Bermuda, let alone like the closer British cousins of Gibraltar or Ulster. The islanders were too distant, in both geographic and ethnic terms. And London had strategic opportunities without having to reward Seychellois toryism. In 1965, several fragments of the southernmost archipelago had been removed from Seychelles to form the new British Indian Ocean Territory (BIOT) along with Mauritius' Chagos archipelago. Thus, England had prepared for the eventuality of an outpost in the Western ocean without having to consult, and eventually to carry, the entire colony. Indeed, after surveying Farquhar, Desroches, and Aldabra islands for prospective naval and air facilities, the UK and the United States decided to locate their interests more centrally, on Diego Garcia in the Chagos.[12]

London was hardly disposed, therefore, to allow a dispensable Seychelles to stand in the way of retrenchment from "east of Suez," a policy formalized in 1968. Her Majesty's Government noted with irritation that the SDP's loyalist impulses were earning Britain international recrimination as a colonial oppressor confronting a recognized "liberation movement" (SPUP). By contrast, truly imperial recalcitrance by the French in Djibouti, Réunion, and the Comoros was only mildly "deplored" by UN and OAU majorities without comparable calls for liberation.[13]

Seychelles' rendezvous with decolonization or "disenclavement" became inevitable. The airfield at Pointe Larue on Mahé originally represented London's compensation in 1965 for transplanting Aldabra, Farquhar, and Desroches to the BIOT. Its inauguration in 1971 ended the isolation which might otherwise have helped justify continued colonial status. Within two years, Seychelles' principal economic activity was tourism, its major domestic industry tourist facility construction, its paucity of farming largely devoted to supplying hotels; its infrastructure was developing to accommodate paying visitors, and its principal attraction to world banking interests was a real estate boom linked to speculation over tourist facilities.

Unaware, perhaps, that his demand for better communications would itself help destroy the case for continued protection by Britain against an intimidating outside world, Mancham greeted the opening of the airport with characteristic ebullience: "We are no longer a thousand miles from nowhere," he wrote, "but halfway to everywhere." [14] Including to independence, against his will. Labor spilled out of the farms and fisheries into new jobs in Victoria, on the roadways, at the airport and resort villages. Even after the first spurts of construction and public works hiring had subsided, Seychelles remained a rapidly urbanizing society with a crippled agriculture and a balance of trade deficit. The once Forgotten Eden no longer had a place for colonialism to hide.

Disowned by Africa for anachronistic toryism, worried by an increasingly restive population at home, faced by London's impatience to evacuate "east of Suez," Mancham yielded to inevitability in 1974. Stepping once more onto SPUP ground, he singlehandedly turned the SDP toward the hitherto unspeakable objective of independence.[15] Carrying their opponents' former banner into the elections of April 1974, SDP candidates managed to win thirteen of the fifteen legislative seats with only 52.4 percent of the ballots against an outraged, outmaneuvered SPUP. Making his metamorphosis complete, Mancham began talking of land reform. He also undertook to repair relations with the African continent and the third world in general. He was rewarded by a cordial reception at the June 1974 OAU meeting at Mogadishu, only a year after the organization's endorsement of SPUP's liberation credentials and his own ostracism as a comprador.[16]

Having adopted its platform, Mancham could generously invite SPUP into a pre-independence coalition. They established a joint negotiating team at the March 1975 constitutional conference in London. Differences of principle between the new partners aborted those discussions, but a second round in January 1976 witnessed an exchange of compromises, preparing for independence in June of that year. The islands would become a republic as demanded by SPUP but the coalition would postpone new elections until 1979, to suit the majority SDP. On June 28, Mancham became President of the Republic, with René as Prime Minister and nine other portfolios attributed to six SDP and three SPUP leaders. Thus a reluctant electorate found its destiny transformed within six years from loyal territory of the Queen in Parliament to the smallest of self-reliant republics.[17]

President Mancham's conversion to nationalism seemed entire. From fervent partisan of the Western cause in world strategies, Mancham even borrowed SPUP's professions of nonalighment and identification with third world interests. He petitioned Britain successfully (some say by prearrangement) for the return of Aldabra, Farquhar, and Desroches at independence, and acted, albeit without permanent effect or great conviction, for curtailment of Seychelles' trade with South Africa. But the new state was not to be abandoned to the vicissitudes of radical neutralism. Following the auspicious lead of polygot Mauritius eight years earlier, Seychelles promptly joined both the Commonwealth and the Francotropic OCAM, suing tirelessly for economic assistance in both languages at once. Moreover, despite his Prime Minister's insistence, Mancham refused to denounce the Anglo-American base at Diego Garcia, for fear of antagonizing Washington and thereby jeopardizing the Pentagon's tracking station which had become Seychelles' largest single employer. For this, among other offenses to the national interest, Mancham was overthrown by SPUP militants in 1977, before his presidency was a year old.

Rejoicing in a benign maritime tropical climate, the Seychellois escape both the ravages of the endemic disease and the treachery of cyclonic seasons which afflict the Mascarenes, Comoros, and Madagascar. Their atmosphere is fresher, more buoyant than Maldives' or Zanzibar's and there are no active volcanoes to shatter serenity, as on Réunion and Grand Comoro. The birthrate remains high whatever Seychelles' fortunes in the world and the population enjoys longevity despite poverty and malnutrition. Numbering 27,444 in 1931, and 60,000 at independence in 1976, that population grows at slightly more than two percent each year. Emigration of labor kept demographic expansion tolerable until the employment bonanzas of the 1970s. Repatriation and retention of labor have brought the male population back into rough equivalence to the female. Voluntary exile had indeed become an important corrective for over-population and political restiveness, at the cost of social imbalances and the loss of industrious elements of society. Small expatriate communities of Seychellois still reside in the United Kingdom, France, Kenya, and Australia, with new channels opening for bilingual and literate islanders (especially women) in Arab countries and in the schools of the African continent.[18]

Census tabulations stopped distinguishing between ethnic groups early in the century, a testimonial to the assimilative mechanism of Seychelles' Creole world, contrasted with Mauritius where "communities" maintain some official identity even now. But social class ascription, even in this relatively homogenous place, tends nonetheless to follow criteria of color. The peaks of the pyramid are occupied by descendants of the early French settlers who inherited this earth for want of accessible others. The forty families of *grands blancs* disapprovingly observe the rising tides of modernity which diminish their feudal entitlements through fiscal policy and minimum wage legislation, competitive labor opportunities, and para-statal marketing arrangements. Family estates are modest in size, compared to those of Mauritius. They are rigorously taxed and tempting to real estate speculators. The latter have probably initiated (or at least refreshed) more large fortunes over the last decade than were ever created in Seychelles by the simple, gracious bounties of coconuts or cinnamon. The aristocrats have themselves turned to the professions, foreign trade, and even innkeeping. Their children are sent abroad in quest of education, employment, and spouses.

Historically on the verge of genteel poverty in their remote homesteads, the Franco-Seychellois never reached the pinnacles of chic, eloquence, or luxury enjoyed by the old plantation families of Mauritius.[19] Nor have they emulated the extraordinary outcropping of literary genius exhibited by the privileged Europeans of Réunion and Mauritius. Seychellois aristocracy resembles the provincial gentry of some "far West" more than the colonial elegance and old world distinction of, say, New England and Philadelphia. As in Réunion (although not Mauritius), the logic of multigeniture and the overall narrowness of opportunity in Seychelles have engendered a lumpen-aristocracy of poor whites (*petits blancs* or *'ti moun'*). These European Creoles have little left but ethnocentric pride to sustain convictions of superiority over the "coloreds" among whom they live. For the island plantocracy maintains two barriers against the pretensions of the compar-atively vulgar—a color bar which limits exogamous marriage and the French language which relegates even wealthy white anglophone parvenus to lower ranks in the cultural geology.

Apart from the *grands blancs* and their impoverished but nonetheless Gallic *petits frères*, a small colony of active and retired British civil servants has quietly served and retired in the congenial islands. This functionary class has become enlarged, if not enriched, by the establishment of travel and tourist firms, contractors, and banks from the English-speaking world, as it had in the 1940s and 1950s with the institution of English language public schools. Even smaller hermetic communities of South Asian Muslims and Chinese conduct most of the islands' wholesale and retail trade, as they do in Mauritius, Réunion, and Madagascar.

Economic growth since the opening of the airport has been dramatic but uneven. The islands' brief period of political adolescence from 1970 to 1976 coincided with a rush of resources into a single industry, the attraction and entertainment of vacationers. Tourist arrivals rose from 1,622 in 1970 to nearly 79,000 in less than a decade. Tourism alone brings in nine-tenths of the Republic's foreign exchange, helping balance an eight to one deficit in the visible trade accounts. It is also directly responsible for 20 percent of the islands' gross domestic product. Those 78,852 visitors kept 2,500 Seychellois employed in 1979, when the traffic reached its peak. Ancillary services and public works accounted for at least as many more jobs. The conversion of productive factors toward tourism was sudden and massive. Capital flowed into coastline real estate and service industries. Imports shifted to the equipment of resorts and hostelries. Labor left the plantations, small farms, and crafts shops, heading for airport building, road improvement, hotel construction, and associated services. In 1980, only 4,000 people, or 17 percent of the labor force, were working in agriculture, forestry, and fishing, contributing ten percent of GNP, half the proportion registered in 1972.[20]

Seychelles' shallow agricultural and manufacturing sectors could not supply tourism's needs in infrastructure and consumable supplies. Imports of construction materials, managerial and other technology, and even food and souvenirs drained out most of the 200 million rupees realized from tourist expenditures in 1979. Filtered through the hands of local wage labor and entrepreneurs, newly created liquidity drove prices high. By its very nature, the construction surge had to be temporary. Only one major airport and so many bungalows are required for the tolerable number of visitors on Mahé and a few accessible outer islands. Implementation of sensible ecological and aesthetic controls on entrepreneurs has weakened somewhat since the euphoric early 1970's, but zoning considerations still limit the expansion of holiday and related facilities on the island. Hence, the sum of 2,500 Seychellois directly employed in the industry is unlikely to rise beyond the rate of increase in labor supply, even if the goal of 100,000 visitors is reached by 1989.

As in so many other transforming economies, however, workers who leave the land for jobs in building trades, industry or services prove recalcitrantly urbanized. The initial move, traumatic as it may be, represents a deliberate, irreversible cultural shift to "modernity." Even dietary preferences have shifted radically, from the cassava (manioc), vegetables, cocunuts, salads, and natural beverages of a rural milieu associated with serfdom to costly imported rice, meat, and fish, and bottled refreshment. As the 66,000 Seychellois drifted on the soft breezes of their new tourist regime, emigration ceased to represent the only logical escape from the suffocating determinism of rural poverty. But the bonanza which kept them home, alienated from their original environment, could not sustain their material expectations. Growth of government services absorbed much labor once public investment took up the slack in private transfers after 1975. Bureaucratic expansion, normal after any independence, imposed new requirements on education and training of manpower, however.[21] It also caused labor shortages in less favored parts of the private sector where wages and job security scarcely competed with civil service employment. Public sector activity contributed to the inflationary trends already stimulated by the expansion of credit in the construction industry. A 54 percent rise in the government budget in 1979 coincided with Seychelles' first current account deficit just as the economy began to encounter the paucities of investment capital and of tourists caused by international recession. Inflation was reduced from twenty to 9.3 percent by a 15 percent revaluation of the Seychelles rupee in March 1981 and by the imposition of price controls; these measures made the islands' tourist services costlier for foreigners. Cheaper alternative sites in Mauritius and the Maldives began to increase their share of the Europeans, South Africans, and affluent Asians attractable by Indian Ocean insular virtues. More or less accurate reports of domestic instability have helped discourage fickle sunbathers and snorkelers from these idyllic shores. Visitor arrivals in Seychelles dropped from a 1979 peak of 79,000 to 47,000 in 1982. They reached 63,000 in quieter 1984, with an average sojourn of 10.8 nights, returning a payments surplus to the island economy.

While the commitment to tourism has long lasting structural impact on Seychelles' economic development, the Republic may not prosper through such specialization alone. The vacation industry remains highly vulnerable to competition between sites and to changing proclivities in speculative investment. It keeps capital and technological formation at low levels, and presses commodity trade out of balance. Experimenting in frontier colonialism, the early inhabitants tried numerous agricultural strategies to make the islands function on the rim of empire. Paradise myth to the contrary, not everything will take root here, although the climate allows year-round fecundity. A luxurious tropical panaorama which greeted early settlers proved under exploitation to be thin and fragile.[22] Topographic formation is too steep on the granite islands, too flat to withstand high winds on the coral bars. Granite soils are easily leached and the coral islands often lack fresh water. Mineral resources are nonexistent except for virtually exhausted guano phosphate banks on the southernmost (Aldabra) group. Experts still argue over the feasibility of wind, tide, and ocean thermal energy in the Seychelles milieu. Once abundant endowments of timber, tortoises, turtles, and whales are all too far depleted to be economically exploitable, and birds eggs have been harvested to the verge of species extinction.

Nevertheless, a diversity of low-cost, lightweight, relatively valuable export commodities like copra, vanilla, cinnamon, and patchouli oils, tortoise shell, guano phosphate, and turtle oil has survived modernity. These commodities help Seychelles surmount the handicaps of isolation, high energy costs, capital scarcity, and international recession. Among the crops introduced by the Mauritian French, cinnamon trees still produce an income for leaf oil producers and exporters on Mahé and Silhouette islands. But the plantations need maintenance, and the other tropical crops are of questionable viability. A high quality cotton had been produced in the early nineteenth century, but it withered in the storm of American competition. Hand-pollinated vanilla, introduced in 1866, remains a minor export, never rivalling the pre-eminence of Madagascar's crop or the quality of Réunion's. Patchouli oil, a blending ingredient for perfumes, suffers from lack of acreage, investment and developmental attention. Recently introduced tea in the Mahé highlands has proved valuable for import substitution only. Tobacco and food crops have never covered domestic needs.

With the slaves emancipated in 1835 went the plantation system, except for the coconut palm, which needed little labor. The palm proved relatively safe here from the high winds which attack it disastrously in Mascarenes, Comoros, and parts of Madagascar. This sub-regional comparative advantage has allowed Seychelles land-owners to work their old plantations with little expense of labor or capital and (ostensibly) little technical improvement. The work of cultivation, harvesting, drying, and transporting coconut products is performed unstrenuously by hand labor and draught animals, all in a rather easy post-colonial reflex.[23] Throughout the nineteenth and early twentieth centuries, coconut oil and copra were Seychelles' staple exports. The tree indeed represents itself as manna for Eden. Husk fiber (coir) is worked into rope and paddings; thatch is used for construction and fuel; the trees lay down their own mulch, and the "milk" and "meat" nourish people and livestock. Almost half the total land surface of the archipelagoes is now occupied by coconut palm and cinnamon groves.

But the Seychelles are no longer basking socially in their equatorial idyll. With skills and wage labor absorbed in tourism and the new service bureaucracies, stagnation afflicts their unregenerated countryside. Government controlled market prices and rising wages deter farmers from taking initiatives to meet expanding markets in the urban and tourist sectors. Traditional crafts have also withered even as demand rose for skilled workmen and for souvenirs made in the country. Moreover, thanks in part to the tourist boom, Seychelles faces a scarcity of good land for expanded production. Thirty percent of the total territory, including entire islands, has been sold to foreign proprietors, most of them speculators uninterested in cultivating the food, textiles, and wood products demanded in the domestic market.[24] Without costly technological improvement, coconut production is becoming gravely inefficient and the plantation land could often be sold more profitably than worked. Thus, cinnamon, vanilla, and copra production has declined along with food staples.

Stagnation in agriculture and the resources put to it has magnified the vulnerability of the islands to world conditions over which they can have no influence. Absentee landlords have for too long neglected tree and factory maintenance, fertilization, parasite control, labor-intensive market organization and prospects for cooperation and integration in the coconut sector. Many of the trees are infected or otherwise underproductive; parasites infest large portions of the granite islands' groves. Opportunities for interlined crops (especially tobacco, potatoes, and vegetables in demand by the tourist market) are precluded by anarchic and cluttered tree dispersion. Labor-employer relations on the more efficient outlying islands remain colonial in all connotations of the term. Their hesitant, benign monocrop has been dilapidating for more than a decade into what Dupon called "a plantation agriculture in crisis, having lost confidence in itself."[25]

By the early 1970s, fishing had already become more profitable than farming for local capital and labor. The principal islands lie outside the cyclone zones, in moderate currents and swells, inhabited by full banks of tuna and other species. Their 200-mile economic outskirts (declared in 1978) cover more square kilometers of exploitable waters than any Indian Ocean power except India and France. Fish became a principal recourse for both protein supply and export growth. Although hand fishing has been a popular occupation for Seychellois Creoles since emancipation, their technology permits capture of only five percent of an estimated annual fish harvest of 45,000 tons in those waters.[26] The primitive industry could scarcely meet domestic demand in the early days of the tourist boom, let alone compete for export markets with Japanese, South Korean, Russian, and other mechanized fleets which harvest these waters.

Unable to attract private resources to so risky a venture, fisheries development has had to be promoted by government services and foreign aid patrons through a painful and often self-contradictory evolution to intermediate technology. New vessels, dock and cold storage facilities as well as vital retraining projects have been started, with aid from Spain, West Germany, Britain, and France. While these technical assistance projects encountered varying luck, the islands have tightened enforcement rules against foreign poaching. They obtain a million dollars in annual licensing fees from European, Soviet, and Asian fleets which comb their part of the ocean.[27]

Relying almost exlusively upon external public capital committed on concessionary terms, Seychelles faces a rising public indebtedness and a period of adjustment to rapidly mounting demands of its urbanizing population. Considerable success in planning, organizing and managing socially responsible development has earned international praise for the World Bank's smallest member. But the islands will have difficulty doubling per capita income within the space of a decade, as they have done twice since 1960. Birthrates remain at 28.4 per thousand despite extensive government family planning programs which must operate against Church resistance. Unemployment reached 14.8 percent in 1985. Yet social and fiscal priorities call for redistribution of income without annihilating the landed and commercial minorities responsible for economic initiative.[28] The remaining rural population must willingly renew commitment to the land and its productivity, requiring rural credit and extension schemes beyond what the administration has been able to provide thus far. A seven percent annual rise in production targeted by the 1985-1989 plan, demands the methodical settlement and development of outlying islands whose prinicipal resources are in plantation agriculture and fishing. Major investments will be necessary to assure jobs and social amenities outside Mahé where Seychellois are accustomed to expect a rapid growth of opportunity.

Seychelles industry once consisted exclusively of copra, coir fiber, and tea processing plants, with at most a dozen regular employees each. To this endowment have been added the usual brewery, soft drink plant, cigarette factory, and plastics manufacturing of an "emerging nation." Together, the islands' fifty plants occupy about five percent of the labor force. An industrial zone exists on Mahé and legislation permits joint ventures, expecially for import substitution and essential needs. Labor costs are already high and social amenities well advanced, however, compared to larger competing Asian and African economies. Little private capital has been manifest except for quick speculative gain. Re-export trade, maritime registration, and a projected international financial facility represent promising but limited (and scarcely labor intensive) prospects. Productive sectors protest against over-taxation for the benefit of educational and social programs which their protagonists consider the islands unable to afford.

Indeed, the ruthless dialectic of practical economics and social justice transpires in island ministates as anywhere else. Among modern Seychelles' social goals are universal free education, full employment, equal rights for women, guaranteed pensions for the elderly, free medical treatment, a school health program, modern housing for all families, and cheap transportation in rural Mahé and outlying islands, whatever the budgetary constraints.[29]

The most active priority is to fit skills and minds to the needs of the economy. The state has nationalized Church schools and made free education available for the first nine years, at the cost of 28 percent of the national budget. Instruction is to take place primarily in Kreol, with English introduced at the fourth year and French in secondary school. Textbooks and pedagogy in the colorful but limited national language are being devised to catch up with policy. At age 16, students may "volunteer" for the National Youth Service which by 1984 was given exclusive jurisdiction over higher secondary education. The Service had reached 1,200 of the 1,500 eligible young Seychellois by 1982. In Tanzanian fashion, overall educational strategy aims at a mental reconversion of the nation's youthful energies toward cooperative national values, at what is often regarded as the sacrifice of intellectual and technical expertice. As Franda observes,

> What many fear, and what seems to be happening already, is a more or less permanent out-migration of the brightest Seychellois to other nations and the institutionalization of a set of second-rate social welfare and technical programs within Seychelles.[30]

Indeed, a thousand expatriate managers and technicians already occupy positions for which Seychellois are deemed unqualified. Less than 200 Seychellois are in post-secondary training in England, other Commonwealth countries and Algeria, to replace the foreign educators, medical personnel, aircraft pilots, accountants, agronomists, and hotel managers who operate the economy. Some of these will certainly remain overseas, wherever their skills, bilinguality and (in many cases) family connections can help them locate, away from the pressures of an egalitarian authority. Thus, the economically, culturally and politically fortunate are replacing the less skilled islanders in the markets of emigration, while the latter stay at home pressing toward urbanity.

As in other blue-skied, golden-beached resorts, political fluctuations have diminished the Seychelles' allure for foreign vacationers in the past seven years. The aimless unrest of the early 1970s soon became focussed on the regime in power. After more than a decade of leadership in a colony, James Mancham lasted only a year as President of the Republic. His carefree, open-arm style had made some friends for the lovely islands among strong and wealthy patrons overseas, but not much of that friendship could be translated into satisfaction of national priorities. His frequent personal missions to Western Europe and North America succeeded in attracting investment and clients for his newly minted haven of repose, but without conspicuous increase in jobs and liquidity.

Moreover, Mancham also seemed to be having too much fun at his prospecting ventures, striking some observers at home and abroad as somewhat frivolous for a chief of state. The year 1976 was rather late for a new third world country to pose as a micro-national open sanctuary for affluent flower people. Mancham was also accused by Prime Minister René of contemplating indefinite postponement of the 1979 elections which SPUP had been anticipating in its long-frustrated bid for power.[31]

On June 5, 1977, while the President was sojourning in London, sixty armed Seychellois disembarked on Mahé and subdued the national police, Mancham having declined to organize a real army to defend his dominion of love. Led by Jacques Hodoul, a Marxist barrister trained in Paris and London, the insurgents had been supplied and assisted by Tanzania to rid the Indian Ocean of its scandalous burlesque of statecraft. Once in control, after two deaths but otherwise little bloodshed, the invaders called on René to assume the authority stripped from "playboy Mancham." Reluctant at first to profit so flagrantly from this irregularity, the Prime Minister was ultimately able to overcome his distaste and accepted the Presidency. He ruled by decree until the promised elections of 1979, ending, at least for the time being, fourteen years of almost archetypal political sibling rivalry with the flamboyant Mancham.

The New Order

Of the same generation as his opponent and predecessor, the 41 year old SPUP leader represents a major departure at least in style and tone of administration. Dour, cautious, diffident, relatively inarticulate, René had risen in fortune as a British educated lawyer-politician from the dignified poverty of his Franco-Seychellois family. Where the prosperous Creole Mancham had sought a complaisant rainbow, René inaugurated a phase of austerity and administrative restraint enveloped in the rhetoric of popular mobilization, scientific socialism, and the discriminations of nonalignment.

Seychelles acquired independence as rustic city-state, a dispersion of scanty human and natural resources that had served little purpose in the colonial world. It had acquired a negative sense of nationality from isolation, the sense of not being anybody else; that identity was reinforced positively from the insular Creole foundation of its way of life. Social classes were interposed without splitting the nation into incompatible communities defined by external metropolitan affinities, as in Mauritius. Yet the rivalries of class interest were sufficiently pronounced to set two parties into competitive orbits and thus to determine local politics.

In the 1970s, local politics became national. Personal loyalties to neighbor politicians started reverberating momentously into principles espoused or opposed by men of state. Face-to-face claims for jobs, scholarships, market licenses, mortgages, foreign exchange, road repairs, water, and other essentials became entangled in a macro-political economy. Such decisions involved considerations of real estate alienation for hotels, encouragement of food production for national needs, payments balances, relations with South Africa and Africa in general, and the perils of nuclear power deployment in a disturbed ocean. Seychellois were of course obliged to adopt attitudes toward issues of contemporary moment, or to support representatives who did so. This requirement began redefining the alternative interests of the new state and thus the very identity of the decolonized islanders.

Inability to dominate the climate of change, to define the terms by which Seychelles came of age, or even to take their passage solemnly, condemned James Mancham and his SDP to obsolescence, even without the aid of Hodoul's coup d'état. Aware of a new set of relations to the external world, a growing number of politically active Seychellois declined to remain loving wards of a paternal universe. Losing credibility as a leader in a modern state, Mancham had insisted on dosing his restive Seychellois with alternative measures of affection and repression, offending the groups which regarded themselves as legitimate participants in a grown-up nation. In contrast to René who invoked the symbolism and strategies applicable to self-respecting states from Tanzania to China, Mancham ignored the consequences of his own political conversion of 1974. Seychelles would use its new police force and customs powers largely to welcome the world to a terrestrial paradise. Government in Mancham's Seychelles consisted in determining which interests were more benevolent than which.

Ironically, Mancham's simple vision of a perpetually dominated Seychelles proved to be at last more consistent, if less honorable, than his succesor's nationalism. Mancham could without reservation encourage self-serving financial and cultural contributions from France, blithely guarantee the longevity of Washington's tracking station, invite vacationers from Johannesburg and food cargoes from Durban, and sell entire islands to Saudi and Iranian royalty, whatever the reflection of such policies on Seychellois national integrity.[32] These policies may have served the interests of a world economic system, profiteering speculators, class and even race repression, but they also promised jobs, capital and indispensable goods and services to an otherwise hapless population. Seychellois nationalism had to be defined in revolt against these established systems, but it offered no material substitute for them. Thus, once in power, the nationalists had to perpetuate Mancham's contrivances substantively, treating them as necessary but transitional contradic tions against a gradually perceptible grain of revolutionary priorities.

That grain has asserted itself distinctly against these constraining realities. Nationalization of property is deferred until Seychelles has more to expropriate for social benefit. René's 1977 doctrine of "positive nonalignment" implies that Mancham's variety was "negative," yet very little substance has changed. Although Mancham naturally interpreted his downfall as an act of Soviet inspired conspiracy,[33] the USSR actually obtained from René few advantages and the United States few disadvantages that Mancham would have reversed. Neither president granted military base rights, for instance, despite occasional rumors inculpating both Mancham and René in this respect.[34] René permitted the United States to renew its tracking station lease in June 1981 for another ten years. Although operated by the U.S. Air Force, the facilties were dismissed as "not really military." Warships of all navies have been equally admissible at Victoria in modest numbers provided their governments declared them to be innocent of nuclear weapons. Since Washington refuses to confirm or deny such attributes, American ships could not enjoy Seychellois hospitality until 1983, when René stopped asking the question. Three "goodwill" visits took place in 1983 and 1984, as the US began catching up with French and Soviet fleets which have called there regularly, sometimes simultaneously, since independence.

For the young polity, the 1977 coup d'état did entail more than a transfer of presidencies from playful brother to sober brother. Within a year, Seychelles had a new constitution, following the Tanzanian model to a considerable extent. The new structure was designed above all to put an end to factional conflict—now that the "right" faction had won—through the instrumentality of the single party. Freedom of association and open dissent are limited in the common interest of the community. In June 1978, Mancham's SDP was outlawed and SPUP transformed itself into the Seychelles People's Progressive Front (SPPF). In this theoretically monolithic state party, a central Executive Committee supervises 23 local branches as well as the National Worker's Union, the Seychelles Women's Association and the National Youth Organization. These bodies were joined in July 1981 by the Seychelles People's Defence Force, a militia composed of most of the able-bodied men on the islands. Thus the party assumes total responsibility for state institutions and for the mobilization of the population behind them. In characteristic formulas:

No element of national policy escapes the vigilance of the Front which assumes a leading role in a nation which acknowledges the primacy of the party over the organisms of the State which are responsible for executing its policy.[35]

Guy Sinon, René's Minister of Administration, became secretary of the party, thus further identifying the country's political and managerial directorates. On Sinon's retirement in 1984 for reasons of health, René, as Head of Party, aborbed the General Secretariat as well.

In June 1979, the Front obtained 96 percent participation for the promised elections, the first since April 1974. Permitting only one presidential candidate on a yes-no ballot, the new system assured René's endorsement by 98 percent of a grateful electorate. He was re-elected in June 1984, again without opposition. However, multiple candidacies are allowed for the 23 elected seats in the National People's Assembly provided that all contestants are endorsed by the party and that the SPPF retains control of all publicity and other campaign activity. On June 23, seventy candidates made the partliamentary run.

In effect, conforming to one-party state experience elsewhere over two decades, unification of political and administrative operations simply transferred normal factionalism to the SPPF's interior. Various personalities have become identified with or against alternative policies and the President maintains his supremacy by preventing individual factions from attaining unequivocal victories. True to its lamentable type, a sycophantic press filters foreign and domestic information to suit the leadership's purposes and helps conceal contradictions between policy and reality.

Under the new system, both consent and dissent have followed slow, tropical trajectories. Administrative reform and new financial institutions sprang impressively into place. Production and marketing incentives have proved more difficult, however, particularly under progressive tax and minimum wage burdens imposed on farmers and artisans. A key institution, the Youth Training Corps, designed to combine secondary and post-secondary education with political indoctrination, had to be modified in October 1979 after 3,000 parents and students protested vigorously in Victoria against its original provisions for compulsory recruitment.[36] The René regime learned a valuable lesson from this unusually forceful display of popular resistance, but the discipline of the SPPF has gradually tightened.

Opposition has come to challenge the regime's existence, if not its policies. At first, opponents of social mobilization simply left the islands, escaping a revolutionary assault on privilege. Hundreds of propertied whites and skilled Creoles emigrated to Australia, South Africa, Kenya, and Mauritius. Eventually, their attitudes crystallized into a movement against the SPPF's regimentation of Seychellois life. Through his first seven years, René has had to evade, or at least denounce, a virtually annual counter coup d'état. Dissident exiles in Paris and London organized a Seychelles Liberation Committee around the convenient if not entirely inspiring presence of the deposed James Mancham. Apart from its direct acts of subversion, the committee has called attention to largely unverified human rights infractions and helped publicize a general temper of instability. Such publicity has seriously debilitating effects on an economy which appeals to expectations of holiday security.

The illegitimacy of the 1977 putsch has haunted René like the ghost of Banquo. To keep Burnham Wood away, he promptly began recruiting soldiers and importing weapons for Seychelles' first army and navy. His undeniable personal sincerity ensured a measure of credibility for the regime, and he has insulated political decisions from military influence as far as possible in this tightly-woven web of elites. The SPPF's social program was intended to summon mass support without open electoral competition. Mancham was to be a good riddance and his global capitalist friends either evicted or at least nudged into the shadows of public life. Yet insecurity has festered in the bright equatorial sunlight.

In November 1979, promptly after the Youth Service Corps disturbances, a new counterplot materialized, resulting in more than a hundred arrests and the withdrawal of two French advisors and a team of naval instructors. The state of emergency prevailed for four months thereafter with a curfew which impeded tourist circulation until August 1980. Accused as a principal conspirator, a French police advisor remained in prison for 73 days against his government's remonstrances. France's naval training mission was dissolved, and Paris recalled its remaining technical assistance personnel. The military team was replaced by Algerians and Tanzanians, as René foreswore military ties henceforth with all but third world brethren.[37] Displaying their customary resiliency, the French eased gradually back into Seychelles, but were no longer entrusted with the republic's security forces. By May 1981, when France, too, voted Socialist, Paris had already persuaded René of its essential good faith. The arrival of François Mitterand at the Elysée stimulated even closer relations. Seychelles' historic progenitor became the embodiment of the "third alternative" to super-power patronage of non-aligned nations. France also soon shared the principal responsibility with her colonial successor, Great Britain, for external economic support of Seychelles.

Another patron of Seychelles' colonial infancy, Mauritius, was also briefly tarnished by the brush of conspiracy. Prime Minister Ramgoolam, skillfully manipulating political life-support devices against a decade-long siege from the left, had been an avuncular companion to Mancham. He openly disapproved of the irregularity of René's assumption of power in 1977 and was generally thought to be inclined to help undo the coup d'état whenever the opportunity arose. Every low point in the oscillations of Seychelles security evoked this suspicion of bad faith on the part of the old administrative metropole. But evidence of complicity never emerged. Eventually, Mauritius recovered from the stigma, and was on the way toward a firmer diplomatic footing in the islands when, two years after the 1979 imbroglio, Seychelles had to fight off an actual invasion.

On November 25, 1981, 46 white mercenaries posing as rugby players arrived at Pointe Larue on a chartered Air Swazi flight, with the objective of overthrowing René's government. Recourse to a contemporary version of Indian Ocean privateering had already succeeded twice in Comoros (1975 and 1978), and, of course, René owed his own presidential accession to an invasion by commandos, although of his own nationality. Representing a variety of origins and civilian occupations, the 1981 mercenary crew had been recruited in South Africa by veteran Irish freebooter Mike Hoare, who had once successfully served Katanga's Tshombe and Zaire's Mobutu. While ex-President James Mancham remained in London, the plot presumed his restoration once the leftist René had been dismissed. Mancham overtly welcomed the enterprise and had even recorded a message to be broadcast on the occasion of its fruition.[38]

Despite their elaborate tactical provisions—including early visits to Mahé incognito by Hoare and an advance planning squad of seven men and one woman—the commandos were immobilized at the airport after a revelatory customs inspection of their baggage. Following a twenty-hour standoff at Pointe Larue, the mercenaries commandeered an Air India plane which had been allowed to land for the purpose, and diverted the craft to Durban. They carried a dead comrade back with them, but had to leave the eight-member advance unit on the island to be apprehended one by one. The repelled invaders were taken into South African custody on arrival in the Indian aircraft.

Thus, two sets of judicial procedures transpired—the trial of the stranded eight conspirators before "popular tribunals" in Victoria, and a South African process at Durban and Pietermaritzburg. In the latter, the four leaders of the raid were charged only with piracy and kidnapping (of the plane, passengers, and Air India crew), and summarily released pending trial. The 41 other surviving commandos were intially freed without arraignment. South African authorities at first perceived no harm in subversive belligerency or "terrorism" outside their own republic, and they were hardly disposed to extradite the perpetrators into the wrathful hands of the Seychellois. Although only 24 of the returning mercenaries held South African citizenship, with eleven Britons, six "Rhodesians," two Irish, one German, and one American completing the complement, all were resident in South Africa at the time of the escapade. Press reports connect the majority of them with various South African security services, suggesting complicity by more senior civil servants and politicians. Using Hoare and other freelancers to lead the raid seems to have been intended to disguise official South African implication. Pretoria's Army inquired into its own role, found instances of purely individual misconduct, divulged no names, and closed the case.[39]

Eventually, South Africa was induced by its political opposition and international opinion to take the case more seriously. Evidence at the skyjacking trial in March 1980 supported certain charges emergent in Mahé that government officials as high as (then) Prime Minister Botha had knowingly facilitated the attempted coup with arms and advice.[40] Although the Court judiciously deplored both the invasion and the intimations of official responsibility in it, the Pietermaritzburg verdicts were relatively light. Hoare was sentenced on July 12 to ten years for air piracy; the others received six-month to five-year terms, some of them reduced or concurrent. Thirty-four were released two months ahead of schedule for good behavior. In March 1983, South African reporters were fined for having published national secrets connected with the raid and the proverbial "cover-up," but not one civilian or military official has been publicly disciplined.

In Mahé, of course, the emphasis was rather different. Information poured out of testimony by a couple of the conspirators, who were released for their pains. Two British, three South Africans, and one Zimbabwean were given severe sentences on July 6, 1982, four of them condemned to death. All six were subsequently pardoned by René and freed on July 23, 1983 after Botha had agreed to spare the lives of three African National Congress members condemned to death in South Africa.

Doing its duty, the United Nations Security Council denounced the aggression against Seychelles and dispatched a tripartite committee of inquiry to Swaziland, South Africa, and the islands in March 1982. The Swazi government was readily exculpated, but the committee was able to develop no new insights into South African behavior.[41] Seychellois allegations of collaboration by Kenyan Minister Charles Njonjo and other reputed friends of James Mancham in Kenya, Mauritius, and Saudi Arabia have been denied and remain unsubstantiated. Njonjo's subsequent break with President Daniel arap Moi and his eventual disgrace for flagrant foreign intrigues appear to substantiate some of the Seychelles' indictment. Kenya was reported to be disturbed over predominant Tanzanian influence on Seychelles' political and military life. Indeed, Tanzania, France, and the USSR all rushed combat forces to Mahé in support of René once the November 1981 invasion alert had reached them. By that time, the Tanzanian-trained Seychellois Army had done its work.[42]

That army was soon to have its own turn at desultory power politics. On August 17, 1982, some 88 noncommissioned officers and private soldiers seized the Victoria radio station and other major institutions, claiming the capture of 239 hostages (actually holding forty or fewer) and demanding redress of a rather confused list of grievances. Some of the mutineers wanted changes in governing personalities and ideological coloration in René's regime; others the expulsion of the 300 remaining Tanzanian military advisors; others improvements in barrack-room treatment of enlisted men. While appealing on occasion for foreign intervention, including South African, the rebels seem to have intended no ultimate threat to René's own authority or the sovereignty of his mass party. In the final confrontation 36 hours later, at least nine of the mutineers were killed, the others captured; most troops had remained loyal and the Tanzanians acquitted their charge. A court martial shrouded in secrecy concluded in April 1983. The public prosecutor, Bernard Rasool, had been fired on August 31, 1982 for demanding full disclosure of the indictments and casualty records.[43] In mid-October 1982, still another reported conspiracy was foiled by police in London after press exposés of machinations among the Manchamite expatriates. They seem to have tried, and failed, again in late 1983, this time in South Africa.[44] Reports of new arrests, minor bombing incidents and dissemination of subversive propaganda continued to reach the overseas press. However futile, these recurrences of Seychellois instability severely jeopardize the political and economic prospects of a diminutive nation in search of institutional solidity and the confidence of investors and vacationers. The November 1981 episode caused 500 tourists to be confined to their hotels for an extra, unplanned week of "leisure." In so remote a place, the publicity quotient alone can effectively sabotage a tourist economy.

Smallest of the Indian Ocean polities, Seychelles has neither the resources nor the scale of production and consumption to exert leverage in world economic decisions. Nevertheless, the decade-old republic has maintained remarkably diverse economic relations and ranged broadly in its diplomatic activity. Traditionally, Britain has supplied the transfers and banking services necessary to assure solvency. But Seychelles has managed better than Réunion, Comoros, or even Madagascar to find markets outside the primary bilateral channel. India and Pakistan buy copra, the United States vanilla; even Mauritius and Réunion are larger customers for Seychelles commodities than the UK. Tourists come from virtually all countries in Western Europe (about 70 percent), from several in Eastern Europe, the Middle East, Japan, and the Asian mainland, and from South Africa and Réunion. Foreign aid arrives from the UK, France, West Germany, Spain, Australia, the EEC, OPEC, and third world sources like Tanzania, India, and Algeria. Seychelles' rupee, independent of Mauritius for eighty years, left its sterling connection in 1979 for a peg on IMF special drawing rights and subsequently for an international "basket" of currencies.

For its size, Seychelles has carved a disproportionately broad path for itself in the outside world. During President Mancham's year as friend of all, enemy to none, relations with the OAU and Commonwealth states turned into full memberships, and Seychelles joined the UN, IMF and, in 1979, the World Bank. The islands' double colonial lineage and complex cultural sources authorized the new republic, like Mauritius eight years earlier, to join Francophone OCAM and the Association for Cultural and

Technical Cooperation (ACCT), occasioning fraternity with the French-speaking third world as well as privileged claims on French generosity. The inculpation of French advisors in the 1979 conspiracy against René clouded these privileges somewhat, but not for long. Unlike South Africa and Kenya two years later, the higher reaches of French authority were never implicated with their minions, and normalization of relations could ensue once Seychellois adrenalin had subsided.

French naval forces represent the strongest permanent contingents in the southwestern ocean and France alone retains imperial territory in that corner of the world (aside from the contested, depopulated BIOT Chagos to the east). Manifestations of French external power remain tolerated as the benign anachronisms of a founding ancestor and old friend with residual legitimate interests in the region—and no unduly alarming influence on world security, even after the parliamentary change of French regimes in March 1986.[45] Detachments of French forces resumed neighborly calls at Victoria and Pointe Larue airfield in early 1981 en route to or from Djibouti, Reunion, and Mayotte. They share honors with the USSR and Tanzania as guardians of Seychellois security, as in the aftermath of the mercenary attack of November 1981. Collectively, these responses demonstrated René's access to friendly security assistance on three levels of world power, notwithstanding his vow to accept direct military assistance exclusively from third world benefactors.[46]

Tanzania, Algeria, and India provide the bulk of Seychelles' earnestly solicited support in the nonaligned third world. The first two are important respondents to that quest in the security arena, while India is assisting development of the coconut industry, dairy and meat production, and forestry. India is also second to Pakistan as a market for copra and other commodity exports from the islands. Dar es Salaam's influence has been most manifest in Seychellois defence and social policy as well. Tanzanian troops sojourned in the islands after the fall of James Mancham in 1977. They were reinforced in 1979 after the expulsion of the French technicians. On November 26, 1981, 400 Tanzanian sentinels began patrolling the airfield and the Mahé coast against a return of the routed mercenaries. Another reinforcement occurred during the August 1982 mutiny. In June 1979, Seychellois units participated with Tanzanian and Malagasy forces in joint maneuvers, demonstrating in microcosm what an Indian Ocean "zone of peace" security force might look like. Precepts enunciated by former President Julius Nyerere of Tanzania serve as principles of SPPF party organization and rural development. Tanzanian acolytes Hodoul and Defense Minister Ogilvie Berlouis habitually outmaneuvered most of their rivals for influence within René's tight cabinet.

While seeking a logically consistent path for microstate nonalignment, factions in the SPPF regime compete for policy openings in a number of directions. Rather than exploit its oceanic position for the favors of a major power, Seychelles "has chosen nonalignment and maneuvering between the powers, causing itself numerous problems that result primarily from the conflict between jet-set tourism and Marxist economics."[47] In June 1984, the widely respected, veteran "pragmatist" Dr. Maxime Ferrari, wearied of the unending internal tensions with René's Marxists, abandoned the Foreign Ministry, betaking himself to Paris and a job in the UN system.[48]

In exchange for some equipment and training for the SPPF organization, the police, and the official Seychelles Press Agency, Moscow has pursued what some Westerners consider a "ruthless friendship" with the René regime.[49] René has followed India's lead in a relatively tolerant approach to Soviet Afghan policy and has accepted Russian navigation in the Indian Ocean as comparatively innocent. The relationship was expressed in a maritime agreement of February 18, 1980, allowing anchorage and use of the airfield for personnel transfers. But René has scrupulously avoided concession of anything resembling a military facility, and all naval calls are rationed. The "positive" quality of nationalist nonalignment also dictated the substitution of North for South Korea in May 1980, as well as unequivocal support for the Palestine Liberation and POLISARIO causes. It entails denunciation of both the Camp David arrangements and American naval power displays in the Indian Ocean and Mediterranean. Unsurprisingly, the American CIA, Wall Street banking interests, and Washington's putative Arab proxies are sporadically if vaguely accused by SPPF commentators of intriguing against Seychellois stability. The naval-air base at Diego Garcia in the BIOT a thousand miles east of Mahé is consistently branded as a threat to that stability despite Anglo-American assurances to the contrary. Yet in June 1981, the Pentagon renewed its lease for the US Air Force's tracking station at La Misère in central Mahé. The base now brings $7.5 million in annual rent (quadrupled since 1963) and employs 180 Seychellois.[50] Food aid and a dozen Peace Corps volunteers represent a $2.4 million assistance item for Seychelles in 1982, rising to over $3.5 million a year later. In 1985, US petroleum product sales generated some $2 million for a number of development projects in Seychelles. Like Moscow, Washington obtains distinct but limited strategic benefit from its modest dose of benevolence.[51]

Feared and denounced, South Africa retains access to Seychelles by hook, crook, and market domination. René's government has evidently joined the ranks of Southern African targets for Pretoria's destabilization activity, entrusted in November 1981 to the officious "Reckies" (Reconnaissance Commandos) at Pointe Larue airfield.[52] South Africa participates with less notoriety in Seychelles' destiny through its ability to undersell any reliable alternative supplier of needed consumer goods, and to fill beds in the islands' tourist hostels.[53] South African Airways must now frequent Mauritius after having been excluded from Seychelles in retaliation for the commando assault, but the supplies and visitors come on other airlines or by sea. Realities of costs and benefits again prevent fruition of the ideological design.

A perpetually peaceful Indian Ocean inspires President René's loftiest visions. His tiny United Nations delegation participates energetically in the General Assembly's ad hoc Committee on the Indian Ocean and he has assumed leadership in the organization of "progressive forces" of the southwestern ocean. Mahé was the site in April 1978 of the first two congresses of sympathetic governments (Madagascar, Seychelles, and Ali Soilih's shortlived revolutionary Comorean regime) together with the Mouvement Militant Mauricien and the Réunionnais Communist Party. The participants, having subsequently formed an Indian Ocean Commission, pledged harmonization of policies in fisheries and transportation development, oceanographic research, industrial specialization, trade coordination, and strategic neutralization of the region. But since then, France and her "neocolonial" Comorean proteges have joined the IOC, helping divert it from ideological pursuits to more mundane, and promising, matters.

René has also given unconditional support to Malagasy President Ratsiraka's call for a conference on the security of oil transportation lanes, reduction of great power warships in the ocean, and the elimination of external bases therein. Modest commercial ties remain between Seychelles and Comoros, even under the latter's uncongenial President Ahmed Abdallah. Pending the MMM's welcome but temporary accession to power on Mauritius in June 1982, René improved his uneasy relations with the conservative Ramgoolam who had once called the 1977 Seychelles coup the work of gangsters. He even applauded Ramgoolam's sharper approach to Mauritius' irredenta over the Chagos during the final stages of the Labour Party's administration in the senior island. Outside the great issues of strategy, the two historically related island nations have cooperated to some extent in transportation, tourism, and scientific research, and Mauritius, too, is a customer for Seychelles copra.

As in most regional collaborative projects, however, closer relations between individual IOC members depend on the availability of external resources and, in most instances, on Western consent. A single European airline's decision to divert its vacationers to Mauritius in 1980 cost Seychelles fully eight percent of its anticipated foreign exchange revenues for the year. The republic's mounting external debt is held in the West. A domestic policy swing to right or left is equally unlikely without another irregular regime change, so delicate is the balance between party ideologues on the one hand and the investors, tourists, and indispensable national elites on the other. Seychelles, like other subordinate states, must continue to juggle contradictory interests in the name of national integrity. "Unfortunately," as Franda concludes,

> the best alternative for the Seychelles might well be the tenuous kind of arrangement it has at present, with foreign influence being confined largely to behind-the-scenes maneuvers that do nothing more than contribute to the mystery and romance, and ultimately to the despoliation, of this most beautiful of places.[54]

Notes

1. Sources on modern Seychelles include Guy Lionnet, *The Seychelles* (Newton Abbot, England: David & Charles; Harrisburg, Penna.: Stackpole Books, 1972);

Marcus Franda, *The Seychelles: Unquiet Islands* (Hampshire, England: Gower; Boulder, Col.: Westview Press, 1982); *Seychelles: Economic Memorandum* (Washington: The World Bank, 1980); Athol Thomas, *Forgotten Eden* (London: Longmans, Green, 1968); John M. Ostheimer, "Independence Politics in the Seychelles," in John M. Ostheimer, ed., *The Politics of the Western Indian Ocean Islands* (New York: Praeger Publishers, 1975), pp. 161–192.

2. Auguste Toussaint, *History of the Indian Ocean*, trans. June Guicharnaud (London: Routledge and Kegan Paul, 1966), pp. 154–157.

3. J.T. Bradley, *History of Seychelles*, 2 vols. (Victoria, Seychelles: Clarion Press, 1940); Franda, *The Seychelles: Unquiet Islands*, Ch. 1; Lionnet, *The Seychelles*, Chs. 4 and 5.

4. Jonathan D. Sauer, *Plants and Man on the Seychelles Coast* (Madision: University of Wisconsin Press, 1967); Franda, *The Seychelles: Unquiet Islands*, pp. 105–110; Lionnet, *The Seychelles*, pp. 32–33; Thomas, *Forgotten Eden*, Ch. 8; D.R. Stoddard, ed., *Biogeography and Ecology of the Seychelles Islands* (The Hague: Ed. Junk, *Monographiae Biologicae*, Vol. 55, 1984).

5. Lionnet, *The Seychelles*, Chs. 8 and 13.

6. Lionnet, *The Seychelles*, pp. 97–98.

7. Jean-François Dupon, *Contraintes insulaires et fait colonial aux Mascareignes et aux Seychelles*, 3 vols. (Lille, France: Atelier de Reproduction des Thèses; Paris: Librairie Honoré Champion, 1977), Vol. 3, Ch. 2, pp. 1303–1306; Lionnet, *The Seychelles*, p. 120; Franda, *The Seychelles: Unquiet Islands*, pp. 33–35.

8. Burton Benedict, *People of the Seychelles*, Ministry of Overseas Development, Overseas Research Publication No. 14 (London: H.M. Stationary Office, 1970), p. 29; Franda. *The Seychelles: Unquiet Islands*, pp. 38–45; Thomas, *Forgotten Eden*, pp. 70–73.

9. Ostheimer, "Independence Politics," pp. 170–174.

10. Colin Legum, ed., *Africa Contemporary Record (ACR), 1973–74* (London: Rex Collings, 1974), pp. B 358–359, C12.

11. Ostheimer, "Independence Politics," pp. 169, 175–178.

12. Jean Houbert, "Mauritius: Independence and Dependence," *Journal of Modern African Studies*, Vol. 19, No. 1 (1981), pp. 83–86; André Oraison, "Les avatars du B.I.O.T.: Le processus de l'implantation militaire américaine à Diégo Garcia," in *Annuaire des Pays de L'Océan Indien (APOI)* (Aix-en-Provence, France: CERSOI, 1979), Vol. 6, 1979, pp. 177–209; Philip M. Allen, *Self-Determination in the Western Indian Ocean*, International Conciliation (New York: Carnegie Endowment for International Peace, 1966), pp. 66–69.

13. Organization of African Unity CM/Res. 302, 202, (XXI), Addis Ababa, May 1973, in ACR *1973–74*, p. C 12.

14 Franda, *The Seychelles: Unquiet Islands*, pp. 105–109; James Mancham, "Foreward," *The Seychelles Handbook* (Victoria: The Government Printer, 1976).

15. James Mancham, Letter to *Times* (London), March 20, 1974; Ostheimer, "Independence Politics," pp. 178–184; ACR *1974–75*, pp. B 260–261.

16. ACR *1974–75*, p. B 260.

17. *Seychelles*, Great Britain, Central Office of Information (London: H.M. Stationery Office, 1976); ACR *1976–77*, pp. B 317–319.

18. Franda, *The Seychelles: Unquiet Islands*, pp. 67–68.

19. Ibid., pp. 33–34; Lionnet, *The Seychelles*, Ch. 7; Dupon, *Contraintes insulaires*, Vol. 3, ch. 2:3:b.

20. Franda, *The Seychelles: Unquiet Islands*, pp. 79–83; Claude Wauthier, *Jeune Afrique* 1118, June 9, 1982; *Seychelles: Economic Memorandum*, p. 7.

21. *Seychelles: Economic Memorandum*, p. 14.

22. Sauer, *Plants and Man*, Chs. 1 and 2; Franda, *The Seychelles: Unquiet Islands*, pp. 105–111; Dupon, *Contraintes insulaires* Vol. 1, Section B, Ch. 3; Lionnet, *The Seychelles*, Ch. 9.

23. Dupon, *Contraintes insulaires*, Vol. 2, p. 796; Franda, *The Seychelles: Unquiet Islands*, pp. 84–85.

24. *ACR 1980–81*, pp. 300–303; *Seychelles Economic Memorandum*, pp. 7–16.

25. Dupon, *Contraintes insulaires*, Vol. 2, p. 810.

26. Franda, *The Seychelles: Unquiet Islands*, pp. 85–92; Dupon, *Contraintes insulaires*, Vol. 1, Section C. Chs. 1–4, *passim*; *Africa News* 16 No. 18, May 4, 1981; *Seychelles: Economic Memorandum*, p. 8. On Seychelles fisheries, see also William Travis *Shark for Sale* (London: George Allen & Unwin, 1961) and F.D. Ommaney, *The Shoals of Capricorn* (London: Longmans, Green, 1952), Ch. 8.

27. Franda, *The Seychelles: Unquiet Islands*, pp. 81–92.

28. *Seychelles: Economic Memorandum*, p. 4.

29. *Africa* 118, June 1981; Wauthier, *Jeune Afrique* 1118, June 9, 1982; *Seychelles: Economic Memorandum*, pp. 14–15; *ACR 1983–84*, pp. B 248–250.

30. Franda, *The Seychelles: Unquiet Islands*, pp. 113; also pp. 91–101.

31. *Ibid.*, pp. 49–53.

32. *ACR 1976–77*, pp. B 317–321.

33. James Mancham, Letter to *Times* (London), June 7, 1977; *ACR 1977–78*, p. B 363.

34. Robert I. Rotberg, "The Socialist Seychelles: More than a Drop in the Indian Ocean," *Christian Science Monitor*, August 27, 1980; Arthur Gavshon, "Seychelles, a Tilt to the West?" *Africa Report* (New York), November-December 1983, pp. 56–59.

35. *The People* (Victoria) 417/014, July 1981, p. 5: Franda, *The Seychelles: Unquiet Islands*, pp. 56–57; *ACR 1978–79*, pp. B 367–369.

36. Franda, *The Seychelles: Unquiet Islands*, pp. 93–97; *ACR 1979–80*, pp. B 296–297.

37. *The Guardian* (London), March 3, 1980; *The Times* (London), June 26, August 2 and 5, 1980; Charles Cadoux, "Chronique politique et constitutionnelle: Seychelles 1978–79: Stabilisation du régime et développement socialiste," *APOI* 6, 1979, pp. 365–382; Franda, *The Seychelles: Unquiet Islands*, pp. 66–67; *ACR 1979–80*, pp. B 297–298.

38. J.P. Langellier, *Le Monde*, November 28, 1981; *New York Times*, December 2, 1981.

39. Patrice Claude, *Le Monde*, March 12, 1982.

40. Christine Abdelkrim, *Afrique-Asie* 255, December 21, 1981; *Le Monde*, December 4, 1981; Patrice Claude, *Le Monde*, January 7, 1982; *ACR 1982–83*, pp. B 254–255.

41. S/RES 496/1981, *UN Chronicle* 19:2, February 1982, pp. 21–24; *Ibid.*, 19:7, July 1982, pp. 25–32.

42. Abdelkrim, *Afrique-Asie*, December 21, 1981; *ACR 1981–1982*, pp. B 247–249, B 250–251.

43. *ACR 1982–83*, pp. B 255–257.

44. *ACR 1983–84*, pp. B 244–245.

45. *ACR 1981–82*, p. B 251; Philip M. Allen, "The Indian Ocean: A New Area of Conflict or a Zone of Peace?" *ACR 1980–81*, pp. A 74–75; Allen, "The Indian Ocean: Very Much at Sea,"*ACR 1981–82*, pp. A 140–141; Philippe Leymarie, *Océan Indien: le nouveau coeur du monde* (Paris: Editions Karthala, 1981), Chs. 9–11.

46. J.P. Langellier, *Le Monde*, January 12, 1982; Franda, *The Seychelles: Unquiet Islands*, p. 125.

47. Franda, *The Seychelles: Unquiet Islands*, p. 125.

48. *Africa Confidential*, Vol. 26, No. 7, March 27, 1985.

49. Drew Middleton, *New York Times*, June 23, 1980.

50. Franda, *The Seychelles: Unquiet Islands*, pp. 117–118; *ACR 1978–79*, p. B 370.

51. Franda, *The Seychelles: Unquiet Islands*, pp. 117–119; Dennis Mullin, *U.S. News and World Report*, March 24, 1980; *ACR 1980–81*, p. B 215.

52. Jack Bourderie, Editorial, *Afrique-Asie* 255, December 21, 1981.

53. Franda, *The Seychelles: Unquiet Islands*, pp. 119–120.

54. *Ibid.*, p. 126.

6

Madagascar:
Riding Its Own Tiger

Virtually a continent, though still an island, Madagascar has been
administratively unified and culturally homogeneous for over a century
without achieving a Malagasy nation state. After juggling European imperial
interests through several decades, the central monarchy of the Merina people
ended abjectly in 1896, despatched by the cannons of the French. The
Indian Ocean's *Grande Ile* emerged from colonial rule in 1960 committed
by treaty to continued respect for multifarious French prerogatives. Two
successive republican governments thenceforth sought to recover the island's
internal cohesion and to find its place in a world somewhat larger than
Overseas France. The 1960 Republic had learned from its French predecessor
to govern Madagascar by disciplined local administrations under central
political control. External resonance was obtained through the high-cultural
network of Francophonia abroad. The resulting integrations were superficial
at best.

Since 1972, these specific colonial legacies have been substantially dis-
mantled. Construction of domestic and international solidarity has followed
more nationalist designs, with revolutionary implications. The traditional
Merina political culture has been resuscitated as a national endowment, and
not by Merina statesmen alone. The momentum of class conflict is accentuated.
A panoply of state establishments is to induce a new justice and to distribute
an elusive prosperity throughout the benumbed, balkanized island. This
Second Republic has declared itself "democratic" and chosen a prominent
role along the slender affinities of the Afro-Asian third world. And still
the pangs of domestic dissent and the trials of dependence on overseas
market economics beset the western ocean's principal island.

From Independence to Independence

Madagascar's nine million people belong to a place larger than all the
islands west of Indonesia combined. The dominant source of this complex
African-Asian culture is in fact that Indonesian insular neighborhood. From
there, the earliest known Malagasy navigated at least 3,500 miles at several

imprecisely specified times through conjectured itineraries of high seas.[1] For the better part of two millenia they have combined with other Asian and Bantu-speaking African people in a unique crucible of ethnicity and insular civilization, penetrated later by Arab and European influence.

Known to ancient mariners as the Island of the Moon among other picturesque identities, Madagascar lay too far south of the regular monsoons to enjoy full frequency in the mercantile traffic along the West Asian and East African coasts. Once the ocean had been penetrated by Europeans from the southwest, however, the great island was given its present name and a change of role. It became a habitual stop in a new maritime power system, a source of slaves for overseas markets, and inevitably, a target for settlement. The usual succession of Portuguese, Dutch, French, and British ships landed on various fringes. But, while other more viable gems of empire still glistened along the continental littorals, only France took the great island seriously as a prospective jewel in its colonial coiffure. Even the French settlement at Fort Dauphin (now Taolanaro) on the southeast coast was abandoned in 1674 after thirty years of vicissitudes in favor of uninhabited Bourbon island (Réunion). Much later, France succeeded in settling offshore at Sainte Marie and Nosy Be in the north and to obtain concessions on the Malagasy mainland. Paris had the presumption to hearken back to the aborted Fort Dauphin experiments, however, as support for its late nineteenth century attempt to legitimize the invasion and appropriation of the Malagasy state.

Beginning in the latter seventeenth century, Madagascar experienced a consolidation of regional realms and chiefdoms into a larger state. Some of the components were favored by European and Arab commerce, including slave traders, others by the mercantile trade's most lethal enemy—potent squadrons of European and American pirates who inhabited Malagasy coasts until the British Navy exterminated them after 1721.[2] Two principal states emerged out of the territorial ferment of this period. With French support, the Sakalava kingdom of the northwest spread south- and eastward over virtually half the island by 1700. The Sakalava soon weakened and ultimately fell to their great rivals, the Merina of the central plateau.[3]

The work of Merina ethnic unification and subsequent expansion was undertaken by the great dynastic founder, Andrianampoinimerina from about 1787. It continued under his successors, beginning with Radama I (1810–1828) who prematurely proclaimed suzerainty over the entire island in 1817. If Radama's pretentions overestimated Merina ability to control Madagascar's other ethnic groups, they were accepted by Great Britain which had been earning a place at Radama's court since 1811. The Merina (often misidentified as "Hova," an appropriate designation for their dynamic class of freemen) were regarded by the British as a force of resistance against post-Napoleonic French ambitions, as well as a source of commercial and cultural opportunity. They prevailed upon Radama to equip and train his armies in triumphant English fashion. The King also agreed to assure vital exports to British Mauritius from east coast concessions and to commission British artisans for monarchical public works. In 1820 he allowed the London Missionary Society to open schools and proliferate culturally throughout the realm, especially in its heartland, Imerina. The Merina today, a privileged fourth of the island population, tend in the majority to be Protestant.

Recovering from their international disaster of 1815, the French responded on behalf of Réunion Island and, ultimately, Roman Catholicism. The flagrancy of European competition under Radama's wife and successsor, Ranavalona I, provoked a strong traditionalist reaction at the court. Anti-European influences induced the Queen to suppress foreign (especially British) activity during most of her reign from 1828 to 1861. Regarded as atavistic and xenophobic from the offended European viewpoint, Ranavalona gave Malagasy nationalism a precocious, anti-imperial precedent for economic, political, and cultural self-sufficiency. Autarchic national spirit confronted the dynamism of British and French technology and language, patterns of organization, alluring consumer fashion, and religious exhortation. Repression of the foreigners and their indigenous followers in turn created an opposition "modernist" faction at Antananarivo, some of it underground, some clustering in the protective ambience of Crown Prince Rakoto. After Rakoto's short-lived reign as Radama II (1861–1863), competing European interests became counterbalanced until the fall of the monarchy, thirty-three years later. This adroit policy was the work of Prime Minister Rainilaiarivony, who married Radama's three royal successors in sequence and thus sustained personal power to the end.

During his three decades as Madagascar's effective ruler, Rainilaiarivony managed to trade concessions with British, French, German, American, and other delegations. He obtained substantial international recognition for the Merina state and stabilized the monarchy's administrative and cultural system throughout some three-fourths of the island. Despite resentment by the diverse peoples of the coasts and the south (often identified in French for convenience as *côtiers*), the Merina domestic imperial system proved internally viable. Betraying some decadence in its last years, the system was to collapse under the direct military assault of European power asserting spurious rights of cultural superiority and flimsy legalisms in the protection of private property claims. Although the great Prime Minister and his queenly spouses revived Britain's initial advantages in Imerina, even converting the entire court to Anglicanism in 1869, they tolerated considerable counter-activity by others. Private French and Roman Catholic establishments prospered in landholding, foreign trade, education, medicine, and other respects, particularly in the provinces. The genial Gascon, Jean Laborde, had served even the distrustful Ranavalona I as polyvalent court engineer after his providential shipwreck in 1831. Laborde died in honor as French Consul at Antananarivo in 1878 but his disputed testament ironically gave France one of several pretexts to subordinate the Merina monarchy which he had served.[4]

During a decade of Gallic encroachment from 1885, the favored British simply looked the other way. Unfortunately for the Malagasy, London had consented to French aggrandizement off the East African coasts in exchange for a free hand in the more valuable Nile region and in the continental fiefdoms of the Sultan of Zanzibar. Thus, another autonomous, cosmopolitan, and essentially cooperative indigenous state became entangled and extinguished in the machinery of late nineteenth century European overseas expansion. As Mutibwa puts it,

> Through contacts with Europeans and as a result of her free and enthusiastic accceptance of foreign ideas and influence, Madagascar had achieved many of those things in the name of which European colonialism was imposed on Africa in the nineteenth century.[5]

To justify the imposition, the authority for such achievements had to be displaced. After a year's hesitation under a militarily enforced "protectorate," the last Queen and her venerable consort were sent to exile. A system of French control supplanted their authority in a country henceforth subjected to deliberate "racial policies."

From a Malagasy perspective, Madagascar is itself only a congeries of discrete "islands" strewn across a rugged landscape. For that matter, the world at large seems only a giant archipelago of Europes, Asias, Africas, Americas (and Madagascar), an enlargement of their own national heterogeneity. Despite its diversity, the country has a tradition of linguistic and cultural coherence and an older political identity than most third world states. All islanders speak dialects of the same originally Austronesian language, carrying various regional admixtures of Arabic, Bantu, English, and French. Cattle raising is universal, even among sedentary forest people of the east. Rice, often grown in irrigated paddy fields, is the staple food, except for some herdspeople of the west and south. Whenever economically and climatically feasible, Malagasy dress tends to be intricately draped. Traditional poetry and proverbial lore reveal a complex animism, stressing the vital presence of the dead and the unborn, the sanctity of family, the moral coherence of the physical universe, and the solemn responsibility of human beings for its welfare. This autochthonous religion still pervades all regions, influencing even the most "westernized" and Islamicized elements of the population.[6]

Madagascar's modern experience follows a consistent historical dialectic. The quest for insular unity is opposed by fissiparous urges toward local autonomy by rural populations and provincial townsfolk. Beginning in the territorial expansion of Andrianampoinimerina's dynasty, central control operated through a class of settlers and professional administrators who appropriated land, operated institutions, and maintained the royal peace. A rough identification of Merina hegonomy with British counsel and trade interest, helped focus côtier anti-colonial resentment against "foreign influence" and, eventually to align the conquering French with coastal peoples against the Merina. Although Merina society was organized on a distinct class basis—the free Hova standing between the *Andriana* nobles and the slaves or the descendants of slaves, called *Andevo*—the imperial experience induced a deep-seated ethnic consciousness, expressed as "Merina versus côtier" hostility.[7]

From the earliest moments of historical conjecture, Madagascar's stronger societies obtained labor from vulnerable neighbors along the Mozambique coast and the Comoro islands. Arab slavers called periodically at ports on both Malagasy coasts for centuries before and after the European incursions into the monsoon seas. From 1500, Portuguese and various other external slave-hunters established their own patterns of commerce in human beings. The nineteenth century ascendancy of Imerina transmitted a new complication to the island's relatively simple dichotomies between free and unfree. Nobility which on the coasts had correlated largely with military prowess and political skill, became identified with the Asiatic ethnicity and culture of the Merina oligarchs. Others who didn't quite "look Merina" could be considered free or attain freedom, but the monarchy was bringing slave labor to the plateau from the conquered coasts. Although some Andriana royalty have relatively dark skin (testifying to very ancient combinations with Africans) and some of the Hova middle class have more recently intermarried, the physiognomies, pigmentation, and hair formations of the Bantu generally implied current or recent slave status (Andevo). Subject peoples were also obliged to contribute scheduled work days to public operations— a practice continued, by the way, under the French and even the Republic despite the abolition of slavery in 1896.

As a result of social labor policies and miscegenation taboos in a large island of widely dispersed population, a remarkably uniform cultural endowment coincides with a pronounced system of classes and political hierarchies sometimes approaching caste discriminations. While their historical grievances may well be more rationally directed toward exploitative classes, some of them non-Merina, the proverbial tribalism of "Hova versus côtier" was available for French divide-and-rule purposes in their own superimposed colonial system.

France did not begin immediately to rule Madagascar as a colony. Following the difficult invasion of 1895, however, the French discovered the danger to their strategic and economic interests in an island capable of rallying around an incumbent monarch, however impotent. Queen Ranavalona III was deported in February 1897, and Madagascar succumbed to the status of a territory of France. For three generations, Paris had to administer in constant tension between the political claims of the deposed but indispensable Merina elites, the insistence of European settlers and concessionaires on classic colonial privileges, and the demands of the coastal and southern peoples that France act on their behalf to secure just balances of opportunity against both.

When General Joseph-Simon Gallieni arrived to govern the island in September 1896, the charge of Colonies Minister André Lebon was to suppress "Hova hegemony" through "the intercession of the chiefs of each distinct people"—the so-called *politique des races*. In reality, Gallieni earned his title to imperial statecraft over the ensuing nine years by establishing realistic lines of policy between the three competitive ethnic-cultural blocs—the Merina, the Europeans and Réunionnais, and the côtiers.[8] Using French and "Senegalese" troops, Gallieni eliminated remaining traces of Malagasy armed resistance, and at first sought the unification of Madagascar without recourse to the Merina political oligarchy. But "Hova hegemony" had been too effective. Gallieni was unable to identify local chiefs of sufficient competence and authority to replace the Merina under the policy of "internal protectorates" (indirect rule) preferred by Lebon's strategy.

Moreover, the density of European and Réunionnais settlers never reached sufficient proportions to warrant the investiture of a colonial charter comparable to that of Algeria, Réunion, or British Kenya. Using his available military forces and appointing whatever chieflings he could find to serve under French authority, Gallieni had to call on the services of Merina "clerk-interpreters" to conduct the affairs of government while seeking to train a more representative cadre of administrators in several regional normal schools.[9]

Gallieni also blocked reconsolidation of Merina political strength through the partition of Imerina into several provinces, called at first "military sectors." An admirer of Merina cultivation, sophistication, and industry, Gallieni (who took a Malagasy wife) anticipated that the Merina should soon qualify for French citizenship under France's assimilationist version of social Darwinism. The Governor nonetheless subsumed all Malagasy under a distinct legal code, the *indigénat*, operating invidiously in favor of Europeans and Réunionnais who were, of course, already citizens.[10] The extraterritoriality implicit in this juridical classification was successfully defended by the privileged settlers until well after World War II. Only 18,000 titles of citizenship were conferred on Malagasy by 1939.

Their access to status as Frenchmen blocked, the Merina retained their cultural and economic superiority over the Malagasy côtiers in practice, if not in policy. As colonial capital in an inevitable centralization of governing institutions, Antananarivo (then Tananarive) obtained the preponderance of educational institutions, commercial headquarters, transportation facilities, and public amenities. Gallieni's provincial training centers were eventually closed for budgetary reasons. The traditional chiefs of the Lebon-Gallieni "tribal policy" were gradually replaced by literate, competent Merina "in greater numbers than in the days of the Queens."[11]

The anomalies of Malagasy society multiplied under French authority. Coastal people still found themselves governed by Merina interlopers acting in the name of a distant, very alien power, and yet the Merina shared indigenous damnation with the côtiers in the estimation of the metropole. Merina manorial landholding had been shattered in Gallieni's "pacification" campaigns, although freed slaves proved inadequate or unwilling to work the available land fruitfully. British competitive interest and the prestige of Anglican Protestantism, cultivated by the Merina, retreated under official pressure in favor of French business and Roman Catholic missions. They were to become emblems of Merina nationalist *revanchisme*.

The French conquest was still recent [in 1939], and it had reduced the former ruling class, the Merina, to the role of second-class citizens by the imposition of the indigenat. They had lost their former positions of command, their privileges and their slaves; and, though for the coastal peoples the French administration merely signified a change of masters from the Merina, these "proud Hova" (as the British missionaries called them) could not easily forget their former status.[12]

The result of the concurrent frustration of French assimilation and tribal policies was an essentially unmanageable colony. France had succeeded simultaneously in aggravating internal Malagasy hostility and stimulating Merina nationalism through as many outlets of expression as that vigorous people could find. What succeeded in French Madagascar was the operation of state-protected neo-mercantilistic companies and settler concessionaires amid the productive resources of the Great Island.

Production, marketing, and distribution developed within prevailing geographic constraints under both the Merina and French imperial regimes. Radical ecological variations occur as the terrain heads from west to east into the winds. Vast distances separating a dozen or more dispersed centers of economic activity allow each of these "islands" primary self-sufficiency and some specialized productive vocation. When the official export of slaves ended under virtuous British influence after 1817, the Merina Kingdom of Radama I remained a major source of timber, beef, and other vital commodities for French Réunion and British Mauritius. Compensation in British arms enabled Radama to extend his father's realm to the east coast. England's weapons were employed, with on the spot advice, against local potentates whose livelihood had theretofore depended on the sale of slaves to the French and the Zanzibari Arabs. Subsequently, under Merina aegis, these chiefs had to undertake the export of foodstuffs, fibers, timber, and other commodities approved by Great Britain.

Even before imposing their protection, with Britain's tacit consent, the French had held their own in nineteenth century Madagascar. They maintained sovereign rights over Nosy Be (originally ceded by the Sakalava crown in exchange for French protection against the Merina) and Sainte Marie (now Nosy Boraha), 1750 legacy of an erstwhile pirate regime. Metropolitan French and Creole settlers periodically took advantage of liberal terms for land use on the east coast and the high interior plateau, as the monarchy and its côtier vassals sought to increase export revenues. Such concessionary practices disturbed communal traditions of landhold, shifting cultivation, and extensive cattle husbandry. Patterns of plantation ownership developed, with labor recruitment and sharecropping for coffee, sugar, fruit, and other cash crops. A Merina manorial aristocracy evolved alongside the European landowners, to be joined subsequently by Arab, Muslim Indian, and Chinese minorities as well.

Parallel with private landholders agricultural production and marketing were regulated by consultative village councils, called *fokon'olona*. With their established rules of procedure, the communities exerted a decidedly peasant-conservative influence on economic evolution. The traditional village system appears to have been transformed by the Merina sovereigns to assure defense, law and order, public works, and local administration as the monarchy expanded its range of control beginning in the late eighteenth century.[13] After several decades of neglect by French and republican authority in favor of more centralized forms of local administration, the fokon'olona were revived by the revolutionary government after 1972. The system's adaptability to new demands of rural modernization and expanding production remains very much in question.[14]

At one time or another, in addition to rice and livestock cultivation, colonial and indigenous plantations were exporting coffee, vanilla, cloves, pepper, groundnuts, cane sugar, bananas, lima beans, cinnamon, tobacco, raphia, sisal, and cotton. A drinkable wine was produced for local consumption on the central plateau. Working for the nineteenth century court, European craftsmen like Laborde established industries to replace or supplement imported capital and manufactured goods from Europe and Mauritius. Laborde even made cannons for the Queen. Processing industries for sugar, vanilla, oils, beef, tobacco, and fibers broadened the island's agriculture. Mining operations were begun by the Merina or the French for mica, graphite, semi-precious stones, and, later, fissionable metals. Royal goldworks continued to produce traces of precious metal through the first years of independence. The 1960 Republic supported meat-packing, fruit processing, cement, cigarette, textile, woodworking, weaving, and beverage industries, and an inefficient oil refinery at Tamatave (Taomasina), but the economy remained anchored in its inherited, diversified agricultural base. After more than a decade of independence, the assets and liabilities described by a sympathetic commentator remained essentially where they had been at the birth of the republic:

> . . . a favourable hydrology over most of the island with a reliable rainfall and no great extremes of climate. The variety of present production, the degree of technology reached in certain regions and the existence of settled villages offer a favourable field for development. The unfavourable factors are that these communities are widely scattered and are linked by indifferent communications, which poses problems of marketing. Traditional marketing structures still result in the peasant's receiving low prices for his products and paying high prices for what he buys. Incentives are thus limited by market opportunities, while advances in technology depend on very extensive capital investments and on the availability of large numbers of technical personnel.[15]

By 1960, a full dozen commodities were being exported in statistically significant amounts from Great Island agriculture and mining industries. French control of production in geographically isolated foyers and a monopoly on transportation to pre-determined metropolitan markets assured the continuity of Madagascar's dependence on those markets. The island's roster of European settler families was modest by Algerian, South African, or Rhodesian standards, although important in comparison with West and

Central African settlement. At independence, the total of about 125,000 foreign residents constituted only 2.3 percent of the population. About 50,000 were metropolitan and Réunionnais French whose numbers were to decline to about 32,000 during the first republican decade. In addition, there were 50,000 Comoreans, mostly in the urban centers, 13,000 Muslim Indians, and 8,000 Chinese dispersed throughout the Great Island. Forty percent of the European and Creole community lived outside the major cities of the island, 6,000 of them estimated to be engaged in agriculture. Identified primarily as tradesmen, the Indians and some Chinese also acquired productive land and entered industrial fields as well.

Despite the modesty of numbers, private colonial interests claimed priority in official solicitude until well after independence. Their presence was felt in the exploitation of raw materials, land and transportation facilities, the production of cheap food and fibers for French and Réunionnais markets, and in their function as consumers of French manufactures, both directly and through the government services they enjoyed. Several oligopolistic trade companies grew out of the old monarchical system of concessions, adding their corporate voices to the demands of the colons and their Réunion island beneficiaries.

After disposing of the monarchy, the French found Madagascar's colonial raison d'être shifting rapidly away from the simple protection of property titles for Jean Laborde's heirs and other citizens. The island's economy lay open to exploitation for the benefit of industrial France. The colonial Government gradually underwrote the production and distribution practices of certain general *comptoirs* and a few specialized corporations (in meat packing and sugar milling, for instance) which dominated importing, exporting, and much domestic marketing until after the revolution of 1972. In a virtual renewal of the pre-capitalist form of charter protection, the companies of Marseille, Lyon, Rochefort, and a few others indulged in typically uncompetitive policies of speculation. Their investment rates and trade volume were kept low, their price mark-ups high. Owning considerable real estate and productive facilities, they enjoyed the services of integrated banks, a European maritime cartel, protectionist tariff schedules, and unlimited heights of financial repatriation. Their market domination, rationally shared with one another and, in restricted areas, with local Indian and Chinese traders, raised the cost of innovation and development prohibitively.

Nevertheless the comptoirs ensured orderly transfers of import and export goods and services while providing revenues for a complaisant state administration, both colonial and republican. They also guaranteed predominance of France and Franc Zone partners in the Malagasy economy. Imperial mercantilism had become sophisticated, its balance sheets articulated by double entries on behalf of metropolitan and overseas partners. For the fiscal burdens of carrying a colony, France thus obtained benefits in private citizen and entrepreneurial prosperity. These genuinely colonial assets ultimately outweighed Madagascar's imperial value as a strategic implantation in the southwestern sea.

The French colonial investment assumed even larger proportions through vigorous cultural evangelism among an eager, sedulous Malagasy population. The island's susceptibility to cultural influence had long been demonstrated in the absorption of various Asian and African influences, in nineteenth century experimentation with Arabic, and later, British linguistic and technical practice. Arabic-speaking and -writing communities (Antalaotra) lived in the north, east, and southeast of the island a millennium ago, and the *Sora-be*, or great writings, of the east coast Anteimoro use Arabic characters.[16] The King James Bible was used to record the vital passages of Andriana and Hova families of the later nineteenth century.

Malagasy assiduity was to be exploited systematically by a new metropole convinced of the importance of its cultural message to overseas interlocutors. While respectful of the rich rhetorical and musical traditions of the Malagasy, the spirituality and the capacity for organization displayed by Merina and other new subjects, Gallieni and his successors patronizingly understood these powers as aptitudes, rather than as cultural achievements. They pursued what they honestly regarded as beneficial assimilationist objectives among a population deemed in need of the precision and productivity of French civilization. Only by mastering France's cultural attributes could a colonial subject hope to obliterate frontiers of race, class, or social status.[17] The "psychology of colonisation" became exemplified for the author before first setting out for Madagascar in 1962, in a lecture by a French academic to an assembly of Malagasy believers in Paris, all of whom seemed to accept his thesis that France had really "donated our language for the expression of your thought."

Colonial cultural policy was pervasively executed through the school system, both public and private-religious. It dominated all socially formative institutions, from hospitals and law courts to banking and commerce to military services and the cinema. That policy converted habits of speech, dress, and hospitality. It determined qualifications for merit and achievement. All institutions of the colonized world reflected a powerful cultural invasion into an already established, flourishing, resilient, and tenacious civilization which simply had not prevailed in technological terms. Madagascar was called to join "Oriental France." Rewards to individual Malagasy, including the liberty to marry Europeans, depended on the acquisition of cultural proficiencies. The laureates in this regard, whose name became legion, nonethless almost invariably retained a normative duality or "double consciousness" testifying to the strength of their Malagasy heritage. From the patronized underground of exotica, a clamorous Malagasy civilization emerged several times during the colonial period. It surged forth in the uprisings of 1971 and 1972, after which a nationalist elite began switching languages back.

While French colonialism dictated social and political reality for three generations, Malagasy nationalism became largely identified with restoration of Merina hegemony. Several major movements of resistance to the French burgeoned in Imerina from the period of World War I through the first phase of independence. Despite the abortion of Gallieni's *politique des races*, the coastal people were consistently treated as hereditary victims of their quondam Merina rulers, hence as allies of the colonial administration. The political evolution of the 1950s and the transfer of competencies in 1960 primarily benefitted a côtier coalition with Roman Catholic influence and settler-comptoir alliances. Although the internal protectorates never materialized, the system of ethno-cultural blocs had effectively repressed Merina political sensibility.

From the outset, the revanchist Merina produced a series of idiomatic but futile combinations against French rule. Some of them operated in quasi-oriental clandestinity; others found support in the French Left and among non-Merina island patriots. Merina agitation continued from inside trade unions, from pulpits, in an emergent Malagasy language press, and among the students sent abroad by government, family, or employer to perfect their assimilibility.

For Malagasy students stranded in France by World War II, and for 10,000 Malagasy troops dispatched there to defend the metropole in Europe's own atavistic controversy, Malagasy nationalism assumed a new, separatist character. National spirit eventually spread over the island in this ebb tide of French prestige. It was reinforced in the successful 1942 invasion of Madagascar by British and South African troops seeking to preempt putative Japanese designs on the island's strategic facilities (then administered by Vichy). Once again, England, ally of Merina kings and queens, seemed to confront discredited French cupidity in the Grande Ile.

When France returned in late 1942 through an armistice with Britain, it was the indomitable Gaullists, not the vanquished regime of Vichy. This change revived Malagasy hopes for an end to colonial humiliation. They were encouraged further by General DeGaulle's Brazzaville declaration of 1944, pledging citizenship and parliamentary representation for indigenous populations. National sentiment was still largely, albeit not exclusively, Merina, thanks to their comparative cultural advantage and their access at Antananarivo to the distant world. A Betsileo teacher, Jean Ralaimongo, had returned from World War I service in Europe and from subsequent association with leftwing labor movements in France, to compaign until his death in 1938 for improvements in Malagasy working conditions and (together with Merina and French agitators) for rights of citizenship. When those rights were acquired under the first postwar Gaullist government, the nationalists began concentrating their efforts on obtaining self-rule. Malagasy claims for autonomy were pressed through the island's elected deputies in the French National Assembly. Parliamentary and provincial council elections of late 1946 and early 1947 were almost monopolized by the Democratic Movement for Malagasy Revival (MDRM), a Merina led but nonetheless universal nationalist party.

French repudiation of MDRM autonomy demands revealed what Malagasy regarded as racist perfidy, particularly when compared with the more respectful reception given similar Indo-Chinese claims. This perception was aggravated by the insouciant restoration of the entire French colonial structure, including the indigénat and forced labor schemes, as though nothing had been changed by the war. The 1942 transfer had left Vichy's civil service relatively intact; settler organizations and their press continued to oppose social and political reforms for Malagasy with pre-war vigor. Out of mass exasperation came the tragic, widespread rebellion of March 1947, the first and most enigmatic of postwar anticolonial upheavals. By December 1948, when the last elements of resistance were eliminated by French troops, Madagascar had lost a conservatively estimated 60,000 to 80,000 dead. Thousands of others emerged embittered from torture and persecution. The MDRM was outlawed and its three Assembly deputies sentenced to death on flimsy evidence for plotting the rebellion. The sentences were eventually commuted to fixed residence and the deputies—Joseph Ravoahangy, Joseph Raseta, and Jacques Rabemananjara—returned to active politics in Madagascar after independence in 1960.[18]

Metropolitian insistence on attributing the 1947 revolt to a primarily Merina conspiracy helped revive the old divide-and-rule ethnic policy. The territory was reorganized into five semi-autonomous, tribally defined provinces. The new structure paid deference to the decentralization of economic life, while defying both the quality of national feeling which had emerged during the war and the homogeneity of Malagasy cultural identity. These antitheses exemplify Madagascar's most characteristic political dialectic, a tension between centrifugal and centralizing forces which no administration has as yet been able to resolve.

The success of the national MDRM raised the specter of Merina leadership over a resurgent, unified Madagascar. Colonial authorities had countered by sponsoring a new populist adversary, the Party of the Malagasy Disinherited (PADESM), with participation almost systematically limited to côtiers. While unfavorably received by the electorate in November 1946 and January 1947, PADESM sat out the 1947–1948 rebellion and then, even without facing organized opposition, fell into splinters. Some of the surviving factions remerged in an orchestrated revival of political activity after a nine year moratorium. Beginning in 1956, they combined into the ultimately victorious Social Democratic Party (PSD) of Philibert Tsiranana, a school teacher from the Tsimihety people of the northwest. During the punitive interim, Malagasy nationalism again found channels of expression in an aroused labor movement, journalism, politically oriented churches, and Marxist study groups.

In the mid 1950s, a relatively sympathetic center-left coalition in Paris, testing the celebrated winds of change, allowed Madagascar to leave political purdah and to participate in the developmental institutions of the empire-wide *Loi Cadre*. By 1958 and the advent of DeGaulle's Fifth Republic, Malagasy political alignments had become largely polarized. Tsiranana's côtier-dominated, non-ideological PSD was able to transfer allegiance to DeGaulle from its original sponsors in the French Social Democratic Party (SFIO). It faced a rough synthesis of radical and bourgeois nationalist factions which had joined in a congress for independence at Tamatave (Taomasina) in May

1958. The resulting Congress Party (AKFM) campaigned against inclusion in the French Fifth Republic while the PSD favored continued affiliation with France in the referendum of October 1958. Acceptance of France's referendary thesis by seventy-seven percent of the voters thrust the PSD into majority status. Tsiranana's party quickly absorbed moderate and conservative opposition and swept all elections through 1972, except for municipal contests in Antananarivo and some other nationalist urban centers.

By virtue of the 1958 referendum, Madagascar joined ten other African territories awarded the title of republic within the French community, albeit without the enjoyment of sovereign rights. Tsiranana thereupon accompanied several other African heads of limited government into junior minister status in the French cabinet. The autonomy designed in 1958 at Paris resembled, ironically, the status demanded by the MDRM in 1946, but the degree of domestic self-rule which had seemed so shocking to French sensibilities then was soon to prove inadequate for self-determination to Africans and Malagasy. Various internal jurisdictions methodically devolved upon the new republic during 1959, but after the secession of Mali from its shortlived union with Senegal, Tsiranana decided to follow the Malians in petitioning Paris for full independence. France concurred, and the remaining attributes of sovereignty were bestowed on Malagasy authority in a series of fourteen negotiated agreements signed April 2, 1960.

Rise and Fall of the Tsiranana Republic, 1960–1972

Following a convention prevailing throughout French-speaking Africa, the Franco-Malagasy agreements transferred powers (not power) to the young republic. They bound its government to articles of respect for essential French interests in the island's economic, cultural, and strategic assets.[19] For more than a decade, the Tsiranana republic lived the scenario cautiously prepared for it in the bilateral agreements. While attributing its "recovery of sovereignty" to General DeGaulle and finding security within a community of Franc Zone republics knotted into French institutions, Madagascar was in fact returning to a stage of qualified sovereignty envisaged under protectorate relationships which had failed realization in the 1880s and 1890s. The island remained headquarters for France's Western Indian Ocean defense forces. The new Malagasy franc (FMG) rode the coasters of metropolitan currency fortunes, pegged by fifty to one to the French franc. Payments clearances operated through the Bank of France, assuring priorities for Franc Zone sources and markets. Unrestricted convertibility between the two francs allowed French residents and companies to repatriate assets rather than spend or invest them in the island economy. A highly centralized education and job qualification system guaranteed France pre-eminence in the training and intellectual orientation of aspiring Malagasy, whether nationalist in persuasion or otherwise. Buildings, statues, street names, and other emblems of colonial prerogative remained in place. The French High Commissioner (ambassador) held the status of diplomatic corps dean, regardless of longevity of accreditation. While the old palace of the Queens remained a historical museum, the ambassador continued to occupy the midcity villa and gardens enjoyed by the line of colonial administrators who had governed at Antananarivo in the name of France.

Honest defenders of the 1960 Franco-Malagasy association correctly, if ingenuously, point out its entirely voluntary nature.[20] The Malagasy Republic could count on substantial privileges in French economic and technical assistance, cultural relations, diplomatic and intelligence exchange, balance of payments stabilization, and the like. But if the relationship was not one-way, it was also astonishingly narrow. Malagasy policy had to be scrupulously coordinated to favor France whenever the latter's interests were directly engaged—as in decolonization disputes, nuclear testing, maintenance of overseas military bases, and the advantages of EEC association. That policy became skeptical and ambivalent where France was not immediately concerned—as in southern African politics and relations with many agencies of the United Nations. It was allowed to display heterodoxy only where France was unharmed by Malagasy deviation—in maintaining ties with Taiwan and, after 1967, with Israel, for instance.[21]

Not saying "non" to France allowed a people to escape the vindictive retaliation which had made a shambles of Sekou Touré's option for Guinean independence in 1958. Malagasy nationalists felt the relationship nonetheless as a means of retaining French supervision without colonial responsibility, assuring the predominance of Paris in a context of states cautioned to honor that predominance. Nationalists resented the protection which the association provided, in their estimation, to the acquiescent government in power. For its part, however, the PSD republic nurtured an almost obsessive concern for regime survival against the restiveness of a highly skeptical population.

By refusing to join the nationalist parties at the May 1958 Taomasina independence congress, the Social Democratic Party demonstrated its fidelity to piecemeal collaborative evolution. It faithfully followed the trajectory enunciated two years earlier in the French Socialist Loi Cadre and extended, with modifications, by DeGaulle. The PSD thus established an alternative to the nationalist drive for dissociation from a Fourth French Republic already at bay over Indo China and Algeria. Fidelity to the beleaguered metropole enabled Tsiranana's party to organize throughout the island without impediment on the part of omnicompetent local administrators. No nationalist faction after the banished MDRM ever developed that opportunity. Their movement broke into local and ethnic identities even with the formation of the AKFM Congress and its claim to represent the MDRM heritage.

Local PSD notables, trade union officials, women and youth section leaders encountered the AKFM in Antananarivo, Antseranana (Diego Suarez), and other cities. They faced and subdued the MONIMA (Movement for Malagasy Independence) in the capital and the South, the Christian Democrats (UDC) in the East, Norbert Zafimahova's Democratic and Social Union (UDSM) on the southeast coast, and other groupings, most of them ephemeral, on their way to identification of the PSD with Malagasy statehood.[22] By 1970, the PSD claimed a million members out of a total population of 7.2 million. The organized opposition had been reduced to the AKFM's capital city redoubt, MONIMA's harrassed avatars in the remote South, and an occasional, ill-fated emergence of a "third force" among various maverick urban politicians. The party's cohesion depended on Tsiranana's considerable personal force and the loyalty of local and regional chairmen who invariably sustained their partisanship through simultaneous elected or appointive office. This relatively new political elite seldom obtained control of major trans-regional production or distribution networks. Those assets were dominated by French, Indian, and Chinese minorities as well as by the old national bourgeoisie of Antananarivo.[23]

Eventually, Tsiranana's party grew top-heavy in a process of aggrandizement by party leaders and diminishing returns for the grass-roots faithful. Regional mandarins continued to obtain patronage for clients and cabinet posts for themselves, but their demands began to exceed individual or collective productivity by the mid–1960s. Initiatives for internal party discipline were urged by party Secretary André Resampa, who served as Interior Minister and later as Vice President and briefly heir-designate to Tsiranana. Reform efforts seldom reached implementation, however. The President insisted on an inclusive, mass-party following for his national leadership even when the returns for party loyalty had thinned out dramatically. Tsiranana's personal standing was demonstrated in a ninety percent reelection victory over several opponents in 1965. He tended, however, to consider his own popularity tantamount to a universal endorsement of his policies and the party which he had founded.

Tsiranana's quest for universality inflated the ranks of party beneficiaries. A huge, academically trained but atrophied civil service furnished the jobs demanded by the expanding labor force. Much of the bureaucracy was composed of Merina and others fundamentally unsympathetic to the PSD. Their activity was subject to a directorial clique of Tsiranana loyalists and regional warlords advancing toward gerontocracy. Tsiranana himself periodically denounced PSD sclerosis and government bureaucratization. He admitted in 1967 that 50,000 functionaries were achieving less than one-fourth that number had produced before independence. Powerless to revise the institutions which sustained his own position and which depended in turn on his prestige, he looked at home for scapegoats and overseas for salvation.[24]

At the epitome of the new Malagasy state, the PSD's development strategy consisted in expansion of agricultural export production, rapid exploitation of mineral resources, a favorable climate for private investment, and increases in tourist revenues. Categoric anti-communism, demonstrations of political efficacy and of steady French favor were supposed to attract European, American, and South African capital toward the island, but residual colonial interests effectively discouraged competition. Projects were inefficiently implemented and the serious improvement needed in infrastructure never obtained adequate financing.

Nor did the overwhelmingly peasant population respond to the PSD's highly politicized, hortatory approach to rural production at the grassroots. An administration of PSD controlled communes was transected by low budget development projects, isolated extension technology and "rural animation" training. The system served to collect taxes and stablize social relationships at subsistence levels without increasing productive investment or the amenities of life in the countryside.[25] Plantation and mining exports were providing the only domestic margins on which development policy could form, but their profits were banked largely in Europe. Moreover, these assets were radically sensitive to market price fluctuations, weather, and other vicissitudes. The flood of peasant sons and daughters to the cities aggravated the urban-rural disequilibrium even farther. Potentially productive, reasonably organized, astute, Tsiranana's Malagasy Republic began to be unable to make its own living.

By 1968, PSD strategy was supported by substantial overseas-financed public investment in "major projects" (*les grandes opérations*).These schemes included some idiosyncratic methods for technical transfer, but lacked the marketing control or fiscal incentives to win over a recalcitrantly skeptical peasantry. Nor did private capital materialize on the scale envisaged in the planning, despite a range of inducements. Foreign monopolies and contractors returned their revenues to Europe and the local sources of capital speculated in real estate and other largely urban opportunities. Net disinvestment was estimated by a sympathetic Tsiranana government official at about fifty million dollars per year.[26]

By the end of the Republic's first critical decade, the island's dependence on French public assistance had begun to cause alarm. From 1959 to 1970, direct French non-military aid had exceeded $400 million and was running at an annual rate of $70 million. French imports and exports had also doubled, still claiming 70 percent of Malagasy foreign trade. French interests owned almost three-fourths of Madagascar's property other than real estate. French investment was solicited and protected with reverence, albeit under diminishing returns for the Malagasy economy.

Yet it was Frenchmen who made that economy function. Notwithstanding rhetorically vigorous campaigns for "malgachisation" of public and private employment, French nationals occupied positions of managerial and technical importance throughout government service and major enterprises across the great island. Europeans, Réunionnais, and Muslim Indians holding French passports operated substantial import and export commerce, light industries, and plantations with a touch of cosmopolitanism characteristic of overseas France. To convert key personnel of banks, businesses, and marketing institutions "too rapidly" would have doubtless altered their operating style, rendering them less accessible to other French institutions. Understandably, resident Frenchmen regarded such a change as ineluctably prejudicial to efficiency. Understandably, Malagasy policy-makers, trained by France, agreed.

In the border arenas of trade, finance, and technology transfer, French economic aid, budgetary guidance, diplomatic advice, and institutional experience stabilized the overall privileged relationship. When necessary, France mediated Malagasy contact with the world external to the French Community and Franc Zone. A vital, and typically Gallic commitment to the universal educational system brought a thousand teachers into Malagasy schools. They accounted for half the total contingent of technical agents (*assistants techniques*) assigned to the island during the 1960–1972 period. Competent Malagasy, many of them Merina, were uninterested in teaching or unacceptable to a national school system, or both. Standards for examinations, school passes, diplomas, and all important civil service and private sector jobs were set in France. The central authority was considered modern because it was French in inspiration and conduct.

But France, too, was faltering again. French political life had been severely shaken in 1968. DeGaulle retired a year later. In Madagascar, economic stagnation was generally acknowledged and the regime could now blame French apathy and stinginess, rather than its own mistakes. A hesitant effort at diversification in investment, trade, and technology led to somewhat ephemeral arrangements with the United States, West Germany, Japan, South Africa, and other partners. Relations with the USSR, China, and allied states were hindered by Tsiranana's personal suspicions of communist intrigue, especially on behalf of the AKFM, which regularly proclaimed its "scientific socialist" orientation. Fearing inundation of his underpopulated island by Asian hordes, the Malagasy President held Peking to be Madagascar's greatest single threat despite an extraordinary absence of any evidence of Chinese interest in the place. A 1964 trade agreement with the Soviet Union was voided by the Malagasy in 1968 after four years of inactivity, in protest over Moscow's military repression in Czechoslovakia. Soviet and other socialist states frequented the island for little more than avowedly scientific and cultural purposes—oceanographic ship calls, for example. While the Moscow "menace" evoked regular alarm within the Tsiranana regime, the USSR seemed content to cultivate its African interests on the continent, considering Madagascar's French allegiances as doubtlessly preferable to the American alternative.

Initiatives from the United States came rarely, and were welcome only if they portended no structural adaptations away from vested French interests. Tsiranana undertook a singularly unproductive visit to the United States in 1964. Americans dug water wells in the provinces, helped build a multinational oil refinery at Taomasina and regularly bought most of the great island's vanilla. NASA operated a major satellite tracking station outside Antananarivo. Washington anonymously subsidized small-scale, relatively effective technical assistance projects by Israel and Taiwan, repaid in Malagasy diplomatic hostility to the Arab states and Peking. But the United States had little effect on productive activity, infrastructure, or cultural and technical affinities. Even the Peace Corps proved ultimately undesirable. When necessary, ritual denunciations of American conspiracies were issued by the President on convenient information from French services.[27]

Tsiranana and South Africa proved more useful to each other. The Malagasy helped promote Pretoria's dalliance in 1969 and 1970 with selected

African states beyond South Africa's immediate chain of neighbors. Encouraged by France, the "dialogue" with Madagascar accumulated a considerable investment portfolio, including several tourist hotels, joint mining ventures, and a new deep-water port on the northwest coast intended to relieve Taomasina of its overflow bunkering traffic after the blockage of Suez in 1967. Some three-fourths of the 8,000 foreign tourists visiting the island in 1971 were South Africans. Their government discreetly opened an "information office" in Antananarivo.

These connections were persistently defended by the Malagasy as of purely business significance, devoid of favor for the detestable practice of apartheid. Nevertheless, Tsiranana habitually complimented Malawi's Kamuzu Banda for his unabashed "realism" over South Africa. He readily accepted the British Conservative decision to supply military spare parts to Pretoria in 1970 in the name of common Indian Ocean security against regional Soviet and Chinese influence. He could not conceive that such weaponry would find use against "our African brethren" in Southern Africa. Madagascar adopted deliberately cool attitudes in OAU debates on Zimbabwe-Rhodesia, Namibia, and the Portuguese territories. Foreign Minister Jacques Rabemananjara, once a nationalist hero, took the lead in the Pretorian rapprochement. "There is no question for the present of establishing diplomatic relations with South Africa," Rabemananjara explained in September 1970.

> Madagascar formally condemns the policy of apartheid. But this does not prevent Madagascar, true to its policy of peace and understanding with everybody, from having good neighborly relations with that country as with all her neighbors.[28]

In contrast to Rabemananjara, his principal rival for the presidential succession, André Resampa, persistently played the African nationalist theme within Tsiranana's broad coalition. As party Secretary and Interior Minister, among the youngest of Tsiranana's barons, Resampa was responsible for the modicum of rejuvenation and discipline tolerated by the President within his universal consensus. Resampa boycotted all the South Africa rendezvous, declined protocolary relations with most Antananarivo embassies, urged revisions of the 1960 agreements (which he had personally negotiated for Tsiranana in Paris). In various ways, including personal incorruptibility, Resampa qualified as dangerously unreliable in the books of the French establishment. His numerous enemies included the French landed and business interests and the protected Asian minorities, as well as the Merina middle class which despised his "African" affinities and his tendency to ride roughly over the AKFM and other opposition.

From his own bailiwick at Morondava on the west coast, Resampa organized autonomous development programs among communal syndicates of local Sakalava and Bara people. These producers and marketing associations exported their lima beans to England, not France, and operated without French or Franco-Asian intermediaries. Their projects included expansion of beef production and organization of a new citrus fruit industry with exclusively Malagasy funds and Israeli technical assistance. Israelis had also been responsible for helping organize the Interior Ministry's efficient security police, the Republican Security Forces (FRS), later transferred into his own office by an increasingly nervous President.

As Resampa's Morondava syndicate became a bellwether for development activity, Tsiranana alternated between approval and suspicion of his ambitious lieutenant. His fluctuations of attitude in turn precipitated moods of anxiety among the sensitive population which itself wanted to know what to make of Resampa. In early 1970, the fifty-eight year old President's health suddenly failed. Tsiranana spent four months in a French hospital. The Republic carried on business in the traditional way through the year, obtaining South African capital, French advice, new PSD majorities in the September parliamentary elections, and suppression of popular discontent—riots, sabotage, vindictive brush fires. André Resampa was clearly interested in operating the shop in the President's absence. He personally supervised formation of the PSD candidate lists, forced several major changes in the unwieldy cabinet after the elections, and had himself promoted formally within the hierarchy. But he did not directly attack the President's authority.

In October, following the PSD parliamentary victory, Tsiranana reorganized his forty-eight ministries into four super-agencies, each headed by a Vice President, all veterans of PSD incumbency, all of them côtiers. He justified the move by reference to his own fragile health and the accumulating burdens of development. Although the quartet included Calvin Tsiebo, hitherto Tsiranana's loyal lone Vice President, precedence and thus heir-apparentness, was explicitly awarded to Resampa. The younger man represented, in the President's words, "the future of the country [and] the socialist orientation which I hold dear." In charge of agricultural and industrial production, foreign and domestic trade as well as his strategic Interior Ministry, Resampa thus assumed czarist powers in a system begging for new energy. He had inadequate occasion to satisfy those appeals, however, despite the vigor which he brought to the task. By the end of the year, Resampa had introduced unused land confiscation measures, investigations of profiteering, aggressive reshuffling of the provincial bureaucracy, and punitive action against bush arsonists and tax evaders. On November 8, 1970, he obtained a PSD resolution to review the advantages and disadvantages of all international cooperation agreements, particularly the ten-year-old accords with France.

But Resampa's heavy-handed, statist coercions never won the confidence of the Malagasy villagers, except, perhaps among his own people of Morondava. In March 1971, the island's impoverished south exploded in revolt against more than a decade of central government neglect. Like France after World War Two, PSD authority had come back with ferocity after betraying its own weakness. Resampa was an exposed symbol of that intolerable reign, the spearhead of its restoration. As unrest spread to the Plateau, a fifth Vice President, the loyal Merina jurist Alfred Ramangasoavina, was appointed and Resampa was demoted to the Agriculture Ministry and the second Vice Presidency. In April and May, he was steadily stripped of power amid rumors, at first denied by Tsiranana, that Resampa had actually connived with the peasant rebels and even plotted the President's assassination. Maintaining the aura of indispensable statesman, Tsiranana reassured the public, and particularly Resampa's enemies, of his own availability for reelection as President in 1972.

On June 1, 1971, bathing in new PSD dithyrambic, Tsiranana put Resampa in jail on absurdly contrived conspiratorial grounds. The charges were never presented to a court and Tsiranana later retracted them entirely. Once his "dear dauphin," Resampa was now supposed to have plotted with an unidentified foreign power to divide the nation and satisfy his overweening ambition. His name was not mentioned at the next party congress in September. The offending alien power, never publicly exposed, was evidently meant to be the United States, even though Resampa had kept a disdainful distance from American officials for over a decade. Later, Tsiranana sought to link Resampa to the Southern Jacqueries led by former Tulear Mayor Monja Jaona, one of Resampa's most implacable foes whose conspiracy had already been denounced by Tsiranana as inspired by Communist China. This implicit Sino-American association via Resampa doubtless produced no little surprise in Peking and Washington. By that time the unoffending American Ambassador, whose principal function had been to induce American private investment into Madagascar's faltering economy, had been summarily sent away with five of his officers.[29]

A year later, after he had resumed full charge of the PSD, secured his own reelection, and been overthrown, Tsiranana recanted his charges against the United States, subsequently withdrawing the accusations against Resampa. By the time the former dauphin was released from detention on Sainte Marie island (Nosy Boraha), on June 8, 1972, Tsiranana himself had fallen from power. The ailing President had gambled in 1972 that neither Washington nor Resampa would possess enough popular sympathy to frustrate his effort to use them as scapegoats for riots and economic disaster. He won, temporarily. Resampa's downfall pleased abundant enemies within and without the party, and the United States was regarded with indifference by most Malagasy. Tsiranana had not calculated, however, on the erosion of his own position from a very different direction.

Under Philibert Tsiranana, Malagasy security had been entirely invested in France. Madagascar represented a major link in an integrated strategic system established in Djibouti, Réunion, Mayotte in the Comoros, with extensions westward across the African continent to Dakar and eastward to Tahiti. France maintained naval, air, and Foreign Legion facilities at Diego Suarez in the north and at Ivato airfield near the capital. French personnel occupied key positions in military and civilian services, including the Presidency's intelligence corps. Training of Malagasy counterparts was in French hands. France had exclusive access to production of thorianite and other fissionable minerals exported from the island. As one of his ministers later assessed Tsiranana's reliance on the limited potency of France in a world polarized among greater forces,

The former colonizer is the middle-level power which can reassure a Tsiranana who feels the need of a power greater than himself, but was seriously disappointed by the United States after his official visit to that country. France guarantees its protection against the external enemy and, on request, the internal enemy as well. Cooperation [read: French aid] assumes diverse shapes, most effectively in the financial arena where the young state is relieved from anxiety over its balance of payments.[30]

Yet the young state felt itself insecurely established in the world. The French relationship was not merely bilateral: it became symbiotic, organic. Anything that weakened France in the southern hemisphere represented a threat to Madagascar. By extension, this concern should include overall Western interests, but Tsiranana was persuaded that the United States and other natural allies failed to appreciate the importance of French and Malagasy security to the struggle against Communism. Soviet arms in Somalia and South Yemen, Chinese deliveries of railway construction supplies to Dar es Salaam, radicalism in Burundi or South Asia, East European training of guerrillas in the wars against Rhodesia and Portuguese Mozambique were all interpreted in the same sense, all subjects of lectures by the Malagasy leader to the Americans and Westerners at large. In his Manichean universe, domestic opponents turned into enemies, subversive of his perfection, prejudicing his version of President Suharto's Indonesian *Pantjasila*. Lurking in all corners of the complex island, these demonic agencies were reflexively identified with the Marxist international, manipulated by some external agency hostile to Malagasy stability.

Very little active hostility has been demonstrated on the part of external agents, but domestic opponents of the regime existed, in spite of Tsiranana's persistence in forging national consensus through the PSD. Although obscured by rituals of acquiescence, nationalist antagonism grew fiercely over the twelve years in which Tsiranana's social democracy reigned. That was a rather longer lease than many others had enjoyed after the dawn of Francophone African republicanism in 1956–1960. But Madagascar was ultimately unable to absorb the disappointments of limited self-determination and the realization of French weakness as thoroughly as Senegal; or to turn Western investment and alien African labor to domestic advantage as emphatically as Ivory Coast; or to obtain French guarantees for regime stability as clearly as Gabon. Experiencing statistical growth without per-ceptible redistribution and international security without independence, the Malagasy lost faith. The main pillars of state authority began crumbling along with the grandeur of DeGaulle and Tsiranana's identification with his mystique.

None of the opposition factions which coalesced against the PSD regime by the early 1970s needed to be "teleguided" from nefarious laboratories in the outer world, as Tsiranana repeatedly charged. Three different forces focused on what seemed to them the incorrigible vacuity of his system. Traditional Merina nationalists, peasant recalcitrants, and urban radicals came to agree on one principle: the PSD regime offered nothing to their respective growing constituencies. Its dynamic had short-circuited into a self-perpetuating bureaucratic state within an increasingly alienated republic.

Through the 1960s, the AKFM (Congress) party interwove several strands of residual Merina nationalism into a vocal but relatively ineffectual parliamentary opposition. Parliament had itself dwindled into an avuncular repository for executive policy statements. The opposition party retained control over the symbolically important, but politically emasculated Antananarivo City Council. Some great landed families and Merina businessmen supported the AKFM, allowing their olympian disdain of the côtier PSD and their resentment of French extraterritorial privilege to be expressed in Marxist terms by the party's ideologues and a cluster of doctrinaire newspapers. AKFM legislative representation declined from nine National Assembly deputies in 1960 to three (of 107) in 1965 and 1970. This trio of MP's, all from the capital, displayed good behavior as the Republic's entitled opposition, taking the government's moderate social democracy at face value and endorsing much of its economic and social legislation. As late as 1970, party President Richard Andriamanjato, a Protestant pastor and perpetually-elected Mayor of Antananarivo, estimated at eighty percent the AFKM's concurrence with the PSD's overall program. Principal quarrels emerged in foreign affairs where Madagascar's flirtation with South Africa and its tight alignment with France offended nationalist, as well as "scientific socialist" sensibilities.

In hindsight, the opposition's strong 1969 and 1970 electoral showing in most of the island's main towns should have been interpreted as more than foreign policy dissent. Nevertheless, the avowedly Marxist AKFM never mobilized popular enthusiasm on a scale broader than its urban bourgeoisie. In 1971, Andriamanjato even had the opportunity to refuse an ambassadorial assignment (to execute the very policy he was rejecting). The post was to be Belgrade, the first Marxist capital perceived as eligible for resident Malagasy diplomacy. That he declined the honor is less remarkable than the fact that, this late in a mortal political crisis, Tsiranana was still seeking to neutralize his political demons by absorbing them.

The incident also testifies to the gradual domestication of the opposition nationalist party. No longer was it a mortal enemy to Tsiranana's universal consensus. Shortly thereafter, the AKFM proved unable to take advantage of purges and defections within the Resampist PSD leftwing. Nor could it profit from the prohibition of its nationalist competitor, the MONIMA party, in 1971. AKFM complicity within the beleaguered system was even to disqualify the party from the impending upheaval in Antananarivo's streets. New urban mass forces had obviously overtaken the sedate, verbalistic opposition. Yet with all its contradictions, the Independence Congress party survived the precipitations of 1972 (although its bastion, the City Hall building, did not). Without a truly revolutionary program, with a dwindling support base under attack from the left, the AKFM has nonetheless been able to offer its organizational acumen and its informational services to each successive power in Antananarivo after 1972. Through this apparatus, and

Rev. Andriamanjato's national prestige as leader of the 1960s opposition, the party has retained a position as representative of traditional nationalism within the Second Republic of President Didier Ratsiraka.

Less conspicuous than the AKFM, but less equivocal in its attitudes, MONIMA appeared and disappeared in the political firmament of the remote South, depending on the fortunes of the peasantry and the fluctuating credibility of the PSD in the area. Conveyor of grievances against pricing and tax discrimination, victim of political strongarming and the arrogance of PSD power acting through local administration, MONIMA realized periodic reincarnations during the Tsiranana 1960s. For leadership, the party benefited from the tenacious, dignified populism of Monja Jaona, once Mayor of Toleara (Tulear) who remains to this day an uncompromising advocate for the revolutionary "wretched of the earth." A few urban sympathizers gave the party a periscope for national affairs beyond the vast and deep Malagasy South. Later, after Tsiranana's fall, Monja has been periodically in and out of President Ratsiraka's governments and had the courage to compaign against Ratsiraka's November 1982 bid for a second term. His strong showing in Antananarivo and other cities during that campaign represented a legible barometer of urban dissatisfaction, much as Andriamanjato's AKFM had done throughout the First Republic.

The final phase of that republic was in fact inaugurated by another in Madagascar's long history of peasant uprisings—this time emerging in April 1971 under MONIMA guidance. The revolt was preceded by years of accumulating complaints against rural neglect and administrative failures, encroaching drought and soil impoverishment, price gouging by hawkers of water, profiteering by PSD notables, exodus of youth, unimproved communications, and rising taxes. The rural population had reacted for years in acts of passive disobedience, pastoral arson, banditry, and increasingly sharp criticism (often in satiric minstrelsy). Finally, as the paternalistic monolith of PSD power seemed first to weaken around its stricken leader and then to return with ferocious ardor under André Resampa, the revolt erupted. On the night of April 1, 1971, three days after the twenty-fourth anniversary of the 1947 rebellion, attacks by several dozen men from all southern ethnic groups struck ten or twelve different armed points in Tuléar Province. Like the earlier great rebellion, the 1971 uprising was evidently well coordinated and, like that assault on French authority, it proved extravagantly ambitious, doomed to futility. After failing to suppress news of the outbreak for a time, the Government declared it terminated on April 4, admitting to thirty dead, all of them rebels. Tsiranana's April 6 radio address appealed for tranquillity and invoked the regime's usual suspects— Maoist China operating through MONIMA seditionists to exploit the illiterate farmers and cattle people of the South. As an opposition newspaper pointed out, genuine Chinese aid should have been able to provide those poor dupes with more impressive insurrectionary implements than the spears and shotguns with which they assaulted police and Gendarmerie posts.[31]

By mid-April, 800 people had been arrested, the unofficial death toll had mounted over 300, and Vice President Tsiebo, a southerner, had filed a

report exonerating local PSD authorities against charges of direct or indirect
provocation. Apparently, there had been no mutinies and no casualties
among the security forces. The revolt was simply a suicidal, if manipulated,
jacquerie by some disgruntled peasants. This was not 1947. Tracked to his
hiding place on the twenty-fourth, Monja Joana was arrested. He claimed
full responsibility for the revolt. MONIMA was banned, but independent
commentators stressed the importance of redressing inequities which the
self-styled Maoist party had only mobilized.[32] An amnesty for some 1,000
militants in mid-May prepared for an extraordinary public reconciliation
between Monja and Tsiranana who visited the rebel leader in his place of
fixed residence. The President promised relief to Southerners now that he
and Monja could jointly blame André Resampa for the underlying causes
of peasant dissatisfaction.

But the Tsiranana state never recovered from the Tulear insurrection
and its urban reverberations.

What the [Social Democratic] system could not contain, either in the non-
Merina PSD left wing or in the traditional Merina AKFM, was the revolutionary
force of a new generation that did not need French standards to define
Malagasy aspirations. This new force did not accept the long-standing myth
of Malagasy quiescence—interpreted by foreigners as supine fatalism, by
missionaries as piety, and by employers as guileless passivity. Acts of violent
protest have indeed been frequent in Malagasy history, and yet they came
invariably as a surprise to authorities. The movement of 1971-1972 is no
exception.[33]

The third source of the Malagasy revolution formed slowly through the
1960s with the confluence of urban opposition factions. These systematic
dissenters had separate agendas and their own reasons for rejecting the
AKFM's mixture of bourgeois-Marxism and ethnic nationalism. The new
contestants ranged from trade unionists irritated by PSD courtship of
business, to students and intellectuals of the generation of 1968 (some of
them French) chafing under "cultural imperialism" and diploma paternalism,
to a growing army of increasingly articulate urban unemployed. This diverse
ethnic and ideological movement found a popular audience through the
press, pulpits, and wind caves of Antananarivo and in certain provincial
towns. Like the epidemic brushfires of Tulear, the gestures of urban protest
multiplied as the government floundered. An ailing President and his arthritic
machine seemed able to offer only appeals to order and patience, denunciations of "teleguided" criminal perpetrators, and falsified claims of social
and economic progress.

Typically for the under-developed world, Madagascar's cities had been
obtaining a preponderance of investment, unproductive employment, subsidized food supplies, and public services. The island had only a tiny
industrial proletariat and a large population of craftsmen, small tradespeople,
and service employees, all of whom eventually found themselves associated
in dissent with the chronic unemployed and miserable transients on the

margins of Antananarivo. The cost of living was rising, a new sales tax began operating in 1971, shortages of essential supplies became habitual, family allowances and minimum wage levels remained where they had been since 1963 (until July 1971, when a ten percent rise triggered a much higher jump in inflation). An improved economic performance in 1970 failed to reach the growing numbers of Malagasy in despair. Soothing statistics could no longer overcome the anxiety evoked by the President's long illness, the harrowing of the ruling circles following his return, and his subsequent Oedipal struggle with Resampa. Nor could Tsiranana's flamboyant recovery of control reassure Malagasy of their universal stake in a dynamic which seemed to be guided, if at all, toward the conspicuous advantage of a few no longer venerable party oligarchs. The chasm widened flagrantly between articulate poor and profiteering rich. For the first time since independence, official corruption became as notoriously endemic as it was said to have been for years on the African continent.

Conceding shortcomings, but avoiding responsibility, the resurrected President pledged a thorough cleansing of the party and bureaucracy which had been allowed (by Resampa) to become exploitatively corrupt. On January 30, 1972, Tsiranana was reelected by a ritualistic ninety-nine percent of the registered vote, contrived by the customary tragi-comical devices of party vote-mongering, chicanery and terrorism (some reports calculate the tally as 120 percent of registered voters). The electoral exercise had obviously lost whatever meaning it once possessed. Even the President no longer seemed to have confidence in his ability to effect change: the same tired faces and tiring ministerial names were appointed to the cabinet after his investiture for the hallowed third term.

On May 11 when his health seemed again in jeopardy and his entire political edifice was crumbling, the most Tsiranana could do was envisage the appointment of a prime minister—a gesture to those who might have accepted his indispensability but not his immortality. During the critical years 1970 and 1971, dynamic Malagasy forces were unpersuaded that the several party convulsions represented in fact the reforms they were portrayed to be. They doubted that the Republic obtained the same advantage from its French association as did its governing clique. Nor could one believe that Tsiranana's acceptance of a third mandate would initiate any benefits not already digested or rejected by the nation, despite the President's apparent recovery from his afflictions of a year earlier and his single-handed assault on the party's Resampist apparatus in mid-1971.

Ironically for social theory, the simmering anger of unemployed and marginal urban populations was brought to boil by the agons of a "spoiled elite," students at the University and a medical college. Intellectuals had always been held suspect by a government of politicians and functionaries. Chronically infested by Merina revanchism, corrupted by juvenile adventure stories from the May 1968 Parisian barricades, the 6,000 University students at Antananarivo were considered cozened by a French Maoist corps of professors and researchers. Radical Frenchmen and their Malagasy accomplices had already been apprehended and/or expelled, one of them in 1969 for clandestinely circulating ridicule of government policy, several more in 1970 for plotting some shadowy iniquity against the President, forty more in 1971 for conspiring against the regime.[34] These were the most sharply ideological expressions of a universal discontent. They focussed ridicule on Madagascar's political, economic, and cultural subservience, the vapidity of socialism under the PSD regime, and the apparent futility of grand development designs by a government unable to keep its own discipline or to execute simple distribution of unexploited pasture land. From Tsiranana's viewpoint, nothing could reconcile what he called spoiled idealistic children to the realities of social responsibility—except the sedative assignment of jobs within the hierarchy. Those assignments had by now become very scarce.

Beginning in 1971 with a strike at the seventy year-old Befalatanana Medical School in the capital, students began to attack the post-colonial supremacy of France over Malagasy education and other national institutions. While the President complained for the record that a few criminals were bedevilling Madagascar's "children" into Francophobia, his government temporized. It made indiscriminate arrests, seeking to extirpate a purely French nest of radicalism. But it also promised to negotiate with France over diploma equivalences, examinations, languages of instruction, and curriculum. Unappeased, and perhaps hearing the distant uproar in rural Tulear, the students resumed their demonstrations, forcing authorities to close the University during four weeks in March-April 1971. A battery of educational reforms was indeed announced during May-September, ostensibly satisfying several demands for a relatively autonomous system (with diploma values still guaranteed by France), but the measures were slow in implementation.[35]

A new series of demonstrations began in early 1972, led again by the Befalatanana medical students whose home-grown diplomas were denied equivalence with the French MD awarded at the University. Again the official reaction was repressive and again the government underestimated the ability of this apparently isolated confrontation to ignite the entire academic sector. The protests spread to other Malagasy cities. By late April 1972, when the Ministries of Education and Health realized the need to mollify the Befalatanana claimants, that dispute had outgrown the original range of grievances. Violating academic liberties, the security police (FRS) attacked the main campus in suburban Antananarivo on May 12 to hunt ring leaders of the disturbances. A succession of plenary arrests and beatings, deportations to the island prison of Nosy Lava, and bloody skirmishes with police brought the University into downtown Antananarivo on May 13. Initiating violence for the first time, the students were thereupon joined by allies across the spectrum of rebellion.

Spanning the gulf between the "modern" intellectuals and less privileged Malagasy urban classes stood an irrepressible if ill-trained and impecunious opposition press. Edited by an older generation of under-educated, politicized

Merina social critics, this "fourth estate" operated within an Aeolian rumor climate around the capital. It was subject to only partially effective government censorship. Repeated seizures of editions and incarcerations of journalists merely invigorated speculation regarding anything the government wished to leave unpublished. This fragile, semi-skilled structure of social commentary was reinforced from certain Protestant Church pulpits in Imerina and even by trade union officials whose function heretofore had been restricted to adjudication of workplace grievances.

Through a social chemistry that remains unclarified even now, the disparate interests of this elder Merina petite-bourgeoisie coincided during 1971-1972 with the blind outrage of a Lumpenproletariat and the fury of the Tulear peasantry. The impact converted a series of otherwise containable student protests into revolutionary concatenation. Commenting prophetically in September 1971 on Tsiranana's campaign to purge Resampa's "progressive revisionists" from the PSD, the Catholic weekly *Lumière*'s astute editorialist, André Ravatomanga, foresaw some of the new circumstances. He held both PSD and AKFM radicalism tame

> compared to other emerging political tendencies which more readily attract a large proportion of young people than the sclerotic ideologies of the two official parties; it is these tendencies which will create the Madagascar of tomorrow.[36]

These new forces did form specific organizations, some of them very much in evidence today. Students and dissident faculty followed the usual pattern of politicized French educational syndicates, while secondary school factions formed satellite committees and action groups in general support of the protest. Leaders emerged out of the urban cauldrons identified in Malagasy as *Zoam* (roughly translatable as "the down and out"). They claimed to represent the inert rabble cowering in doorways and lining pavements of the billowing towns where excitement cost money and work was rare. These proletarian standard-bearers suddenly crossed ideological lines in May 1972 to join the street manifestations of the comparatively privileged student and professional intellectuals. The alliance was almost spontaneously coordinated in the streets by the KIM (Action Committee of the Protest Movement). Police over-reaction and Tsiranana's uncontrolled threats on the radio during the May 12-13 crisis rendered the country ungovernable. Thirty-four were killed in rioting; five of the 375 students deported to Nosy Lava died; a French-language newspaper office where some Government troops had retreated from the mobs was burnt; the Antananarivo City Hall, citadel of the loyal AKFM opposition, also went up in flames.

All of Tsiranana's instruments of domestic control entered the lists against rebellion. They included the urban police, Gendarmerie, special security forces (FRS), the PSD's action teams, and the controlled broadcasting media. Only the Army remained out of action. A largely ceremonial force disciplined by its French and French-trained officers, Madagascar's regular armed forces had always shunned political action. Neglected, aloof, they stayed intact during the entire extended episode of 1971-1972, when the security police and Gendarmerie were embroiled in controversial repression. Ultimately Tsiranana put the Republic into the hands of his Army commander—but not before making his move for rescue by the French.

France had indeed much to lose in a nationalist revolution in Madagascar, and Tsiranana had reminded her of the prospect at every opportunity. Maoist and Moscovite manipulations, whether of students, peasants, or city mobs, could do Overseas France no good. Merina vendettists would frequent anybody's table to accumulate crumbs for their eventual banquet of power. Communist and even American corrupters were espied in machinations among down-at-heel journalists, holier-than-thou clergy, ambititous frondistas, and susceptible schoolboys.

A typical tale, perhaps, and one which the vain-glorious old strategist DeGaulle would have understood. But insecurity festered in Madagascar's sea-locked imagination and DeGaulle's successors were unimpressed by the regime's petition for redemption. Madagascar occupied a subdued corner of the world for French interests, even after 1967, when vital Europe-Asia traffic redirected itself from Suez to sail copiously past the Great Island. Intelligence reports displayed little peril from global conspiracy. Americans occasionally made half-hearted efforts to appeal to one Malagasy group or another, but the United States was preoccupied in losing Indo China once more for the West. On May 4, Tsiranana had even admitted he'd been "deceived" about an American role in Resampa's alleged plot of the previous year. With this confession, the entire conspiracy obsession began to dissolve, even for those who had been inclined to believe it earlier. In any case, France knew better. Tsiranana was a liability and the May 1972 tempest, while surprising in its vehemence, showed no sign of external manipulation on the part of the aliens conjured up by the paranoiac President.

Indeed, no external factor was needed in the rapid implosion of otherwise disparate forces on the great island. They did it by themselves, in the loosely shared drive to dispose of what they deemed a corrupt, cowardly, incompetent regime which had refused to understand its own warnings. France had seen such superannuated structures topple before, making way for new forces of purification, only to reconstitute themselves without jeopardizing serious French interests.

France was doubtless in a position to intervene in May, 1972. She maintained 4,500 troops on the island, a third of them just outside Antananarivo. It was apparently President Pompidou who decided against releasing them into what was already a popular uprising with anti-colonial nationalist features. His refusal left Tsiranana no choice. On May 18, the President gave full executive powers to General Gabriel Ramanantsoa, a sixty-five year-old Merina aristocrat with unimpeachable credentials as military servant of both the French and Malagasy Republics. With Ramanantsoa as Chief of the Government of Public Security, Tsiranana remained titular head of state without function or ability to influence the form of order to which the state was to return. He had to accept the release of 2,000 political prisioners, including André Resampa. A year of censorship, searches, and subpoenas by a mysterious investigative committee never saw the particulars of Resampa's indictment.

Monja Jaona, also liberated in June, promised to support any government that demonstrated its good faith to the people. Unlike' some members of the old regime and its loyal opposition, both Monja and Resampa refrained from fawning flattery of the new leadership. Nevertheless, like the PSD and AKFM, Monja's MONIMA party prepared for a return to politics, this time, with new alliances among the urban poor (the Zoam).

In the capital, however, a series of highly agitated "seminars," coordinated by the radical intellectual KIM, prevented reconciliation with the old politics. Like so many other third world military caretakers, Ramanantsoa developed a tolerance, if not a veritable taste, for extended control in the name of civil security. A referendum held on October 8, 1972 invested the General with a five-year mandate to recreate the Malagasy state. Tsiranana was thus formally deposed. Enraged, the former President went into partial retirement, warning against the triumph of "Merina tribalism"—a striking admonition from a côtier protagonist of national reconciliation who had recently devised a government of four côtier vice presidents.

The Revolution Comes

During his two and one-half years as military dictator, Ramanantsoa sought diligently to forge an indigenous Malagasy national order, deliberately balancing continuity with innovation. He had to accommodate not only the energies liberated by a fulminating multitude, but the underlying claims of an agitated population, urban and rural, desperately seeking change. Unaccustomed and ill-adapted to politics, the General took the job seriously. He knew that the 1972 rebellion represented more than a barrack-room putsch. The presidency required more than a simple substitution of khaki uniform for seersucker costumery on an essentially accommodating figure-head. Loyal as he was to the France he had once served, Ramanantsoa also knew that Madagascar required a substantial departure from the hallowed relations of privilege established with the old colonizer in 1960.

For better or worse, what the French had failed to perceive in 1972 was that Malagasy labor militants, students, intellectuals, frustrated functionaries, street rabble, and rural pitchforkers had managed to synthesize into a positive force. Their common enemy was a colonial presence protected by a collaborating regime. They wanted jobs, which had become scarce. But, as an organized movement, they would not accept a mere substitution of labels on the local beneficiaries of a structural status quo. Nor did they challenge one opportunistic band simply in order to shift opportunity to another, as Tsiranana in his bunker, seemed to believe. Their intention was to change the fundamental relationships between authority in Antananarivo, the Malagasy population, and the rest of the world.

The revolution of 1972 challenged what it perceived, accurately or otherwise, as a continuing occupation of the country by European profiteers, privileged settlers, influential bureaucrats, and a foreign army whose purposes were at best indifferent to Malagasy interests. Madagascar was not yet governed by Malagasy. For all its claim to nationwide representation, the PSD had decayed into a complaisant bourgeoisie, self-serving and unredeemable. Malagasy nationalism had emerged as a legitimate movement transcending the casual rhetorical patterns of coup d'état regimes elsewhere. This movement had joined, for a time at least, an agitated peasantry with militantly organized urban factions. The existence of another, older, nationalist force in the Merina AKFM party and its satellite groups was only afterward to become acknowledged as a contradiction in radical Malagasy nationalism.

But the PSD was still very much alive. Tsiranana and his followers disputed revolutionary transition at every step, even after the referendum of October 8 which deposed them by 96.4 percent (with a 16 percent abstention rate). They were able to mobilize their own urban factions in Taomasina, Antseranana, and other northern centers in favor of established (including French) military, educational, and commercial interests. That legitimacy was threatened, as the PSD saw it, by a return to the even more alienating hegemony of the Merina. Although rejected again in elections to the consultative National People's Development Council (CNPD) a year following the referendum, it was this ethnically conscious thermidorean force which, through a succession of military mutinies and other disturbances, ultimately forced Ramanantsoa's resignation in February 1975.

While satisfying neither the impatient radicals nor their vengeful PSD opponents, the Ramanantsoa transition set in motion most of the dynamics which led to the establishment of a new republic by his successors after 1975.[37] An extraordinary atmosphere of open debate followed the heady experience of May 1972. New parties formed, along with the surviving AKFM and MONIMA, to represent the discredited PSD and the Zoam-KIM urban alliance. The 162-member CNPD began meeting in October 1973 to stabilize the fervor of the turbulent "seminars" organized by KIM as a source of constitutional and policy advice to Ramanantsoa's Supreme Revolutionary Council (CSR). Substantial modifications in educational, judicial, fiscal, labor, commercial, and landholding institutions emerged from this ferment, many of them enacted by executive decree. Notwithstanding the radicals' overt denunciation of Ramanantsoa as a temporizing "gradualist" and bourgeois Bonapart, this was in fact a period of pluralistic fermentation hitherto unprecedented in modern Malagasy society.[38]

Ramanantsoa's administration prepared for the orderly nationalization of the banking system, heretofore entirely owned by foreign proprietors. It took on other sectors of the economy regarded as critical to the nation's integrity, or subject to unusual opportunity for exploitation—insurance, foreign trade, transportation, energy, mining, pharmaceuticals, alcoholic beverages, the cinema. In September 1973, a strict investment code replaced Tsiranana's liberal forms of enticement to overseas capital. The number of foreign civilian residents, which had declined by six percent after independence in 1960, fell again by a total of 14,000 (14 percent) in 1972 and 1973. Most of the émigrés were French metropolitans, Réunionnais, and Comoreans holding French passports. Ramanantsoa's Interior Minister, former Gendarmerie commandant Colonel Richard Ratsimandrava, presided over the design of a modified fokon'olona revival to mobilize productive forces in decentralized authority and assure greater egalitarian distributive mechanisms in the countryside. The majority of delegates elected to the consultative CNPD were chosen by fokon'olona. But productive mobilization remained unachieved.

Foreign relations under Ramanantosa soon abandoned the Francophone security network, turning toward an almost relentless version of nonalignment. This translation of nationalism entailed, among other moves, cancellation of agreements with South Africa, Israel, and Taiwan as incompatible with fidelity to third world principles. The OAU, shunned by Tsiranana for its verbose radicalism, replaced France's preferred African-Malagasy Common Organization (OCAM) as Madagascar's principal forum for interchange with African states. Windows were thrown open on a hitherto unknown world, introducing mixed breezes from China, North Korea, the Soviet Union, Tanzania, and Libya, and with mixed results.

The architect of the new internationalism was Navy Captain Didier Ratsiraka, Foreign Minister and previously Tsiranana's military attaché in Paris. A French-trained Betsimisaraka from the east coast, Ratsiraka undertook the laborious renegotiation of the 1960 agreements with France, beginning in January 1973. Malagasy sovereignty itself, he said, was henceforth unnegotiable. When the talks appeared stalemated in mid-March over the issue of French base rights at Diego Suarez (Antseranana), Ratsiraka appealed directly to President Pompidou. When France insisted on the rights of her nationals to repatriate assets under free convertibility guarantees, Madagascar left the Franc Zone. On June 4, although eight new agreements were signed in Paris, they were qualitatively unlike their predecessors, and the umbilical was severed. France had shifted from protecting metropole to the status of a foreign power. The bases at Ivato and Diego Suarez were evacuated on orderly timetables. France's military, financial, and employment resources were transferred for the most part to Réunion and, in smaller doses, to Djibouti and Comorean Mayotte—all at the time still parts of Overseas France.[39]

Both Ratsimandrava and Ratsiraka were to succeed Ramanantsoa in 1975, the former for a single week only before his assassination on February 12. Although elaborately investigated, the murder remains unsolved. On June 15, following a second military interregnum managed by Ramanantsoa's Army successor, General Gilles Andriamahazo, the thirty-nine year-old Ratsiraka was chosen President by the CSR. Ratsiraka's immediate priority was to constitute a Second Republic, renouncing the continuity which Ramanantsoa had scrupulously tried to respect. The constitution was approved in a new referendum on December 21, 1975 and Ratsiraka's presidency was endorsed simultaneously, by a 92 percent majority. The new President's rapid ascent to power represented a testimonial to his efficacy as Foreign Minister, ultimately a less constricted job than the Interior portfolio carried by the unfortunate Ratsimandrava. Ratsiraka had been able to carry the revolution to notable achievements abroad while domestic tranquillity and economic prosperity lingered beyond reach at home. French imperialism, South African racism, Israeli, Taiwanese, and other interests seemed to fall readily under the barrages of Malagasy nationalism, whereas domestic enemies remained recalcitrant. Shortly after his inauguration in June 1975, Ratsiraka expelled the NASA tracking station from Imerintsiatosika near the capital. He then resumed the nationalization of foreign-owned enterprise, including the old mercantile establishments which had dominated Malagasy foreign trade since the turn of the century.

Ratsiraka's early triumphs endeared him to the entrenched middle class of Antananarivo, the mostly Merina merchants, landowners, bureaucrats, and intellectuals eager to supplant the French in the indivisible name of national sovereignty. These interests are said to be responsible for his rise to power.[40] As more conservative observers kept warning, however, these revolutionary adventures did not necessarily improve Madagascar's chances for international autonomy, let alone economic and social development. A country of nine million people, growing at an annual rate of 2.5 percent, required new productive resources, revenues, markets, and employment opportunities to replace the role which France had played. That role, even if no longer tolerable, had entailed viable, broad-based support as a matter of reciprocal self-interest. France was to remain a contributor, among others. But initial reactions of the Giscard government, which succeeded the late President Pompidou's administration in May 1974, were scarcely sympathetic to the nationalization of French property, restrictions on investment and currency convertibility, or neutralization of the island's strategic assets. For a while, French assistance sagged in proportion to the French stake in the island's prosperity.

Some relief arrived in the rush of newly recognized friends. The USSR and North Korea made explicit commitments to domestic and internal security, but they scarcely replaced the revenues and employment realized from erstwhile French military expenditures, or the American tracking station, for that matter. China kept Ratsiraka from having to default on South Africa's loans, but Peking did not care to build the hotels or port installations originally contracted by Pretoria. Socialist countries sent teachers and technicans but only began to replace the repatriated French personnel in critical Malagasy institutions, or the Israeli advisors in Resampa's Morondava development showcase. There was Soviet help for a number of major projects, like a flour mill at Taomasina, for which Tsiranana had once been prepared to grant timber monopolies to a single private investor from Dakar. Nevertheless, development assistance became dominated by multilateral agencies—a nationalist improvement of a kind, perhaps, over dependence on a single main source of bilateral aid.

The French relationship survived in altered form and it blossomed gratifyingly after the May 1981 election of Socialist President François Mitterand. Without the privileges embodied in the 1960 agreements, France has remained the Great Island's principal trade partner, source of technical assistance and commercial lending. It also acts as intermediary with the IMF and the eleven-nation Club de Paris which holds most of Madagascar's $1.6 billion (1984) public debt. An informal arrangement with the Bank of France supported the Malagasy franc (FMG) until April 1982, but the currency and the nationalized banks depend on multilateral institutions for liquidity and equilibrium. By 1981, French aid had risen to about half its 1970 rates, reaching the $100 million annual level in 1983 and 1984. About 600 French technicians (450 of them teachers) are working in the country, compared to 2,000 a decade earlier.

After its dramatic redirection of external affairs, the Ratsiraka administration sought marked changes in domestic political institutions. Reinforced by the referendary and election victory of December 1975, Ratsiraka and his CSR collected congenial political parties into a loose National Democratic Revolutionary Front (FNDR) to administer by consensus under the authority of the President and his Council. The FNDR reflects the continued diversity of Malagasy loyalties over geographic, ethnic, class, and ideological persuasions. These differences have prevailed over the integrative mission of the Front, allowing participating parties and personalities to represent their respective constituencies openly. The FNDR has suffered periodic defections by both MONIMA and the Militants for Power to the People (MFM) which had appointed itself heir in late 1972 to the Zoam-KIM alliance of the previous May. In practice, Ratsiraka and his Prime Minister, Lieutenant Colonal Désiré Rakotoarijaona, and their relatively balanced ministerial cabinet governed through the President's own Advance Guard of the Malagasy Revolution (AREMA). Strongest participant in the FNDR, AREMA is itself a sprawling dispersion of socialist ideologues, middle class nationalists and outright opportunists from the Tsiranana PSD, which AREMA resembles in some rather embarrassing respects.

The AKFM of Andriamanjato and veteran secretary Gisèle Rabesahala also remains active within the Front, but without the solid electoral appeal it once exerted in Merina Antananarivo and on occasion, other urban centers. In the 1977 elections to the new National People's Assembly (ANP), the AKFM obtained sixteen of 137 seats; 112 went to AREMA. Defending the purity of the 1972 revolution, both MFM and MONIMA refused to campaign, charging presidential favoritism for AREMA. Seven of the remaining seats went to the People's National Unity (VONJY) party, repository of Tsiranana-Resampa social democracy. The old PSD's avatar, the Malagasy Socialist Party (PSM), has been prohibited on the grounds of insincere socialism and affinities to French imperialism. Many PSD defectors have joined the triumphant AREMA, which obtained almost 90 percent of local government offices at the 1978 fokon'olona elections. The remaining two ANP seats are occupied by the Catholic-labor Union of Christian Democrats

(UDECMA), another chip off the old PSD block. A veritable epidemic of elections in 1983 and 1984 confirmed the predominance of Ratsiraka's AREMA, by now identified by a nation of peasants with the "foreign", despised, intimidating governing establishment (*fanjakana*).

While dependent on the support of loyalists within AREMA, Ratsiraka has managed to keep the Front intact and to neutralize prospective opponents from the liberal Right and the ideological militant Left. From these extremes, the President appears vacillating, improvising sporadic compromises between Malagasy stability and the egalitarian revolution. That such criticism can be tolerated in an otherwise tightly repressive environment testifies more to the regime's insecurity than to its liberality. Many opponents, including André Resampa, wait their turn in self-imposed exile. (Tsiranana died in seclusion on the island in April 1978.) Others languish in prison under circumstances that have elicited recrimination from international human rights watchers—Mitterand's otherwise sympathetic French Socialist Party included. Police, Gendarmerie, and a clutch of security services control overt dissent, preserving the President from a reported succession of conspiracies while seeming impotent in the face of urban and rural banditry and intermittent demonstrations of discontent.[41]

However closely this portrait resembles the last years of Philibert Tsiranana, Ratsiraka has sought to guide his republic into a new mood of collaboration and self-reliant prosperity. But he has been obliged by circumstances to dominate, and thus vitiate, the political process through centralized authority and increasingly orthodox fiscal and economic policy. Although beset by factionalism, executive authority has weakened or preempted all other constitutional institutions—legislative, juridical, economic, military, and cultural. Excessive responsibility may be convenient to Ratsiraka, but it has hardly increased his popularity. His reelection on November 7, 1982 for a second seven-year term, was anything but easy. The peasantry's patriarch, Monja Jaona, scored impressively, even in the cities where the generation of May 1972 voted its conscience (or abstained in protest). In the capital, with a twenty-five percent abstention rate, especially among the MFM's youthful adherents, Ratsiraka received the AKFM's endorsement and yet beat Monja by less than 4,000 (of 25,000) votes.[42] The MONIMA leader thereupon spent another eight months in fixed residence for contesting the returns.

Legislative elections, due earlier the same year, were postponed until August 28, 1983, in order to shield the President's campaign from the indignities of provincial and personal recriminations. His AREMA party thereupon recorded 85.4 percent of the ballots, increasing its parliamentary contingent from 112 to 117 seats out of a total of 137. The AKFM dropped from sixteen to nine seats and had to share Antananarivo's eight MP's with AREMA, Vonjy, MONIMA, and MFM. Despite the return of the last two parties from their 1977 boycott, voter apathy prevailed throughout the island. The abstention rate was officially put at 26 percent, with 38 percent absent in the capital and 41 percent in disaffected Mahajanga.

The Second Republic's 1975 charter, elaborated in Ratsiraka's own *Red Book*,[43] ordains pursuit of the Ramanantsoa-Ratsimandrava program for decentralized development of agricultural production and rural society. It pays homage to the utility of indigenous communal institutions, proverbial wisdom, ancestral precedent, and individual community. Authentic tradition must nevertheless be freed from atavistic superstition and xenophobia, blamed on the distortions of French rule and Tsiranana neocolonialism. This utopic vision proved difficult to inspire and manage on a nationwide scale, and the results have been disappointing, whether measured against popular standards or Western criteria of modernization. Fokon'olona have been dominated by new technical and political agencies designed to animate and focus rural energies. Without success in promoting production, circulating food supplies into cities, or providing consumer goods to the peasantry, the system has jeopardized authenticity by imposing central power and the interference of a technocratic elite.[44]

Madagascar's more conventionally socialist program has in turn been compromised by unresponsiveness in the industrial and mining sector— much of it prejudiced by adverse international price circumstance. State agencies substituted for foreign enterprises after 1972 have proved almost persistently unproductive. The best that can be expected of the island in the near term is agricultural self-sufficiency, internal transportation improvement, and a recovery of agricultural exports, all requiring foreign generosity. They also require world coffee markets to clear, vanilla to be sold directly rather than through black markets, and fratricidal disputes with Indonesia over the clove trade to cease.

As in many other third world debtor nations, IMF strictures on Malagasy fiscal policy have forced liberalization of domestic and external commerce as part of the price of international balance of payments support. These "reforms" have been salutary in statistical terms. Already a new family of private Western and Arab banks has formed its "Club of London" to negotiate with Ratsiraka's beleaguered socialists over their growing commercial debt (about $200 million in 1984). The corresponding official "Club of Paris" has, in its own great city, thrice accorded Madagascar a new schedule for public debt service since 1981, reducing the cost to a mere 35 percent of 1984 imports (from 55 percent the preceding year). The ideological price, however, has proved very high.

Starting its second decade beset by international vicissitudes as well as habitual Malagasy reticence, the Second Republic retains much of the social inequity and economic torpor of the first. Gaps remain between rich and poor, urban and rural incomes, Merina and côtier advantages. Regressive landholding patterns have proved more resilient than anticipated. So has adult illiteracy, despite the enormous expansion and diligent reform of the educational system. Bureaucratic corruption and incompetence have taken their toll on the revolution. Industry has been constrained by post-colonial restrictions on capital and currencies; mining and agriculture wallow in low productivity, anomalies of resource allocation, bureaucratic dishonesty, and labor apathy.[45] A 1974 tourist expansion scheme to accommodate 40,000 visitors by 1977 (five times the 1971 total), 200,000 by 1985, a half million by 1995, has been overtaken by recessionary realities. Eighty-five percent of the population, a wary, wizened peasantry, shrugs at perpetual policy-by-exhortation while producer prices remain repressed and the bureaucratic elite subsists conspicuously. Peasants grow enough food to survive, pay taxes (the most onerous of which were abolished early in the revolution), and barter for necessities in primitive, "informal" local markets. For wage earners, food, oils, flour, soap, and sugar remain in chronic short supply. Overall per capita production has declined by eight percent since 1969–1971, according to FAO statistics, with agriculture slipping six points from 1977 to 1981 alone. A rice-devouring population is obliged annually to import 200,000 tons of the staple grain which it once exported to neighbors and Europeans.[46]

If the structure of Malagasy economics has been transformed in a decade of revolutionary politics, the majority of Malagasy seem still to await their share in the revolution. The country remains profoundly rural in character but only 40 percent of the gross domestic product comes from agriculture. Towns have increased their share of the population from ten to 15 percent in a decade, but without industrial or commercial expansion to mitigate their proportionate drain on productive resources. Massive nationalizations from 1975 endowed the public sector with 70 percent of national production by 1978, as opposed to 20 percent in 1970, but in the main this change reflects the replacement of French colonial companies and plantations as well as small rural traders by state companies. A huge structure of over 300 public corporations and self-managed fokon'olona collectives, Army enterprises, public banks, and energy utilities, sugar and textile plants, meat packing and machinery producers has been substituted for the old private entities without a metamorphosis of production and distribution or, indeed, an improvment in efficiency. Weaknesses of economic structure, failures in performance, committed without compensatory gains in social justice, constitute the nation's most agonizing trouble. The vast international borrowing campaign launched in 1977 to replace expropriated private capital and to quadruple national income by the year 2,000, has propelled the external debt to beyond 50 percent of 1983 GNP, as exports stagnated.

After this long phase of debilitating reorganization, the economy seemed in 1984 to begin a positive response to the urban austerity and market liberalization prescribed by Western therapists as the sole remedy for underdevelopment. Whether the results will vindicate the claims of "non-ideological" market pragmatics remains to be confirmed in the experience of Malagasy farmers and urbanites. Whatever its outcome, the process represents a defeat for revolutionary nationalism.

Despite bottlenecks and planning fiascos, the regime has improved roads, air transport and telecommunications services, introduced rural production incentives, expanded agricultural credit, applied "rural animation" techniques to modern, self-managed communes. Western assistance is being applied to critically needed irrigation, transportation, and farming methods. Food processing, textile, timber, mining, and chemical industries have been selectively dosed with foreign exchange and imported technology (from France, China, and the USSR) according to rationally devised priorities. The catastrophically inefficient state marketing board for agriculture (SINPA) has given way to relatively open rural markets.

Without disturbing the lucrative plantation system which still furnishes the bulk of Malagasy export revenues, the Government has opened 5,000 new hectares of land for rice production. But to satisfy the demand of a growing population, without continuing to import Asian rice, 20,000 new hectares will have to go into production each year and yields per hectare will have to rise substantially. Land is available, since less than five percent of the total island surface is cultivated (ten percent of estimated arable surface). Almost half of that is under inefficiently produced paddy. A National Investment Fund, fed by the national banking system using pension funds and public subsidies, operates in all sectors, with particular attention to sugar milling, textile manufacture, machinery, and meat packing. Domestic capital has thus far proved unresponsive to public borrowing and market stimulation. Construction and crafts languish without investment. Madagascar's coal, lignite, graphite, bauxite, and other resources remain underutilized. New ferro-nickel, uranium, and chromium deposits are only beginning to be worked. Like the coffee plantations of the east coast, the vanilla forests of the northeast, the sugar and pepper estates of the east and the north, the cotton, sisal and raphia fields of the south, these assets are often situated in isolated geographic pockets of intense wealth. This economic archipelago has never enjoyed systematic linkages between primary and secondary production or between production and consumption. Its segregated resources remain severally connected, if at all, with separate overseas markets, sources of finance, and technology. Depressions or crises in one area can scarcely respond to ameliorations elsewhere.

Madagascar needs to become an economic system, with a privileged role for agricultural production. State administrations throughout the twentieth century have acknowledged this desideratum without discovering the way to achieve it. Suspicious farmers, caught between the rhetoric of communalization and the imperatives of central controls, habitually refrain from what they regard as perilous overproduction beyond sheer subsistence needs. Coffee, cotton, vanilla, and other plantation exports depend on meteorological vicissitudes, radically fluctuating world prices, and technological renewal currently unavailable under prevailing austerity constraints. International recession and high costs have forced the Taomasina oil refinery out of business. The hastily nationalized shipyards at Antseranana have failed to recover from the French Navy's forced departure in the mid-1970s.

With exports barely covering seventy to 75 percent of imports through 1983, fiscal policy has had to accommodate IMF disapproval of unnecessary expenditures, urban consumer subsidies, and imports. Austerity has cut the government deficit in half from over 18 percent of GDP in 1980; subsidies for urban consumers have been reduced and currency devaluations have further eroded purchasing power while lowering inflation to under ten percent in 1984. SINPA and other public sector liabilities have vanished or metamorphosized; a new investment code offers opportunities to private capital; expropriated French businesses have finally been promised the full compensation demanded by Western creditors as a gauge of Malagasy good faith. Even partial compliance has begun dismantling the regime's socialist investment and services program. In return, a phased loan of SDR 143 million, augmented by standby credits and by emergency donations from the World Bank and other agencies, has increased liquidity and helped restore payments stability. A 15 percent devaluation of the FMG in May 1982 responded only halfway to IMF demands, but a second 15 percent was taken in March 1984, after which the Paris "Club" (and, separately, the USSR) agreed to reschedule debt service. Removal of price subsidies for urban consumers and rationalization of certain state corporations have helped to precipitate political repercussions—including voter apathy and turbulence among city youth. More than half the Malagasy population is now under twenty years of age, and the jobs they seek in the towns do not exist.

Dissatisfaction still overflows in this large, disjunctive terrain with its distant, dense pockets of population, its distrust of external authority, and its lingering manorial politicians and rapidly bureaucratizing local governments. Constant shifts of ministers and key personalities testify to ideological fermentation while Ratsiraka retains his precarious seat. Serious rioting re-erupted again in late 1980 and in November 1981. It reappeared intermittently and throughout the island during and after 1982 as the urban population came increasingly to resent the inability of the revolution to satisfy the essential demands made on it. Riots among politicized youth gangs have become murderous. The Catholic clergy, virtually alone, speaks out publicly against injustices, and priests have been assassinated for their candor. Failures and contradictions of government are as always widely discussed throughout the island in the multitude of "languages" to which Malagasy resort to express their irrepressible opinions.[47]

To put a new republic together with the fragments of several ancient systems and a partially shared élan from 1972, Ratsiraka must depend on a far more congenial international climate than he has experienced thus far. Accumulating petroleum debts, mostly to Algeria for relatively expensive crude, and the subsequent world recession destroyed all expectations of an economic resurgence at the close of the retrenchment phase in 1979–1980. While diligent in some sectors of Malagasy society (security, education, and rural technology, for instance), the Republic's new socialist friends have not been able to substitute their services for Western capital and markets. Nor has tighter alignment with African aims and purposes produced more than inspirational results. French technical and financial assistance resumed part of its role in Malagasy economics even before the arrival of the congenial Mitterand at the Elysée, but the former metropole has not consented to drop manna from heaven. It still operates without the political and military context in which economic commitments once automatically justified themselves on grounds of French self-interest. That interest becomes all the more important as Madagascar deals with a new, conservative majority in Paris from March 1986.

The United States continues second in importance as a Malagasy client, particularly for vanilla.[48] Japan, West Germany, and other partners have joined a balance of East and West, while Algeria, Libya, and other Arab funding sources compensate modestly for Madagascar's third world (or at least, anti-Israeli) allegiances. Hence, a broad portfolio of Malagasy liabilities, including the arduous IMF dialogues and the Paris and London "Clubs" of hard lenders, has only partially replaced the omnibus system of Franc Zone guarantees—the "neo-colonial" channel of interest-free liquidity transfers through the Bank of France, for example.

While clothing the Malagasy national spirit in controversial forms of socialism at home, Ratsiraka has been able from the outset to express the Republic's external purposes more successfully in neutralist terms. In vigorous displays of pacifism, the Malagasy condemn both US and Soviet military deployments in the putative zone of peace. Reaction to Soviet initiatives, including operations on Afghanistan, display greater nuance than the response to Western strategy, however, and Russians are reported to be operating a radar station for Mozambique Channel monitoring at Mahajanga.[49] Despite international rumors to the contrary, however, Ratsiraka has refused to compromise essential Indian Ocean neutrality. Antseranana has not been opened for regular naval vessels, nor has it been leased to one fishing fleet or another. The French and American navies beat Soviet ships there in April 1984 after the passage of an especially destructive cyclone. To the extent that Ratsiraka is obliged for his personal and official security to Soviet, North Korean, and affiliated protectors, his "socialist-oriented" regime remains at least theoretically susceptible to their influence, while the West provides the resources for national recovery and international market persuasion. The nationalist dialectic has as yet no obvious synthesis, but the long-term realities seem to portend enhanced priority for the French case in Madagascar, and with that case, the Grande Ile's interest in subregional development among the islands of the Indian Ocean.

French political and military presence in Réunion remains tentatively tolerated in Antananarivo. That presence is still preferable to the exercise of Super Power *droits de seigneur* among weak and dependent clients. France suffered some recrimination for retaining Mayotte against the will of the Comorean majority, but distaste for President Ahmed Abdallah has limited Malagasy enthusiasm for defending the rights of the archipelago that was once administratively and economically tributary to Antananarivo.

Madagascar pursues its own claim against France for the recovery of the uninhabited islets of the Glorieuses to the north, Juan de Nova, Bassas da India, and Europa in the Mozambique Channel. These flecks of land had been separated from the Madagascar territory just before the independence settlement of 1960. Used by the French military for scientific research, weather prediction, and other oceanic exclave advantages, the islets have been administered from Réunion in defiance of Malagasy protests. While Paris argues its case for sovereignty on the basis of nineteenth century appropriation rights over uninhabited and unclaimed territory, Madagascar is supported by UN General Assembly resolutions, the OAU, and various third world sympathizers. Even the French Socialist Party had urged accommodation to the Malagasy position before its leaders obtained the power to decide the question in the 1981 elections.[50] International pressures induced both the Giscard and Mitterand governments to "negotiate" the fate of the islets with Madagascar, eternally if necessary. Without giving up their suit, the Malagasy have sought of late to avoid public furor with France over these residual atoms of empire.

The islets question symbolizes the constraints of international reality impinging on the aspirations of the Great Island of the Western Indian Ocean. Ratsiraka's standing invitation to stage a global conference at Antananarivo on the Zone of Peace project has been politely ignored for years by most members of the UN's ad hoc committee, including France and the USSR. Madagascar's passion for the zone of peace has energetically spent itself upon a decade of inconclusive assizes in that committee. Moreover, its example of militant decolonization has also been restricted to the narrow southwestern area in which alone Madagascar casts a sizeable shadow.[51] There, the Malagasy experience has doubtless exerted influence on the abbreviated Soilih revolution in Comoros, the conversion of Seychelles into a socialist state, the gradual and ephemeral triumph of the Mauritian Militant Movement (MMM), and perhaps the emerging fortunes of the Réunionnais Left. After hesitant beginnings and the 1978 setback by Abdallah and his mercenary allies in Comoros, a constellation of regional interests has begun to take shape in the neighborhood. Shape at least . . . if not life, as yet.

Notes

1. For speculation on the provenance of the Malagasy, see Note 5 to Ch. 1; also Hubert Deschamps, Histoire de Madagascar (Paris: Berger-Levrault, 1961), pp. 13–17; Nigel Heseltine, Madagascar (New York: Praeger Publishers, 1971), Ch. 2; Michel Mollat du Jourdin, "Les contacts historiques de l'Afrique et de Madagascar avec l'Asie du Sud et du Sud-Est: le rôle de l'Océan Indien," Archipel: études interdisciplinaires sur le monde Insulindien, #21 (Paris: CNRS-SECMI, 1981), pp. 35–53.

2. Hubert Deschamps, Les Pirates à Madagascar (Paris: Berger-Levrault, 1949).

3. Raymond K. Kent, Early Kingdoms in Madagascar, 1500–1700 (New York: Holt, Rinehart & Winston, 1970), Ch. 5.

4. Deschamps, Histoire, pp. 182–189; Edouard Ralaimihoatra, Histoire de Madagascar, 4th ed. (Antananarivo: Editions de la Librairie de Madagascar, 1982), Chs. 7 and 8; Kent, Early Kingdoms, Ch. 6.

5. Phares M. Mutibwa, The Malagasy and the Europeans: Madagascar's Foreign Relations, 1861–1895 (Atlantic Highlands, N.J.: Humanities Press, 1974), Preface, p. xiv.

6. Richard Andriamanjato, Le Tsiny et le Tody dans la pensée malgache (Paris: Présence Africaine, 1957); Maurice Bloch, Placing the Dead: Tombs, Ancestral Villages,

and Kinship Organization in Madagascar (London and New York: Seminar Press, 1972); Bakoly Domenichini-Ramiaramanana, *Du Ohabolana au Hainteny: Langue, littérature et politique à Madagascar* (Paris: Karthala, 1983).

7. Robert Archer, *Madagascar depuis 1972: la marche d'une révolution* (Paris: Harmattan, 1978); Césaire Rabenoro, *Les relations extérieures de Madagascar de 1960 à 1972.* (Thèse d'Etat, Université Aix-Marseille III, 1981), p. 316.

8. Deschamps, *Histoire*, pp. 237, 246; Virginia Thompson and Richard Adloff, *The Malagasy Republic: Madagascar Today* (Stanford University Press, 1965), pp. 15–20; Heseltine, *Madagascar*, pp. 144–149.

9. Deschamps, *Histoire*, pp. 246–247; Heseltine, *Madagascar*, pp. 84–85, 146–149.

10. Deschamps, *Histoire*, p. 247; Relaimihoatra, *Histoire*, pp. 239–241.

11. Deschamps, *Histoire*, p. 261.

12. Heseltine, *Madagascar*, p. 155.

13. For discussions of village communities, see George Condominas, *Le Fokonolona* (Paris: Berger-Levrault, 1961); Gérard Althabe, *Oppression et libération dans l'imaginaire; les communautés villageoises de la côte orientale de Madagascar* (Paris: François Maspero, 1969); Yves Prats, *Le développement communautaire de Madagascar* (Paris: Librairie Générale de Droit et de Jurisprudence R. Pichon et R. Durand-Auzias, 1972); Jean Claude Rouveyran, *La logique des agricultures de transition: l'exemple des sociétés paysannes malgaches* (Paris: Ed. G.P. Maisonneuve et La Rose, 1972); Dominique Desjeux, "Réforme foncière et civilisation agraire: le cas de Madagascar," *Le Mois en Afrique* 184–185 (April-May 1981), pp. 55–61; Andriamanjato, *Le Tsiny et le Tody*, pp. 38, 73–74; Paul Ramasindraibe, *Fokon'olona* (Antananarivo: Imprimerie de la Mission Catholique, 1962); J. Dez, "Un des problèmes du développement rural: la diffusion de la vulgarisation agricole," *Terre Malgache, Tany Malagasy* No. 1 (Antananarivo: Université de Madagascar, n.d.), pp. 41–70; Jacques Tronchon, "L'idéologie Fokonolona et l'insurrection de 1947," *Lumière* (Fianarantsoa, Madagascar), 1985 (June 23, 1974).

14. Andrianarivo Ravelona Rajaona, "Le Dinam-Pokonolona: mythe, mystique ou mystification?" (Paper delivered to December 1981 Colloque on Indian Ocean History at Aix-en-Provence, France; reprinted *Annuaire des Pays de l'Océan Indian*, APOI, 1981); Desjeux, "Réforme foncière," pp. 55–61.

15. Heseltine, *Madagascar*, p. 219.

16. See Kent, *Early Kingdoms*, Ch. 3; Ralaimihoatra, *Histoire*, pp. 45–53; F. Fanony and N.J. Gueunier, "Quelques directions pour l'étude de l'Islam Malgache." (Paper presented to Colloque d'Histoire Malgache, Majunga, 13–18 April 1981).

17. Heseltine, *Madagascar*, p. 156, for instance. Note the classic "debate" on the subject between [Dominique] O. Mannoni, *Prospero and Caliban: The Psychology of Colonization*, trans. Pamela Powesland (New York: Praeger, 1964) and Frantz Fanon, "The So-Called Dependency Complex of Colonized Peoples," in *Black Skin, White Masks*, trans. Charles Lam Markmann (New York: Grove Press, Inc., 1967), pp. 83–108.

18. Jacques Tronchon, *L'Insurrection malgache de 1947: essai d'interprétation historique* (Paris: François Maspero, 1974); Pierre Boiteau, *Contribution à l'histoire de la nation malgache* (Paris: Editions Sociales, 1958); Ralaimahoatra, *Histoire*, pp. 274–287; Heseltine, *Madagascar*, pp. 178–184; Frank Raharison, "Les notables et l'insurrection de 1947," *Cahiers du Centre d'Animation Culturelle, d'Information et de Documentation* (CACID) (Paris: Malagasy Embassy, 1980); Raymond William Rabemananjara, *Madagascar sous la Rénovation Malgache* (Paris, 1951).

19. Edward M. Corbett, *The French Presence in Black Africa* (Washington: Black Orpheus Press, 1972); Y.G. Paillard, "The First and Second Malagasy Republics: the Difficult Road of Independence," in Raymond Kent, ed., *Madagascar in History: Essays from the 1970s* (Albany, California: The Foundation for Malagasy Studies, 1979), pp. 298-354; Philip M. Allen, "Madagascar and OCAM: The Insular Version of Regionalism," *Africa Report* (January 1966), pp. 13-18; Allen, "Francophonie considered," *Africa Report* (June 1968), pp. 6-15.

20. Heseltine, *Madagascar*, pp. 191-200.

21. Rabenoro, *Relations extérieures*; Harry Bryce Qualman, *Limits and Constraints on Foreign Policy in a Dependent State: Madagascar under the Tsiranana Regime* (Ph. D. diss., Johns Hopkins University 1975); Philip M. Allen, "Madagascar: The Authenticity of Recovery," in John M. Ostheimer, ed., *The Politics of the Western Indian Ocean Islands* (New York: Praeger Publishers, 1975), pp. 55-59; Allen, "Madagascar and OCAM;" Allen, *Self-Determination in the Western Indian Ocean*, International Conciliation series 560, (New York: Carnegie Endowment for International Peace, 1966).

22. Thompson and Adloff, *The Malagasy Republic*, pp. 101-112, a detailed account of the party structure, with some errors; André Ravatomanga, Editorial, in *Lumière*, May 9, 1971, one of a series of remarkable political analyses by this extraordinary journalist during the long crisis.

23. Archer, *Madagascar depuis 1972*, pp. 9-17.

24. For an account of the decline of the Tsiranana Republic, Allen, "Madagascar: Authenticity of Recovery;" Pascal Chaigneau, *De la Première République à l'orientation socialiste, processus et conséquences d'une évolution politique* (Thèse 3ème cycle en Sociologie Politique, Univ. de Paris X, 1981), Vol. 1, pp. 403-468; Chaigneau, *Rivalités politiques et socialisme à Madagascar* (Paris: Centre des Hautes Etudes sur l'Afrique et l'Asie Modernes, CHEAM, 1985), pp. 51-68.

25. For penetrating discussions of anomalies in rural development policies, see Althabe, *Oppression et libération*; Rouveyran, *Agricultures de transition*; Chaigneau, *Première République*, Vol. 1; Jean-Pierre Raison, *Les Hautes Terres de Madagascar*, 2 Vols (Paris: ORSTOM-Karthala, 1984); Prats, *Développement communautaire*; Dominique Desjeux, *La Question agraire à Madagascar: administration et paysannat de 1895 à nos jours* (Paris: Harmattan, n.d.).

26. Rabenoro, *Relations extérieures*, p. 306.

27. Ravatomanga, Editorial, *Lumière*, August 8, 1971; Allen, "Rites of Passage in Madagascar," *Africa Report* (February 1971), pp. 24-27.

28. Interview with Agence France Presse, September 3, 1970; also *Rand Daily Mail* (Johannesburg), November 30, 1970.

29. Allen, "Rites of Passage" and "Authenticity of Recovery," pp. 45-49; Ravatomanga, Editorials in *Lumière*, June 6 and August 8, 1971.

30. Rabenoro, *Relations extérieures*, p. 331; author's translation.

31. *Hehy* (Antananarivo), April 16, 1971.

32. *Lumière*, April 11, May 2 and 9, 1971; *Le Monde* (Paris), May 8, 1971.

33. Allen, "Authenticity of Recovery," p. 47.

34. *Lumière*, October 17, 1971.

35. *Ibid.*, April 20, May 30, June 27, July 18, October 17, 1971.

36. André Ravatomanga editorial in *Ibid.*, September 5, 1971.

37. Supplement to *Jeune Afrique* (Paris) 716 (September 28, 1971), pp. 29-73.

38. Siradou Diallo in *Ibid.*, 646 (May 26, 1973) and 647 (June 2, 1973); Chaigneau, *Première République*, Vol. 2, pp. 468-637.

39. *Marchés Tropicaux et Méditerranéens* (Paris), June 8, 1973; Colin Legum, ed., *Africa Contemporary Record 1973-74* (London: Rex Collings, 1974), pp. B 200-202; *Africa Confidential* 64-67 (November and December 1973).

40. *Ibid.*, pp. 612–621; Archer, *Madagascar depuis 1972;* "P.R.N." in *Le Monde,* 7–8 April 1985.

41. Sennen Andriamirado, *Jeune Afrique* 1121 (June 30, 1982); *Afrique Nouvelle,* January 13, 1982; J.C. Pomonti, *Le Monde* October 1, 1981; J.P. Langellier, "Madagascar: la révolution essoufflée," *Le Monde Hebdomadaire* (Paris) 1692 (2–8 April 1981); Charles Cadoux and Jean du Bois de Gaudusson, "Madagascar 1979–1981: un passage difficile," *APOI* 7 (1980), pp. 357–387.

42. J.P. Langellier, *Le Monde,* November 10, 1982.

43. Didier Ratsiraka, *La Charte de la révolution Malgache* (Antananarivo: Gouvernement de Madagascar, 1975).

44. Paillaird, "The First and Second Malagasy Republics," pp. 343–344; Allen, "Authenticity of Recovery," pp. 62–67; Rajaona, "Le Dinam-Pokonolona;" Christian Roux, "Le recentrage et la restructuration de l'économie malgache depuis 1974," *Le Mois en Afrique* 15 No. 176–177 (August-September 1980), pp. 81–97; *ACR 1982–83,* pp. B 214–216; *ACR 1983–84,* pp. B 192–207; Roland Razafindramanto, *Essai de bilan politique, économique et social de la période révolutionnaire socialiste Malgache, 1975–1982* (Mémoire en relations internationales, Univ. Aix-Marseille III, 1982–1983); Philippe Hugon, "Chronique Economique et Démographique; Madagascar," *APOI* V, 1978, pp. 423–433; Jean-Louis Calvet, "Chronique politique et constitutionnelle: Madagascar," *Ibid.,* pp. 319–346; Jacques de Barrin in *Le Monde,* 21, 22, 23 March 1985; *MTM* 3 May 1985.

45. *Madagascar: Recent Economic Developments and Future Prospects,* World Bank Country Study (Washington: The World Bank, 1980), pp. 5–14; *ACR 1980–81,* pp. B240–242, 247–254; *Ibid.,* 1982–83, pp. B 215–220; "NAP" in *Afrique Nouvelle* (Dakar) 1670 (July 8–14, 1981); Cadoux and Du Bois de Gaudusson, "Madagascar 1979–1981;" Roux, "Recentrage et restructuration."

46. Langellier, "La Révolution essoufflée;" see also Desjeux, "Réforme foncière et civilisation agraire;" Yves Prats, "Les nouvelles institutions socialistes du développement économique en République Démocratique Malagasy," *APOI* IV, 1977, pp. 15–24; *ACR 1983–84,* pp. B 198–207.

47. Roger Jouffrey, "Didier Ratsiraka et le socialisme malgache," *Afrique Contemporaine* 115 (May-June 1981); Cadoux and Du Bois de Gaudusson, "Madagascar 1979–1981," parts 2 and 3; *Africa Confidential* (London) Vol. 25: 13 and Vol. 26: 13; *Jeune Afrique* (Paris) 1261, March 6, 1985; Sennen Andriamirado in *Ibid.,* 1071, July 15, 1981; Pavageau, *Jeunes Paysans.*

48. The announcement of a new "formula" by the Coca-Cola Corporation in early 1985 sent panic into the vanilla market, where the American soft drink consumes about 30 percent of the product, much of it contributed by Malagasy sources; the corporation had also been rumored dumping large quantities on the glutted market at fifty-five dollars per ton, rather than the Malagasy price of seventy dollars. Coca-Cola's retraction of the formula change saved an entire agricultural industry for the Great Island, which has already lost market influence to cheaper synthetics. See *Africa News,* July 29, 1985, *Africa Report* (September-October 1985), p. 45.

49. See Jacques de Barrin in *Le Monde,* May 5–6, 1984; *ACR 1984–85* (chapter on Madagascar); *Africa Confidential,* Vol. 26 No. 13.

50. Philippe Leymarie, *Océan Indian: le mouveau coeur du monde* (Paris: Editions Karthala, 1981), p. 217; Charles Cadoux, "Esquisse d'un panorama politique des pays de l'Océan Indien," *APOI* 1 (1974), p. 53.

51. Leymarie, *Océan Indien,* pp. 53–55, pp. 355–356.

7

A Latin Afro-Asia:
Islands in Communion

However well hidden from the emulative eye of history, Madagascar, Comoros, the Mascarenes, and Seychelles recommend themselves, as islands will, to mankind's proverbial quest for sanctuary. Exclaves of ourselves, they exemplify modes of asylum against the prisons of landed society. Yet, captured in their turn by the blank sea, islands become both secure and vulnerable. They reveal in flagrant, often garish relief the typical rumors of the blood, the blends of race and mixtures of the mind so readily diffused over continents, so quickly dissolved on the open oceans, yet so indicative of humanity.

In the vast ocean of affairs between landmasses, the people of the south western islands occupy an obscure but essential place. Theirs is a region waxing and waning in strategic value, and they are tangled in the flux. Yet they, too, act and react, and their cultures become trammeled, liberated, and trapped again in the crucibles of change. Africans, Asians and Europeans cross one another here and now as they have done over centuries, reflecting counterpoints of history and vicissitudes of social process known on a larger scale in the continents. Understanding the plights and purposes of these authentic Indian Oceanites may help enlighten the world's way into time ahead.

There is good reason to consider the seaward Mascarenes and their erstwhile Seychelles and Chagos dependencies somewhat separately from the landward Malagasy and Comoros islands. Final spots of the habitable planet to obtain a permanent population, the Mascarenes, Seychelles, and Chagos were converted from geographic property into societies for the sake of Europe's precious Cape-to-Indies passage. They participated briefly in a lively but abrasive interspersion of mercantile systems until the definitive reorganization of the Indian Ocean at Paris in 1814. From then on, they disappeared from historical contention. Mauritius and Seychelles became tributaries to English industrial metabolisms, Réunion a lost projection of France, and the Chagos a virtual nonentity in the scatterings of British empire. Later in the nineteenth century, Madagascar, Comoros, and even Zanzibar joined the seaward archipelagoes as territories of Europe, sacrificing in turn their principal identity within the oceanic and East African region. (As a significant exception at about the same time, the Asiatic Maldives acquired only indirect, or "protected," connection to Britain, retaining their traditional Sultanate and answering to the authority of Ceylon.)

Lessons of Insular Dependence

None of these expropriations was perfect, Seychelles retaining close association with Mauritius and finding export opportunities in India, Madagascar developing new sub-colonial relationships with both Réunion and the Comoros. Nevertheless, nineteenth century industrial colonialism ended the autonomy which all the insular societies had enjoyed, whether as Afro-Asian polities or as exclaves of free Europeans. Gradually, their productive forces were concentrated by imperial design on specialized market lines for the metropole, which undertook for its part to supply the islands' need for survival.

It is this concomitance of narrowly focused, relatively efficient production and abject dependence on external sources for essential needs that prevails today, even in Madagascar, the largest and most versatile of the island economies. Self-sufficiency, diversification of production, "import substitution," and export innovations naturally represent serious objectives for the islands; but conversion from their specialized imperial functions has proved exceedingly difficult, especially in a world system organized to limit decision-making on the periphery. Their economic organization, patterns of costs and prices, fixed investment, labor skills, and an entire social structure are dedicated to doing one thing well (or at least cheaply) and expecting every other thing to come from abroad. Here, Madagascar's several economic zones, virtually sealed from one another, act in simulation of the "archipelago" mechanism which prevails on the separate smaller islands of the region. The particles are divided and regulated by their respective overseas correspondents. Seychelles is no more an exception than Madagascar: the belated arrival of air communications in the early 1970s simply caused a peremptory transformation from a specialized, dependent, inefficient plantation economy to a specialized, dependent, relatively efficient tourist mono-industry.

This structural dependence is not merely the pernicious work of colonialism. It goes with utter insularity, defined by geographic isolation and political obscurity. Exposed ineluctably to the ocean, to what it brings and what it takes away, the southwestern islands have no continental recourse at their backs. They belong nowhere else but at sea. Whoever crosses that sea first or most persistently can claim its sealocked prizes.

France finally staked that claim after Portugal and Holland had waived the privilege and while England was preoccupied in larger parts. The French East India Company and Crown created settler societies *ex nihilo* on the Mascarenes and Seychelles and later competed successfully for landward prizes. Madagascar and the Comoros were wrenched politically away from

a continent dominated by British, Germans, and Portuguese. Carried out
to sea, they joined their fate symbolically to the truly oceanic, pluralistic
isles. A more substantial integration of all the islands, once so clearly
envisioned by the great Mahé de Labourdonnais, proved politically impossible
after 1814. By then, Great Britain had permanently appropriated bold
Mauritius and its erstwhile dependencies—Rodriguez, the Chagos, Agalega,
the Cargados Carajos, the several Seychelles groups—all but Réunion and
a few flecks to the west and south. Even independent Madagascar was
falling into the British sphere.

From the late nineteenth century all the islands, seaward or landward,
French and British, were being used primarily as territories for economic
exploitation. Only Réunion could retain its truly colonial character in an
affective reciprocity between a privileged settler class and its metropolitan
cousins. Economic exploitation became imperialism's raison d'être in the
entire area once France's bungled experiments in "protective" relationships
had worn out on Madagascar and Comoros, as England's had done in the
disintegrating empire of Zanzibar. Today, all but Réunion are politically
independent, all but Réunion belong to the under-endowed strata of the
complex third world.

Much has changed and changed rapidly in the southwestern islands over
the past two decades. New forces have overcome the resistance of a stratified
social system and the economic alignments so agreeable to privileged classes
and metropolitan counterparts.[1] Viewed politically, the transformations have
been wrought by the irreversible visit of postwar nationalism in the smaller
islands, and a return of national sensibility in Madagascar. Culturally, two
generations of insular society have indelibly absorbed standard twentieth
century patterns of work, social intercourse and leisure. Contrasted with
the casual improvisations of plantation colonialism, the State has become
a sudden colossal presence, giving and taking away in administrative perpetuity. Cities and their inhabitants have drawn far from retrograde rural
society while intensifying their demands both on agricultural production
and ancestral values imputed to the mythical land. Urban joys and problems—
mass communications and machinery, nuclear family life and regimental
education, upward wage pressures within self-protective bureaucracies, the
helplessness of urban unemployment, new measures for time and space,
new languages and symbol systems—have tumbled like avalanches on large
communities of Creole, Asian, Malagasy, and African alike.

There is an international dimension to this "modernizing" process. Island
societies have found their tongue in a universe no longer limited to the
audiences of a metropole. Their political parties, trade unions, universities,
and diplomatic missions speak out to that world through various media
tuned to register, if not always to hear, what they have to say. No longer
do their virgin trees crash soundlessly in the forests of oblivion.

The southwestern ocean has emerged from obscurity through a complex
parallelogram of factors. Its nationalisms were impelled by attenuated "winds
of change," impeded by metropolitan France and England who encouraged

a different independence. Their arrival has been broadcast by salesmen of new technology, applauded by choruses of the third world at large. Most crucial in the island evolution, as so often elsewhere, has been the emergence of a nationally sensitive middle class. The product of multiplying population, expanded schooling, liberalized franchise, broadening employment opportunity (especially in the public sector), and the insemination of anti-colonial ideas, everywhere this class has spilled out in complex and contradictory terms.

New national forces have operated with varying intensity in each island society as both vicious opponent and reluctant collaborator of the established oligarchies. In Madagascar, bureaucratic and commercial nationalism has had to accommodate the living memory of a tragically deposed monarchical system as well as the abused heritage of ancient rural communities. In Mauritius, nationalism assumed its first identity among colonially mystified city Creoles and commercial Asians. "Nationalism" for Réunionnais must be expressed through delicately nuanced advocacy of social change among a rapidly urbanizing Creole population which regards itself as truly French. Comorean nationalism had to incubate overseas before it arrived headlong in 1975 among the unprepared but fervent youth of the archipelago. It has since retreated abroad and underground, leaving a new, more complex sensibility of "modernization" to confront the restored regimes of religious custom and quasi-feudal patronage. A similar sensibility took hold more readily among educated and organized Creoles in Seychelles, although this most avowedly radical of the island movements has been obliged, ironically, to operate with utmost discretion against the dictates of an uncongenial establishment.

The timing of statehood and institutional maturity has depended on the relative efficacy of these national bourgeoisies. A rough national consensus was able to develop everywhere as colonial power receded, but its acquisition of political control had for better or worse to await the arrival of nominal independence. Once again, Réunion may represent the exception, for a tense debate rages today over the very existence of a Réunionnais nation. Its outcome will depend less on sterile academic definitions than on the degree to which insular expectations can be satisfied within the decentralization framework of Socialist France and on the flexibility ultimately allowed in Réunion's longterm allegiance to the French Republic.

In all cases, popular loyalty to the nationalist elites was secured, or refused, through direct personal relationships. It was the transactions of local "politics," family prestige and bread-and-butter party programs, rather than the legitimacy of offices, the appeal of ideologies, or the operation of national institutions, that determined how people understood and expressed their interests. Madagascar's comparative bulk, its decentralized cultural geography and deeply carved class structure render mass loyalties particularly susceptible to this primacy of local services and political personality.

As these societies evolved toward national self-consciousness, their new classes have come to behave, like their opponents, in accordance with certain overseas allegiances, however opaque the connection may be to mass constituencies. At first these external affinities operated as reflections of metropolitan party or trade union models as in the case of the Réunionnais Left, the Malagasy AKFM's "scientific socialism," and the early Mauritius Labour Party. More recently, nationalist regimes and oppositions have tried to tune their doctrines to international or third world precedents, as demonstrated in Ali Soilih's abortive Cultural Revolution in Comoros and F.A. René's use of Tanzanian ideals in Seychelles.

The importance of such external models consists not in how well they transplant but in their utility as sources of filtered information and activist vocabulary for island consensus or elite solidarity. They thus help determine insular public attitudes on such complexities as "great power presence," multinational corporate interests, and third world demands in global economics. Where allowed to compete, as in Mauritius' and Réunion's pluralistic marketplaces and through the ebullient underground channels of Madagascar and Comoros, the various antitheses of world politics tend to trickle into the hardened local party ideologies. Their influence creates distortions between existential program and international outlook. Where only one thesis is legitimate, as in Seychelles and on the surfaces of Comoros and Madagascar, the result is a decided public apathy toward the exhortations of power. In political practice, however, the island nationalisms have proved to be both unique and eclectic. They defer to older European strategies and to inspirational friendships with India, Algeria, China, or Tanzania. At the same time, they contend with the peculiar constraints of the insular, post-colonial microcosms which they inhabit.

The national movements have by and large failed to encourage a metamorphosis of rural life and agricultural production along with the inevitable transformations of their urban environments. If anything, the countryside has become more impoverished, less productive, more stagnant, less responsive to innovation than under colonial and post-colonial regimes. The tragedy of Indian Ocean nationalism consists primarily in having expanded urban opportunity so dramatically as to beggar the entire rural neighborhood. It consists secondarily in having to sully its national integrity through concessions to the overseas market economy which alone can guarantee the stability of that new urban edifice.

In the invidious interplay of priorities, all the island polities suffer from the common discrepancy of sensibility between the state and society, the official and the "real" country. The greatest application of state resources to urban and rural change has taken place where France had most influence over institutions—Réunion, Madagascar, and Comoros. Yet the most appreciable conversions of technology, capital and labor resources have actually occurred through the influence of market forces in the more permissive environments allowed by Britain in Seychelles (with negative results) and Mauritius (more fortunately). New competing labor markets and real estate speculation have drained Seychellois agriculture in favor of tourist-related industry. Mauritius lacked such alternatives, for there the rural-urban dichotomy is too closely congruent with Asian-Creole communal cleavage. Its Hindu smallholders and canefield labor force sustained both the nationalist movement and the campaigns of agricultural diversification, innovation, and cooperative association. Mauritians have made much of the fiscal limitations on state intervention, compared with Réunion and Madagascar which use greater public resouces (including foreign aid) for contrived rural development schemes or even more overwhelming urbanization.

Whatever the cause, and with Mauritius' partial exception, the south-western Indian Ocean countryside retains what Dupon regards as the vestigial shell of a demoralized plantation colonial past. At its worst, this atavism is manifested in the Mascarenes and Seychelles by lack of individual initiative, spiritual defeatism, feudal dependence of the weak on the strong, supine acceptance of European cultural superiority, irresponsibility among the powerless, and overbearing chauvinism by manorial masters.[2]

Dupon's analysis extends by and large to Comoros as well, for the period of flagrant reform in landholding and rural structure lasted less than three years, ending abruptly in 1978, and then evaporated. The old relations between Comorean aristocratic privilege and peasant subservience have since been restored, endorsed once again in political clientage and ceremonial liturgy. As in the Mascarenes and Seychelles, Comorean class oppositions between plantation proprietors and peasant, share-cropper, or field laborer correspond to ethnic divisions: the Zanzibari-Arab aristocracy retaining its paternal eminence much like the European plantocracy of the eastern archipelagoes. Class superiority tends to correlate with landholding, educational privilege, import-export business activity, and contract bonanzas for public works and foreign aid projects.[3]

Although more complex in social composition, with residual patterns of communal land ownership and decision-making, rural Madagascar resembles the other societies. Its countryside is deplorably stagnant in production, unresponsive to diversification, subject to prolonged paternalism, inclined to aggravate its own predicament by exporting the most dynamic population to the towns or overseas. Rising urban living costs and consequent wage demands have induced governments (largest of the urban employers) to subsidize food and other essentials in town while keeping the domestic agricultural market depressed, thus intensifying the undertow away from rural life. Where surplus food is produced, it is often bartered through parallel markets for consumer necessities, rather than sold through the contrivances of the State.[4]

The infernal twin specters of urban unemployment and rural suffocation stalk all regimes in the area, from Comoros' conservative restoration to the would-be radical mobilizations of Seychelles and Madagascar, the prudent reformers of Mauritius, and even France's successive administrative bene-factors of Réunion. Frustrated by the recalcitrance of their rural dilemmas, the new state systems have been able to improve on their colonial predecessors primarily in their willingness to offer comparatively egalitarian access to expanding urban opportunities. These include the bristling military institutions of Madagascar, Seychelles, and Comoros, rapid bureaucratization everywhere, and flourishing new private sectors in Mauritius and Seychelles. Always insufficient to satisfy expectations of upward mobility, these urban prospects reproduce the very conditions which brought nationalism to power in each place after the acquisition of titular independence. They are the conditions which the distant French administrations have been encouraging in Réunion, albeit without characterizing their welfare policies in anything like "national" terms.

The urbanity on which nationalism prospered proved morally indigestible to some of the beneficiaries. Here as elsewhere, the urban Western model for development has repelled national consciences by the apparent egoistic profligacy of its market technology. Yet, the neo-Marxist competitor has failed to demonstrate more than the ability to maintain a bureaucratic class. Efforts to revitalize society on some other basis have been implemented, and stultified, in the two insular societies of the region not originally created by Europe. After nine years, Madagascar has yet to realize its audacious experiment in a decentralized cooperative society founded on the revival of traditional rural forms of organization. Ali Soilih's more expeditious schemes to metamorphose the Comoros failed against the resistance of both modern and traditional elites. Perhaps all the islands have been too successfully westernized to substitute radically devised communal standards for the conventional indices of consumer prosperity, personal status, and professional success. On the other hand, they seem not sufficiently modern to satisfy those criteria by material progress in Western terms—or to carry agriculture along with prospering industry and services. Caught between a problematic present and a visionary future, the islands still risk the fate apprehended by Dupon—the isolation of separate, subjected, spuriously modern island entities which have lost their own traditions without generating new creativity.[5]

While social changes multiply of their own momentum and indigenous regimes modify popular symbolism toward national objectives, the material foundations of dependence change hardly at all. Primordial relations to sources of capital, credit, technology, food and raw materials, transportation, supplies of specialized products and tourists, markets for monocultures and for emigrant labor have remained remarkably stable from the pre-independence epoch. Standing at large in a suddenly busy sea, the southwestern islands again occupy a zone of international concourse, while remaining on the periphery of strategic and economic reality as defined by world power. These five clusters of islands and their dusting of islets suffer from the geographic disadvantages identified by Percy Selwyn in his 1975 policy paper for UNCTAD—remoteness of location, paucities of resources, and limited scale of activity.[6] They are dependent on external exchanges with larger, remote powers in a relationship which they can neither improve substantially nor renounce. That stable dependence requires the concentration of capital and other resources on specialized exportable production to the neglect of food production and other essentials of subsistence.

Wherever the markets may be for the undifferentiated commodities of plantation agriculture, mining, or tourism, their managers enjoy far greater discretion than do the islands to accept or reject prevailing price and other dictates. The international companies which conduct the trade at both ends are free to buy or sell within their own kaleidescopes of comparative market conditions. Their diversified interests, informed management and astute accountancy, oligopolistic control of technology, and wide-ranging speculative habits permit postponement of satisfactions not allowed a subsistence economy. Given this freedom of action, notwithstanding the domestic political importance of the companies' correspondents in the islands, terms of trade will almost inevitably operate to the disadvantage of the dependent economy. Powerlessness thus vitiates conventional cost and benefit calculations of comparative advantage.

Each island economy has been grafted onto a system over which it has little influence. It functions tributarily, subject to others' needs and terms of operation. The illustrations have become virtually universal for underdevelopment. While the European Communities will deliberate on sugar prices and import quotas for Mauritius' benefit, and France will open European sugar markets advantageously to Réunion, the islands cannot even think of establishing their own sugar refineries for fear of differential shipping tariffs established to protect metropolitan refining.

Once encountered, balance of payments anomalies can be remedied only through fiscal and monetary policies acceptable to orthodox macro-economists in Western banks, governments, and international lending organizations. The International Monetary Fund, World Bank, European Development Fund, and multilateral banking consortia have come to replace traditional Franc Zone adjustment mechanisms for Madagascar's budgetary deficits and imbalance of payments. Paris assumes direct responsibility for departmental Réunion and subservient Comoros (especially for Mayotte) and still accepts a leonine burden of Malagasy debt. But official France seeks as far as possible to displace its burdens of fiscal and commodity stabilization onto the European Community, commercial banks, and the IMF, while maintaining maximum bilateral influence on policy orientations. Britain withdrew that kind of responsibility years ago from Mauritius and Seychelles in order to go "west of Suez."

Whether implemented by governments, banks, or multilateral agencies, the conditions for stabilization shrink the range of experiment open to leaders of fragile societies. They thus willy-nilly assure retention of the privileges enjoyed by prevailing island elites. Progressive taxation, rising minimum wages, and large-scale social benefit programs have eroded some of that privilege even in Réunion and Comoros where the aristocracy has remained intact. Still, the overseas financial and commercial networks have sustained the essential material superiority of the *grands blancs* of all the Mascarenes and Seychelles, the Arab nobility of Comoros, the remaining planter and commercial interests in Madagascar. Ironically, all these protected groups had previously sought to secure their prerogatives by futile political opposition to the nationalist movements which they had regarded as inevitably calamitous threats.

For the entrenched island establishments, nationalism runs against the needs of security. Colonial patronage, however negligent, was once regarded as essential to the survival of the insular societies, usually identified with the eminence of class. Whenever obliged to support an indigenous political faction or to acknowledge the imminent end of overt colonial rule, the aristocracies invariably favored the closest possible constitutional, economic, and cultural association with the metropole. Acceptable to most metropolitan interests, this option produces the regimes (stigmatized rhetorically as neo-colonial) of Philibert Tsiranana's PSD in Madagascar, James Mancham's SDP in Seychelles, Ahmed Abdallah in Comoros; in Mauritius, the association with European and South African interests has provoked periodic coalitions with the wishfully titled Mauritius Social Democratic Party (PMSD) which helped draw Ramgoolam's Labour Party and Jugnauth's socialism to the right of center. Tsiranana, Ramgoolam, Mancham, and Abdallah all enjoyed power in an independence arrangement with the metropole. Regime viability, confused with state security, kept that arrangement attractive, at an acceptable cost in economic options. The overall pattern is of course far from unique. Sooner or later, if only by default, the determinisms of security have induced most weak Indian Ocean nations from the Persian Gulf to the seacoasts of ASEAN into a complex, hesitant engagement with dominant Western trade and financial systems. For nationalists entangled in this web of dependence, recourse to the "socialist option" permitted credible claims of "progressiveness" while entailing a second dimension of political and/or security reliance on Soviet sponsors.

Forced to accept a purely Western determinism at the outset, however, the original regimes of the southwestern islands generally consented to exchange economic and social initiatives for metropolitan security assurances. Both partners agreed that the foreign enemies of the one were domestic threats to the other. As in most of the littoral states, island majorities eventually discovered—with alacrity and intensity in Comoros and Seychelles, more gradually in Madagascar and Mauritius—that the advantages of the security equation devolved upon a relatively small faction with direct interest in its maintenance. A popular surge of resentment against this state of postcolonial subordination—moving at differing pace and intensity from island to island—ultimately eliminated the consenting regimes without necessarily altering the fundamental economic and social realities which they had been protecting. This transformation seems consistent with the primary phenomenon of nationalism identified here—namely, generalized access to urban opportunity. But the successor regimes, after redefining external enemies and domestic opponents, encountered similar obstructions to their national goals. The constraints operating against full social trans-formation in the Comorean case invited counter-revolution. In Madagascar, Mauritius, and Seychelles (and with appropriate variations, French Réunion), the retarded dynamics of social change have likewise had serious repercussions for the regimes in power—policy stalemate, insolvency, and civil unrest in Madagascar, several violent efforts at destabilization in Seychelles, collapse of the nationalist coalition in Mauritius nine months after its belated electoral triumph, and an intrepid resurgence of the tory Right in Réunion.

Despite their vicissitudes, the islands' embattled leaderships have manifested considerable ingenuity in devising new political and military relationships compatible with their respective conceptions of national interest. In one way or another, all ruling factions have discovered that identification of enemies and accommodation to protective power do not assure prosperity, modernization, or even stabilizing self-confidence. Among the divers solutions proposed for the syndrome of the sea-locked, the best security has seemed in practice to consist in the least onerous protective relationship consistent with need. A lighter, dispersed burden of security arrangements no doubt recommends itself to any small country which has felt the blocking bulk of a single protecting power—or the tangle of competing sponsors experienced by Seychelles in 1977-1979. Being smothered in security hardly enhances a ministate's ability to conduct foreign relations, let alone to overcome constraints of economic impotence.

To make the align-nonalign option meaningful, a state must be able to withhold something another power might wish to possess. None of these islands has the weight to impress itself upon power realities. Even in solidarity, their leverage would amount to small change, compared to the population, resource density, and geopolitical importance of, say the ASEAN complex, the Arabian peninsula entente, or the "frontline" coalition facing South Africa. As tributary economies with chronic payments problems, rising debt, and relatively low per capita claims on international development aid, the islands have few bargaining assets to begin with. They may refer vaguely to strategic location along tanker routes, but even there the islands have little to withhold except port and airfield facilities of uncertain value to one or another external power. These installations were developed and occupied by the colonial powers—and in the cases of Réunion, Mayotte, and Diego Garcia, are still so occupied.

The early independence regimes (including Abdallah's) did not hesitate to extend such rights to the ex-colonial, cum protecting power. Both Mauritius and Madagascar forged central security arrangements with their respective metropoles while professing—and in Mauritius' case, implementing—broader affinities among other presences of the Indian Ocean. Under Prime Minister Ramgoolam, with the mercurial Gaetan Duval as intermittent foreign minister, Mauritius conducted a positive "all-horizons" foreign policy for fourteen years beyond independence. It ranged swashbucklingly over a buyer's market in a form of open neutrality that welcomed Soviet, Iranian, French, British, and American fleets at Port Louis, some of them simultaneously. But, declining to organize military forces of its own, Ramgoolam's Mauritius obtained British security assurances by treaty. Until the Diego Garcia controversy boiled into embarrassment for Ramgoolam, Britain enjoyed privileged telecommunications and transportation facilities as well as intervention responsibilities in the event of civil disturbance. Ramgoolam's nationalist successors profess a different, more hermetic variant of nonalignment, with special favors for and from none. Both Mauritian regimes have courted particularly close relations with India, origin of the island's majority population and mounting star of Indian Ocean regional aspirations, but in neither case has this association entailed unusual security arrangements.[7]

During his twelve years in power after independence, Philibert Tsiranana persistently alluded to Madagascar's historic office as a "bridge" between Africa and Asia, while never himself quite trusting any traffic on the bridge except French. The military aspects of the cooperation agreements of 1960 governed Malagasy security until 1973. They authorized French force deployment on and around the island and provided for exclusive French guardianship over the evolution of Madagascar's own military, paramilitary, and intelligence agencies. On the periphery of this bilateral arrangement, Tsiranana could diffuse the Great Island's international audience, occasionally straining at the essential umbilical, to dally with the United States, United Kingdom, West Germany, Israel, or South Africa—until France called a halt to his experiments. Never did Tsiranana seriously consider trying his luck with the Communist or radical third world interests which he regarded as infernally motivated. Hence, his policy of diversification lacked the outrageous scope of Mauritius' behavior during the heyday of Ramgoolam-Duval dialectics.[8] Tsiranana's successors have accepted Soviet, North Korean, and other Socialist ministrations in the security arena. But France has been neither restored nor replaced as privileged protector in Madagascar. The great naval base at Diego Suarez (now Antseranana) remains without a tenant, and the abundant Malagasy ports and airfields receive rare foreign military callers.

Although gratuitously declaring his regime among the fraternity of the nonaligned, Ahmed Abdallah has reaffirmed prenationalist French authority over Comorean security. In truth, he had little choice—even less, perhaps, than Djibouti's President Gouled Aptidon who has retained French military supremacy in his strategic country since independence in 1977, earning precious little reproach from the customary critics of alignment. France was still occupying Mayotte in Comorean territory when Abdallah returned to power in May 1978. It seemed only prudent to make the French forces welcome on the entire archipelago, avoiding frictions and perhaps generating inducements for reintegration of Mayotte. Moreover, Paris was leading a surge of international pressure against Abdallah's retention of his white mercenary militia. The neo-corsair crew seemed about to become a permanent instrument of state security. France represented the sole eligible respectable alternative to those "ghastlies." Many of them have nonetheless retained less conspicuous roles in the islands under the suspicious eye of Abdallah's French military advisors. Rivalry between his mercenary-trained palace guard and the Frenchified army has jeopardized Comorean domestic tranquillity, violating the insular nationalist faith that the simplest security is the best security.

Seychelles has also had to manage a complicated political-military situation. The islands spent a full year without any such arrangements under its first President, James Mancham, who made everybody equally at home. Thus, Mancham was defenseless against a small force of invading irregulars who disposed of him by taking him at his word. Beginning in 1977, the islands became strenuously militarized in the cause of national mobilization, and were able to repell their own "ghastly" commando attack in 1981. President René has used a variety of sponsors for military equipment and training, including Tanzania, Algeria, the USSR and, for a two-year period, France as well. Since 1979, however, Tanzania has assumed the active role in internal security, while Soviet and French naval units hover avuncularly around Port Victoria in times of stress. Crowded as the scene is, René's SPPF government has maneuvered autonomously in foreign political affairs, granting few privileges to external forces—but at serious cost to Seychelles' peace and quiet.

Like René and like the nationalists in Mauritius, Madagascar's President Ratsiraka declares his nation's nonalignment to be "positive." The adjective ordinarily implies some activity, but policy seems limited here to diplomatic postures in response to the acts of others. External power moves which appear compatible with one's own perceptions of security are approved; those which intrude into the Indian Ocean for reasons less legitimately linked to zonal tranquillity are repudiated. Although both super powers profess only the healthiest motives, American deployments and base installations appear less justified to the positively nonaligned than corresponding Soviet moves. The distinction derives in part from the local company they keep. South Africa, Israel, and Pakistan are regarded as more troublesome than Ethiopia, South Yemen, India, or even Libya, Syria, or Vietnam. However logical these discriminations, the Diego Garcia base looms far more ominously than France's busy installations in Djibouti, Réunion, and Mayotte, or the Soviet anchorages at Socotra, Aden, and the Ethiopian Red Sea coast. Nevertheless, all intrusions into the general neighborhood have proved tolerable if the alien power behaves quietly and brings some token of deference. Distrustful as they are of Western motives, especially when NATO interests, Israel, or South Africa can be associated therewith, none of the nationalist island regimes has been willing to concede security assets in any direction that might seriously alienate another protecting power. Their solicitude is founded less, perhaps, on the delights of austere defense arrangements than on the contributions committed by the several metropolitan powers to island finance and commerce. So the West's ideological disadvantage is ransomable through international economic and cultural cooperation.

Although prejudiced by close association with American machinations, Britain's scanty, senescent power has come to be tolerated on a relative par with the French in an ocean which readily forgets the storms of its troubled past. Like Abdallah in the Franco-Comorean dispute over Mayotte, all Mauritius governments have adjusted philosophically to the offense of Diego

Garcia, conducting relations of utmost cordiality with the Anglo-American trespassers on the Chagos. Seychelles refrains from recrimination against Britain, even in times of tribulation for the René regime.

Still, it is the French reputation that is the most charmed in this corner of the world. Revolutionary Madagascar has achieved substantial reconciliation with France following a period of obligatory discord in 1972–1973, as the island disengaged from Tsiranana's elaborate treaty relationship. Like Mauritius and Comoros, Madagascar has discreetly pursued its unreconciled grievance with Paris over the Mozambique Channel islets and Les Glorieuses. As we have noted in our chapters treating the islands respectively, French colonial and post-colonial strategy has skillfully encouraged reconciliation at each turn of fortune's wheel. French Indian Ocean policy has in fact manifested remarkable continuity, reminiscent of Tory influence over England's approach to Rhodesia in the 1960s and 1970s. The Gaullist bloc championed by Michel Debré has persistently determined France's fundamental orientation to the ocean from the outset of the Fifth Republic through the Giscard and Mitterand administrations into the current Mitterand-Chirac condominium.

Integration in the Quartier

Severely over-ridden by economic reality, the islands make a brave show of neutral opinion in the outside world, and go seeking a securer peace in their own region. Other obstacles, discussed in our final chapter, have frustrated the Indian Ocean states' search for a general autonomous system of collective security, economic development, and diplomatic consensus. The emergence of India as a new pole of organization for the greater region remains controversial for the present, and problematic in the future. At the moment, while joining the Zone of Peace quest and exploiting opportunities for cooperation with burgeoning New Delhi, the islands rely increasingly on each other to resonate their modest initiatives in security, development, and political conciliation. What latitude they have comes in part from an enlarging mutuality of nationalist experience. Their chances for reinforcement are also favored, however ironically, by intense French cultivation of their respective institutions and elites. Common access to the heritage of France, acquired at varying depth and some sacrifice of cultural autonomy, provides a valuable, enduring medium for the cohesion which the islands propose among themselves.

After her eviction from India during the late eighteenth century, France lacked continental territory in the region until her protectorate over Djibouti was accomplished in 1888. Sporadic assertions of French interest in other parts of East Africa were dissuaded by British and German pressures. They were finally renounced in 1885, in exchange for a free hand in Madagascar and the Comoros. France had already obtained predominance over Mayotte, the southeasternmost Comoro, as well as on Nosy-Be just off Madagascar's northwest tip and Sainte Marie (now Nosy Boraha) opposite the Great

Island's northeast coast. The settler colony on Réunion was clamoring for intervention in Madagascar, and the official French residents of Antananarivo had persuaded Napoleon III to "offer" protection to the Merina regime in the early 1860s. France and her Réunionnais sought to support and expand plantation and mining concessions and to protect exclusive trade privileges in the vast, under-populated breadbasket next door. Acting with what imperial Europeans regarded as impertinent autonomy in international affairs and in the treatment of foreigners at Antananarivo, the Merina monarchy gave France numerous pretexts for intervention. English benevolence may have been fondly anticipated by the Malagasy in a potential crisis with France, but the British henceforth proved supremely indifferent to the plight of the Merina court.

British rule in Mauritius and Seychelles concentrated mainly on the formal economic and political allegiance of the island societies. Despite occasional afterthoughts, London allowed prevailing French practice to continue determining language, law, and jurisprudence, the arts, and all other institutions in perpetuity. That influence was transmitted through the late colonial period, albeit with some mid-twentieth century competition from English as a language of high political and economic affairs. Bilingualism became an asset for the powerful, the learned, and the ambitious, but not a necessity for the rest of Mascarene and Seychelles society. Britain had made her covenant with the French aristocracy. Unlike Quebec, surrounded by Anglophonia, the islands gave little cause for English intrusion on French prerogatives while essential loyalties of flag and flagship remained intact. Cultural homogeneity has proved strong among the Mascarenes (Réunion, Mauritius, Rodriguez) and between them and the Seychelles, despite their different constitutional destinies. All the main Creole (Afro-Asian-European) communities—their own language based solidly on French and their faith monopolized by Roman Catholicism—joined the white upper classes in resisting decolonization longest and most intrepidly.[9]

Even without that critical mass of original European settlers or Creole converts, the deepest oceanic cultures of Madagascar and the Comoros have also been strongly permeated by French influence. By 1880, Britain was tolerating French intervention in the zone between East Africa and Mauritius. France first asserted "protectorates" (of metropolitans and Réunionnais, mainly) over Madagascar and the three remaining Comoros, but those regimes hardened into direct military, then political control. Refusing linguistic status to indigenous Malagasy, Comorean Swahili or Arabic, or Réunion's Creole, the French established their language as the obligatory medium for social-economic progress and political participation. Aspirants to any official or social privilege throughout the island zone necessarily absorbed not only the parlance but also the French ways of organizing, building, criticizing, teaching, buying and selling, running a railroad, deploying an army, eating, drinking, and making merry. Their distinctive cultural endowments notwithstanding, Malagasy and Comoreans were treated with the condescension reserved for colonial Africans. Their evolution demanded the intervention of civilization, the technology of the white mask over the Afro-Asian soul. Malagasy, Comorean, and Réunionnais societies were bombarded by an invidious, essentially chauvinist barrage of ideas and institutional standards. French metropolitan policy far transcended the minimal political and commercial orientation which sufficed as imperial control for Britain in the islands to the east.[10]

Francophone facility represents not only a medium for contact among all the islands. It also entails valuable political advantages for France in the entire region to this day. Despite the brutality of its "civilizing process" among the African, Asian, Malagasy, and Creole populations of the colonial period, France suffers relatively little local criticism of its continuing sovereign and military presence in the region. Without overt manipulation by Paris, the leaders of Francophone societies can make allowances for France that are normally denied to any imperial cause. In the case of Réunion and Mayotte, it is even possible that African and mulatto populations might legitimately prefer to remain under the Tricolor, rather than jeopardize their happiness in the ruinous self-determination that has derelicted so much of the third world.

By virtue of natural abundance, Madagascar once occupied a central position across the partitions of the Anglo-French island quarter. The late colonial and early independent phases reduced Comoros, Réunion, and even proud Mauritius to mere stages on the air and maritime circuits between Europe and the Great Island or lands eastward. Supplies of Malagasy beef and rice have helped keep the smaller islands provisioned for nearly two centuries. Tens of thousands of Réunionnais and Comoreans carrying French passports settled in Madagascar after 1896, at times coming to dominate particular occupations and markets. Seizing the advantage of their putative bilinguality, many English teachers from Mauritius served in Malagasy schools both before and after 1960. While the Great Island's trade advantage stayed favorable, convertible Malagasy franc remittances from these workers helped keep intrazonal payments in balance. French sugar planters and millers in Madagascar benefitted from intensive technological exchanges between research and development institutions in Mauritius and Réunion, particularly in strategies against disease and meteorological devastation. Vanilla growers on Madagascar, Réunion, and Comoros have also occasionally pooled technical and commercial lore.

Seychelles was usually too distant for this much intimacy. Once separated from Mauritius' jurisdiction in 1903, that obscure colony on the Mombasa-to-India steamship route scarcely knew its neighbors to the south. This isolation ended in 1971, however, when Mahé's airport put Seychelles onto the map of modern tourism and official junketing. Seychelles could thereupon file for affiliation with Comoros, Madagascar, Réunion, and Mauritius in a number of consultative undertakings. The Indian Ocean Tourist Alliance (ATOI), an intergovernmental marketing council, was established in 1967 under French aegis. After succumbing to South African domination, the council dissolved in Madagascar's upheavals after 1972.

Before yielding to the combustions of that year, Malagasy President Tsiranana periodically considered prospects for fraternal influence by the Great Island among the southern continents. In practice, Malagasy initiatives proved rare and rather ephemeral. Mauritius under Ramgoolam evinced interest in regional economic integration, but Tsiranana seldom met Ramgoolam and had little enthusiasm for the return of the illustrious, Asian-populated Ile de France as pivot of the Indian Ocean. What Tsiranana conceived was an almost exclusively conservative, anti-Communist political association extending from South Africa, Portuguese Mozambique, and Kenya through the grand arc of Arabia and South Asia to the Philippines, with the Malagasy-led islands as links and linguists. Such concert was to serve Western interests as well as the stability of the ocean as a whole. Primarily, however, the idea was a way of reinforcing French attention to the islands' economic and security needs. Returning from a visit to Paris in July 1969, Tsiranana told his people, "I sought to represent to my interlocutors all the islands of the Indian Ocean whose harmonious development is necessary to guarantee peace in that part of the world."[11]

Paris seems to have shown little enthusiasm for a Malagasy mission of oceanic integration. Problems of heterogeneity, geopolitical mass and discrepancies in colonial heritage limited what even the few neighboring islands might accomplish toward sectoral unity.[12] France maintained satisfactory ties with radical states like Somalia and Sukarno's Indonesia which Tsiranana considered beyond some ideological pale. From its complicated diplomatic position in Eastern Europe and China, Paris could never indulge the Malagasy President's pure Marxophobia. It was not persuaded that Soviet arms in the region, Chinese railroad supplies to Dar es Salaam, or Eastern European training for Southern African liberation movements constituted threats to French interests in Madagascar, Réunion, Comoros, or Djibouti. While maintaining her own strategic trade links with ostracized South Africa, France was unlikely to second Tsiranana's blatant encouragement of a regional guardianship by the Pretorian pariah.

Moreover, any project for Indian Ocean integration beyond France's own *quartier* would have inevitably entailed consultations with the United States and United Kingdom over the role of the Francophone islands—an unwelcome concession for Gaullist policy. Even NASA's station on the Great Island was regarded in Paris as an unnecessary American foot in the Malagasy door. Tsiranana might not be denied the freedom to bargain with NASA, although he could be prevented from accepting more insidious intrusions like the US Peace Corps or major agribusiness ventures. The Malagasy acquiesced for a time in British military use of Majunga (Mahajanga) airfields for surveillance of the 1966 international embargo against Rhodesian trade through the Mozambique port of Beira, but that mission was eventually cancelled by French pressure at Antananarivo.

Ironically for Tsiranana, the integrative moral influence he sought did emerge rather dramatically after his downfall in 1972. Even then, its manifestations revealed Madagascar's inadequacy for ambitious substantive political and economic leadership. Radical dynamics in the Great Island gave courage and example, if not direct assistance, to the nationalist forces which moved successfully in Comoros and Seychelles three and five years, respectively, after the Malagasy experience in 1972. Those events had repercussions in Mauritius and Réunion as well. For once, the previously isolated Mauritian Militant Movement (MMM) and Réunion Communist Party (PCR) could make use of a nearby interlocutor regime during their increasingly successful electoral campaigns. In April 1978, these five "progressive" governments and parties began the political and diplomatic coordination that the deposed Malagasy leader had once envisioned for a far different set of objectives. The progressives' meeting at Mahé (Seychelles) called for self-determination in Réunion, demilitarization of the Indian Ocean, dismantling of the Diego Garcia base, and other regional desiderata totally opposed to the old Tsiranana orientation.

These pronouncements produced little effect in the greater world, although useful consultation sharpened the participants' behavior in UN, OAU, and other international forums. It has also obviated some actual conflict between those participants themselves. Madagascar has ceded its claim on Tromelin island, allowing Mauritius to confront the immovable French by itself on that issue. Abrasions over maritime and fishery rights can also be adjudicated in the multilateral Mahé forum. In the most serious neighborhood dispute of all, the exasperated Malagasy population of Mahajanga had turned on the city's huge and comparatively prosperous community of Comoreans in early 1977, murdering thousands and forcing the repatriation of 20,000 to their impoverished homeland. Without directly blaming the Ratsiraka government for the pogrom (as others did), Comorean leader Ali Soilih found his Malagasy counterparts to be less than forthcoming in settling the painful aftermath of the riots. Still, the fact that Madagascar and Comoros agreed to meet in April 1978 during an intense bilateral crisis testifies to the conciliatory influence of the progressives' concert. Comoros stopped receiving invitations to progressive conclaves after May 1978 when Soilih had fallen in Abdallah's counter-putsch. Relations with Madagascar remained unsatisfactory.[13] Containing only two functioning governments, the Mahé group soon declined into desuetude.

The MMM electoral victory of June 1982 compensated for the loss of Comoros, however, and brought the forum back to life. Overcoming reciprocal distaste between Ramgoolam and Mauritius' more nationalist neighbors, the island's new leaders improved regional cooperation measurably. The Réunion PCR's legitimacy in the group was also enhanced through the inclusion of French Communists in President Mitterand's cabinet in June 1981. Bolstered in its specific gravity, and with expectations of neighborhood free trade and political, economic and cultural integration, the loose concert of progressives turned itself in July 1982 into a tripartite Indian Ocean Commission (IOC). Observers from France (sitting on behalf of Réunion) and from Abdallah's Comoros attended 1984 meetings and the two governments were made full IOC members the following January, even though Abdallah remains an albatross for his nationalist neighbors. Comoros had already been woven into air and sea transport patterns with Madagascar, Mauritius, and Réunion. It is also among the fifteen signatories of the UN Economic Commission for Africa's May 1981 East and Southern African Preferential Trade Agreement. The IOC even contemplates an ambitious expansion to include friendly but distant partners like India and Australia.

While far from rivalling the Association of Southeast Asian Nations (ASEAN) in either economic mass or strategic position, the IOC has sought to put some concrete into the foundation of a flourishing Latin Quarter. With modest external assistance, particularly from the European Development Fund, island ministries developed schemes for regional cooperation in tuna fishing, renewable energy development, air and sea transportation, navigation aid, and telecommunications, as well as joint undertakings in tourism and crafts, beef and rice marketing (based in Madagascar), cement and plate-glass fabrication.[14] Full membership for France—as Réunion's sovereign—promises to augment the reality of cooperative action: for up to then, the progressive partners could more easily denounce the American base on Diego Garcia than find the grounds for inter-island trade, employment creation, and shared industrial resource allocation. They still confront strong European monopolies over sea and air traffic connecting them to their patron-partners abroad. Transportation of bulk sugar, coffee, and copra exports, with little compensatory weight in returning bottoms, is constantly subject to upward rate fluctuations, aggravating the islands' chronic terms of trade vicissitudes.[15] They have little to buy from one another and, while theoretically eager to promote agricultural and industrial divisions of labor, they have few resources to invest in complementarity of production. Their resources are even scantier when it comes to persuading established producers with traditional European "connections" to curtail wasteful duplication on behalf of regional pies in the sky.

The islands don't just competitively "produce the same thing," of course, although there is serious duplication among them in sugar, vanilla, copra, cloves, perfume oils, and tourist facilities. But they all do *need* the same benefits from outside—in raw materials, finance capital, foreign exchange, market quotas and price guarantees, food and consumer imports, technology, and accessible communications. Very little of this can be supplied from within a five-island network or even over a broader, more elaborate system with East African and South Asian partners. Ruinous competition in bidding for these benefits could be reduced and the pooling of applications might apply somewhat greater leverage on overseas suppliers. For the time being, however, dependence on those sources is largely bilateral, minimally discretionary for the island economies, and essentially competitive.

Highly promising joint research and development projects are annually coordinated among governmental and private institutions within the Indian Ocean Association of Institutions of Reasearch and Development (AIRDOI). These undertakings touch on regional interests in ocean fishing, energy resource development, communications, public health, Creole studies, and many other areas of joint concern. They are particularly important in the Mascarenes and Seychelles, although Madagascar and Comoros participate in principle. Incompatibilities between Mauritius' largely private research centers (including the admirable Sugar Research Institute) and their governmental counterparts in Réunion have been smoothly regulated by AIRDOI and other mediators. Exigencies of funding nevertheless keep such projects at the mercy of international and Western donor agencies which acknowledge little stake in regional coordination. AIRDOI's efficacy has been restricted primarily to examination and endorsement of project viability without the means for assuring implementation of the most valuable initiatives. Lacking its own endowment, AIRDOI is constantly jeopardized as a credible mediator between the islands.

The islands have a clear interest in mutual collaboration to reallocate their respective assets and liabilities nationally, to obtain multipartite distribution of benefits and costs of investment, to enhance their bargaining power overseas, to share needed information and technology, maximize their exchange reserves, and establish benefical migratory employment flows. Yet the very forces which weakened each of the islands individually—poverty of resources, isolation, overpopulation, inadequate infrastructure, speculative development of specialized but vulnerable export crops—now prevent them from forging combinations of strength.[16] They are all bound by rigid rules of commercial exchange, credit, and services within traditional networks established to ensure their very existence as economies. Even joint participation in tourist networks has turned competitively against them. Despite their real diversity, one island seems, at least during international recessions, to have the same assets as the other islands. A once relatively coherent system of shipping and air transportation was operated monopolistically by Air France, Messageries Maritimes, and the ocean freight conference SIMACOREM. This mixed blessing for integration has been disrupted in recent years by the easy achievement of bilateral connections with Europe, India, East and South Africa.

The islands have few reserves of their own to convert to the purposes of relative self-sufficiency or interzonal collaboration. The available overseas acquisitions have to be used primarily to ensure, or to adjust to, the status quo on which survival depends. All populations have developed predilections for rice, which can be produced in quantity only on Madagascar. Yet even the big island imports rice for its own subsistence, although it continues to sell beef (corned and on the hoof) to Réunion, Comoros, Mauritius, and East African markets. They all import the other grains, meat, dairy products, and vegetables which might be cultivated domestically only at the sacrifice of resources now devoted to lucrative export agriculture and tourism. Egress from the cycles of stagnation, unemployment, and post-colonial subordination requires a benevolent effort from abroad as well as a determination not yet realized in the insular social metabolism. However benign its regional patronage, India has been able to enhance only specific projects of bilateral and limited importance, while the regional service rendered by

Mozambique and even Tanzania has been primarily ideological. The economic power of the Arab world has operated half-heartedly and at cross-purposes in the islands without providing much more than marginal alleviation of current financial and labor pressures. The more substantial role of South Africa in general trade and capital formation can be expanded without political stigma only in Comoros, where economic opportunities are weakest.

Current IOC members tend to look to the continent behind them for substantive cooperation far more than their predecessors did. Occasions have arisen in transportation and tourism, the production and exchange of textiles and complementary agricultural products, fisheries development, oceanographic and other research, telecommunications, pooled education, and training personnel. Some of these endeavors enjoy United Nations sponsorship. An eight-nation treaty on East African marine pollution has been promoted by the UN's Environmental Program (UNEP). Others are more spontaneous. Tanzania has contributed military assistance for Seychelles and rural development advice in Seychelles and Madagascar. Kenya is a veteran trade partner of the islands, especially Mauritius. The achievement of independence since 1975 by Mozambique, Djibouti, and Zimbabwe, all with differing but notable affinities with the islands, should help broaden their dialogue with Eastern Africa. The limitations on such cooperation are virtually self-evident. All the regimes are cautious, constrained by internal quandaries, preoccupied by pre-emptive external relations. Excluding South Africa—a main source of preoccupation, not of resolution—only Mauritius and Kenya have the mature private sectors to realize economic relations without cumbersome governmental good offices.

The quest for area solidarity continues nevertheless, and not without some long-range prospects. For all its futility in securing the Indian Ocean as a self-regulating Zone of Peace, the UN's multilateral diplomacy has opened exploitable avenues of intercourse among the zone's inhabitants— or at any rate, among their foreign offices. The mere prospect of enhanced access to information on technology, markets, and financing practices could help each partner in pursuit of viability, multilateral or otherwise. A more tranquil East and Southern Africa could improve prospects for broader cooperation. But the island economies remain nonetheless separate wards of international patrons.

The islands' own prospects for generating regionally useful surpluses are concentrated on two economies—the Malagasy and the French, operating through Réunion. Traditionally a supplier of food and other necessities, a nucleus for transportation connections, a more or less indulgent recipient of immigrant labor, a processor and re-exporter of petroleum products, Madagascar theoretically has the resources to act as an engine for gradual inter-island development. It has a diversified agriculture with much open land, raw materials including some mineral wealth, and sources of energy. But the Great Island's productivity has declined tragically over two decades, while indebtedness rose precipitously and foreign exchange reserves disappeared. Malagasy economic strength must be applied in the short run to maintaining current budgetary and payments equilibrium under IMF controls, rather than to the creation of surpluses which could help enliven new circuits of transaction for smaller neighbors. Mauritius, Réunion, Comoros, and Seychelles have all bypassed Madagascar in developing new transport connections with their principal overseas partners. Their population pressures could be alleviated by emigration to the Great Island only at the expense of Madagascar's already doubtful social cohesion.

Seychelles, Comoros, and especially Mauritius operate economies of limited means and overriding constraints, with little good land left for exploitation and little unexhausted production technology for intensification or diversification.

By contrast, Réunion has been able to draw and even waste lavish resources from the metropole. Here, French investment strategy transcends the usual logic of costs and benefits. It has aimed since the mid-1960s at finding satisfactory formulas of departmental integration and after 1972 at accommodating military and business operations evicted from Madagascar. Réunion's operating budgets compare with those of Madagascar, which has twenty times its population. This investment produces disparities in wage and consumption levels that could threaten any design for resource allocation between Réunion and the poorer islands.

Réunion obtains constant recompense for its allegiance to France in what Dupon calls a "colonial pact." The island's airfield, road system, hydroelectric complexes, telecommunications, new port facilities, and equipment parks are extraordinary. They testify to the ability of a metropolitan patron to reproduce the perquisites of industrialized Europe in an otherwise impoverished, unproductive, distant Eden of colored people.[17] While Seychelles, Madagascar, Mauritius, Comoros, and the East African littoral countries scramble for piecemeal improvements in their underdeveloped fishing fleets, for instance, Réunion alone has joined the major trawler nations in exploiting the resources of the deep from Antartica through the tropical waters of their common ocean.

These cardinal advantages in living standards could help generate regional economic production, but they also militate against Réunionnais enthusiasm for closer integration with the region. Bilateralism afflicts all the islands' integration ambitions, but it has its most compelling logic in French Réunion.[18] Thus, Paris still holds the essential key to integration. From 1981 to 1986, Socialist France enjoyed extraordinary freedom of movement throughout the subregion. Paris had even earlier resumed major economic and social partnerships in Madagascar and Comoros after brief interruptions. French relations with Britain's former Mauritius and Seychelles colonies are *primus inter pares*, thanks both to the historic cultural heritage and to the curiously "cohabitational" appeal of Gaullism with European socialism.

France would have little competition if it chose to act as a patron of regional coordination, a responsibility which neither Britain nor any other power wishes to undertake. If Paris should decide to take an expensive but prestigious gamble in regional patronage, it could use Francophone affinity and ideological homogeneity to correct the disparate banking and credit, currency, trade, and legal systems among the islands. It must also combat French interest in the pre-eminence of Réunion as an exception to the poverty of independence, a beacon for European loyalism in a sea of nationalist misery. The claims of three regional partners against French retention of Mayotte and other islands may also have to be settled, if France wishes to promote full cooperation in such a project.

As signatories of the Lomé agreement between the European Communities and the African, Caribbean and Pacific states, the independent islands now sell bilaterally to Europe. To start an integrative process, they might try to increase sales to Réunion if they can produce what the island needs at appropriate prices and if France lowered the island's imposing tariff barriers. Mauritius has begun to do this, for a variety of manufactured items and for vacation packages. Mauritians even invest capital in Réunion, taking advantage of French guarantees and protected markets for Réunion's costly exports to the metropole, as contrasted with their own hard-pressed economy and redistributive politics. Madagascar has also resumed sales of beef and beef products to Réunion, although Malagasy exports worth eighty-five million French francs represented only 1.3 percent of the Réunionnais import bill for 1983. Some interest has been shown by Réunion capital in the newly reopened Malagasy investment market, but thus far, the two close neighbors remain far from reproducing the symbiotic economics that once inspired and guided France's colonial control over the Great Island.

France, particularly as a member of the IOC, could encourage both the development of export capacity in the other islands and the receptivity of Réunionnais to such products. Already struggling to restore its own deteriorating trade balances, however, Paris could multilateralize the Réunion market only at a sacrifice to its own exporters who now sell profitably there. Moreover, that market of barely one-half million people can scarcely be expected to generate opportunities for a full region of twelve million, whether France finances the development or not.

It is not only privileged Réunion which might resist regional integration. Each of the islands has developed its own responses to the stimuli of world interests. They were populated, after all, by varying accretions of Africans, Asians, and Europeans in unequal proportions, different susceptibilities to miscegination, conflicting overseas loyalties. They evolved for a century and longer under different colonial policies—true settler colonialism in Réunion contrasting with protection of concessionary agribusiness in Comoros, hard industrial bargains for Mauritius, somnolent subsistence in Seychelles, and a shifting, complex, often contradictory combination of strategies in Madagascar. Its very size and expanse of resources, prospective self-sufficiency, cultural originality, and deep history distinguish the Great Island radically from the Mascarenes and Seychelles, linked as these smaller islands are by undersea geological, as well as oceanic and historical conditions. While closer to Madagascar in many respects, the Comoros remain culturally distinct as insular southern outposts of Muslim Africa.

Indeed, using ethnic and socio-linguistic logic, Cadoux attributes these islands to separate "families" of the greater Indian Ocean—Comoros to the Arab-Muslim north, Mauritius and a segment of Réunion to the Hindu subcontinent, Seychelles, Réunion, Rodriguez, and part of Mauritius to the Creole family, and Madagascar to the Indo-Malayan east.[19] This diversity of origins has not prevented cultural affinities under French influence or cooperative economic aspirations in the IOC, but it could obstruct a deeper process of integration. The result of diverse internal evolutions and metropolitan ministrations is a rich, colorful patchwork interlaced by vital geographic, political, and cultural crossovers. The capital, technology, and management needed for development of the real correspondences and for correcting the discrepancies are maintained by France and the Western powers in general. (These proprietors include South Africa whose "necessary evil" role is circumscribed by inveterate hostility.) Unless such resources are made more liberally available, the aspirants to multilateral cooperation remain trapped in bilateral financial and commercial conduits leading to their preoccupied patrons.

The IOC or alternative sponsors of regional integration will thus need more than affective solidarity to mobilize existing linkages against the odds of insular pluralism and bilateral dependence. They are unlikely to find those new means in the economic exchanges which put the islands at chronic disadvantage. Perhaps the islands can use their strategic location for diplomatic leverage, but that asset remains to be proved in the tough manipulation of international power. Until they exploit some such advantage, the five island polities seem condemned to ask others for generosity in intensifying their otherwise symbolic convergence of interest. A common Francophone medium will of itself not correct the contemporary plight of nationalism compromised in the machinery of military and economic security. In this destiny, the islands of the proverbial Latin Quarter stand as a microcosm for Indian Ocean societies at large.

Notes

1. Most studies of these transformations remain fragmentary or monographical. The most useful syntheses appear in Jean-François Dupon, *Contraintes insulaires et fait colonial aux Mascareignes et aux Seychelles*, 3 vols., (Lille, France: Atelier Reproduction des Thèses; Paris: Librairie Honoré Champion, 1977); Raj Virasahmy, ed., *Characteristics of Island Economies* (Port Louis, Mauritius: University of Mauritius, 1977); John M. Ostheimer, ed., *The Politics of the Western Indian Ocean Islands* (New York: Praeger, 1975); Philip M. Allen, "New Round for the Western Islands," in Alvin J. Cottrell and R.M. Burrell, eds., *The Indian Ocean: Its Political, Economic, and Military Importance* (New York: Praeger, 1972), pp. 307–329; in articles and essays collected annually in *Annuaire des pays de l'Océan Indien (APOI)* (Aix-en-Provence, France: Presses Universitaires d'Aix-Marseille, CERSOI, from 1974); and periodically in *Archipel: études interdisciplinaires sur le monde Insulindien* (Paris: CNRS-SECMI).

2. Dupon, *Contraintes insulaires*, vol. 3, pp. 1214–1218.

3. Ibid., pp. 1191–1195; Jean Benoist, "Perspectives pour une connaissance des sociétés contemporaines des Mascareignes et des Seychelles," APOI 1 (1974), pp. 223–233.

4. Dupon, Contraintes insulaires, vol. 3, pp. 1209–1212; Percy Selwyn, "External Dependence of Small Plantation Islands," in Virasahmy, Characteristics, pp. 1–21; J.M. Boisson, Edmond Lauret, and Serge Payet, "Emergence historique et adaptation des rapports de production dans le cadre d'une économie de plantation insulaire: le cas de la Réunion," in Ibid., pp. 103–163; Gérard Althabe, Oppression et libération dans l'imaginaire (Paris: François Maspero, 1969); Dominique Desjeux, La question agraire à Madagascar (Paris: Harmattan, n.d.); Jean-Claude Rouveyran, La logique des agricultures de transition (Paris: G.P. Maisonneuve et LaRose, 1972); Colin Legum, ed., Africa Contemporary Record (ACR), 1982–83 (New York and London: Holmes & Meier, Africana Publishing), pp. B 214–215.

5. Dupon, Contraintes insulaires, vol. 3, p. 1620.

6. Percy Selwyn, Small, Poor, and Remote: Islands at a Geographical Disadvantage, UNCTAD Policy Paper, February 1975 (Brighton, England: University of Sussex, Institute of Development Studies, 1978).

7. A.R. Mannick, Mauritius: The Development of a Plural Society (Nottingham, England: Spokesman, 1979), p. 161; Philip M. Allen, "Mauritius: The Ile de France Returns," in Ostheimer, Politics, pp. 208–213.

8. Harry Bryce Qualman, Limits and Constraints on Foreign Policy in a Dependent State: Madagascar Under the Tsiranana Regime (Ph.D. diss., Johns Hopkins, 1975); Césaire Rabenoro, Les Relations extérieures de Madagascar de 1960 à 1972, (Thèse d'Etat, Université Aix-Marseille, 1981); Philip M. Allen, "Madagascar and OCAM: The Insular Approach to Regionalism," Africa Report (January 1966), pp. 13–18; Allen, "Madagascar: The Authenticity of Recovery," in Ostheimer, Politics, pp. 28–45.

9. Benoist, "Perspectives;" Robert Chaudenson, "La situation linguistique dans les archipels créolophones," APOI 1 (1974), pp. 155–182; Dupon, Contraintes insulaires, vol. 3, part B, esp. pp. 1214–1218.

10. Benoist, "Perspectives," pp. 232–233; Alix D'Unienville, Les Mascareignes: Vieille France en mer indienne (Paris: Albin Michel, 1954); Frantz Fanon, Black Skin, White Masks, trans. Charles Lam Markmann (New York: Grove Press, Inc., 1967), Ch. 4.

11. Info-Madagascar (Tananarive), August 2, 1969, author's translation.

12. Allen, Self-Determination in the Western Indian Ocean, International Conciliation 560 (New York: Carnegie Endowment for International Peace, 1966); Allen, "Mauritius: The Ile de France Returns," pp. 223–225.

13. ACR 1977–78, p. B 194; Ibid., 1978–79, pp. B 186–192, 196–197.

14. For instance, Yin Shing Yuen (Tian Shung), Pour une intégration régionale entre l'Ile Maurice et d'autres îles du Sud-Ouest de l'Océan Indien (Thèse doctorat 3ème cycle, Université de Lyon II, 1980), part 2; Jonathan M'Haruia, "Un Marché commun pour l'océan Indien," Afrique-Asie (Paris) 257 (January 18, 1982), pp. 58–59; "Indian Ocean Pact," Africa Now, May 1983; Marchés Tropicaux et Méditerranéens (MTM) (Paris), 20 July 1984; African Economic Development (AED) (London), 22 June 1984.

15. Charles Cadoux, "Esquisse d'un panorama politique des pays de l'Océan Indian," APOI I (1974), p. 76, n. 97; see regular summaries in The Economist Intelligence Unit (EIU), Quarterly Economic Review of Madagascar, Mauritius, Seychelles, Comoros (London).

16. Discussed in Cadoux, "Esquisse," pp. 47–77.

17. Dupon, *Contraintes insulaires,* vol. 2, p. 866; André Scherer, *La Réunion,* Que sais-je? (Paris: Presses Universitaires de France, 1980), pp. 99–111.

18. Boisson, Lauret, and Payet, "Emergence historique."

19. Cadoux, "Esquisse."

PART THREE

Paradoxes of Security, Reality of Power

8

Authority and Security
in the Zone of Peace

For a half millennium, the political economy of the Indian Ocean has braided itself into a dynamic wreath of alignments with and against major external powers. Before 1500, the local participants had been fragmented into myriad alliances and antipathies of a centrifugal yet never quite anarchic system. The distinct saw-lines between sub-regions of this huge crescent puzzle were blurred from time to time by the expansion of regional powers, as in the several tidal flows of Indian states in the center, mercantile Arab penetrations in the west and their concomitant investment of Islam along virtually all the coasts. By then, Indian religions had spread throughout central and eastern Asia. Political and commercial classes developed their own linkages through the Malay language in the East, Swahili in the West.

A glacially slow process of integration was aborted by the early sixteenth century Portuguese invasions from the southwest. European successors drew local populations away from an internally coherent commercial system to an externally determined heterogeneity of embattled trading alignments. Strings were plucked in Lisbon and The Hague, London, Paris, and Berlin, and the once interdependent Afro-Asian partners danced to imported tunes. To secure the commerce against ambitious rivals and nautical pickpockets, Europe sent the fleets.

Security and insecurity are temperamental responses to more or less rationally apprehended circumstances of protection. The temper of security depends on an assurance of applicable power (military, economic, diplomatic, geographic situation) adequate to nullify conceivable threats to the integrity of a system. To suit calculation, a system is analyzed into component interests—domestic tranquillity, coastal imperviousness, facility of trade routes, and the like. Security policy in the imperial age was determined by the minimal requirements of a dominant power against both local resistance and external competition. The controlling authority recruited and cultivated local collaborators through political promotion, economic affiliation, or outright compulsion. It met external challenges through combinations of military and diplomatic resources. Regional equilibrium took a multipolar shape around 1625. This was the age of the great trading companies with territorial endowments. In the region, the charters competed with one-another, with the Portuguese crown, and, later, with a resurgent Arab power from Oman.

Mercantile security then as now required the standard instumentalities of "classic" imperialism. For this purpose, sovereign power buttressed, and eventually replaced, the forces directly commanded by the charter companies. Strategic points and gates of access had to be held, coastlines rendered congenial, and hinterlands harmless. Some choice terrain, however acquired, was reserved for colonization by European and, less frequently, by favored indigenous, settlers. Manpower was shifted across what used to be state borders; technical expertise transferred down from Europe (although much was learned locally in manufacturing and maintenance, transportation, management, and style of consumption). Today, decades after the end of European colonization, the external state still guards its national markets while resident administrations contract for migrating labor and technology. Alignments persist in the post-imperial ocean, but the allegiance of subordinates inside the region does not always signify transcendance of the external power's security interests when the two systems find themselves in dispute over strategic priorities.

Repercussions of Nationalism

New like everybody else at the overseas imperial business, Portugal proved adequate to its demands only in Brazil. Yet Lisbon persevered for the spice and glitter of trade and the grandeur of the Faith until superior force backed her away from the most desirable holdings in India, East Africa, and the eastern islands. Recognizing similar limitations in better times, hard-headed Holland withdrew into the choicest portions of the East, holding only essential supply bases in Africa to serve clearly specified ends. When French strategy and policy failed at crucial points during the eighteenth century, diplomacy and paramilitary bravura almost compensated. But only England maintained the consistency of larger purpose and persistence of execution required to perfect the imperial architecture. She managed this by establishing India as a displaced imperial nucleus, surrogate of the Crown, suzerain of the seas. This was a strategic device never undertaken for Portuguese Goa, Dutch Batavia, or the Ile de France. After the post-Napoleonic settlement. England's erstwhile great rivals were tolerated wherever their presence was not incompatible with British imperial purpose and the primacy of India. Security obtained in a hierarchial arrangement of military power. Britain undertook directly to resist southward pressure from Russia and, later in the century, to deflect bumptious German intrusions along the peripheries away from India.

Prior to World War Two, Gandhi's great movement notwithstanding, Indian Ocean nationalism failed to draw large populations away from British, French, and Dutch authority. Australia and South Africa, with their critical mass of Europeans, were exceptional. But the war weakened imperial power in full view of its subjects. Nationalist parties could mobilize successfully once that power no longer bulwarked overseas authority. Nationalists in capital territories—India, Indonesia, Kenya, Indo-China, Israel—were among the first to grasp the implications of metropolitan enfeeblement. Collateral territories—Burma, Sri Lanka, Jordan—arrived more smoothly at independence before the end of the 1940s. Shortly thereafter, nationalism redirected politics in Egypt and Iran. But the metropoles, recovering from their conspicuous power lapse, resisted nationalist threats wherever they could—most dramatically in Indo-China, Madagascar, and Kenya, later, more equivocally, in Mozambique, Iran, and Egypt. They eventually re-established authority, particularly in Africa, in cooperation with new, cosmopolitan classes outside the central nationalist movements.

Independence was often proclaimed upon a relatively nominal re-contracting of responsibilities among national elites, with explicit or concealed powers reserved to European governments or nationals. Statehood thus obstructed, or at least delayed, the veritable "decolonization" of institutions. That stage, when realized in most Indian Ocean societies, begins with a reapportionment along nationalist perspectives of access to opportunity and privilege. Jobs and property once monopolized by Europeans or surrogates became increasingly available to autochthonous claimants. These new beneficiaries rarely penetrated levels of genuine authority without considerable struggle.

During this interim period of selective transfers of responsibilities in most Indian Ocean societies, bilateral partnerships prevailed between metropolitan institutions—bureaucratic, educational, commercial, military—and their respective indigenous heirs. These links provide security for both partners. The nationalist alternative which transcended such arrangements in India, Indonesia, and Tanzania encountered difficulty elsewhere in challenging this cosmopolitan security. Madagascar has provided our own case study in this respect. But the challenge was having its cumulative effect in other places, heading toward either gradual autonomy or social crisis, as demands for autonomy neared the crucial levels of authority sketched in the following schema.

Stages of Nationalist Penetration

1. Opposition to direct European control over policy and opportunity.
2. Opposition to Europe's designated recipients for transfers of responsibilities within institutions.
3. First Stage Decolonization: a) Redistribution of jobs and property. b) Diversification of external alignments.
4. Decolonization of Authority: a) Transformations of institutions and benefits. b) Autonomous external policy.

Through the decade of the 1960s, nationalism also found the imperial world becoming transformed by the operation of new, transcendant external power. No longer resticted to highly volatile European and East Asian theatres, the alarums of global cold warfare began crossing the terrain of Commonwealth and Communauté. After the Berlin and Cuban crises of 1961–1962, the East-West confrontation was tacitly acknowledged as too dangerous to keep in proximity to nuclearized northern heartlands. The great rivalry was expatriated to battlefields prepared by third world animosities. Without actually firing a shot into the region, the Soviet Union and United States came eventually to re-enact some of the choreography of political clientage and selective economic privilege that had been staged over centuries by West Europeans in the Indian Ocean. The regional consequence was a second relegation of British and French authority, a new security quest for local interests, and a fresh lift in the sails of the nationalists.

During this change of climate, both national and global forces were inexorably stretching the fibers linking Indian Ocean societies to Britain, France, and Portugal. Interpenetrating demands of national autonomy, imperial authority, and global interest effectively diffused the old imperial structures into a new web of responsibilities. National and global authority undertook certain financial, military, and technological charges relinquished (willingly, by and large) by imperial authority. Decolonization was the high purpose, but it was more effectively pressed for reasons of security than on political or ethical principle. The quest for national security in the 1960s and 1970s normally engendered a portfolio of strategic alignments. Diversification was the rule even when external threats were largely invented or exaggerated to substitute for genuine domestic enemies. In this quest, national systems had to be fitted into the larger structures, with inevitable outbreaks of rejection and recrimination, aimed at both the United States and the USSR. Here the remaining imperial authority often acted to assure the mesh of systems. The Baghdad Pact (CENTO), Southeast Asia Treaty Organization (SEATO), the Australia-New Zealand-US agreement (ANZUS), and access by the American Middle East naval force (MIDEASTFOR) to Bahrein represent some of the more formal versions of this process. Here and there, even France has mediated between world power and national security interests in the Indian Ocean. For want of such available mediation, the Soviet Union operated with East European, Cuban, North Korean, and for a time, Chinese collaborators in a shifting ensemble of sponsorship for national states and guerrilla factions.

Few nationalist movements proved strong or resolute enough to dissolve their respective imperial establishments entirely. For the most part, enfeebled imperial powers remained profoundly tenacious, in search of assurance for their residual stakes in the area. London and Paris could even present themselves as alternatives to Soviet or American patronage. The intercession did weaken Moscow's and Washington's direct influence on national policy in the zone. They yielded some responsibilities to indigenous institutions, others to the global powers, retaining certain deep-seated rights of institutional process and market management. Security policy moved once again toward congruence with still dependent systems of economic growth and social privilege. The old wreath of alignments was not essentially unravelled in the postwar surge of self-determinations. It was diversified, recontrived, and reinforced, certain strands replaced, others loosened. National and global fibers joined the weave. Japan and China re-entered as secondary or alternative patrons, with their own interests to protect. Sources of security were diffused, competition born among them. The old links of capital and commodity markets, technology, cultural influences, and political class sponsorship adapted and survived. Or, as in Indonesia, Tanzania, Madagascar, Mozambique, Comoros, they returned in new or multilateral form after revolutionary hiatus,

In general, national policies of Indian Ocean residents have been able to determine the identity of flagrant enemies and conspicuous allies, the resolution of domestic conflicts, the rules of election and distribution of offices, the relations between elites and political parties, nationalization of middle- and most upper-level jobs, adjustments between rural and urban priorities, UN voting options, and associated rhetoric. The Southwestern islands of this study epitomize the attainment of this first stage of nationalist decolonization. Each had at least one substantive shift in regime during the 1970s (1981 and 1986 in Réunion). Variously and with clearly delineated consequences, they have sought diversity in external partnerships, undertaken public appropriation and redistribution of jobs and limited property holdings, and launched programs of social amelioration, progressive taxation, universal education, authentication of vernacular languages, and ideological (or rhetorical) exaltation of the "children of the earth." These strategies have been replicated throughout the Indian Ocean without jeopardizing crucial bilateral arrangements in the management of economic options and external security.

For their part, the global powers and their syndicated multilateral combinations (including much of the disposition of OPEC investment capital) have undertaken a different agenda. They seek to determine armament levels and military technology, access to industrial and "high" technology, the operation of capital markets and interest rates, the viability of currencies, some of the migrations of labor, some behaviour in multinational organizations, and the perils of contagion from conflicts generated by local combustion. But, with the growing self-reliance of resident belligerents, the great powers have encountered obstacles to direct intervention, stigmatized as expatriation of their "East-West rivalry" into the zone.

By and large, the erstwhile imperial powers (Britain, France, Portugal) have retained influence over which elites shall prosper in the Indian Ocean. Metropolitan norms for socio-economic expectations have prevailed remarkably. Cultural and economic institutions operate in large continuity with colonial and post-colonial standards. Europe remains a major market for labor and a source of technology. More important, perhaps, Europe's endorsement of third world elite legitimacy has become essential in the new circumstances of domestic insecurity and global anxiety. French or British experience decides the cultural nexus betwen technology and social status.

New partners and new competitors also speak to shifting interests within the region's societies. Japan, China, and a roster of middle powers—including OECD and COMECON members, and third-world pace-setters like Algeria, India, and Tanzania—have begun to share responsibilities and exert influence in localized spots throughout the Indian Ocean. With France and Britain, they have multiplied international alignments and tightened the great weave.[1]

As in the decades of mercantilist competition, the Indian Ocean still responds to the claims of disputing external powers. Intra-regional hostilities are available for coercive or diplomatic exploitation from outside. Although the new polities might have preferred to assure their own security autonomously or through their own collective combinations, the imperial experience effectively divided them from one another. That experience has also separated their domestic politics into a broil of hostile factions variously responsive to external stimulation. Whether through traditional nationalism or pre-arranged elite promotion, genuine responsibilities were conferred on conventional nation states, frustrating the regional or sub-regional imagination which alone might have conquered the divisons among them. Yet, the fragility of their institutions invites a progressive establishment of the new external powers. At the least, those powers provide arms and technology for antagonists, a bulwark for local authority. They may thus characterize their own presence as a guarantor of the preservable status quo.

Whatever the restraint shown in global policy, anxieties are inspired on the littoral by any appearance of alien might. Too easily may great powers betake themselves to these waters so far from European and American heartlands. Errant deities may destroy riparian mortals for sport. Or they may encourage local champions to do so, expecting a share of advantages. Indian Ocean residents have trouble understanding what real interests super powers could entertain in the region.[2] These apprehensions complicate the balance between state security and national autonomy. National ritual, particular or collective, requires eviction of the mighty heirs to Britain's establishment. A clamor surges for ways to bell the global cat. This militancy is not merely rhetorical, for by starting in categorical rejection, third world states from Kuwait to Indonesia are able to raise the price and reduce the prejudice of their collaboration.

However repugnant, global power will remain. Consenting regimes naturally seek to take advantage of major power proximity, turning presence into participation. In local conflict, advantage is seized through bilateral security guarantees from one or more of the principal interlopers. As some of these affiliations evolve into relations of clientage and privilege, intra-regional suspicions inevitably grow in the very incubator of the non-aligned movement. As privilege settles on its local favorites, domestic opposition rises against flagrant manifestations of economic and strategic dependence.

Thus, instability festers in pursuit of its antithesis. Accommodating regimes have given way since the late 1960s to more radically nationalist successors in Somalia, South Yemen, Madagascar, Ethiopia, Mozambique, Seychelles, Mauritius, and Iran. Sri Lanka, Bangla Desh, Pakistan, and Zimbabwe have swung away from categorical nationalism, while Comoros and Sudan have shifted in both directions. Thailand, Kenya, Mozambique, Seychelles, Egypt, Sudan, North Yemen, and Oman have felt the buffet of discontent with their respective international options. As local frictions flair tragically into warfare, interested observers permit themselves to speak of arcs of instability, flashpoints, and tinderboxes. Great power presence become all the more justified in a suddenly materialized "strategic triangle" from the Persian Gulf to the Cape of Good Hope to the verges of Indo China.[3]

Thus, a systematic adjustment toward new forms of national security after Britain's evacuation east of Suez has inadvertently contributed to regional insecurity and domestic instability. When the illusory Zone of Peace was pronounced by the United Nations in 1971, it was already too late, but the proclamation has served as a hortatory twinge to consciences already implicated in conflict.

The protection of greater powers may be desirable or even necessary, but it exacts its economic price. The security of incomplete states often requires webs of mandatory weaponry, financial credit, and market prescription. Such relationships are inevitably construed, correctly or otherwise, as ideological subordination, with prospects of global importance. Participation appears to entail influence. But the option of an overseas patron becomes most attractive whenever the alternative is to yield to a neighbor whose very proxmity gives it a positive, pernicious, and unlimited interest in redefining the client's identity. To some riparians, a minimal imposition from a contemporary "super power" with limited interests seems lighter than the weight of the old colonizers, Britain and France, or the pressures of nearer forces like China, India, Iran, or South Africa. To others, however, including the island polities of our middle chapters, new imperial energies intimidate far more powerfully than the alternatives of Francophone or Commonwealth allegiance in an eternally open sea. Thus far, few Indian Ocean riparians have enjoyed the luxury of not having to choose.

This study represents a depiction of such third world sensibilities under pressure. Great power freedom of encroachment is both rejected and accommodated by the dependent residents of a turbulent, poverty-ridden, strategically coveted zone. Neither the heart of the world nor a region still seeking its identity, the Indian Ocean presents a re-enactment of some parable of the medieval forest or American West. Beset by anxieties, local inhabitants seek the protection of the disinterested powerful, even though all intrusions are in principle more or less unwelcome. The powerful enjoy privileges and functions beside mere bullying and protecting the weak. They own the tools, the local mills and banks, the water rights, the police force, the judges and juries of society, so that to choose sides inevitably has serious economic and cultural implications. At the least, the global alignments frustrate the emergence of potential regional or sub-regional powers like India, Iran, Indonesia, Saudi Arabia, South Africa, or Ethiopia. Governing elites are induced to think globally, against cultural tendencies toward national or regional values. National security thus has an ironic relation to national idiom.

Nonalignment, Trap of Nationalists

The Indian Ocean has scant prospect for regional integration while external powers sustain their bilateral influence over policy in third world states under accommodating management. Where that influence weakens, as Kapur argues, significant local powers can bargain for relative autonomy. Regional or sub-regional arrangements can develop around those new "middle power" centers, even as the external power remains fervently engaged.[4] Kapur invokes the examples of India, South Africa, and Israel to demonstrate how this process can evolve in the direction of neighborhood security contrivances without great power enforcement, a new emancipation for Indian Ocean residents. He has perhaps underestimated economic and cultural inhibitions on autonomy in regimes so tightly linked to world market structures as are Israel and South Africa (and maybe India as well). The thesis may also overstate the integrative impact on neighborhood truce arrangements, even in relatively autonomous cases like those being cultivated by Israel, Syria, and other Levantine antagonists, by India and Pakistan, and possibly by South Africa, Mozambique, Angola, Zimbabwe, Swaziland, Lesotho, and Botswana. Kapur has prophetically described how the gradual "structuring" of conflict can lead to locally autonomous truce. But a truce expresses battle-weariness under conditions that may prove transient. It does not prevent profound enmity from re-emerging in new conflict once those conditions have changed and the warriors have recovered their wind.

Nor is it clear that the substitution of relatively autonomous rulers for an accommodating neo-colonial elite will itself produce the dynamics of regional collaboration. The succession of Malagasy administrations after 1972 intensified real gestures of amity in their part of the zone. Yet, without active participation by France, substantive integration would have advanced little farther than under Tsiranana's Francophile démarches. Nationalism and regional integrity may ultimately be capable of synthesis in the Indian Ocean, but thus far they have operated at cross purposes. During the senescence of England's imperial authority after World War Two, India naturally contemplated perpetuation of her central stabilizing role, albeit now as a fully sovereign agent with exemplary spiritual impact upon the region.[5] Gandhi's movement wedded individual conscience to the demands of national solidarity. The nation in revolt transcended confessional differences until it had reached the brink of success. Failing tragically to sustain the integrity of a Hindu-Muslim nation, Indian nationalism lost its claim to universality, thereby becoming less menacingly imperial in the perceptions of neighbors. Furthermore, India's glaring socio-economic weakness and her vicious disputes with Portugal, Pakistan, and China revealed the new state's provisional unfitness for regional hegemony. During the gradual unravelling of the European colonial fabric, other claimants to authority were visited by nemesis—Sukarno's ambitious Indonesia, Reza Pahlevi's Iran and imperial Ethiopia, as well as Iraq and Ethiopia under their current militant rulers.[6] The prejudice of nonalignment has frustrated local pretensions to leadership more effectively than those of the major powers against whom it was devised.

Sprung from the profundities of India's anti-colonial experience, authenticated in 1955 at Bandung, reposing in the periodic assizes of a broad multilateral movement, nonalignment degenerated into the reflex of hapless nationalisms in external affairs. For the weakest Indian Ocean states, it represents at most a wistful design for a common homestead in the balkanized place where they happen to reside. Alignment—understood as the reciprocal accommodation by two or more partners to interests of high priority—has been forced on most Indian Ocean states by the circumstances of dependence. That is, the transactions of economic viability, political stability, and military security allow the external partner a greater degree of penetration into the institutions of the weaker. Only a few—India for instance—have succeeded in diversifying their dependence without jeopardizing security and only Iran since 1980 has conducted overt belligerency free of compromising association with global power. Nonalignment has become a rear defense of nationalism. It has no higher, no forward demiurge. When in jeopardy, it quickly concedes to its opposite, super- or secondary-power influence. Entangled in a world market system which sustains both political and economic stability, national leadership can seldom reserve resources to assure security—including acquisition of arms and defense technology—outside that system. The most hopeful recourse, as illustrated in Tanzania, Madagascar, Burma, and Seychelles, is to refuse complicity to major powers, hoping either that enemies will not react, or that a secondary power, France or China, for instance, will help if they do.

As a positive alternative to bipolarization, nonalignment has had little effect on global realities. But it does have a purpose at the ideological junction of nationalism and regional autonomy. Fashionably declared dead, unable to convene at Baghdad in 1982, or to overcome the Moscow-wards bias imparted by its Cuban presidency from 1979, the nonaligned assembly managed nonetheless at New Delhi in March 1983 to return to its Indian Ocean hearthstone. There it took aim against the twin trammels of economic and strategic subservience, the least illusory if most intransigent of international objectives.[7] The movement continues to function as a third world caucus within the UN Conference on Trade and Development (UNCTAD), the World Bank and IMF, the General Agreement on Tariffs and Trade (GATT), and the European Community's dialogue with African, Caribbean, and Pacific economies. In these debates, anti-imperialism is brandished in order to clear a path for third world interests into the forbidden center of economic decision. Other studies must assess the longterm prospects of this effort toward the proverbial new world order. Here, we may consider only the strategic implications of the movement.

A Zone for the Peace

During the early 1970s, Indian Ocean states entered a second stage of foreign policy evolution after Bandung. Seeking a diplomatic community to frustrate external intervention and end the half-millennium cycle of obeisance to "northern" power, they have rallied behind the ambiguous call for a zone of peace. The concept incubated in various receptacles, emerging in the Lusaka nonaligned conference in 1970 as a least common denominator of rival national interests. Since then, Resolution 2832 (XXVI) of the 1971 UN General Assembly has provided the test for exploration of zonal sanctuary. Passed with only sixty-one votes against fifty-five abstentions including most of the decisive external powers, the controversial resolution enunciates three main principles:

1. It declares the ocean (within as yet unspecified borders), its air and sea space "for all time as a zone of peace;"
2. It asks the "great Powers" to consult with littoral states in order to curb their military presence in the zone, to eliminate bases and related facilities, as well as nuclear weapons "and any manifestation of great Power military presence in the Indian Ocean conceived in the context of great Power rivalry;"
3. It anticipates a system of collective security implemented by littoral and hinterland states with cooperation from outside users of the ocean, to prevent "any threat or use of force against the sovereignty, territorial integrity and independence of any littoral or hinterland State" in contravention of the UN Charter, but otherwise guaranteeing "the right to free and unimpeded use of the zone" under international law.[8]

In its original form, the peace zone would only insulate, not pacify, the several theatres or sub-regions of the zone. By attributing all their security problems to large external sources, local states could continue with impunity toward their separate goals, stirring neighborhood conflicts as they proceed. At its best, the idea would prevent the outside powers from raising the level of theatre conflicts through massive sponsorship of local belligerents. At its worst, it would permit those powers to influence policy without engaging their own presence in a risk of conflict. If the current Namibean stalemate is an example of the worst, the Iran-Iraq war lugubriously represents the "best" obtainable example of how the zone of peace principle would work. The West and on occasion the USSR reject the contention of Resolution 2832 attributing zonal insecurity to their global rivalry, although each side is pleased to explain how much the other side all alone contributes to the problem. Insecurity, most external participants agree, originates chiefly in neighborhood imbroglios. They doubt the ability of Indian Ocean residents to police these controversies without benign intervention.

But the zone of peace debate has reached levels of far greater maturity and complexity than the original resolution augured. Since 1980, after associating the major UN and maritime powers in its consultations, the debate has delivered a lucid annual demonstration of the recalcitrance of global consensus on first principles of security. (See Appendix 2.)

Excluding only South Africa and Israel from otherwise universal participation by Indian Ocean resident states, the UN's ad hoc Committee on the Indian Ocean is charged with recommending modes of implementation of the resolution. Under perpetual leadership from Sri Lanka, the committee has spent the years since 1971 in ostensibly fruitless deliberation. Apart from annual reiterations of the peace zone thesis in successive resolutions of the General Assembly, the now forty-seven delegations have managed only to clarify the irreducible controversies of definition, objective, and interest among their Western, Socialist, and non-aligned factions. Such elucidation is of considerable benefit to statesmen and scholars, but the committee has been unable to define the objective conditions of security in the zone of common concern. In 1979, before admitting the major powers to their forum, the littoral and hinterland residents of the zone conferred in virtual unanimity among themselves on the perils of foreign deployment in the region. Singapore and Australia alone took exception to the conference communiqué, and India disputed her interlocutors' prohibition of the nuclear capacity which she alone possessed.[9] Thereafter, once the committee was enlarged to include the permanent members of the Security Council and most of the major maritime frequenters of the ocean, substantive consensus became impossible. Even the worldwide Colombo conference on the subject, demanded by UN majorities since 1980, has been postponed six times by disagreements over its terms of reference.

The committee's NATO states, including France, behave in veritable unanimity and with general support from Australia and others in the region.[10] They demand an "improvement in the political climate" of the area, meaning primarily withdrawal of Soviet troops from Afghanistan and resolution of the war between Iran and Iraq, before a universal meeting can be successfully launched. To confer on zonal peace while enemies occupy local territory would, in Western eyes, imply legitimization of the very aggression which the resolution seeks to abolish. Proponents of an immediate conference, including the socialist group and majority of resident states, insist that such improvements represent a desirable consequence, not a precondition, of fruitful open debate. The three committee blocs even disagree over the geographical boundaries of the eventual peace zone (the West wishing to obstruct the action of "adjacent" powers like the USSR), the conditions under which armed vessels and aircraft of external powers might be welcome as innocent transients of the zone, and the feasibility of excluding nuclear weapons from an area which includes at least three current nuclear powers (India, France, and Britain) as well as several postulants to such arsenals.

Western reservations to Resolution 2832 and its sequels also deplore the emphasis on security perils from the sea, while ignoring the destabilizing threat of (Soviet, Vietnamese, Libyan) continguous land-based power. They accuse the Socialist and nonaligned parties of using obsolete naval doctrines to obscure the real threats to peace. Thus for the West, a successful conference must be preceded by deliberate "harmonization" of the concepts to be discussed. Western governments are prepared to await a new climate of mutual confidence or détente like that prevailing around the negotiation of the 1975 intra-European Helsinki accords.

The Soviet Union understandably rejects the infernal "linkage" between its proclaimed rescue of the Afghan revolution and the putative security menace of great power presence. Although the USSR also abstained on the original 1971 resolution, Moscow and its allies have been glad since then to join the third world majority on as many issues as possible. They help castigate their adversaries for subverting the devoutly wished Colombo conference through unnecessary preconditions. The Socialist group objects only to any abridgement of the rights of maritime usage, navigation of straits and canals, and access to fisheries and other resources in the open sea. Like the West, the Soviet group declines to be considered a foreign presence on the high seas, rejecting privileges of domesticity for littoral states in an open ocean. Aware that the United States will refuse to follow suit, the East group offers assurances against transportation of nuclear weapons and the establishment of military bases, (however the term is defined) in the zone. They would agree to a freeze on existing military assets and on maneuvers in the ocean provided all other external parties gave similar undertakings.[11] Moscow could even accept a nuclear-free zone comparable to the Latin American area covered by the 1967 Treaty of Tlatelolco, a step which France has also been willing to contemplate, but not the other Western participants.

In Soviet opinion, Washington has deceitfully postponed the peace zone conference in order to increase its capacity for military intervention and space war in the unoffending region. The West contends that Soviet forces, particularly in Soviet Asia, have also been strengthened behind the veil of peace zone equivocation. Each side attributes its own moves to legitimate purposes of self-defense and protection of allies. Each is self-appointed guardian of whatever peace prevails.[12] To the UN majority, it is just this military presence of extra-regional powers "in the context of their rivalry" which has invariably aggravated, if-not provoked, the disputes that are to be eliminated by systematic enforcement of a zone of peace. Despite the manifold discord of their committee, the resident Indian Ocean states have persuaded UN majorities that contentious external presence encourages "grave and ominous developments" which threaten regional, hence global, stability.[13] After years in which regional antagonists, like the global blocs, used the committee to denounce one another, a substantial third world consensus has recently begun operating in the debates. This harmony prevails in matters of procedure, at least. All littoral and hinterland delegations more or less agree on the desirability of a world conference, if not on the substance of every issue to be resolved there. They have followed leadership by Sri Lanka, India, and Madagascar in endeavoring to obtain an acceptable charge for those assizes. This focus has allowed the committee's animators to avoid recriminations among riparian disputants albeit without obtaining East-West agreement on any principal issue. By 1983, their efforts to strike compromises began antagonizing even the hitherto conciliatory Soviets, and the United States had taken to threatening resignation from the committee, as from other malfunctioning UN organisms.

Although a forum for elucidation and third world consensus has considerable political value, it seems unfortunate that the UN debate has failed to follow the 1982 New Delhi nonaligned conference's rediscovered priority for economic relations—a more promising field for regional solidarity than the desultory assault on great power security privileges. Those powers sit in the committee as well as in the ocean, and are not about to negotiate themselves out of either. The cat will reject his new bell unless he enjoys wearing it. It is evidently not within fine, rationalized debates over who is peace-loving that the world will arrive at guarantees for Indian Ocean stability.

If the Zone of Peace movement has foundation, it may inhere in urging the concept of a zone for development, rather than in futile formulae for its peace. Considered geostrategically, the ocean only mediates between several indigenous theatres or sub-regions within each of which conflict is acutely and regularly threatened. The global powers understandably decline responsibility, as Arabs and Israelis, Iraqis and Iranians, Indians and Pakistanis, Somalis and Ethiopians, North and South Yemenis, South Africans and Mozambicans, Tanzanians and Ugandans enact their agons of propinquity. Moscow and Washington have little to do with the origin of Southeast Asian conflicts which threaten the stability of Thailand and thus of the entire ASEAN complex. They do not provide the dozens of domestic disputes which rage throughout a region composed of latterday nation states with contrived boundaries.

Great powers with extensive global investments can nevertheless hardly be indifferent to the implications of these conflicts. Most proximity wars have been kept from spreading, and some have been resolved, by apprehension that one if not both the global leviathans might intercede, with incalculable prejudice to the viability of local states. Direct intervention has occurred within the last decade only in Ethiopia (and abortively by the US in Iran). It has afflicted the zonal hinterland—in Indo China, Afghanistan, Angola, and Lebanon—at the behest of national regimes and with ambiguous consequences. Indirect action and intimidating military demonstrations have been more frequent, but they have also aimed generally at re-stabilizing unruly circumstances on the littoral.

The circumscription of local conflicts is thus owed in part to great power self-restraint, reinforcing the insulation between theatres of the region. The ocean itself pleads innocent to the offenses of its murderous peripheries. Thanks to the absence of navies and of alternative means to extrapolate force, these aren't specifically Indian Ocean conflicts, but rather continental Middle Eastern, East or Southern African, and Southern or Southeastern Asian disputes. But perhaps turning continents inside out isn't so futile as it might seem. The denizens of these shores, unable to disengage their vital interests from the continental theatres which preoccupy them, have defaulted to others the responsibility for pacifying the energies which circulate among them. From theatre to theatre, the regional linkages are, if not fully creative, at least purged of contagion from the turbulent continents. What has not been externally pacified are the passions circulating *within* certain theatres where great power authority is either impotent—as in Southern Africa and the Persian Gulf—or stalemated, as in the African Horn and South Asia. It is within these theatres that Kapur's expectation of sub-regional settlements may materialize once hostility between a local power and its neighbors has proved first futile then manageable.

Precedent for imperial insulating authority, on the other hand, refers back to the ocean's great trading system before 1500. As in the Roman Mediterranean, commercial intercourse was assured by one or more of the participants among interlocking, embattled, yet mutually insulated continental foyers. Local warfare, piracy, slave raids, and invasions troubled the coasts and the interiors of each theatre; yet, the maritime circuits operated intact and prosperously. After three centuries of epidemic warfare infecting both residents and European penetrants, the *pax brittanica* restored that relative tranquillity under radically changed conditions for what had ceased to be autonomous societies. From 1810 until 1942, conflicts in the ocean basin were again localized.

Following the second World War and through the slow relinquishment of Britain's authority, the old system prevailed, albeit with serious organic defects. The British patrimony has now been diffused and the new imperialists are indeed competitive—while secondary powers defend their holdings in the region. Zone of peace proposals cannot resolve the implications of sub-regional "hegemonies" like those of India, South Africa, or Australia, so they ignore the phenomenon. If anything, the peril of external patrons consists in the encouragement extended to dynamic "clients" (Pakistan, Israel, South Africa, or Iraq, Ethiopia, Vietnam) to exert influence beyond their borders. Or at least, the patrons often fail to prevent such extensions and they supply the instruments of coercion. In that sense, the bellicosity of East and West has been displaced to Southern theatres of truculence.

But the United States, USSR, Japan, China, and most of Europe dispose themselves throughout the Indian Ocean with a primary (if not vital) interest in regional stability. As in the ancient Indian Ocean, stability today is good for business. Whether regional patriots like it or not, the minimal condition of a zone of peace is at hand: greater powers keep some local and theatre conflicts on the periphery from infecting other theatres and the zone as a whole. While even benign imperialism remains offensive to the dignity of the client, its contemporary incarnation offers greater overall security to the Indian Ocean than to peoples entangled in theatre disputes elsewhere. Or it would, if only the new bipolar imperialism were as efficacious as it is feared to be.

Wars have raged in the Middle East and South Asia beyond the logic of East versus West. Susceptible at times to external remonstrance, these conflicts prove nonetheless capable of erupting and perservering with alarming self-sufficiency. Some were resolved with help from within the region—in Kuweit (1971), Iran and Iraq (1975), and the Yemens on several occasions. Others—Oman's Dhofar rebellion, the 1965 Indo-Pakistani conflict, the long

Sudanese civil war, the independence of Zimbabwe under majority rule, and part of the Arab-Israeli saga—obtained constructive mediation from one external source or another. Still others proved impervious to the ministrations of external might, running their course to triumph or stalemate— *viz.*, China's conquest of Tibet in 1950, Indonesia's annexation of West Irian (1962) and India's of Goa (1961), Portugal's downfall in Africa, the tripartite Bangla Desh secessionary war, Tanzania's eviction of Idi Amin in Uganda, and the mercenary deposition of Ali Soilih in Comoros in 1978. Currently, the Iran-Iraq war, South African intervention in Angola, Mozambique, Swaziland, and Lesotho, and the Lebanese and Southeast Asian conflicts just outside the region, have also resisted outside influence. Civil turbulence, as in Burma, Sri Lanka, Pakistan, India, the Kurdish provinces of Iran and Iraq, Zimbabwe, Ethiopia, Sudan, and the Yemens, once again prove highly recalcitrant. The great powers seem mainly able to frustrate distant enemies, not to prevent conflicts of propinquity. Inter-theatre insulation is helpful, but far from sufficient for regional security.

Today's Indian Ocean residents cannot remain satisfied with minimal shelter from neighboring conflicts. Massive power intrusions into the oceanic realm may assure a very general condition of peace, but they do so on the wrong terms. Too many lives are lost, too many resources squandered in disputes, however attributed, however well-contained. Refugee relief burdens have become immense. Intimidation, even to minimize conflict, offends national sensibility, jeopardizing any more acceptable medium for cooperation. Third world peace zone advocates disguise the relationship, claiming local consensus on overall conflict resolution without imperial intrusion—whereas they agree in reality only on the affronts of clientage. If India, Iran, Israel, South Africa, Saudi Arabia, and the ASEAN partners could successfully disengage strategic presence from economic determinism in their respective neighborhoods, the zone of peace might be built, stone by stone, from the ground up.

The most constructive element of Resolution 2832 is not the proclamation of what cannot exist, or the eviction of those who won't leave. It consists in envisaging a form of collective or collaborative autonomy among all states interested in the well-being of the region. Logically, Article three of the resolution, calling on the local residents to concert action, should take priority over the first two articles, which have obtained far more attention thus far. Participating states would be obliged to renounce the use of force (except in the usually ambiguous instances of self-defense) and to repudiate nuclear weapon development. They would combine to enforce these rules on themselves. A new system could then evolve, constructed laboriously while alien powers remain on the scene, not suddenly erected in the anarchy that might ensue upon their withdrawal.

How a regional system might emerge—through pluralist concert or under impetus by one or more strong indigenous powers—remains open to speculation. Ideally, it should evolve through transnational cultural inter-action. But, more realistically assuming dependence on prevailing state institutions, systematic collaboration could benefit from a somehow benign, respectful leadership of India at its vortex. Centrality and sheer size have helped India make the most of her ambivalent historical experience as imperial headquarters. The great republic's claim to leadership in the 1980s rests less on the initiatives of outraged third world morality than on real industrial and technological dynamism. This sixth of the world's atomic powers advances ineluctably in the channels of modernity despite social and political turbulence. India has even begun the development of an oceanic navy and merchant fleet, thus perhaps correcting the historical deficiencies which had opened the old congeries of nabob principalities to European conquest.[14]

In the larger region, India's growing ability to assert technical industrial, diplomatic, and military power must always assume importance to her immediate neighbors. This has become dramatically manifest since the fall of the Iranian monarchy, the perpetuation of Egypt's exile in the Arab world, and the distractions of South Africa in her own agitated orbits. Despite domestic dissension and the repercussions of the Soviet Afghan venture, India has managed in fits and starts to induce confidence in her wary neighbors, to be available for service to technologically handicapped partners in the Gulf and East Africa, and to play an enviable role of Third World champion, both at home and among the major powers. While still limited, India's ability to project economic strength has been manifest in the provision of trade credits, middle-level industrial units, joint venture capital, and useful technical assets to Sri Lanka, Bangla Desh, Maldives, Nepal, Mozambique, Mauritius, and other needy neighbors.

Uncontrollable civil war in Sri Lanka, inevitably interesting Southern India's huge Tamil-speaking population in the fate of their three million Hindu brethren across the narrow Palk Strait, has extended perilous opportunities for effective peace making to Prime Minister Rajiv Gandhi. Even under his mother, Indira Gandhi, before her assassination in late 1984, New Delhi managed to avoid implication in theatre hostilities, to maintain a sovereign distance from the sectarian tribulations which claim other Indian Ocean residents. If the martial preoccupations of East and South Africa, Arab Middle East, and Southeast Asia can be insulated in perpetuity, India's opportunity for zonal leadership could enhance the region's audience in Moscow, Washington, Paris, and London.

While Russian, Cuban, and Vietnamese forces remain in overt belligerence on the region's outskirts, the Western position in the central Indian Ocean continues to be sensitive but sound. India's preponderant trade and financial inclinations toward the United States, European Communities, and Japan offset her over-publicized security links with the USSR.[15] The Gandhi governments have had to overcome Washington's distasteful prejudice, notably in sending the fleet to the Bay of Bengal during the Bangla Desh secession of 1971 and in military commitments to Pakistan and China against putative Soviet lusts through Afghanistan. India has scrupulously diversified military procurement. She practices an essentially nationalist approach to world politics, with a complex of relatively mature, competitive institutions resistant to the penetrations of clientage. New Delhi alone has successfully, if tentatively, developed regional ambitions in the interstices left by East-West competition. Western cooperation remains nonetheless crucial in the quest.

India's expectations of zonal influence depend on scrupulous avoidance of aggressive guises in her delicate relations with Pakistan, Bangla Desh, Sri Lanka, and China. The aggressor stigma has already nullified leadership pretensions of Iran, Iraq, and Ethiopia in their respective theatres and beyond. Vietnam, South Africa, and Israel remain politically stigmatized as pariahs, whereas New Delhi has maneuvered to obtain footholds of confidence, even in that most obscure of Muslim states, the Republic of Maldives.[16] The welfare of India's own Islamic minorities in the face of recurrent Hindu hostility will tell critically for or against her leadership credentials in the South Asian, Middle Eastern, and other sectors. In any event, it is by no means certain that Indian Ocean nationalism will accept such leadership from "one of their own" any more readily than it has from relatively disinterested external authority.

Extending their chronic rivalry beyond the sub-region, India and Pakistan compete for influence in the Arabian peninsula.[17] Both supply labor, arms, banking services, and military and managerial technology in exchange for petroleum and capital resources. This competition runs deeply beneath the diplomatic promise of bilateral reconciliation launched in late 1982 at historic meetings between Indian and Pakistani leaders. Political party machinations in India's part of disputed Kashmir, suspicions of Pakistani meddling in Kashmir and Punjab separatism, and Indira Gandhi's use of military force to quell the Sikh rebellion in Punjab state keep the prospects for reconciliation in persistent doubt.

For its part, Pakistan has sought to appear independent of American strategic prerogatives, while requiring Western and Chinese assurances against both Indian and Soviet strength on its frontiers. Common apprehension over the durability of the Afghan war and Soviet occupation in the north, the consequent floods of refugees into Pakistan, and the bellicosity of revolutionary Iran encourage the tender rapprochement betweeen Islamabad and New Delhi. Despite their serious differences, both India's democracy and Pakistan's confessional military regime share apprehension over any zonal disturbances which might attract direct super power intervention, by land or by sea.

Conclusion: Powers and Purposes

Theatres of portentous local conflict—Northeast and Southern Africa, the Arabian-Persian Gulf area, South and Southeast Asia, for instance[18]—manifest certain principles in the destinies of nations and the temper of security.

1. In each sub-region, the constellation of factors underlying actual and potential conflict pertain more to continental relationships outside the ocean

than to conditions on the littoral or at sea. Yet, as the southeastern islands demonstrate, the oceanic profile can be seriously disturbed by rapidly changing power balances in the impinging theatres.

2. Only rarely if at all has great power rivalry been the cause of conflict, although external partisanship can act as either catalyst or deterrent to hostilities between local antagonists. Indian Ocean security and insecurity are primarily affected by resident, not external, initiatives.

3. While subject to comparable constraints, Japan, China, France, and Britain play important roles within the theatres of turbulence. Vietnam has strong impact throughout Southeast Asia. Australia, India, Tanzania, South Africa, Saudi Arabia, Israel, and other regional bellwethers exert ideological, military, and even economic influence at their various stations around the zone. Most of these "secondary" or local powers have acted more often and more overtly than the United States or USSR to sustain favored conditions in the region.

4. Armament levels are steadily, even precipitously, rising throughout the region. The nuclear proliferation peril correlates with anxieties in such "cornered" regimes of high technological potential as Iran, Pakistan, South Africa, and Israel. External competition has persistently exacerbated the latent dangers of this situation.

5. Security depends not merely on national relations with external powers, but on the relations between regimes and their respective populations. True to the melancholy experience of third world societies, Indian Ocean institutions have with few exceptions substituted the stewardship of governing groups for consultation of the public interest. Ruling factions—radical, technocratic, bourgeois, or pretorian—have tended to confuse their cause with society's. The process of perversion seldom returns toward democratic ideals of participation. Crises of security readily become pretexts for repression, so that the map of endemic conflict coincides by and large with the roster of deteriorating liberties. Appeals to justice receive very mixed returns across the region. Acolytes of East and West are found among the most vigorous violators of humane norms. Part Two of this study explored remarkably wide variations in the interplay of national security and regime policy across the Southwestern islands.

6. Radical contrasts in living standards within theatres (South Asia, for instance) can of course provoke domestic unrest and interstate aggression. Perhaps even more serious is the wide and growing disparity between theatres of relative prosperity (Southeast Asia and Middle East) and theatres of mounting social desperation to the west and south. This existential anomaly endangers the evolution of regional solidarity as espoused in the diplomatic pretensions of the peace zone. Apart from latent reminiscences of historical linkages, a modicum of Indian Ocean regional coherence has been constructed essentially on the shared consciousness of "not being the North." As parts of the sentimentally integrated zone increase their resemblance to that "North"—moving into the stage of full national decolonization, for instance—the prospect of solidarity with unfavored societies will vanish. The zone

of peace is divided into turbulent theatres and ruled by contingencies of highly uneven socio-economic need.

7. East-West polarization has tended to obscure the fundamental advantage enjoyed by the United States and its allies in virtually all Indian Ocean relationships, regardless of overt strategic alignment. Western sympathizers or clients control all gates of access to the Indian Ocean basin. Western lines of transport are realistically threatened by no tangible enemy among the residents of the basin. This security prevails even in the celebrated instance of the Cape of Good Hope, whatever the outcome of current political, racial, and ideological ferment in South Africa. Any alternative regime to the present, whatever its color or political alignment, would have little alternative but to watch hundreds of ships pass around the Cape daily, and to keep markets and mineral supplies open to those who hold the capital, technology, and international influence to exploit those resources.[19]

England's imperium has passed into the hands of a northern consortium in which the USSR acts as an outside but often collaborative partner. Cold war intensifications since 1980 notwithstanding, Moscow cooperates with the West by (1) ensuring against escalation or contagion of local conflicts to levels which risk simultaneous engagement (hence confrontation) of both global powers, and (2) posing little or no attractive (hence, expensive) alternative to the market system within which financial, commercial, and technological choices are made by national leaders—except, perhaps, in the area of arms sales.

By protecting regimes and patronizing responsive institutions, the great global presence has much to do, albeit indirectly, with the conditions determining the rights and liberties of populations. That presence is maintained by a strategy seeking the defense of real interests. To the extent that those interests join the external powers to resident societies—or at least, to regimes—the responsibility of the powers can be crucial—and critical. Before casting definitive judgment on the exercise of that responsibility, however, local parties, rival powers, and suspicious bystanders should appreciate (if not endorse) the independent logic by which both the United States and the Soviet Union justify their forceful frequentation of the Indian Ocean.

First, both powers have interest in assuring continuity between their respective economies (and those of their northern allies) and regional sources of commodities, markets, and investment opportunity. With the putative, but doubtful, exception of Arabian-Persian oil, lines of access to such assets entail little mortal rivalry. Nor do Western designs on ocean-floor resources necessarily menace the well-endowed Soviet colossus.

Secondly, since these continuities engender far-ranging deployments, a global power must be sensitive to isolated changes in pressures and attitudes anywhere in the zone. A concern for global networks of commerce, finance, ideology, or security requires both the US and USSR to trace the implications of events far beyond the immediate theatre of occurrence, and to insist on the right to be present as potentially dangerous situations evolve. Inconvenient as the presence may be, this is an obligation owed by world power to itself.

Thirdly, each power has undertaken to help guarantee the security of friendly residents of the region in the event of local or external destabilization. These undertakings assume various forms, some of them—in the African Horn, for instance—potentially volatile, but in any case, they are devised with consenting local regimes.

Finally, a narrower logic of competitive reciprocity issues from somewhere beyond the first three considerations. As each power goes about its "own business," the United States sees Moscow as prime beneficiary of any lapse in world order; the USSR regards Washington reciprocally, as ultimate obstacle to the legitimacy of Soviet global behavior—behavior which Moscow considers symmetrical to American action. As the clumsy machineries of state assert their rational interests, irrationality festers in the partisan spirits of the contestants. Each side becomes suspicious of the other's tendency toward unreasonable defense of its commitments. Each tends to overstress the other's capacity and propensity for mischief. It insists on a compensatory right of counter-balance, even at the risk of the proverbially escalating spiral. Here, on the broad margins of miscalculation, lurks the third world's nightmare of great power rivalry.

Critics of East or West may readily dispute the legitimacy of any of the four claims for great power interest in the zone of peace. From the standpoint of nonpartisan resident spokesmen, nothing in these pretensions gives either super power a right to patrol waters, to intimidate local belligerents from offshore, or to convert local insecurity into serfdom within armaments systems and economic dispensations. They should nonetheless appreciate the intensity with which such arguments are sustained by virtually all contenders for authority in Washington and Moscow. The Indian Ocean "presence" has become accepted on both sides as an irreducible principle in their respective conceptions of global status. The tenacity of these judgments allows little hope for the zone of peace vision or the suspension of strategic power rivalry invoked by the first two operative articles of 1971 UN Resolution 2832. Prospects may nonetheless exist for increased acceptance of collective security responsibility by the two super principals and, ultimately, among all interested parties, as envisaged in the neglected third article of that resolution.

The logic of the Soviet Union's Indian Ocean presence combines: (1) a need to behave in reciprocity to the United States as a global power; (2) an insistence on the right to ply the southern maritime link between western and eastern extremities of the USSR; (3) a solicitude for friendly regimes in the basin; and (4) concern for Western strategic advantages (including deep-sea and space technology) in such proximity to the vulnerable Republics of the Soviet South.

Moscow's assets for these purposes are considerable. Red Sea ports at Massawa and the Dahlak islands receive the peripatetic navy; at any given time, a formidable fleet of two dozen ships (half of them combat vessels) collects there and in the waters off Aden and Socotra island in the People's Democratic Republic of (South) Yemen (PDRY). The units available for such assignments grow in number and quality as the overall navy expands in accordance with the USSR's conception (identified with Admiral Sergei Gorchkov) of great power standing. Using its treaty privilege to navigate the Dardanelles, and enjoying frequent Suez Canal passage, the Soviet Black Sea and Mediterranean forces thus make steady contact with bases at Cam Ranh Bay, Vladivostock, and Petropavlovsk.[20]

That fleet is substantially over-balanced by American units of varying strength (including one or two carrier groups) spreading between their own Mediterranean and Pacific concentrations, using Diego Garcia (BIOT) as a way station. Since 1980–1981, units in the Persian Gulf, Arabian Sea, and Gulf of Aden, have enjoyed access to facilities in Oman, Somalia, Egypt, and Kenya, in addition to the long-standing arrangements at Bahrein. Accommodating regimes, including the precarious, strident government of President Siad Barre in Mogadishu, are compensated for their pains by development aid and (increasingly) military support.[21]

The pace of circulation of these forces and the concomitant metamorphosis of Diego Garcia have increased steadily since the 1960s, ratcheting upward along with Soviet response levels. A permanent American presence was not anchored in doctrine, however, until January 1980. It was then that President Jimmy Carter declared access to the Persian Gulf to be of vital interest to the United States. In effect, Carter was warning Soviet forces to remain landlocked at the Afghan distance, while barring the Iranian revolution from the West's lifeline of economic resources. A naval network and a new Rapid Deployment Force (CENTCOM) obtained justification beyond their controversial utility as strategic instruments for American eco-political control, domination of oceanic resources, maritime surveillance of outer space, or other advancing technological conquests. They assumed the more conventional charge of protecting established Western industries dependent on oil and gas.[22]

That dependence pertains more closely to America's allies than to the United States (or, Soviet needs or designs for that matter). And, unlike Moscow's solitary fleet, United States power is complemented by considerable deployment of allied forces. Although the United Kingdom served notice of its incapacity to represent global interests "east of Suez" after 1968, British withdrawal has by no means been total. Forces were removed from Aden, Trincomalee, Massirah, Gan, Singapore, Seychelles, and Simonstown, but Diego Garcia remains English property; Hong Kong is a British foundation until 1997, and Britain retains defense responsibilities under agreements with Australia, New Zealand, and several Persian Gulf states. She supervised a partially effective embargo against Rhodesia's Mozambique Channel trade during the first decade of that colony's rebellion. The Royal Navy has retained a small presence along with American vessels at Bahrein and has scheduled maneuvers in other sectors of the ocean. British diplomatic and cultural influence remains impressive, especially among the fifteen Commonwealth members in the region.[23]

The French Indian Ocean navy by itself ranks with the Soviet in size and fire power. The bulk of that force, supported by ground troops and air power, is stationed at Djibouti, at the head of Ethiopia's only secure link to the sea. In addition to the 4,500 troops and an average of twenty ships with 1,500 marines stationed there by agreement with the young republic (whose own security is thereby ensured), France maintains a Southern Zone detachment of 3,000 men at its Overseas Department of Réunion. This includes Foreign Legion and Gendarmerie units on Mayotte in the Comoro archipelago and radio facilities at a number of points in the Mozambique Channel and Antarctic. Paris has managed to magnify its economic and cultural offerings in Madagascar, Mauritius, and Comoros, inducing those states to insulate such business from their irredentist grievances in the far-flung islets and Mayotte.[24]

French disagreements with the United States elsewhere have scarcely afflicted informal Indian Ocean coordination. With proverbial Gallic dexterity, French President Mitterand has been able to follow the parallel policy lines of his conservative predecessors in this area of the world. The advent of a conservative ministry under Jacques Chirac in March 1986 reinforces that coordination. Paris continues to cooperate closely in Western strategy when such matters as petroleum access are at stake, while persuading third world interlocutors of French bona fides as a stabilizing alternative to alignment between Moscow and Washington. To the extent that these ambiguities remain credible among vocational neutrals like India, Mozambique, Tanzania, Madagascar, and Seychelles, a partly Socialist France provides a decided asset for the less equivocal West.

Finally increasing naval capacity in Japan and China must also be added to the Western side of the bipolar Indian Ocean balances.

Exposed to Islamic scrutiny in Afghanistan and its own Muslim Republics, Moscow's credentials are·entangled in the ambiguities of counter-revolution. Ethiopia must be bolstered flagrantly in its prolonged resistance against Islamic secessionists in Eritrea and Tigray, whose Arab sponsors include the Soviets' ally, Iraq. President Saddam Hussein's beleaguered Iraqi regime in turn requires help from Saudi Arabia, Jordan, and other Arab anti-Communists, as well as from France, thus reducing Soviet influence in Baghdad. And yet, the commitment to Hussein encumbers Russian efforts to attenuate the profound animosity emanating from Tehran. The USSR is caught by another Mideastern contradiction in supplying both North and South Yemen in their sporadic fratricide. Somalia, Egypt, the Arabian conservatives, and (with recent nuances) Sudan regard themselves threatened by the dubiously efficacious alliance, encouraged by Moscow, of Libya, Ethiopia, and the PDRY. Considered geostrategically, moreover, the Soviet position is substantially inferior to the aggregated Western advantages—in the exposure of the southern USSR to both subversion and submarine- or air-launched missiles, in naval force levels, and in space technology. The fleet's friendly seaports are especially vulnerable to the instability of the ocean's celebrated "choke-points"—Aden and Socotra (PDRY) close to Bab-el Mandeb, Massawa on the Red Sea coast between those straits and Suez, Mozambique in the channel leading to the Cape of Good Hope.[25]

These are the realities, not the preference or the mythology, of Indian Ocean deployments. Western policy might as well be devised in conformity with the imperious interests implied in those realities, rather than the perilous romantics of East-West confrontation.

East-West competition does of course affect the Indian Ocean. World power alters any strategic situation by merely asserting its own presence. Unilateral gains and losses get recorded in the "zero sum" rivalry of the nuclear champions. The United States and Soviet Union joust with each other in a spiralling reciprocity of parries and thrusts across the oceanic crescent. While each side views the other as seeking permanent strategic superiority, each move seems designed to maintain dynamic stability—and to convey a destabilizing perception of the opponent. The mechanism of security swings through its point of equilibruim like a seesaw on which neither rider quite recognizes the necessity of the other. In one pocket after another, the energy of contagious dispute has already traveled cyclically from periods of intense if non-belligerent military intervention, through interludes of relative relaxation, back to further intensification. In 1977–1978, as the toleration period called "détente," was expiring, Washington and Moscow even indulged in modestly promising bilateral discussions of reductions in Indian Ocean force levels. President Carter unilaterally suspended the negotiations in February 1978, realizing that quantities of power had little to do with security, and that, in any case, the Western advantage simply took care of itself.[26] Thus another light on the marquee of détente went out, and the awkward bipolarity of presences continues. From an Afro-Asian viewpoint, the prospect of US-USSR deliberations over oceanic security only perpetuated the impotence of residents menaced by thermonuclear folly from both quixotic Communism and an inscrutable Occident.

But the ocean has not broken into East-West halves. It has kept regionally inchoate without turning into a hemispheric mirror of the frozen North. Influence and privilege can be acquired without necessarily prejudicing the assets of the global antagonist—as in the Latin Quarter islands and perhaps eventually in South Africa. Regimes may change and disputes burst into the open without either engaging the great powers directly or threatening the ability of Western states (including Japan) to conduct relations satisfactorily in the region. Western financial, technical, and commercial pre-eminence, challenged at few points in the zone, determines the direction and intensity of security alignments, even while external influence on local initiatives and outcomes remains limited. The real losses in these relations, if any, come from a sacrifice of economic flexibility and national prerogative by the weaker states or their governing elites. They have even less room for maneuver once their credit positions or payments quandaries have obliged them to be responsive to norms of viability imposed by OECD partners or Western-dominated multilateral organizations. As regimes turn over, successful opponents discover themselves under comparable constraints.

The tolerability of great power presence frustrates certain national purposes, represented at one extreme by a ponderously resurgent India, and at the other by the impotent decolonization effort of the insular Southwest. Most of the active belligerents, from Pretoria to Baghdad to Bangkok, seek tangible forms of patronage by one or more external powers. It is the quieter cultural dynamic of nationalism which resents the invidious implications of such patronage. Cultural and economic tribute to a market (or socialist) metropole imposes a burden overriding the consolations of relative stability. The outside powers have trammeled institutional autonomy, not troubled the peace. They have actually helped insulate the region from concatenations of theatre conflict; they have here and there assured substantial measures of economic growth, while inhibiting full national determination and regional collaboration. These have become the fundamental costs and benefits of entertaining major power in a troubled third world sea. India has much to gain, and the islands little to lose, from relinquishment of that external power, provided the general peace is somehow kept and that capital, technology, and markets somehow remain accessible. For the time being, most resident societies are unwilling to take either of those risks.

More secure from strategic intimidation and more dependent economically than its inhabitants like to admit, the Indian Ocean must contend with both realities as it struggles to realize its great motivating myth of regional autonomy. It may be impossible in the short run to emancipate governing institutions from penetration by external powers, but if so, the problem does not inhere in some malicious turn of global naval strategy. A locally-determined zonal security system cannot happen until its emergence promises some control over the underlying circumstances of internecine disputes. Like the foundations of cultural and economic subordination to external power, these conflicts transpire unaffected by the fragile third world consensus in UN deliberations. The ocean is indeed a welter of battlegrounds, domestic and sub-regional, and great powers must look after their interests in the zone. If nobody else, then at least their major clients want them to do so. One way or another, they have helped keep the guns of the Levant, the Gulf, the Horn, the Afghan mountains, the Mozambican bush, and the Kampuchean countryside from firing into nervous, non-belligerent neighbors. But external ministrations may by now be having diminished effect on the outcomes of these struggles. Some secondary and local influences might be operating more effectively on them at present—India for instance, or Saudi Arabia, Australia, Egypt, or Zambia. While the wreath of eco-strategic alignments stays intact, another, more locally autonomous presence may be announcing itself—pacificatory, as Kapur predicts, or otherwise.

In this process, it is surely premature and perhaps self-contradictory for zonal patriots (most of them Indian, Jasjit Singh,[27] for instance) to ask local naval forces to swell to the point at which they will expell the foreigners from the seas. For one, their armaments and desperately needed resources must come, with strings attached, from the intruders themselves. The deployment of power in the Indian Ocean remains unimpressed by arguments that trade and political relations proceed most fluently in the absence of military coercion. Each party imputes such malice to its rivals alone. No state can renounce capacity for appropriate response if it considers itself prejudiced by a rival's behavior. Nor can Eastern or Western forces be disengaged from the region on the grounds that residential friends can best solve their problems without external intrusion. In most instances, that intrusion is invited, even if it proves relatively ineffectual. However unwelcome, the intruding powers will inevitably apprehend portents of disequilibrium in locally negotiated balances. Such perceptions of prejudice demand that the alarmed power and its friends be on the spot. And if all other justifications should expire, great power global prerogatives remain as an irreducible pretext for lingering in Indian Ocean, and any other, waters. Free passage through expanses of international seas is not to be construed as a natural condition of those seas: it is a conventional right which must be asserted and defended, even if nobody thinks of denying it.

No cause is served by blaming global powers for inviting themselves into the Indian Ocean. Economic and political circumstances alone provide adequate warrant for that presence. The resident states may vote resolutions of eviction, but they have yet to convince themselves of prospects for solving their own differences without recourse to external intervention. There is evidence that such prospects are growing but in the absence of mechanisms to render them reliable, most residents and all external frequenters of the ocean require other guarantees against contagion from endemic local disputes. Great power cooperation would presumably provide more security in that regard than great power enmity, but since the rivalry exists in a local context of contention and insecurity, each power has adequate reason for taking direct interest in the affairs of the region. Despite current practice, defending that interest should be possible in tandem, or preferably in concert, with all residents and partners in an inclusive, not exclusive, zone of peace.

Notes

1. For background, see Barbara Ward, *The Rich Nations and the Poor Nations* (New York: W.W. Norton, 1962); Mahbub ul Haq, *The Poverty Curtain: Choices for the Third World* (New York: Columbia University Press, 1976), esp. Chs. 8 and 9; Dieter Braun, *The Indian Ocean* trans. by Carol Geldart and Kathleen Llanwarne (New York: St. Martin's Press, 1984), Part II; K.P. Misra, *Indian Ocean Politics: an Asian-African Perspective* (University of Maryland School of Law, Occasional Papers/ Reprints Series in Contemporary Asian Studies, No. 1, 1978).

2. See, for example, K. Rajendra Singh, *The Indian Ocean: Big Power Presence and Local Response* (New Delhi: Ramesh C. Jain, 1977); Singh, *Politics of the Indian Ocean* (New Delhi: Thomson Press India, 1974); G.S. Barghava, *South Asian Security After Afghanistan* (Lexington, Mass.: D.C. Heath, 1983); Captain V.K. Bhasin, *Super Power Rivalry in the Indian Ocean* (New Delhi: S. Chand & Co., 1981); Misra, *Indian Ocean Politics*.

3. See Larry W. Bowman, "African Conflict and Superpower Involvement in the Western Indian Ocean," in Larry W. Bowman and Ian Clark, eds., *The Indian Ocean in Global Politics* (Boulder, Col.: Westview Press, and Nedlands, W.A.: University of Western Australia Press, 1981), pp. 89, 98-99; Philip M. Allen, "The Indian Ocean: A New Area of Conflict or a Zone of Peace?" in Colin Legum, ed., *Africa Contemporary Record (ACR), 1980-81* (New York and London: Holmes & Meier, Africana Publishing, 1981), pp. A 72-79; Philippe Leymarie, *Océan Indien: le nouveau coeur du monde* (Paris: Karthala, 1981); Patrick Wall, ed., *The Southern Oceans and the Security of the Free World* (London: Stacey International, 1977); Ashok Kapur, *The Indian Ocean: Regional and International Power Politics* (New York: Praeger Special Studies, 1982), esp. Introduction and Chs. 1, 2, and 3.

4. Kapur *Indian Ocean*, Ch. 2.

5. C.S. Venkatachar, *Sea Power in the Indian Ocean*, Eastern Economic Pamphlets No. 22 (New Delhi: Eastern Economic Ltd., 1953); Marcus F. Franda, "The Indian Ocean: A Delhi Perspective," Fieldstaff Reports (Hanover, New Hampshire: American University Fieldstaff), Asia Series, March 1975; André Bellamal, "L'Inde et son environnement géostratégique," *Revue de la Défense Nationale* (Paris), Aug.-Sept. 1981, pp. 79-93; Kavalam Madhava Panikkar, *India and the Indian Ocean: An Essay on the Influence of Sea Power on Indian History* (London: George Allen & Unwin, 1945, 2nd ed. 1951).

6. Ferenc A. Váli, *Politics of the Indian Ocean Region: The Balances of Power* (New York: The Free Press, 1976), pp. 46-55.

7. Zdenek Cervenka, "Twenty Years of Nonalignment: How the Movement Lost Its Way from Belgrade to Havana," *ACR 1980-81*, pp. A 47-63. For a more optimistic prognosis of the nonaligned movement, see Didier Ratsiraka, *Stratégies pour l'an 2000: du tiers monde à la troisième puissance mondiale* (Paris: Editions Afrique Asie, 1979).

8. UNGA Res. 2832 (XXVI), December 16, 1971. See Appendix I. For the morphology of the resolution, see Misra, *Indian Ocean Politics*, pp. 9-15.

9. *Report of the Meeting of the Littoral and Hinterland States of the Indian Ocean*, UNGA 34th Session,. Supplement No. 45, A/34/45, August 28, 1979.

10. For Australia's position in Indian Ocean affairs, see Henry S. Albinski, "Australia and the Indian Ocean," in Bowman and Clark, *Global Politics*, pp. 59-86; Kim C. Beazley and Ian Clark, *The Politics of Intrusion: The Super Powers and the Indian Ocean* (Sydney: Alternative Publishing Coop., 1979), Part 3; Coral Bell, "The Indian Ocean: An Australian Evaluation," in Alvin J. Cottrell and R.M. Burrell, eds., *The Indian Ocean: Its Political, Economic, and Military Importance* (New York: Praeger Publishers, 1972), pp. 203-217; Robert O'Neill, "Australia and the Indian Ocean," in Wall, *The Southern Oceans*, pp. 177-189.

11. UNGA Ad Hoc Committee on the Indian Ocean, *Summary Records*, 1983, A/AC.159/SR.214, April 18, 1983.

12. *Ibid.*, SR.204, February 7, 1983 and SR.228, August 8, 1983; see also Philip M. Allen, "The Indian Ocean: Very Much at Sea," in *ACR 1981-82*, pp. A 138-140.

13. *Report of the Aid Hoc Committee on the Indian Ocean*, UNGA Official Records, 37th Session, Supplement No. 29, A/37/29, November 24, 1982.

14. Panikkar, *India and the Indian Ocean*, p. 7; Franda, "The Indian Ocean: A Delhi Perspective;" Venkatachar, *Sea Power*; Pervaiz Iqbal Cheema, *Conflict and Cooperation: Pakistan's Interests and Choices* (Canberra: Canberra Papers on Strategy and Defence No. 23, Australian National University, 1980).

15. Bellamal, "L'Inde et son environnement;" Bargava, *South Asian Security*, esp. Ch. 9.

16. See Clarence Maloney, *People of the Maldive Islands* (Bombay: Orient Longman, 1980); Martin Adeney and William K. Carr, "The Maldives Republic," in John M. Ostheimer, ed., *The Politics of the Western Indian Ocean Islands* (New York: Praeger Publishers, 1975), pp. 139–160; Ranjan Gupta, *The Indian Ocean: A Political Geography* (New Delhi: Marwah Publications, 1979), pp. 20–28; Urmila Phadnis and Ela Duttluithui, "The Maldives Enter World Politics," *Asian Affairs*, Jan.-Feb. 1981, pp. 166–179.

17. See Cheema, *Conflict and Cooperation*; Ali A. Mazrui, "Changing the Guards from Hindus to Muslims: Collective Third World Security in a Cultural Perspective," *International Affairs* (London) 57:1 (Winter 1980–1981), pp. 1–20.

18. The region can be carved variously. Váli, Cheema, and others organize it into six areas of study, three of them along the African littoral, one in the Gulf-Arabian Peninsula, and two in Asia; Braun treats Australia separately, separates the Southwestern islands from the African continent into a seventh sub-region, merging Eastern and Southern Africa into a single theater.

19. See Larry W. Bowman, "The Strategic Importance of South Africa to the United States: An Appraisal and Policy Analysis," *African Affairs* (London), April 1982, pp. 159–191; Patrice Claude, *Le Monde*, October 15, 1981. These analyses correct the "indispensable white South Africa" thesis implicit in conventional Western treatments, *viz.* Wall, *The Southern Oceans*. But for a new, Western-oriented assessment, see Roger D. Spegele, "Revisionism in South African International Relations: A Realist Critique," in *International Journal on World Peace* (New York), Vol. II, No. 3, July-Sept. 1985, pp. 53–62.

20. Geoffrey Jukes, "Soviet Naval Policy in the Indian Ocean," in Bowman and Clark, *Global Politics*, pp. 173–188; Leymarie, *Nouveau coeur du monde*, Chs. 6 and 7; Bradford Dismukes and James M. McConnell, *Soviet Naval Diplomacy* (New York: Pergamon Press, 1979); Elmo R. Zumwalt, Jr., "Gorshkov and His Navy," *Orbis* 24:3 (Fall 1981), pp. 491–510; Donald C. Daniel, "Sino-Soviet Relations in Naval Perspective," *Orbis* 24:4 (Winter 1981), pp. 787–803.

21. See Claudia Wright, "Implications of the Iraq-Iran War," *Foreign Affairs* 59:2 (Winter 1980–1981), pp. 275–303; Alvin J. Cottrell and Associates, *Sea Power and Strategy in the Indian Ocean* (Beverly Hills, Calif.: Sage Publications, 1981); "Oil and the Gulf: A Survey," supplement to *Economist*, July 28, 1984; Singh, *Big Power Presence*, Ch. 1; Ashok Kapur, "Carter's Diplomacy and the Indian Ocean Region," in Bowman and Clark, *Global Politics*, p. 136; Harvey Sicherman, "Reflections on Iraq and Iran at War," *Orbis* 24:4 (Winter 1981), pp. 711–718; Rouhollah K. Ramazani, "The Strait of Hormuz: The Global Chokepoint," in Bowman and Clark, *Global Politics*, pp. 7–20; Adeed I. Dawisha, "Iraq: The West's Opportunity," *Foreign Policy* 59:2 (Winter 1980–1981), p. 134; Eric Rouleau, "La diaspora palestinienne du Golfe," *Le Monde*, June 15, 16, 17, 1982.

22. See Jasjit Singh, "Indian Ocean: Geopolitics and Super Power Rivalry," II, *Mainstream* (New Delhi), November 3, 1983, pp. 10–14; See also Steven C. Goldman and Wayne A. Schroeder, "The Geopolitics of Energy," *Policy Review*, Summer 1981, pp. 95–113; Cottrell et al, *Sea Power and Strategy*; Richard Cottam, "The Iran-Iraq War," in *Current History* (Philadelphia), January 1984, pp. 9–12; Leymarie, *Nouveau coeur du monde*, Chs. 4 and 5; Braun, *The Indian Ocean*, pp. 139–149; For the Rapid Deployment Force, see John D. Mayer, Jr., "Rapid Deployment Forces: Policy and Budgetary Implications," Congressional Budget Office, February 1983; James P. Wooten, "Major Legislation of the Congress," No. 9, Congressional Research Service, January 1983; Thomas H. Moorer and Alvin J. Cottrell, "The Search for U.S. Bases in the Indian Ocean: A Last Chance," *Strategic Review* 8:2 (1980), pp.

30–38; Kenneth N. Waltz, "A Strategy for the Rapid Deployment Force," *International Security* 5:4 (Spring 1981), pp. 49–73; Francis J. West, Jr., Testimony Before Senate Committee on Armed Services, 97:2, March 12, 1982, cited in Mayer, "Rapid Deployment Forces," p. 15.

23. See Váli, *Politics of the Indian Ocean Region*; Singh, *Big Power Presence*; Beazley and Clark, *Politics of Intrusion*; Cottrell and Burrell, *Political, Economic, and Military Importance*, Chs. 1, 4, 18, 19; Braun, *The Indian Ocean*, pp. 93–94; Leymarie, *Nouveau coeur du monde*, Ch. 13.

24. *Ibid.*, Chs. 9–11; Drew Middleton, in *New York Times*, May 1, 1981; Allen, "Very Much at Sea;" Amiral Henri Labrousse, "L'Europe et l'océan Indien: perspectives politiques et stratégiques" (paper delivered to Colloque International on l'Europe et l'Ocean Indien, Aix-en-Provence, France, December 1981, reprinted in *APOI* 8:1981; Bernard Dyle, Stratégie et l'Océan Indien," *Revue de Défense Nationale* (Paris), July 1981, pp. 155–160.

25. Singh, "Geopolitics," I, *Mainstream*, October 27, 1984, and II, *Ibid.* November 3, 1984; Eric Rouleau, "Qui menace les chaikhs du Golfe?" in *Le Monde*, May 11, 12, 13, 14, 1982; *Economist*, June 2, 1984; James H. Noyes, *The Clouded Lens: Persian Gulf Security and U.S. Policy*, 2nd ed. (Stanford: Hoover Institution Press, 1982).

26. Rear Admiral R.J. Hanks, "The Indian Ocean Negotiations: Rocks and Shoals," *Strategic Review*, Winter 1978; Ashok Kapur, "Carter's Diplomacy;" George W. Shepherd, Jr., "Demilitarization Proposals for the Indian Ocean," in Bowman and Clark, *Global Politics*, pp. 223–247; Braun, *The Indian Ocean*, pp. 68–72. For alternative interpretations of great power motives, see Singh, "Geopolitics," II; Henry Trofimenko, "The Third World and the U.S.-Soviet Competition: A Soviet View," *Foreign Affairs* 59:5, Summer 1981, pp. 1021–1040; Kapur, *Regional and International Power Politics*; Cottrell and Burrell, *Political, Economic, and Military Importance*; W.A.C. Adie, *Oil, Politics, and Seapower: The Indian Ocean Vortex* (New York: Crane, Russak, 1975); Váli, *Politics of the Indian Ocean Region*; Monoranjan Bezboruah, *U.S. Strategy in the Indian Ocean: The International Response* (New York: Praeger Publishers, 1977); Singh, *Big Power Presence*; Bowman and Clark, *Global Politics*; Leymarie, *Nouveau coeur du monde*; also recurrent analyses by Labrousse, beginning in *APOI* No. 1 (1974) and the author's own analyses in *ACR*, beginning in 1980–81.

27. Singh, "Geopolitics," I and II. See also Ratsiraka, *Stratégies pour l'an 2000*.

Tables and Maps

TABLE 1
Indian Ocean Littoral and Hinterland Countries[a]
by Sub-Region

Sub-Region, Country	Inde- pendence	Area (sq.km.)	Population 1984/85 (mn)	GNP p/cap. US$. 1983
Southeast Asia, Oceania				
Australia	1901	7,682,300	15.45 ('83)	10,780
Burma	1948	678,030	35.31 ('83)	180
Indonesia	1945	1,919,443	173.0	560
Malaysia	1963	50,806	15.27	1,870
Singapore	1965	616	2.56	6,842 ('84)
Thailand	Historical	514,000	50.6	810
South Asia				
Bangladesh	1971	144,020	99.0	130
India	1947	3,166,828	748.0	260
Maldives	1965	298	.2	400 ('82)
Pakistan	1947	803,943	88.0	390
Sri Lanka	1948	65,610	14.9 ('81)	330
Hinterland				
Afghanistan	Historical	636,266	17.15	168 ('82)
Bhutan	1910	46,600	1.29	80 ('81)
Nepal	Historical	141,400	16.48	170
Persian Gulf, Arabian Peninsula				
Bahrain	1971	661	.4 ('83)	10,360
Iran	Historical	1,648,000	45.19	2,160 ('77)
Iraq	1932	438,446	15.4	3,020 ('80)
Israel	1948	20,770	4.15	5,360
Jordan[b]	1946	91,000	3.35	1,710
Kuwait	1914	24,280	1.7	18,180
Oman	1956	105,000	1.5 ('82)	6,240
Qatar	1971	11,437	.3	21,170
Saudi Arabia	1927	2,400,000	12.4	8,000
United Arab Emirates	1971	92,100	1.23	21,340
Yemen (PDRY)	1967	287,682	2.5	510
Yemen (Arab Repl.)	1918	195,000	7.7 ('80)	510

TABLE 1, cont.
Indian Ocean Littoral and Hinterland Countries

Sub-Region, Country	Inde-pendence	Area (sq.km.)	Population 1984/85 (mn)		GNP p/cap. US$. 1983	
Northeast Africa						
Djibouti	1977	23,000	.3		480	('81)
Egypt	1936	1,001,447	48.3		700	
Ethiopia	Historical	1,221,900	42.0		140	
Somalia	1960	630,000	5.27	('83)	250	
Sudan	1956	2,505,809	20.56	('83)	400	
East Africa						
Kenya	1963	582,600	19.5		340	
Tanzania	1961	939,704	21.73		290	('84)
Hinterland						
Burundi	1962	27,834	4.92	('83)	240	
Rwanda	1962	26,330	6.03		270	
Uganda	1962	236,860	13.99	('83)	220	
Zambia	1964	752,620	6.65		580	
Southern Africa						
Mozambique	1975	784,961	13.53		270	('80)
South Africa	1910	1,140,519	23.43		2,450	
Hinterland						
Botswana	1966	582,000	1.05		920	
Lesotho	1966	30,340	1.47		470	
Malawi	1964	94,082	7.1		210	
Swaziland	1968	17,400	.6		890	
Zimbabwe	1980	390,308	8.67		780	('84)
Southwestern Islands						
Comoros[c]	1975	2,236	.5		320	('81)
Madagascar	1960	594,180	9.91		290	
Mauritius	1968	1,865	1.0	('83)	1,150	
Reunion	Dependent	2,512	.55		3,710	
Seychelles	1976	440	.06		2,400	
BIOT	Dependent	125	0[d]		---	

TABLE 1, cont.
Indian Ocean Littoral and Hinterland Countries

Sources: composite, adapted from Statesman's Year-Book 1986–87 and various independent sources.

Notes

    a.   Hinterland: landlocked countries with primary maritime access through the Indian Ocean littoral.

    b.   Includes West Bank.

    c.   Includes Mayotte.

    d.   Transient military and construction personnel on Diego Garcia only.

TABLE 2
The Southwestern Islands

Islands	Status	Social Composition	Regime Type	Global Alignment
BIOT (Chagos Archipelago)	British Territory.	Military & contractor personnel only. Permanent pop. transferred to Mauritius in 1966.	British military headquarters.	US-leased air and naval base.
Comoros	Independent Repl. fr. France 1975 (exc. Mayotte).	Swahili speaking Antalaote (Bantu), some Arab, Malagasy, European. Patriarchal Islamic society.	Post-colonial "federation" under elected authoritarian Pres. Ahmed Abdallah.	Western, esp. France (despite Mayotte irredentism), conservative Arab states.
Madagascar	Independent Repl. fr. France 1960.	Unique Asian-African variations among coastal & Plateau ethnic groups. Small, important minorities of Asians (Pakistani, Chinese) and Europeans.	Centralized, multi-party executive & legislature controlled by elected Pres. Didier Ratsiraka & indigenous Socialist ideology.	Nonaligned Third World champion; strong political ties with Socialist bloc, econ. relations with West (esp. France). Indian Ocean and inter-island leadership aspirations.
Mauritius	Independent from UK 1968.	Indian majority (more than ½ Hindu). Large Creole (African-Malagasy-Asian-European) & Pakistani minorities; small Chinese & European minorities.	Commonwealth parliamentary pluralistic democracy. Majority coalition under PM Aneerood Jugnauth (social democrat).	Western, esp. UK, France but with Third World reservations on example of India.

Mayotte	French Territory separated fr. Comoros.	Comorean with strong Creole & Malagasy elements.	French military & civilian institutions. Repr. in French Parliament.	French naval and Foreign Legion base.
Reunion	French Overseas Department.	Creole majority (African-Malagasy-Asian-European); large French & Asian (Indian, Pakistani) minorities.	Elected Regional & General Councils; pluralist. Relatively decentralized admin, French Prefect.	Headquarters for French Southern Indian Ocean Navy and Air Force. Econ. dependence on France & EEC.
Seychelles	Independent Repl. from UK 1976.	Creole majority (African-Asian-European); large French, British & Asian (Indian) minorities.	Centralized one-party State under elected Socialist Pres. Albert René.	Nonaligned. Good relations with UK, France, USSR, Tanzania.

TABLE 2, cont.
The Southwestern Islands

Islands	Political Parties	Nationalist Movement	Press-Labor-Education
BIOT	None.	None, apart from some "home-land" agitation in Mauritius.	None.
Comoros	Union for Comorean Progress (UPC) formed 1982 to support President.	Various exile groups in France, Madagascar, East Africa press to overthrow Abdallah.	Govt-controlled minimal press. Rudimentary labor movement. Slow educational development under colonial & Koranic domination.
Madagascar	Natl Front (FNDR) of 6 parties dominated by President's AREMA.	Insular & Third World patriots contend for influence on Ratsiraka (vs. Marxists and pro-West factions).	Pluralist but heavily censored press in Antananarivo. Unions allied with major parties. Vernacular educational expansion.
Mauritius	Shifting constellation of nat'l & ethnic groupings. Ctr-Right in power since 1983.	Mainly in opposition MMM which won 1982, lost 1983, elections. Some residual communal chauvinism.	Pluralist, lively press under increasing Government pressure. Labor organizations affiliated with majority or MMM parties. Literate pop. but overcrowded, defective post-colonial schools.
Mayotte	Dominated by Mahorais Peoples Movement (MPM).	None. Main debate is between loyalist MPM & French commitment to reintegrate island with Comoros.	No remarkable press or labor institutions. Education expanding from rudimentary condition thanks to French subsidies.

Reunion	Multiparty system polarized as in France; slight current majority for Right.	Marxist Left seeks home-rule short of independence for purposes of socio-economic redistribution. Right & Center remain loyalist.	Pluralistic, highly politicized press & labor, congruent with party patterns. Education nearly universal, but in tension between French "equivalence" and insular Creole populism.
Seychelles	Single party Seychelles Peoples Progressive Front, held together by Pres. René.	Officially embodied in SPPF, although constrained by economic dependence.	Gov't controlled, immature press & labor organizations. Education expanding from colonial system to universality and primacy of Creole language.

238

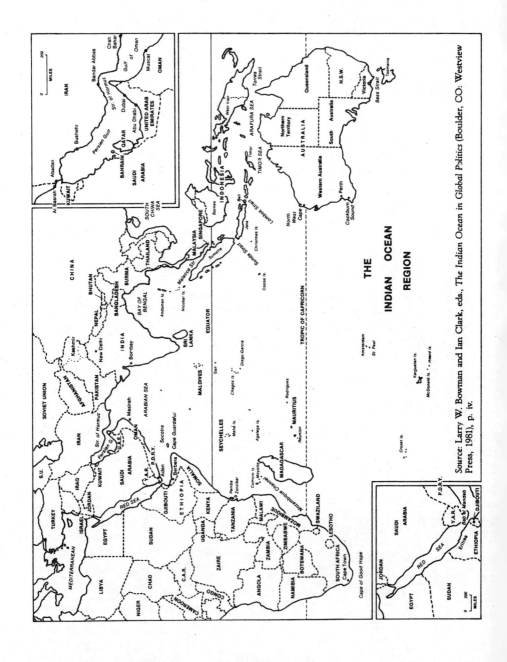

Source: Larry W. Bowman and Ian Clark, eds, *The Indian Ocean in Global Politics* (Boulder, CO: Westview Press, 1981), p. iv.

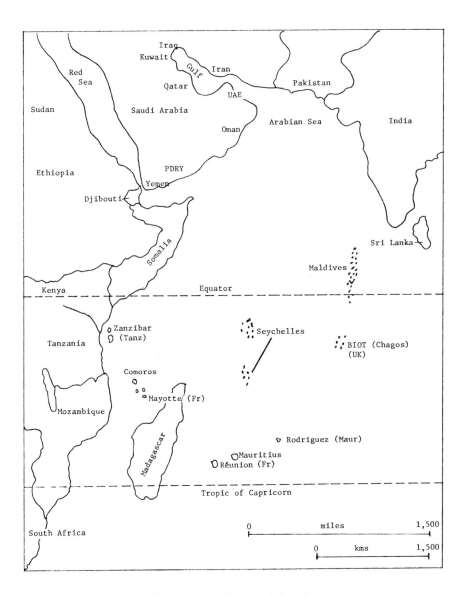

Western Indian Ocean with Islands

Appendix 1

UN General Assembly Resolution
Declaring the Indian Ocean a Zone of Peace,
Resolution 2832 (XXVI), December 16, 1971

The General Assembly,

Conscious of the determination of the people of the littoral and hinterland States of the Indian Ocean to preserve their independence, sovereignty and territorial integrity, and to resolve their political, economic and social problems under conditions of peace and tranquillity,

Recalling the Declaration of the Third Conference of Heads of State or Government of Non-Aligned Countries, held at Lusaka in September 1970, calling upon all States to consider and respect the Indian Ocean as a zone of peace from which great Power rivalries and competition as well as bases conceived in the context of such rivalries and competition should be excluded, and declaring that the area should also be free of nuclear weapons,

Convinced of the desirability of ensuring the maintenance of such conditions in the area by means other than military alliances, as such alliances entail financial and other obligations that call for the diversion of the limited resources of these States from the more compelling and productive task of economic and social reconstruction and could further involve them in the rivalries of power blocs in a manner prejudicial to their independence and freedom of action, thereby increasing international tensions,

Concerned at recent developments that portend the extension of the arms race into the Indian Ocean area, thereby posing a serious threat to the maintenance of such conditions in the area,

Convinced that the establishment of a zone of peace in an extensive geographical area in one region could have a beneficial influence on the establishment of permanent universal peace based on equal rights and justice for all, in accordance with the purposes and principles of the Charter of the United Nations,

1. Solemnly declares that the Indian Ocean, within limits to be determined, together with the air space above the ocean floor subjacent thereto, is hereby designated for all time as a zone of peace;

2. Calls upon the great Powers, in conformity with this Declaration, to enter into immediate consultations with the littoral States of the Indian Ocean with a view to: (a) Halting the further escalation and expansion of their military presence in the Indian Ocean; (b) Elminating from the Indian Ocean all bases, military installations, logistical supply facilities, the disposition of nuclear weapons and weapons of mass destruction and any manifestation of great Power military presence in the Indian Ocean conceived in the context of great Power rivalry;

3. Calls upon the littoral and hinterland States of the Indian Ocean, the permanent members of the Security Council and other major maritime users of the Indian Ocean, in pursuit of the objective of establishing a system of universal collective security without military alliances and strengthening international security through regional and other co-operation, to enter into consultations with a view to the implementation of this Declaration and such action as may be necessary to ensure that: (a) Warships and military aircraft may not use the Indian Ocean for any threat or use of force against the sovereignty, territorial integrity or independence of any littoral or hinterland State of the Indian Ocean in contravention of the purposes and principles of the Charter of the United Nations; (b) Subject to the foregoing and to the norms and principles of international law, the right to free and unimpeded use of the zone by the vessels of all nations is unaffected; (c) Appropriate arrangements are made to give effect to any international agreement that may ultimately be reached for the maintenance of the Indian Ocean as a zone of peace;

4. Requests the Secretary-General to report to the General Assembly at its twenty-seventh session on the progress that has been made with regard to the implementation of this Declaration;

5. Decides to include the item entitled "Declaration of the Indian Ocean as a zone of peace" in the provisional agenda of its twenty-seventh session.

Recorded Vote:

In favour: Afghanistan, Algeria, Bhutan, Burma, Burundi, Cameroon, Ceylon, Chad, China, Colombia, Congo, Costa Rica, Cyprus, Egypt, El Salvador, Equatorial Guinea, Ethiopia, Ghana, Guinea, Guyana, Iceland, India, Indonesia, Iran, Japan, Jordan, Kenya, Khmer Republic, Kuwait, Laos, Lebanon, Liberia, Libya, Malaysia, Mali, Malta, Mauritania, Mexico, Morocco, Nepal, *Nicaragua, Nigeria, Pakistan, Panama, Qatar, Romania, Saudi Arabia, Somalia, Sudan, Swaziland, Sweden, Syria, Togo, Trinidad and Tobago, Tunisia, Uganda, United Republic of Tanzania, Uruguay, Yemen, Yugoslavia, Zambia.

Against: none.

---

*Later advised the Secretariat it had intended to abstain.

Abstaining: Argentina, Australia, Austria, Belgium, Bolivia, Brazil, Bulgaria, Byelorussia, Canada, Central African Republic, Chile, Cuba, Czechoslovakia, Dahomey, Denmark, Dominican Republic, Fiji, Finland, France, Greece, Guatemala, Haiti, Honduras, Hungary, Ireland, Israel, Italy, Ivory Coast, Jamaica, Lesotho, Luxembourg, Madagascar, Mongolia, Netherlands, New Zealand, Norway, People's Democratic Republic of Yemen, Peru, Philippines, Poland, Portugal, Rwanda, Senegal, Singapore, South Africa, Spain, Thailand, Turkey, Ukraine, USSR, United Kingdom, United States, Upper Volta, Venezuela, Zaire.

Absent: Albania, Bahrain, Barbados, Botswana, Ecuador, Gabon, Gambia, Iraq**, Malawi, Maldives, Mauritius, Niger, Oman, Paraguay, Sierra Leone, United Arab Emirates.

**Later advised the Secretariat it had intended to vote in favour.

Appendix 2

UN General Assembly Resolution on the Indian Ocean as a Zone of Peace, December 1986

A/RES/41/87. *Implementation of the Declaration on the Indian Ocean as a Zone of Peace*

Date: 4 December 1986
Adopted without a vote

The General Assembly,

Recalling the Declaration of the Indian Ocean as a Zone of Peace, contained in its resolution 2832 (XXVI) of 16 December 1971, and recalling also its resolutions 2992 (XXVII) of 15 December 1972, 3080 (XXVIII) of 6 December 1973, 3259 A (XXIX) of 9 December 1974, 3468 (XXX) of 11 December 1975, 31/88 of 14 December 1976, 32/86 of 12 December 1977, S-10/2 of 30 June 1978, 33/68 of 14 December 1978, 34/80 A and B of 11 December 1979, 35/150 of 12 December 1980, 36/90 of 9 December 1981 and 37/96 of 13 December 1982, 38/185 of 20 December 1983, 39/149 of 17 December 1984, 40/153 of 16 December 1985 and other relevant resolutions,

Recalling further the report of the Meeting of the Littoral and Hinterland States of the Indian Ocean,*

Reaffirming its conviction that concrete action for the achievement of the objectives of the Declaration of the Indian Ocean as a Zone of Peace would be a substantial contribution to the strengthening of international peace and security,

Recalling its decision, taken at the thirty-fourth session in resolution 34/80 B, to convene a Conference on the Indian Ocean at Colombo during 1981,

Recalling also its decision to make every effort, in consideration of the political and security climate in the Indian Ocean area, and progress made

---

*Official Records of the General Assembly, Thirty-fourth Session, Supplement No. 45 (A/34/45 and Corr.1).

in the harmonization of views, to finalize, in accordance with its normal methods of work, all preparations for the Conference, including the dates for its convening,

Recalling further its decision, taken at its fortieth session in resolution 40/153 concerning the convening of the Conference at an early date not later than 1988,

Recalling the exchange of views in the *Ad Hoc* Committee on the Indian Ocean in 1986,

Noting the exchange of views on the adverse political and security climate in the region,

Noting further the various documents before the *Ad Hoc* Committee,

Convinced that the continued military presence of the great Powers in the Indian Ocean area, conceived in the context of their confrontation, gives urgency to the need to take practical steps for the early achievement of the objectives of the Declaration of the Indian Ocean as a Zone of Peace,

Considering that any other foreign military presence in the area, whenever it is contrary to the objectives of the Declaration of the Indian Ocean as a Zone of Peace and the purposes and principles of the Charter of the United Nations, gives greater urgency to the need to take practical steps towards the early achievement of the objectives of the Declaration,

Considering further that the creation of a zone of peace requires co-operation and agreement among the States of the region to ensure conditions of peace and security within the area, as envisaged in the Declaration of the Indian Ocean as a Zone of Peace, and respect for the independence, sovereignty and territorial integrity of the littoral and hinterland States,

Calling for the renewal of genuinely constructive efforts through the exercise of the political will necessary for the achievement of the objectives of the Declaration of the Indian Ocean as a Zone of Peace,

Deeply concerned at the danger posed by the grave and ominous developments in the area and the resulting sharp deterioration of peace, security and stability which particularly seriously affect the littoral and hinterland States, as well as international peace and security,

Convinced that the continued deterioration of the political and security climate in the Indian Ocean is an important consideration bearing on the question of the urgent convening of the Conference and that the easing of tension in the area would enhance the prospect of success being achieved by the Conference,

1. *Takes note* of the report of the *Ad Hoc* Committee on the Indian Ocean and exchange of views of the Committee;**
2. *Takes note* of the discussions on substantive matters in the Working Group established in accordance with the *Ad Hoc* Committee's decision of 11 July 1985;***
3. *Emphasizes* its decision to convene the Conference of the Indian Ocean at Colombo as a necessary step for the implementation of the Declaration of the Indian Ocean as a Zone of Peace adopted in 1971;
4. *Notes* that the *Ad Hoc* Committee has been unable, during its four weeks of work in 1986, to complete preparatory work relating to the convening of the Conference on the Indian Ocean and urges the Committee to continue its work with vigour and determination;
5. *Requests* the *Ad Hoc* Committee, taking into account the political and security climate in the region, to complete preparatory work relating to the Conference on the Indian Ocean during 1987 in order to enable the opening of the conference at Colombo at an early date soon thereafter, but not later than 1988, to be decided by the Committee in consultation with the host country, with a clear understanding that if preparatory work is not completed in 1987 serious consideration will be given to ways and means of more effectively organizing work in the *Ad Hoc* Committee to enable it to fulfil its mandate;
6. *Emphasizes* that the Conference called for in General Assembly resolution 34/80 B and subsequent resolutions and the establishment and maintenance of the Indian Ocean as a zone of peace require the full and active participation and co-operation of all the permanent members of the Security Council, the major maritime users and the littoral and hinterland States;
7. *Decides* that preparatory work would comprise organizational matters and substantive issues, including the provisional agenda for the Conference, rules of procedure, participation, stages of conference, level of representation, documentation, consideration of appropriate arrangements for any international agreements that may ultimately be reached for the maintenance of the Indian Ocean as a zone of peace and the preparation of the draft final document of the Conference;
8. *Requests* the *Ad Hoc* Committee at the same time to seek the necessary harmonization of views on remaining relevant issues;
9. *Requests* the Chairman of the *Ad Hoc* Committee to consult the Secretary-General at the appropriate time on the establishment of a secretariat for the Conference.

***Official Records of the General Assembly, Forty-first Session, Supplement No. 29* (A/41/29).
****Ibid.*, para. 12.

10. *Renews* the mandate of the Ad Hoc Committee as defined in the relevant resolutions and requests the Committee to intensify its work with regard to the implementation of its mandate;

11. *Requests* the Ad Hoc Committee to hold two preparatory sessions in 1987 each of a two-weeks' duration for completion of preparatory work;

12. *Requests* the Ad Hoc Committee to submit to the Conference a report on its preparatory work;

13. *Requests* the Chairman of the Ad Hoc Committee to continue his consultations on the participation in the work of the Committee by States Members of the United Nations which are not members of the Committee, with the aim of resolving this matter at the earliest possible date;

14. *Requests* the Ad Hoc Committee to submit to the General Assembly at its forty-second session a full report on the implementation of the present resolution;

15. *Requests* the Secretary-General to continue to render all necessary assistance to the Ad Hoc Committee, including the provision of summary records, in recognition of its preparatory function.

Selected Bibliography

Two serial publications contain original, reliable, and often penetrating studies on the western Indian Ocean:

Annuaire des pays de l'Océan Indien (APOI). Aix-en-Provence: Université d'Aix-Marseille, Centre d'études et de recherche sur les sociétés de l'Océan Indien (CERSOI), 1974 to date.

Legum, Colin, ed. *Africa Contemporary Record (ACR)*. London: Rex Collings to 1977; New York and London: Africana Press, Holmes & Meier, 1978 to date.

Other useful periodical coverage appears in:

The Economist Intelligence Unit, *Quarterly Economic Review of Madagascar, Mauritius, Seychelles, Comoros*. London: The Economist Intelligence Unit, Ltd.

The Economist weekly. London: The Economist Newspaper, Ltd.

Le Monde daily, weekly and *Le Monde Diplomatique*. Paris: Le Monde.

Marchés Tropicaux et Méditerranéens (MTM), weekly. Paris.

Adie, W.A.C. *Oil, Politics, and Seapower: The Indian Ocean Vortex*. New York: Crane, Russak & Co., 1975.

Albany, Michel, ed. *A la découverte de la Réunion: Tout l'univers réunionnais de ses origines à nos jours*. 10 vols projected. Saint Denis (Réunion): Favory, 1980.

Allen, Philip M. *Self-Determination in the Western Indian Ocean*. International Conciliation. 560. New York: Carnegie Endowment (1966).

——— and Ostheimer, John M. "Africa and the Islands of the Western Indian Ocean," *Munger Africana Library Notes* 35 (1976). Pasadena: California Institute of Technology, 1976.

Althabe, Gérard. *Oppression et libération dans l'imaginaire: les communautés villageoises de la côte orientale de Madagascar*. Paris: François Maspero, 1969.

Andriamanjato, Richard. *Le Tsiny et le Tody dans la pensée malgache*. Paris: Présence Africaine, 1957.

Archer, Robert. *Madagascar depuis 1972: La marche d'une révolution*. Paris: Harmattan, 1978.

Ballard, Admiral G.A. *Rulers of the Indian Ocean*. Boston and New York: Houghton Mifflin, 1928.

Beaton, Patrick. *Creoles and Coolies: Five Years in Mauritius*. 2nd ed. Port Washington, N.Y.: Kennikat Press, 1971.

Beazley, Kim C. and Clark, Ian. *The Politics of Intrusion: The Super Powers and the Indian Ocean*. Sydney: Alternative Publishing Coop. Ltd., 1979.

Bellamal, André. "L'Inde et son environnement géostratégique." *Revue de la Défense nationale.* Aug/Sept. 1981.

Benedict, Burton. *Indians in a Plural Society: A Report on Mauritius.* London: H.M. Stationery Office, 1961.

_____. *Mauritius: Problems of a Plural Society.* London: Pall Mall Press, 1965.

_____. *People of the Seychelles.* 3rd ed. London: H.M. Stationery Office, 1970.

Bennett, Norman R. *A History of the Arab State of Zanzibar.* London: Methuen & Co. Studies in African History 16, 1978.

Benoist, Jean. "Perspectives pour une connaissance des sociétés contemporaines des Mascareignes et des Seychelles." *APOI* 1 (1974): 223–233.

Bezboruah, Monoranjan. *U.S. Strategy in the Indian Ocean: The International Response.* New York: Praeger, 1977

Bhargava, G.S. *South Asian Security After Afghanistan.* Lexington, Mass.: Lexington Books (D.C. Heath), 1983.

Bloch, Maurice. *Placing the Dead: Tombs, Ancestral Villages, and Kinship Organization in Madagascar.* London and New York: Seminar Press, 1972.

Boiteau, Pierre. *Madagascar: Contribution à l'histoire de la nation Malgache.* Paris: Editions Sociales, 1958.

Bouillon, Antoine. *Madagascar: le colonisé et son âme: Essai sur le discours psychologique colonial.* Paris: Harmattan, 1981.

Bowman, Larry W. and Clark, Ian. *The Indian Ocean in Global Politics.* Boulder, Colorado: Westview Press; Nedlands, W.A.: University of Western Australia Press, 1981.

Bradley, J.T. *History of Seychelles.* 2 vols. Victoria (Mahé), Seychelles: Clarion Press, 1940.

Braun, Dieter. *The Indian Ocean: Region of Conflict or "Peace Zone?"* trans. Carol Geldart and Kathleen Llanwarne. New York: St. Martin's Press, 1983.

Cadoux, Charles. "Esquisse d'un panorama politique des pays de l'océan Indien." *APOI* 1 (1974): 47–77.

Chagnoux, Hervé and Haribou, Ali. *Les Comores.* Que sais-je? No. 1829. Paris: Presses Universitaires de France, 1980.

Chaigneau, Pascal. *Madagascar: de la Première République à l'orientation socialiste, processus et conséquences d'une évolution politique.* Thèse IIIème cycle en Sociologie Politique, Université de Paris X, 1981.

_____. *Rivalités politiques et socialisme à Madagascar.* Paris: Centre des Hautes Etudes sur l'Afrique et l'Asie Modernes, 1985.

Cheema, Pervaiz Iqbal. *Conflict and Cooperation in the Indian Ocean: Pakistan's Interests and Choices.* Canberra Papers on Strategy and Defence, No. 23. Canberra: Australian National University, 1980.

Chittick, H. Neville and Rotberg, Robert I., eds. *East Africa and the Orient: Cultural Syntheses in Pre-Colonial Times.* New York and London: Africana Publishing, 1975.

Corbett, Edward M. *The French Presence in Black Africa.* Washington: Black Orpheus Press, 1972.

Cottrell, Alvin J. and Burrell, R.M. *The Indian Ocean: Its Political, Economic, and Military Importance.* New York: Praeger, 1973.

Cottrell, Alvin J. and Associates. *Sea Power and Strategy in the Indian Ocean.* Beverly Hills, Cal.: Sage Publications, 1981.

Coupland, Reginald. *East Africa and Its Invaders: From the Earliest Times to the Death of Seyyid Said in 1856.* Oxford: Clarendon Press, 1938.

Delmas, Claude. "De Vladivostock à Diégo-Garcia: tension dans les eaux asiatiques." *Politique Internationale* 5 (1979).

Deschamps, Hubert. *Histoire de Madagascar.* Paris: Berger-Levrault, 1961.

————. *Les Pirates à Madagascar aux XVIIème at XVIIIème siecles.* Paris: Berger-Levrault, 1949.

Desjeux, Dominique. "Réforme fonçière et civilisation agraire: le cas de Madagascar." *Le Mois en Afrique* 184–185 (1981).

Desjeux, Dominique. *La question agraire à Madagascar: Administration et paysannat de 1895 à nos jours.* Paris: Harmattan, n.d. (probably 1979).

Dismukes, Bradford and McConnell, James M. *Soviet Naval Diplomacy.* New York: Pergamon Press, 1979.

Djalili, Mohmed-Reja. *L'Océan Indien.* Que sais-je? 1746 (1978). Paris: Presses Universitaires de France, 1978.

Dossier Réunion. Bulletin d'Information du CENADDOM (Centre National de Documentation des Départements d'Outre-Mer) 48 (1979). Talence, France: CENADDOM, 1979.

D'Unienville, Alix. *Les Mascareignes: vieille France en mer indienne.* Paris: Albin Michel, 1954.

Dupon, Jean-François. *Contraintes insulaires et fait colonial aux Mascareignes et aux Seychelles.* Lille, France: Atelier de Reproduction des Thèses; Paris: Librairie Honoré Champion, 1977.

————. "L'Océan Indien et sa bordure: présentation géographique." APOI 1 (1974).

Durand, Joyce and Jean-Pierre. *L'ile Maurice: Quelle indépendance? La reproduction des rapports de production capitalistes dans une formation sociale dominée.* Paris: Editions Anthropos, 1975.

Dyle, Bernard. "Stratégie et Océan Indien." *Revue de Défense Nationale* (July 1981).

Favoreu, Louis. *L'ile Maurice.* Paris: Berger-Levrault, 1970.

Flobert, Thierry. *Les Comores: évolution juridique et socio-politique.* Travaux et mémoires de la Faculté de Droit et de Science Politique d'Aix-Marseille 24. Aix-en-Provence: CERSOI, 1976.

La France de l'Océan Indien: Madagascar, les Comores, le Réunion, la Côte Française des Somalis, l'Inde Française. Collection Terres Lointaines 8. Paris: Sociétés d'Editions Géographiques, Maritimes et Coloniales, 1952.

Franda, Marcus F. "The Indian Ocean: A Delhi Perspective." American Universities Field Service *Fieldstaff Reports,* Asia 19:1 (March 1975).

————. *The Seychelles: Unquiet Islands.* Boulder, Colorado: Westview Press; Hampshire, England: Gower, 1982.

Fuller, Jack. "Dateline Diego Garcia: Paved-Over Paradise." *Foreign Policy* 28 (Fall 1977).

Graham, Gerald Sanford. *Great Britain in the Indian Ocean: A Study of Maritime Enterprise 1810–1850.* Oxford: Clarendon Press, 1967.

Gupta, Ranjan. *The Indian Ocean: A Political Geography.* New Delhi: Marwah Publications, 1979.

Heseltine, Nigel. *Madagascar.* New York: Praeger, 1971.

Houbert, Jean. "Mauritius: Independence and Dependence." *Journal of Modern African Studies* 19:1 (1981).

Indian Council of World Affairs. *Defence and Security in the Indian Ocean Area.* New York: Asia Publishing House, 1958.

Ingrams, William Harold. *Arabia and the Isles.* 3rd ed. New York and Washington: Frederick A. Praeger, 1966.

Jouffrey, Roger. "La République de Djibouti et ses activités économiques." *Afrique Contemporaine* 133, Jan-Feb-Mar. 1985, pp. 33–42.

Kaushik, Dépéndra. *The Indian Ocean: Towards a Peace Zone.* Delhi: Vikas Publications, 1972.

Kapur, Ashok. *The Indian Ocean: Regional and International Power Politics.* New York: Praeger Special Studies, 1982.

Kent, Raymond, ed. *Madagascar in History: Essays from the 1970s.* Albany, California: Foundation for Malagasy Studies, 1979.

————. *Early Kingdoms in Madagascar, 1500–1700.* New York: Holt, Rinehart & Winston, 1970.

Kerr, Alex, ed. *The Indian Ocean Region: Resources and Development.* Boulder, Colorado: Westview Press; Nedlands, W.A.: University of Western Australia Press, 1981.

Labayle, Henri. "L'Océan Indien, zone de paix: le désenchantement." *APOI* 7 (1980).

Labrousse, Amiral Henri. "L'Europe et l'Océan Indien: perspectives géopolitiques et stratégiques." *APOI* 8 (1981).

————. "Océan Indien: 'nouveau coeur du monde.'" *Monde en Développement* 21 (1978).

Lamballe, Alain. "La France et l'Océan Indien." *Civilisations* 30:1-2 (1980).

Lenoir, Philippe. "An Extreme Example of Pluralism: Mauritius." *Cultures* (UNESCO) 6:1 (1979).

Leymarie, Philippe. *Océan Indien: le mouveau coeur du monde.* Paris: Karthala, 1981.

Lionnet, Guy. *The Seychelles.* Harrisburg: Stackpole Books, 1972.

Luce Report, The: A Time for Decision. Sessional Paper 8 (1958). Port Louis, Mauritius, 1958.

Maloney, Clarence. *People of the Maldive Islands.* Bombay: Orient Longman, 1980.

Mannick, A. Ramaoutar. *Mauritius: The Development of a Plural Society.* Nottingham: Spokesman, 1979.

Marsaud, Jean-Louis. "Les extensions de juridiction sur les espaces maritimes dans l'Océan Indien." Aix-en-Provence: CERSOI pamphlet, 1978.

Martin, E.B. and C.P. *Cargoes of the East.* London: Elm Tree Books, 1978.

Maurice, Pierre. "Le cloisonnement des échanges extérieures des pays de l'Océan Indien." *APOI* 1 (1974).

Mayer, John D. "Rapid Deployment Forces: Budgetary Implications." Washington: congressional Budget Office, February 1983.

Meade, J.E. and others. *The Economic and Social Structure of Mauritius: A Report to the Government of Mauritius.* London: Methuen & Co. Ltd., 1961.

Miller, Norman N. "The Indian Ocean: Traditional Trade on a Smuggler's Sea." *American Universities Field Service Field-Staff Report,* Africa-Asia 7 (1980).

Misra, K.P. *Ocean Politics: An Asian-African Perspective.* Occasional Papers/Reprints Series in Contemporary Asian Studies No. 1. University of Maryland School of Law, 1978.

Moorer, Admiral Thomas H. and Cottrell, Alvin J. "The Search for U.S. Bases in the Indian Ocean: A Last Chance." *Strategic Review* 8:2 (1980).

Mouvements de populations dans l'océan Indien. Actes du 4ème Congrès de l'Association historique internationale de l'océan Indien et du 14ème Colloque de la Commission Internationale d'Histoire Maritime. St. Denis, Réunion, September 1972. Paris: Honoré Champion, 1979.

Mutibwa, Phares M. *The Malagasy and the Europeans: Madagascar's Foreign Relations, 1861–1895.* New York: Humanities Press, 1974.

Newitt, Malyn. *The Comoro Islands: Struggle Against Dependency in the Indian Ocean*. Boulder, Colorado: Westview Press; London: Gower, 1984.

Noyes, James H. *The Clouded Lens: Persian Gulf Security and U.S. Policy*. Stanford: Hoover Institution Press, 1982.

Oberlé, Philippe. *Afars et Somalis: le dossier de Djibouti*. Paris: Présence Africaine, 1971.

Ommanney, F.D. *The Shoals of Capricorn*. London: Longmans, Green & Co., 1952.

Oraison, André. "Les avatars du B.I.O.T.: le processus de l'implantation militaire américaine à Diégo-Garcia." *APOI* 6 (1979).

————. "L'Océan Indien à la croisée des chemins." *Revue de Droit International de Sciences diplomatiques et politiques* (Geneva) April-June 1977.

Ostheimer, John M., ed. *The Politics of the Western Indian Ocean Islands*. New York: Praeger Publishers, 1975.

Ottino, Paul. "Madagascar, les Comores et le Sud-Est de l'Océan Indien," Projet d'enseignement et de recherches. Antananarivo: Université de Madagascar, December 1974.

Panikkar, Kavalam Madhava. *India and the Indian Ocean: An Essay on the Influence of Sea Power on Indian History*. 2nd ed. London: George Allen & Unwin, 1951.

Paturau, J.M. *The Sugar Industry of Mauritius*. Port Louis, Mauritius, 1962.

Periplus maris Erythraei: The Periplus of the Erythrean Sea: Travel and Trade in the Indian Ocean by a Merchant of the First Century. Translated and annotated by Wilfred H. Schoff. London: Longmans, Green & Co., 1912.

Phadnis, Urmila and Dutthuithui, Ela. "The Maldives Enter World Politics." *Asian Affairs*, Jan-Feb. 1981.

Prats, Yves. "L'Océan Indien: zone stratégique." *APOI* 1, 1974.

————. *Le Développement communautaire à Madagascar*. Paris: Librairie Générale de Droit et de Jurisprudence R. Pichon et R. Durand-Auzias, 1972.

Qualman, Harry Bryce. *Limits and Constraints on Foreign Policy in a Dependent State: Madagascar under the Tsiranana Regime*. Ph.D. dissertation, Johns Hopkins University, 1975.

Rabenoro, Césaire. *Les relations extérieures de Madagascar de 1960 à 1972*. Thèse d'Etat, Université Aix-Marseille III, 1981.

Rajaona, Andrianaivo Ravelona. *Essai sur la coopération entre pays en développement: Etude sur la problématique à travers la coopération entre pays en développement*. Thèse de Doctorat en Droit, Université Aix-Marseille III, 1985.

Rees, David. "Strategic Problems of Indian Ocean Defence." *Asia Pacific Community* 11 (1981).

"La Réunion sous le vent du changement." Supplement to *Le Monde*, March 13, 1982.

Rouveyran, Jean-Claude. *La logique des agricultures de transition: l'Exemple des sociétés paysannes malgaches*. Paris: Editions G.P. Maisonneuve et LaRose, 1972.

Roux, Christian. "Le recentrage et la restructuration de l'économie malgache depuis 1974." *Le Mois en Afrique* 15:176–177 (1980).

Saint-Pierre, Bernardin de. *Voyage à l'Isle de France, à l'Isle de Bourbon, au Cap de Bonne-Espérance, etc. par un Officier du Roy*. Neuchatel, France: Imprimerie de la Société Typographique, 1778.

Sauer, Jonathan D. *Plants and Man on the Seychelles Coast: A Study in Historical Biogeography*. Madison: University of Wisconsin Press, 1967.

Scherer, André. *La Réunion*. Que sais-je? 1846. Paris: Presses Universitaires de France, 1980.

Selwyn, Percy. *Small, Poor, and Remote: Islands at a Geographical Disadvantage.* Brighton, England: University of Sussex, 1978.

Seychelles. Central Office of Information. London: H.M. Stationery Office, 1976.

Seychelles Handbook, The. Office of the President. Victoria, Mahé, Seychelles: Government Printer, 1976.

Simmons, Adele Smith. *Modern Mauritius: The Politics of Decolonization.* Bloomington: Indiana University Press, 1982.

Simon, Sheldon W. *The ASEAN States and Regional Security.* Stanford: Hoover Institution Press, 1982.

Singh, Jasjit. "Geopolitics and Super-Power Rivalry," *Mainstream,* October 27 and November 3, 1984.

Singh, K. Rajendra. *The Indian Ocean: Big Power Presence and Local Response.* New Delhi: Ramesh C. Jain, 1977.

_____. *Politics of the Indian Ocean.* Delhi: Thomson Press (India), Ltd., 1974.

Stoddard, Theodore Lothrop, and others. *Area Handbook for the Indian Ocean Territories.* Washington: U.S. Government Printing Office, 1971.

Thomas, Athol. *Forgotten Eden: A View of the Seychelles Islands in the Indian Ocean.* London: Longmans, Green & Co. Ltd., 1968.

Thompson, Virginia and Adloff, Richard. *The Malagasy Republic: Madagascar Today.* Stanford: Stanford Univeristy Press, 1965.

Titmuss, Richard Morris. *Social Policies and Population Growth in Mauritius.* Sessional Paper 6 of 1960. London: H.M. Stationery Office, 1961.

Toussaint, Auguste. *Histoire des Iles Mascareignes.* Paris: Berger-Levrault, 1972.

_____. *History of the Indian Ocean.* Translated by June Guicharnaud. London: Routledge & Kegan Paul, 1966.

_____. *La Route des îles: contribution à l'histoire maritime des Mascareignes.* Paris: Ecole Pratique des Hautes Etudes, 1967.

Tronchon, Jacques. *L'insurrection Malgache de 1947: Essai d'interprétation historique.* Paris: François Maspero, 1974.

UNESCO. *Historical Relations Across the Indian Ocean.* General History of Africa, Studies and Documents, Vol. 3, Report and Papers of the Meeting of Experts Organized by UNESCO at Port Louis, Mauritius, from July 15 to 19, 1974. Paris: UNESCO, 1980.

United Nations General Assembly. Ad Hoc Committee on the Indian Ocean. *Annual Reports* and *Summary Reports,* 1972 to date.

United States Department of the Army. *South Asia and the Strategic Indian Ocean: A Bibliographic Survey of Literature.* D.A. Pamphlet 550-15, April 1973.

United States General Accounting Office. *Financial and Legal Aspects of the Agreement on the Availability of Certain Indian Ocean Islands for Defence Purposes.* Report of the Comptroller General of the United States B-184915, 1976.

Váli, Ferenc A. *Politics of the Indian Ocean Region: The Balances of Power.* New York: The Free Press, 1976.

Venkatachar, C.S. "Sea Power in the Indian Ocean." Eastern Economic Pamphlets 22. New Delhi: Eastern Economic Ltd., 1953.

Vibhakar, Jagdish. *Afro-Asian Security and Indian Ocean.* New Delhi: Sterling Publishers, 1974.

Villiers, Alan. *Monsoon Seas: The Story of the Indian Ocean.* New York: McGraw Hill Book Co., Inc., 1952.

_____. *Sons of Sinbad: The Great Tradition of Arab Seamanship in the Indian Ocean.* New York: Charles Scribner's Sons, 1969.

Virasahmy, Raj. *Characteristics of Island Economies.* Seminar Papers. Port Louis, Mauritius: University of Mauritius, 1976.

Virpsha, E.S. *Southern Africa and the Indian Ocean: A Study in Power Strategy.* London: Markham House Press, 1969.

Patrick Wall, ed. *The Southern Oceans and the Security of the Free World: New Studies in Global Strategy.* London: Stacey International, 1977.

Waltz, Kenneth N. "A Strategy for the Rapid Deployment Force." *International Security* 5:4 (1981).

Watt, D.C. "Britain and the Indian Ocean: Diplomacy before Defence." *The Political Quarterly* 42:3 (1971).

World Bank, The. *The Comoros: Problems and Prospects of a Small, Island Economy.* World Bank Country Study. Washington: The World Bank, 1979.

————. *Madagascar: Recent Economic Developments and Future Prospects.* World Bank Country Study. Washington: The World Bank, 1980.

————. *Seychelles: Economic Memorandum.* World Bank Country Study. Washington: The World Bank, 1980.

Yin Shing Yuen (Tian Shung). *Pour une intégration régionale entre l'île Maurice et d'autres îles du Sud-Ouest de l'Océan Indien (les Comores, Madagascar, la Réunion, les Seychelles).* Thèse Doctorat IIIème cycle, Université de Lyon II, 1980.

Zakheim, Dov S. "Towards a Western Approach to the Indian Ocean." *Survival* (London) 22:1 (1980)

Index